BABY BLUES **15** SCRAPBOOK

BABY BLUES:
UNPLUGGED

P9-AEU-316

Other Baby Blues® books from Andrews McMeel Publishing

Guess Who Didn't Take a Nap?
I Thought Labor Ended When the Baby Was Born
We Are Experiencing Parental Difficulties. . . Please Stand By
Night of the Living Dad
I Saw Elvis in My Ultrasound
One More and We're Outnumbered!
Check, Please. . .
threats, bribes & videotape
If I'm a Stay-At-Home Mom, Why Am I Always in the Car?
Lift and Separate
I Shouldn't Have to Scream More Than Once!
Motherhood Is Not For Wimps

Treasuries

The Super-Absorbent Biodegradable Family-Size Baby Blues®
Baby Blues®: Ten Years and Still in Diapers
Butt-Naked Baby Blues®

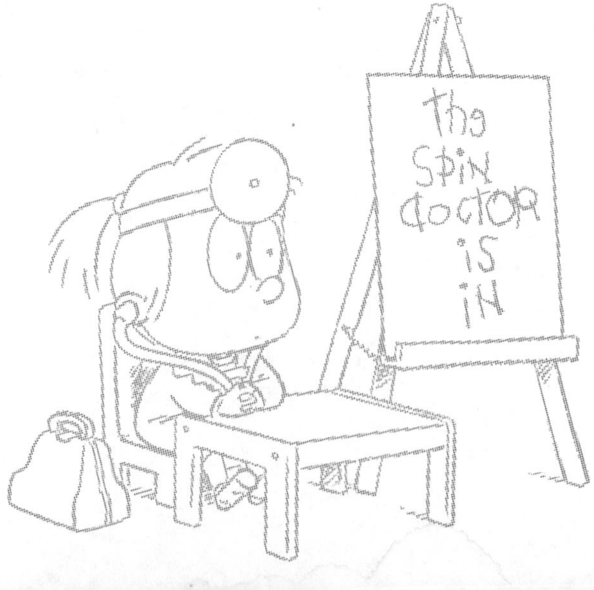
the
SPIN
doctor
is
in

BABY BLUES **15** SCRAPBOOK

BABY BLUES:
UNPLUGGED

BY RICK KIRKMAN
AND JERRY SCOTT

Andrews McMeel
Publishing

Kansas City

Baby Blues® is syndicated internationally by King Features Syndicate, Inc. For information, write King Features Syndicate, Inc., 888 Seventh Avenue, New York, New York 10019.

Baby Blues: Unplugged copyright © 2002 by Baby Blues Partnership. All rights reserved. Printed in the United States of America. No part of this book may be used or reproduced in any manner whatsoever without written permission except in the case of reprints in the context of reviews. For information, write Andrews McMeel Publishing, an Andrews McMeel Universal company, 4520 Main Street, Kansas City, Missouri 64111.

03 04 05 06 BAH 10 9 8 7 6 5 4 3 2

ISBN: 0-7407-2323-5

Library of Congress Control Number: 2001095911

Find *Baby Blues* on the Web at
www.babyblues.com

——— **ATTENTION: SCHOOLS AND BUSINESSES** ———

Andrews McMeel books are available at quantity discounts with bulk purchase for educational, business, or sales promotional use. For information, please write to: Special Sales Department, Andrews McMeel Publishing, 4520 Main Street, Kansas City, Missouri 64111.

To Abbey and Cady from their very proud dad.

—J. S.

To Sukey: There can never be enough thanks for being the wonderful mother
you are to our daughters.

In remembrance of Sparky Schulz, whose every strip was a cartooning lesson.

—R.K.

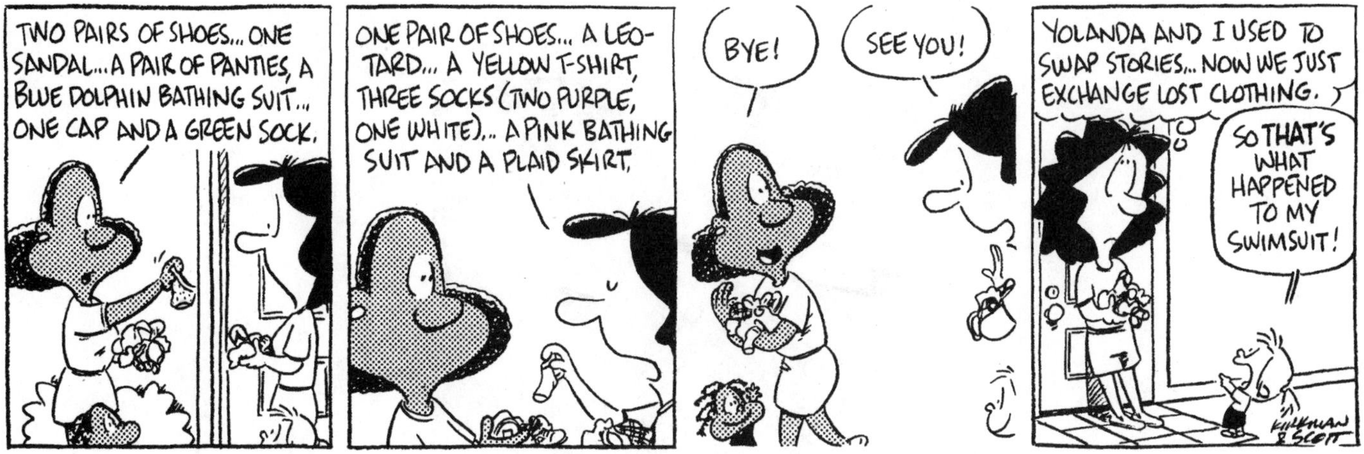
TWO PAIRS OF SHOES... ONE SANDAL... A PAIR OF PANTIES, A BLUE DOLPHIN BATHING SUIT... ONE CAP AND A GREEN SOCK.
ONE PAIR OF SHOES... A LEOTARD... A YELLOW T-SHIRT, THREE SOCKS (TWO PURPLE, ONE WHITE)... A PINK BATHING SUIT AND A PLAID SKIRT.
BYE!
SEE YOU!
YOLANDA AND I USED TO SWAP STORIES... NOW WE JUST EXCHANGE LOST CLOTHING.
SO THAT'S WHAT HAPPENED TO MY SWIMSUIT!
KIRKMAN & SCOTT

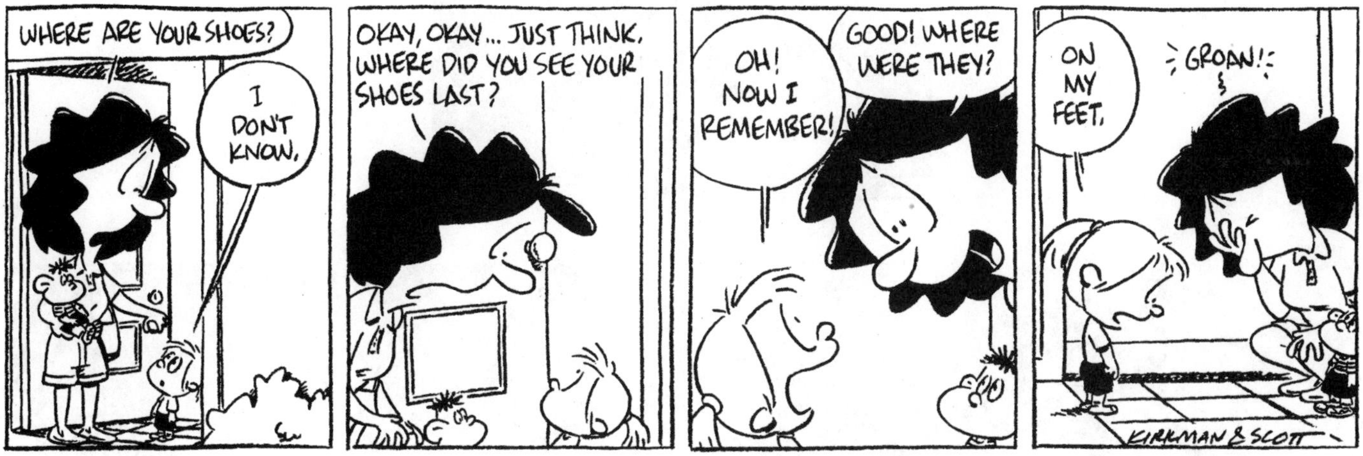
WHERE ARE YOUR SHOES?
I DON'T KNOW.
OKAY, OKAY... JUST THINK. WHERE DID YOU SEE YOUR SHOES LAST?
OH! NOW I REMEMBER!
GOOD! WHERE WERE THEY?
ON MY FEET.
GROAN!
KIRKMAN & SCOTT

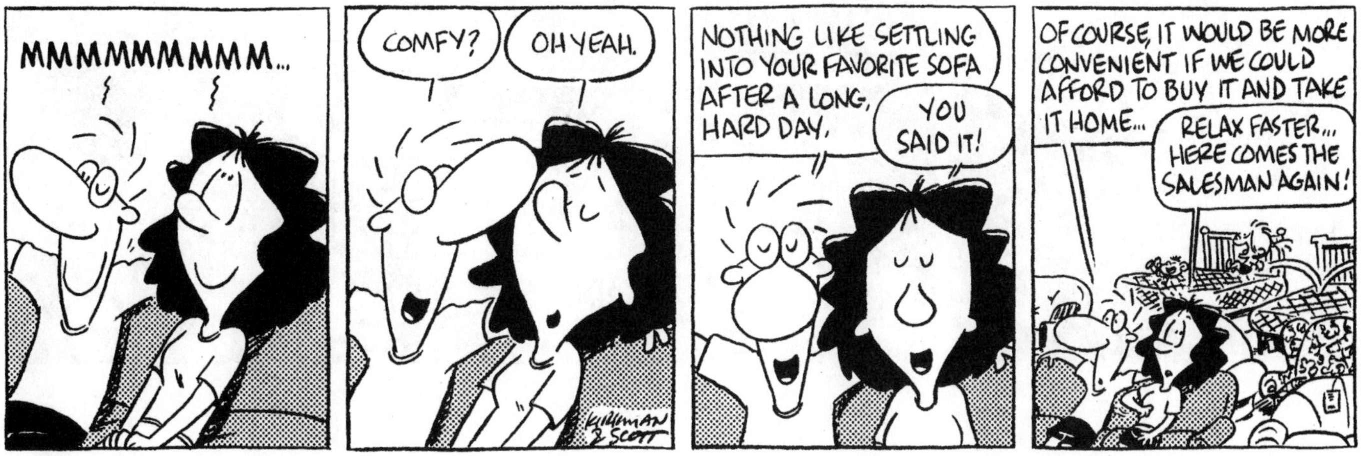
MMMMMMMMM...
COMFY?
OH YEAH.
KIRKMAN & SCOTT
NOTHING LIKE SETTLING INTO YOUR FAVORITE SOFA AFTER A LONG, HARD DAY.
YOU SAID IT!
OF COURSE, IT WOULD BE MORE CONVENIENT IF WE COULD AFFORD TO BUY IT AND TAKE IT HOME...
RELAX FASTER... HERE COMES THE SALESMAN AGAIN!

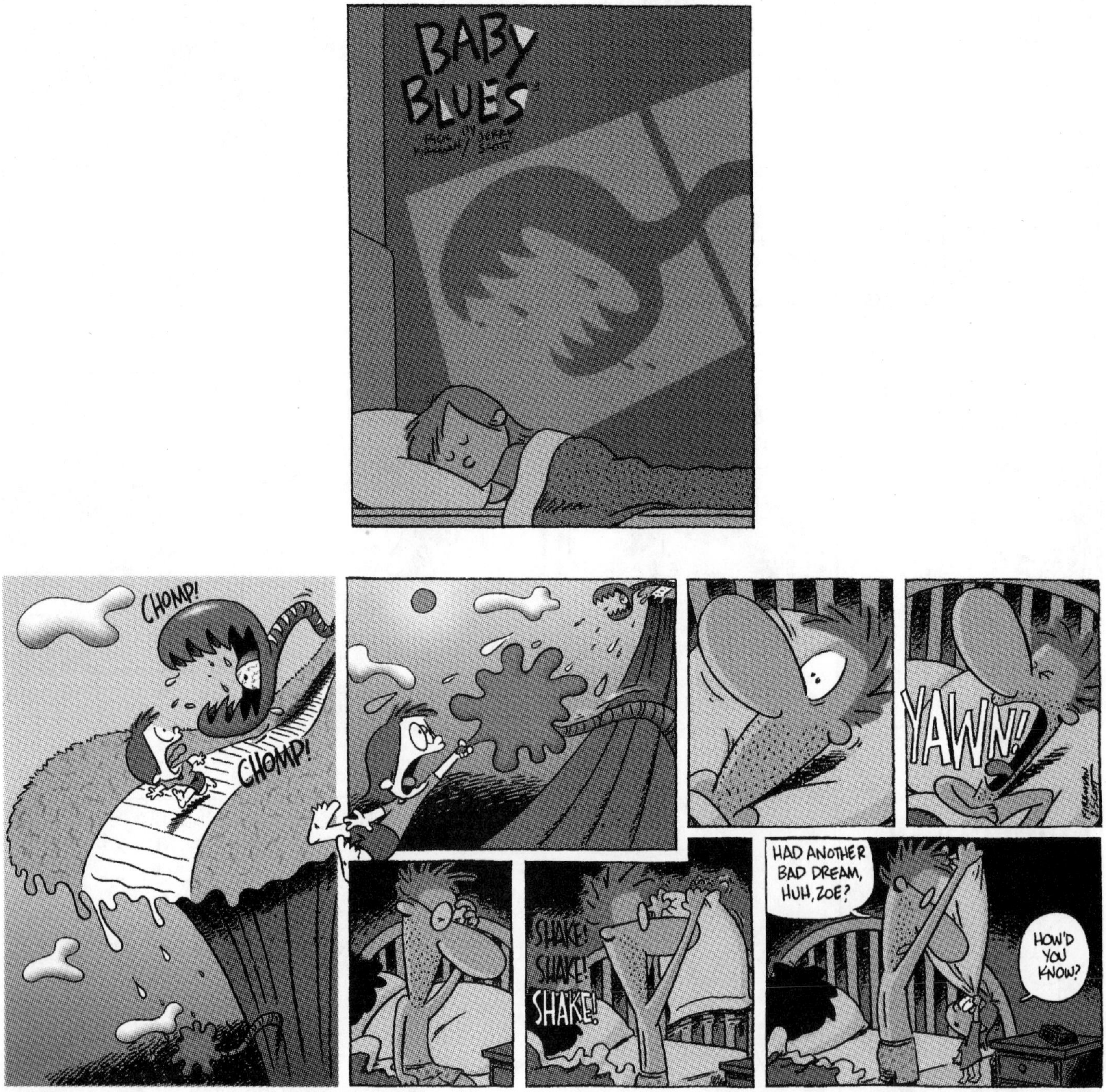
BABY BLUES
RICK KIRKMAN / JERRY SCOTT
CHOMP!
CHOMP!
YAWN!
SHAKE!
SHAKE!
SHAKE!
HAD ANOTHER BAD DREAM, HUH, ZOE?
HOW'D YOU KNOW?

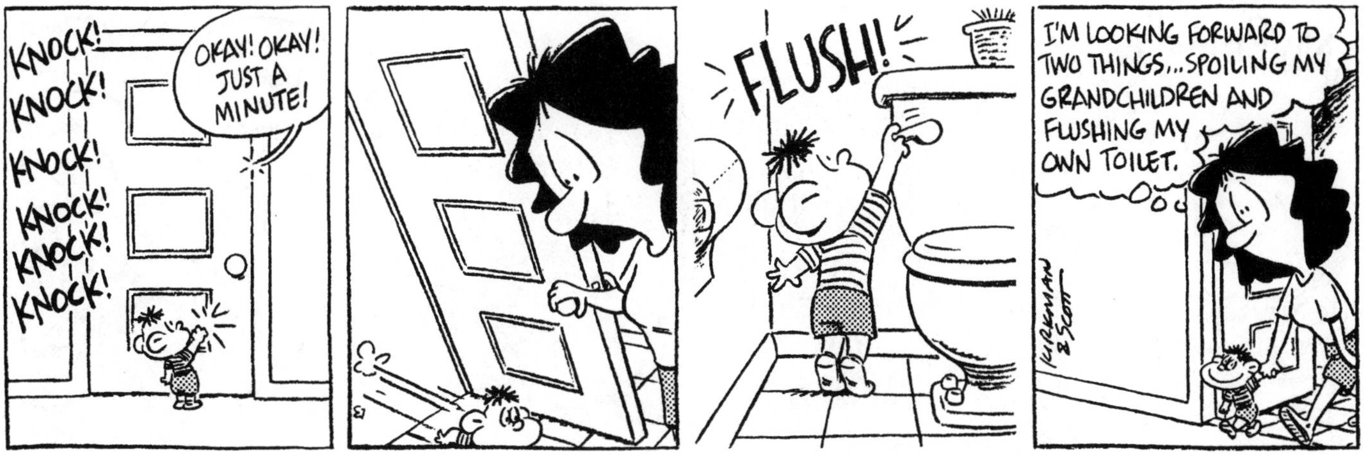
KNOCK! KNOCK! KNOCK! KNOCK! KNOCK! KNOCK!
OKAY! OKAY! JUST A MINUTE!
FLUSH!
I'M LOOKING FORWARD TO TWO THINGS... SPOILING MY GRANDCHILDREN AND FLUSHING MY OWN TOILET.
KIRKMAN & SCOTT

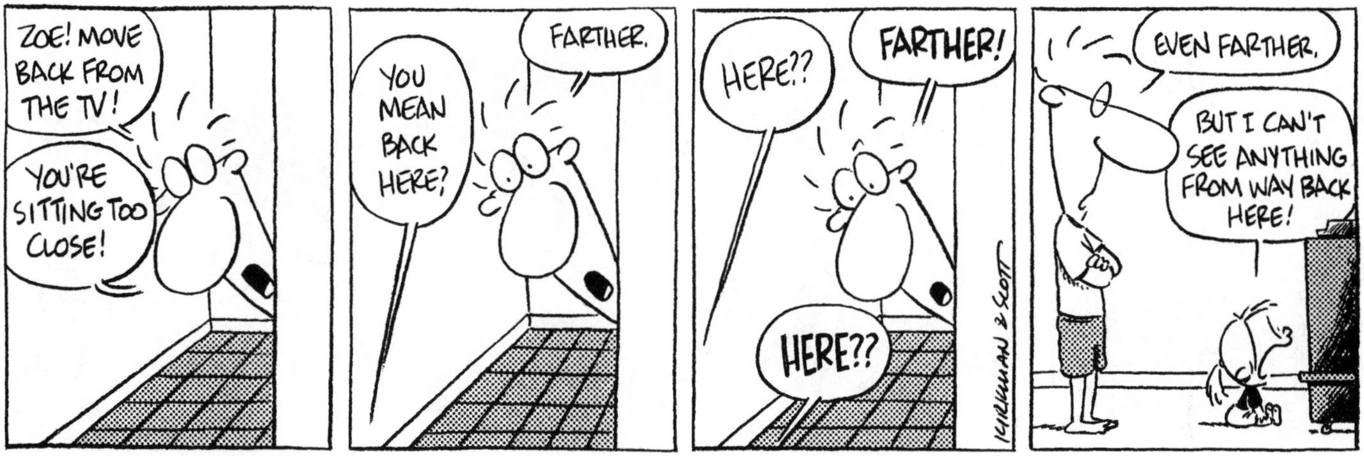
ZOE! MOVE BACK FROM THE TV!
YOU'RE SITTING TOO CLOSE!
YOU MEAN BACK HERE?
FARTHER.
HERE??
FARTHER!
HERE??
KIRKMAN & SCOTT
EVEN FARTHER.
BUT I CAN'T SEE ANYTHING FROM WAY BACK HERE!

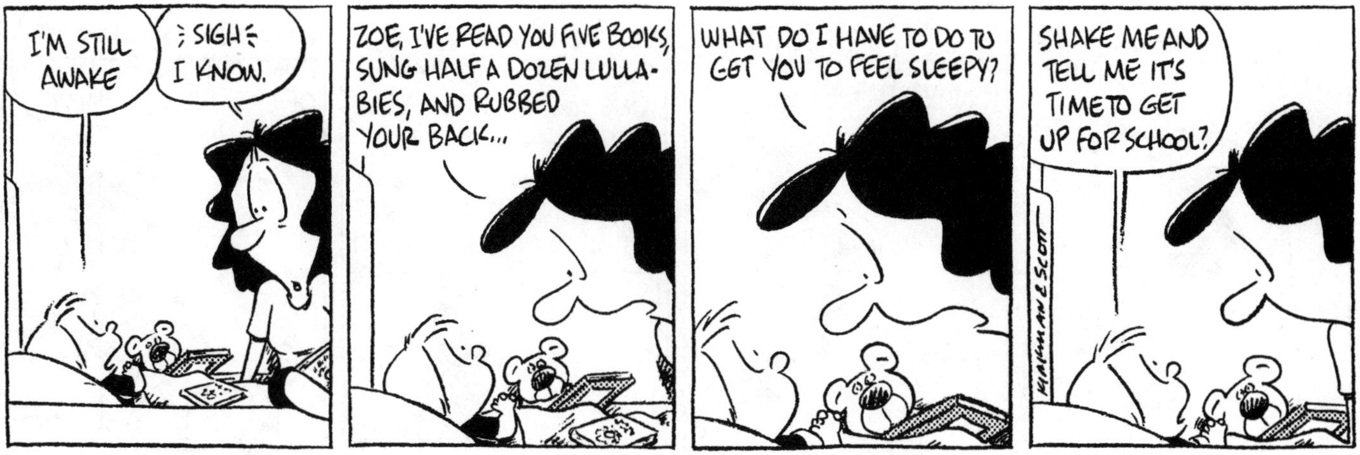
I'M STILL AWAKE
SIGH I KNOW.
ZOE, I'VE READ YOU FIVE BOOKS, SUNG HALF A DOZEN LULLABIES, AND RUBBED YOUR BACK...
WHAT DO I HAVE TO DO TO GET YOU TO FEEL SLEEPY?
KIRKMAN & SCOTT
SHAKE ME AND TELL ME IT'S TIME TO GET UP FOR SCHOOL?

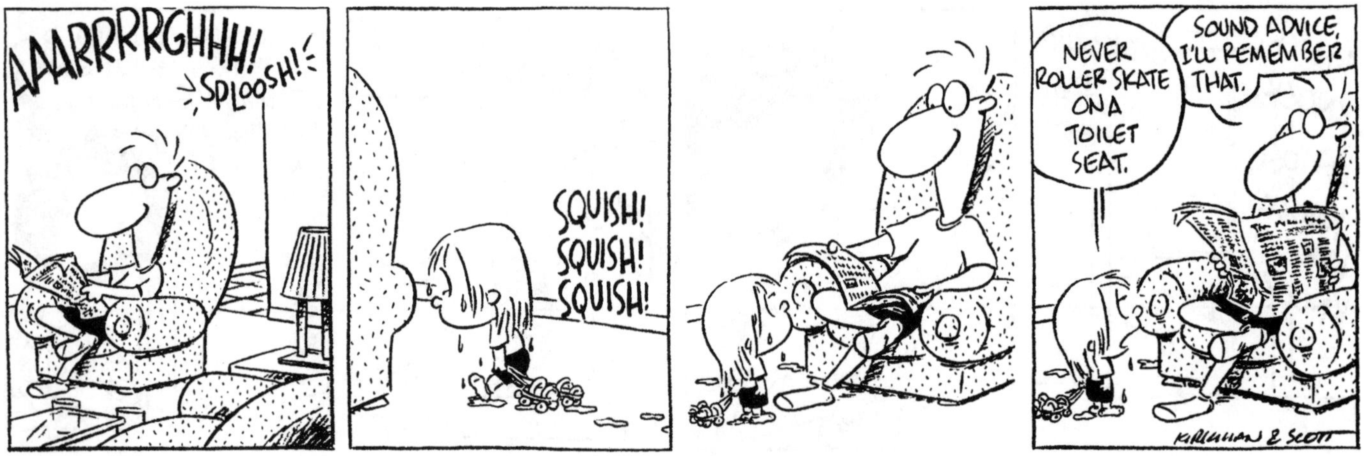
AAARRRRGHHH!
SPLOOSH!
SQUISH! SQUISH! SQUISH!
NEVER ROLLER SKATE ON A TOILET SEAT.
SOUND ADVICE, I'LL REMEMBER THAT.
KIRKMAN & SCOTT

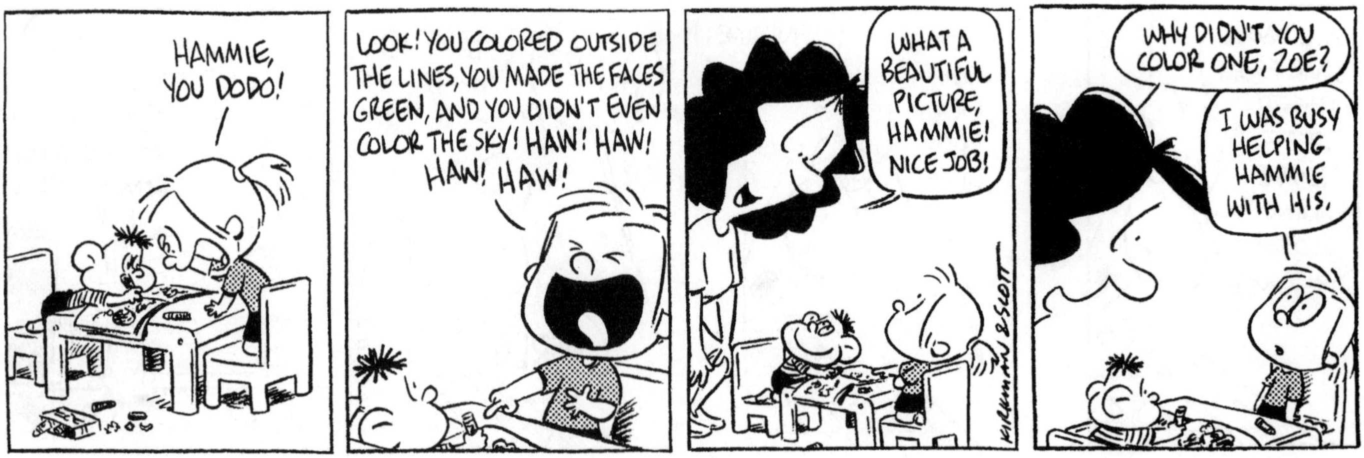
HAMMIE, YOU DODO!
LOOK! YOU COLORED OUTSIDE THE LINES, YOU MADE THE FACES GREEN, AND YOU DIDN'T EVEN COLOR THE SKY! HAW! HAW! HAW! HAW!
WHAT A BEAUTIFUL PICTURE, HAMMIE! NICE JOB!
KIRKMAN & SCOTT
WHY DIDN'T YOU COLOR ONE, ZOE?
I WAS BUSY HELPING HAMMIE WITH HIS.

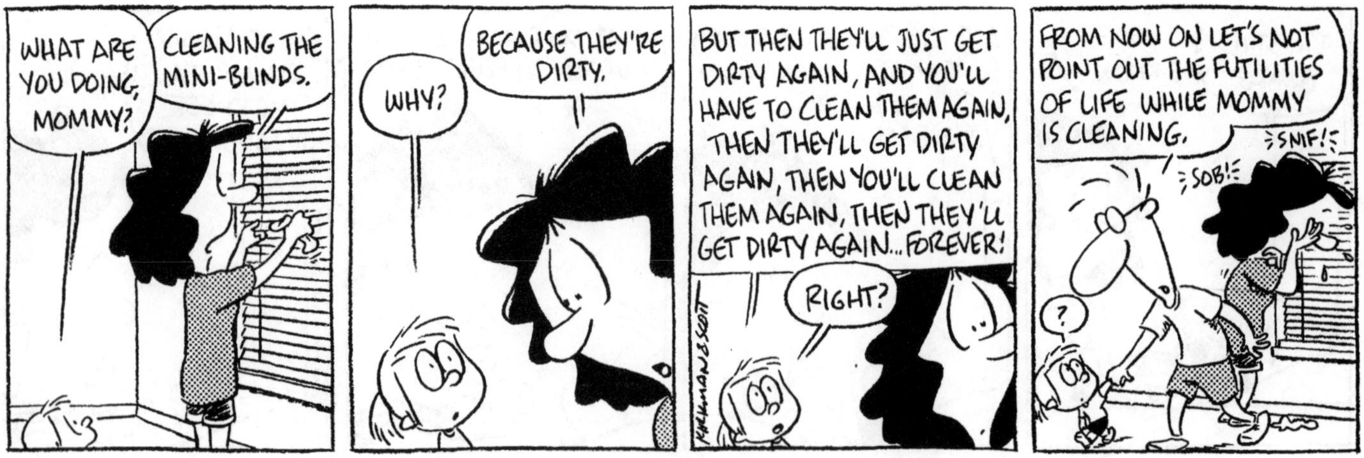
WHAT ARE YOU DOING, MOMMY?
CLEANING THE MINI-BLINDS.
WHY?
BECAUSE THEY'RE DIRTY.
BUT THEN THEY'LL JUST GET DIRTY AGAIN, AND YOU'LL HAVE TO CLEAN THEM AGAIN, THEN THEY'LL GET DIRTY AGAIN, THEN YOU'LL CLEAN THEM AGAIN, THEN THEY'LL GET DIRTY AGAIN... FOREVER!
RIGHT?
KIRKMAN & SCOTT
FROM NOW ON LET'S NOT POINT OUT THE FUTILITIES OF LIFE WHILE MOMMY IS CLEANING.
SNIF!
SOB!
?

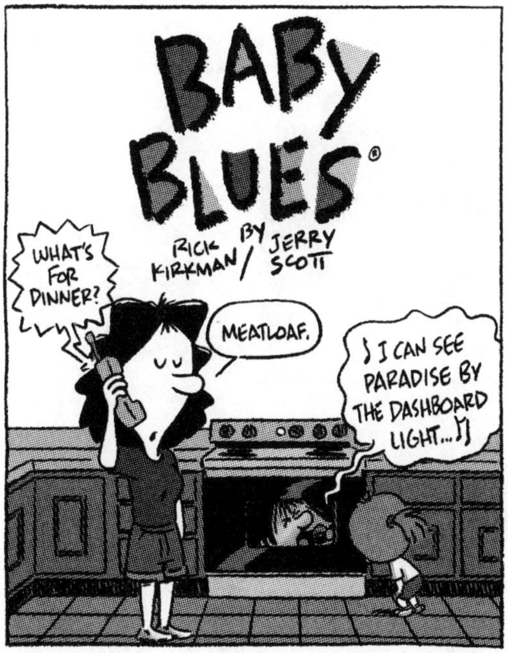
BABY BLUES®
BY RICK KIRKMAN / JERRY SCOTT
WHAT'S FOR DINNER?
MEATLOAF.
I CAN SEE PARADISE BY THE DASHBOARD LIGHT...

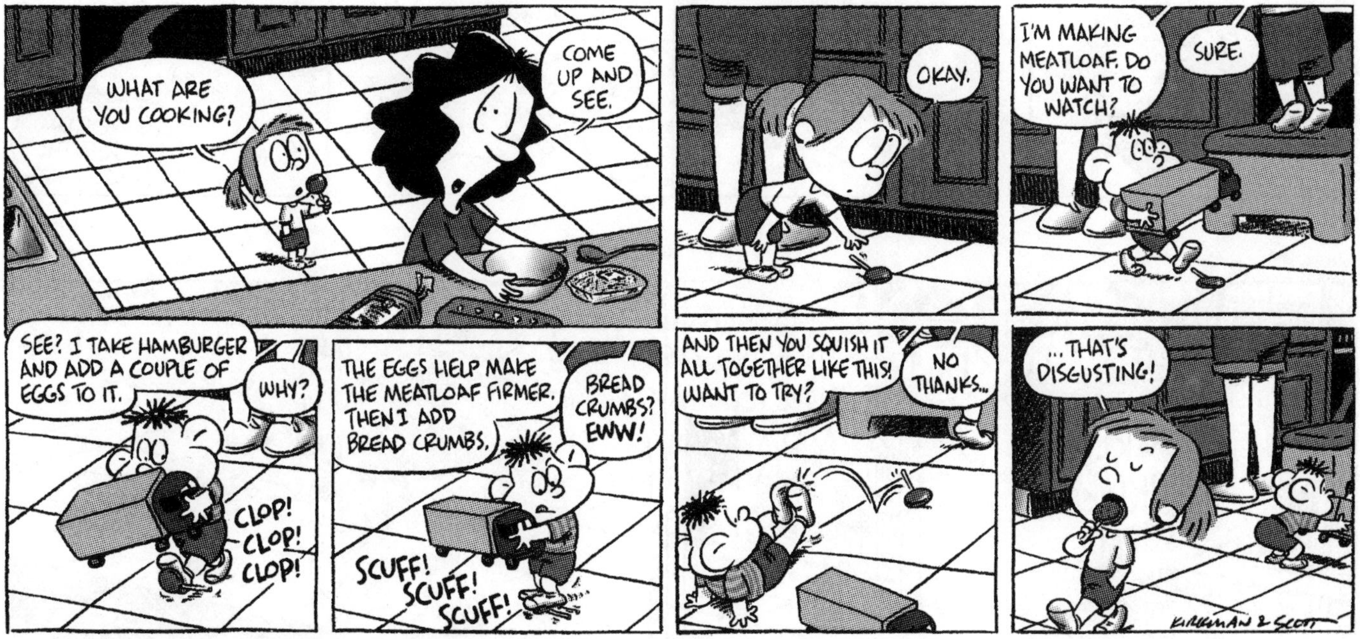
WHAT ARE YOU COOKING?
COME UP AND SEE.
OKAY.
I'M MAKING MEATLOAF. DO YOU WANT TO WATCH?
SURE.
SEE? I TAKE HAMBURGER AND ADD A COUPLE OF EGGS TO IT.
WHY?
CLOP! CLOP! CLOP!
THE EGGS HELP MAKE THE MEATLOAF FIRMER. THEN I ADD BREAD CRUMBS.
BREAD CRUMBS? EWW!
SCUFF! SCUFF! SCUFF!
AND THEN YOU SQUISH IT ALL TOGETHER LIKE THIS! WANT TO TRY?
NO THANKS...
...THAT'S DISGUSTING!
KIRKMAN & SCOTT

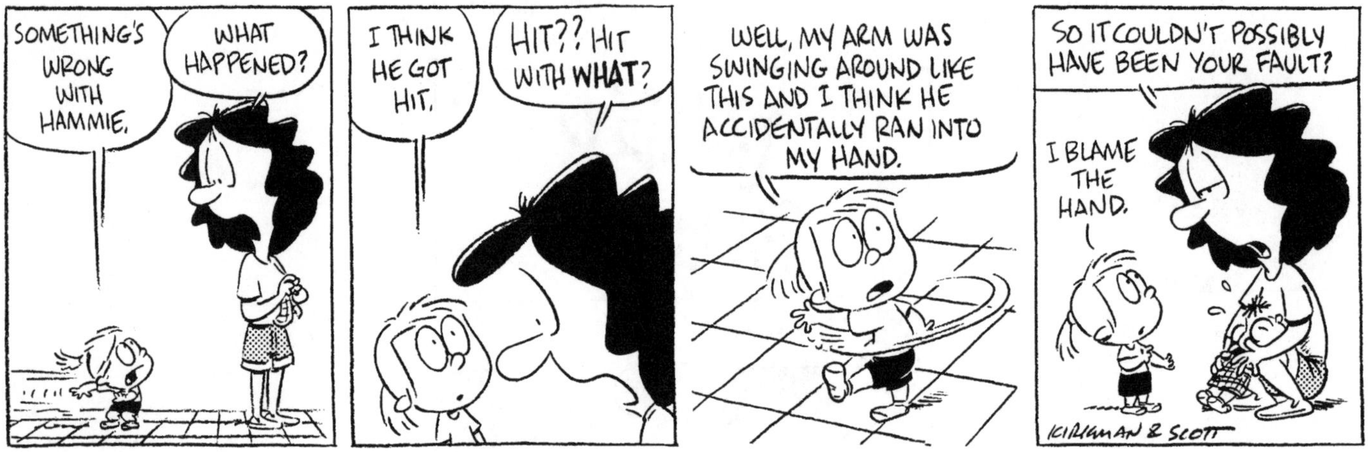
SOMETHING'S WRONG WITH HAMMIE.
WHAT HAPPENED?
I THINK HE GOT HIT.
HIT?? HIT WITH **WHAT**?
WELL, MY ARM WAS SWINGING AROUND LIKE THIS AND I THINK HE ACCIDENTALLY RAN INTO MY HAND.
SO IT COULDN'T POSSIBLY HAVE BEEN YOUR FAULT?
I BLAME THE HAND.
KIRKMAN & SCOTT

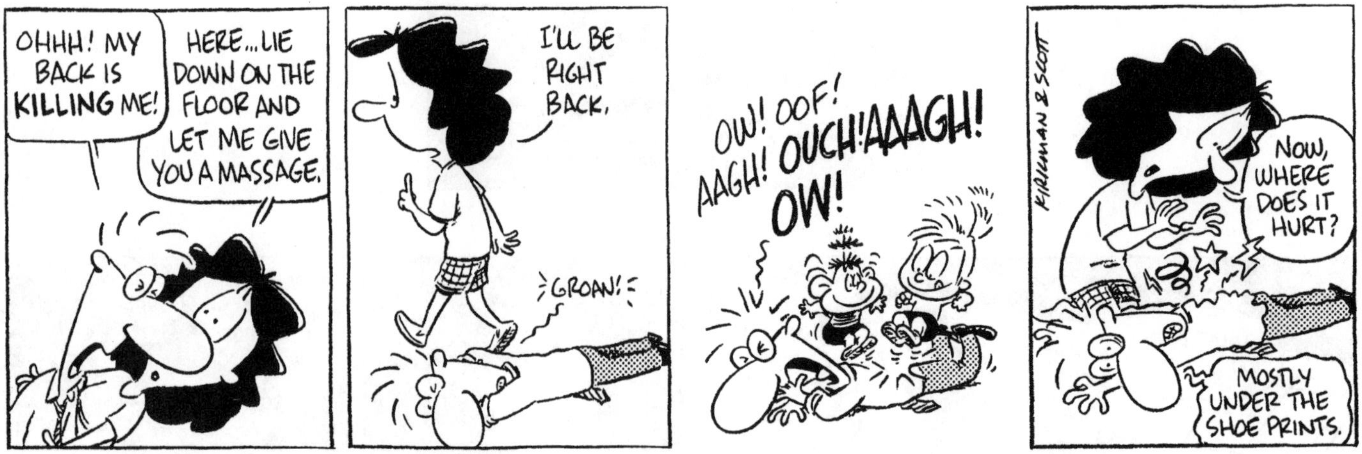
OHHH! MY BACK IS **KILLING** ME!
HERE...LIE DOWN ON THE FLOOR AND LET ME GIVE YOU A MASSAGE.
I'LL BE RIGHT BACK.
GROAN!
OW! OOF! AAGH! OUCH! AAAGH! OW!
KIRKMAN & SCOTT
NOW, WHERE DOES IT HURT?
MOSTLY UNDER THE SHOE PRINTS.

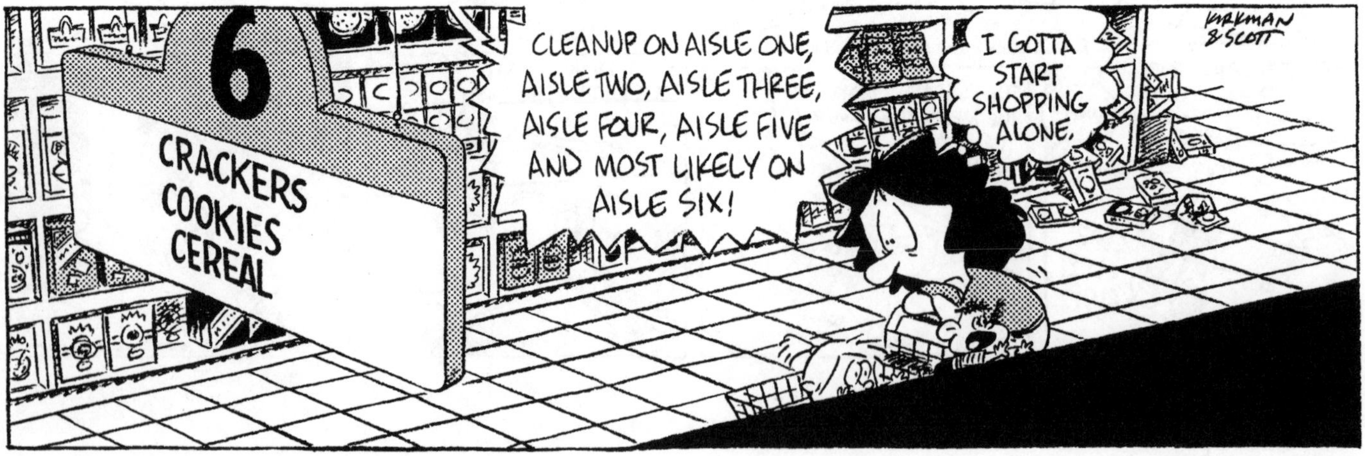
6
CRACKERS
COOKIES
CEREAL
CLEANUP ON AISLE ONE, AISLE TWO, AISLE THREE, AISLE FOUR, AISLE FIVE AND MOST LIKELY ON AISLE SIX!
I GOTTA START SHOPPING ALONE.
KIRKMAN & SCOTT

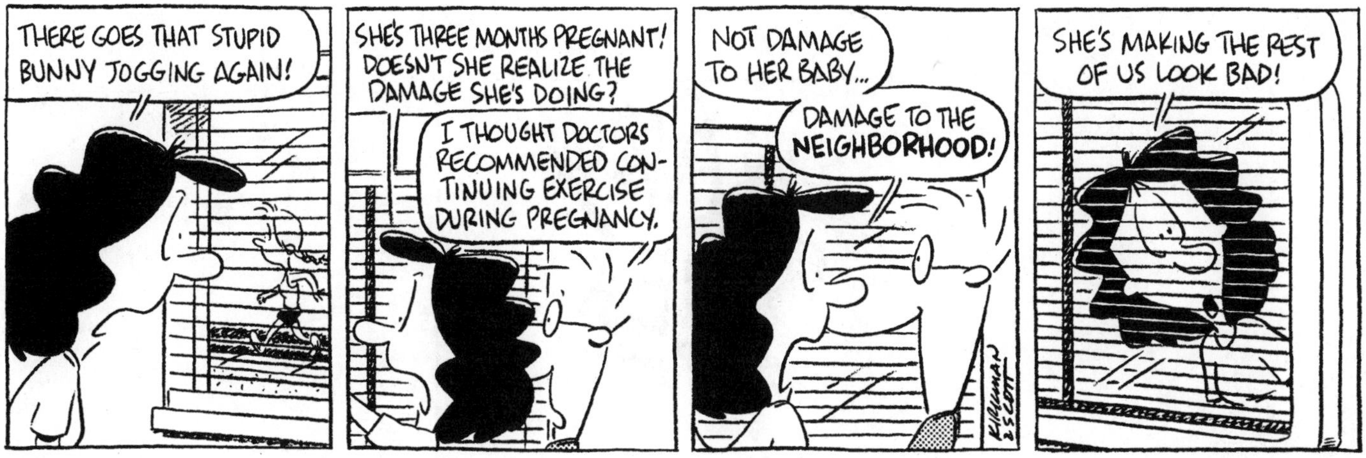
THERE GOES THAT STUPID BUNNY JOGGING AGAIN!
SHE'S THREE MONTHS PREGNANT! DOESN'T SHE REALIZE THE DAMAGE SHE'S DOING?
I THOUGHT DOCTORS RECOMMENDED CON-TINUING EXERCISE DURING PREGNANCY.
NOT DAMAGE TO HER BABY...
DAMAGE TO THE NEIGHBORHOOD!
SHE'S MAKING THE REST OF US LOOK BAD!

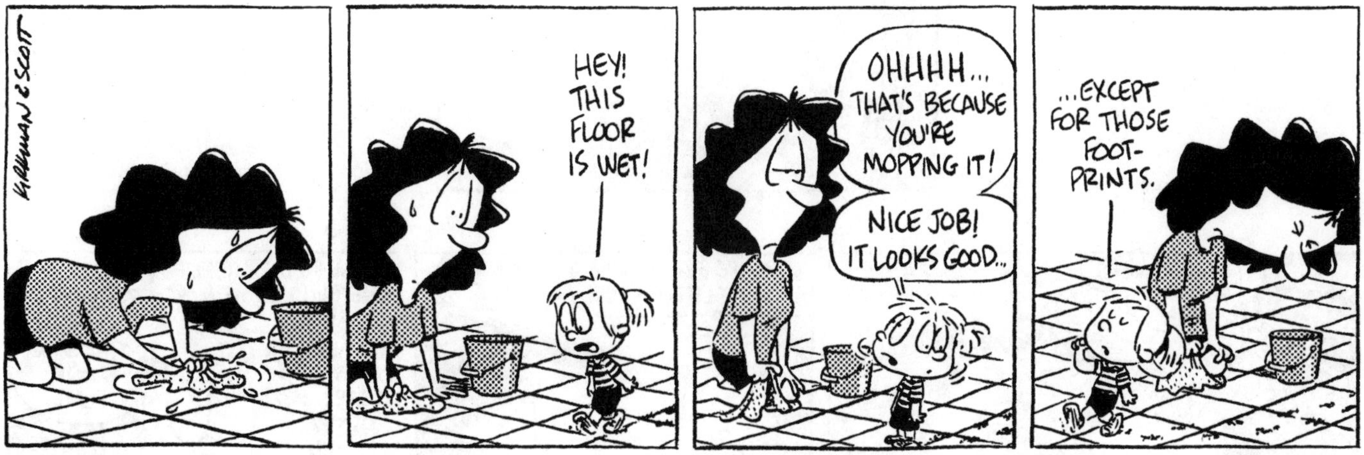
KIRKMAN & SCOTT
HEY! THIS FLOOR IS WET!
OHHHH... THAT'S BECAUSE YOU'RE MOPPING IT!
NICE JOB! IT LOOKS GOOD...
...EXCEPT FOR THOSE FOOT-PRINTS.

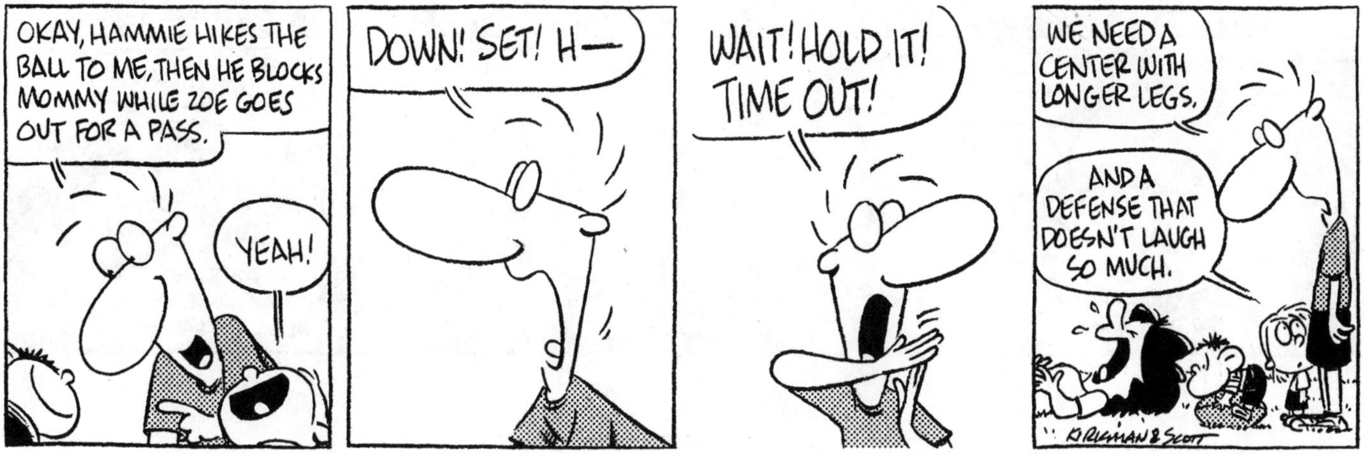
OKAY, HAMMIE HIKES THE BALL TO ME, THEN HE BLOCKS MOMMY WHILE ZOE GOES OUT FOR A PASS.
YEAH!
DOWN! SET! H—
WAIT! HOLD IT! TIME OUT!
WE NEED A CENTER WITH LONGER LEGS.
AND A DEFENSE THAT DOESN'T LAUGH SO MUCH.
KIRKMAN & SCOTT

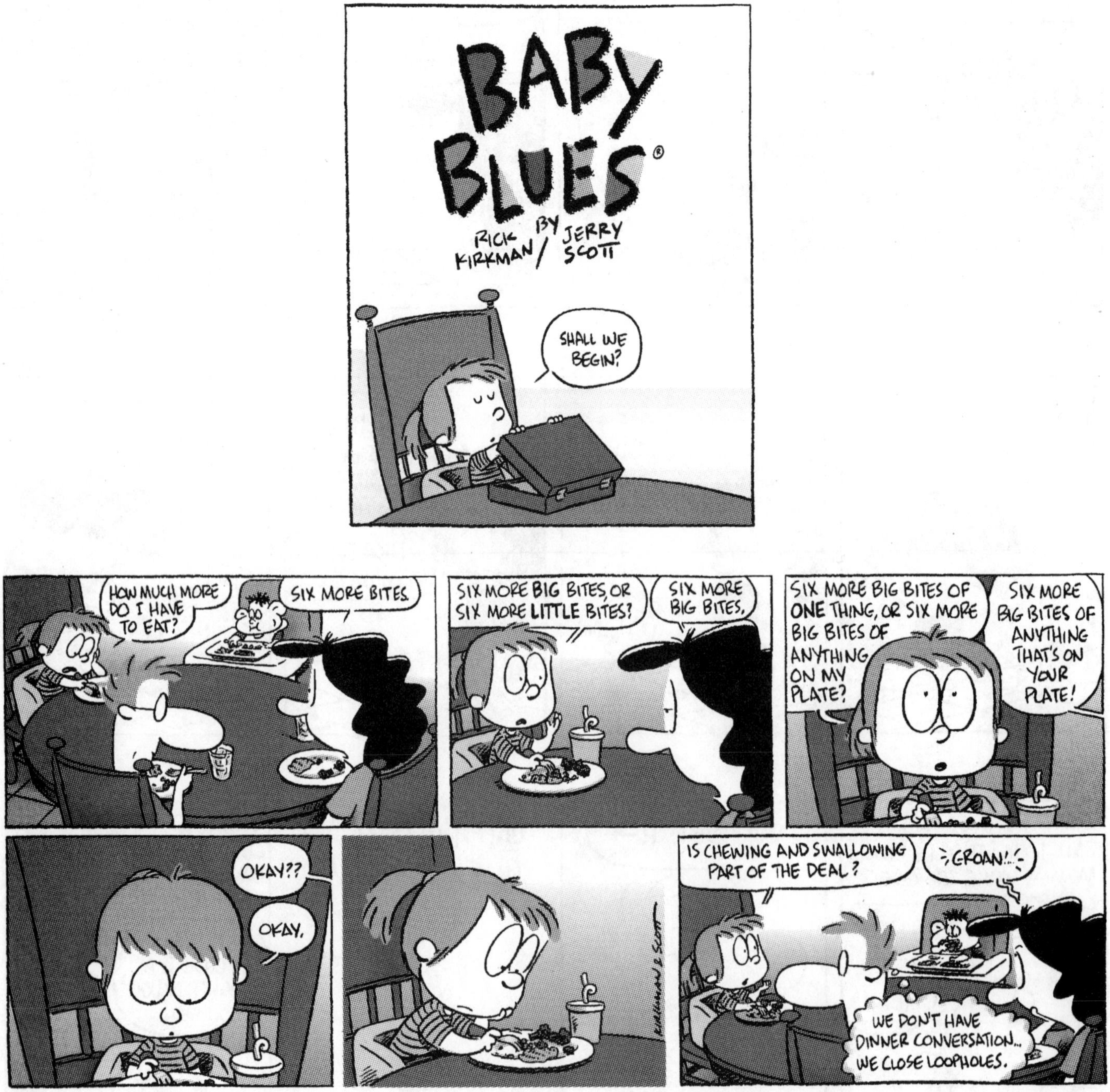
BABY BLUES®
BY RICK KIRKMAN / JERRY SCOTT
SHALL WE BEGIN?
HOW MUCH MORE DO I HAVE TO EAT?
SIX MORE BITES.
SIX MORE BIG BITES, OR SIX MORE LITTLE BITES?
SIX MORE BIG BITES.
SIX MORE BIG BITES OF ONE THING, OR SIX MORE BIG BITES OF ANYTHING ON MY PLATE?
SIX MORE BIG BITES OF ANYTHING THAT'S ON YOUR PLATE!
OKAY??
OKAY.
KIRKMAN & SCOTT
IS CHEWING AND SWALLOWING PART OF THE DEAL?
GROAN!
WE DON'T HAVE DINNER CONVERSATION... WE CLOSE LOOPHOLES.

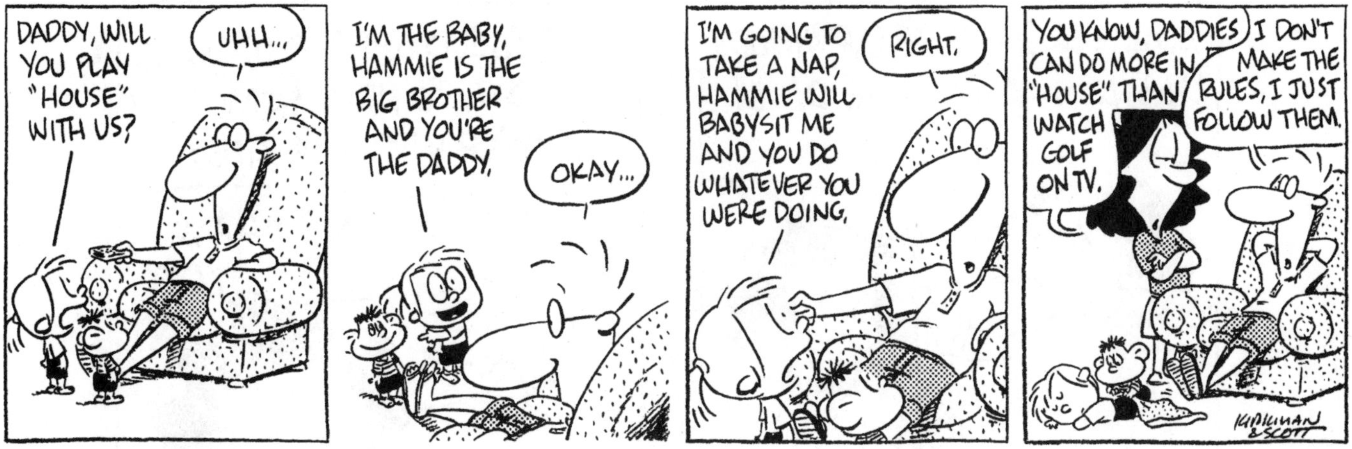
DADDY, WILL YOU PLAY "HOUSE" WITH US?
UHH...
I'M THE BABY, HAMMIE IS THE BIG BROTHER AND YOU'RE THE DADDY.
OKAY...
I'M GOING TO TAKE A NAP, HAMMIE WILL BABYSIT ME AND YOU DO WHATEVER YOU WERE DOING.
RIGHT.
YOU KNOW, DADDIES CAN DO MORE IN "HOUSE" THAN WATCH GOLF ON TV.
I DON'T MAKE THE RULES, I JUST FOLLOW THEM.
KIRKMAN & SCOTT

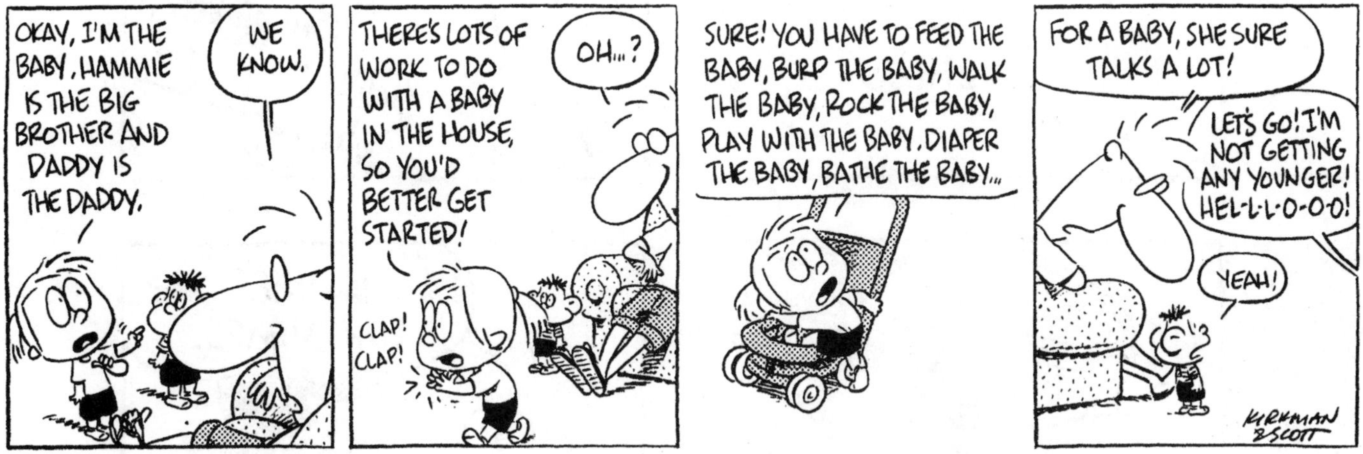
OKAY, I'M THE BABY, HAMMIE IS THE BIG BROTHER AND DADDY IS THE DADDY.
WE KNOW.
THERE'S LOTS OF WORK TO DO WITH A BABY IN THE HOUSE, SO YOU'D BETTER GET STARTED!
OH...?
CLAP! CLAP!
SURE! YOU HAVE TO FEED THE BABY, BURP THE BABY, WALK THE BABY, ROCK THE BABY, PLAY WITH THE BABY, DIAPER THE BABY, BATHE THE BABY...
FOR A BABY, SHE SURE TALKS A LOT!
LET'S GO! I'M NOT GETTING ANY YOUNGER! HEL-L-L-O-O-O!
YEAH!
KIRKMAN & SCOTT

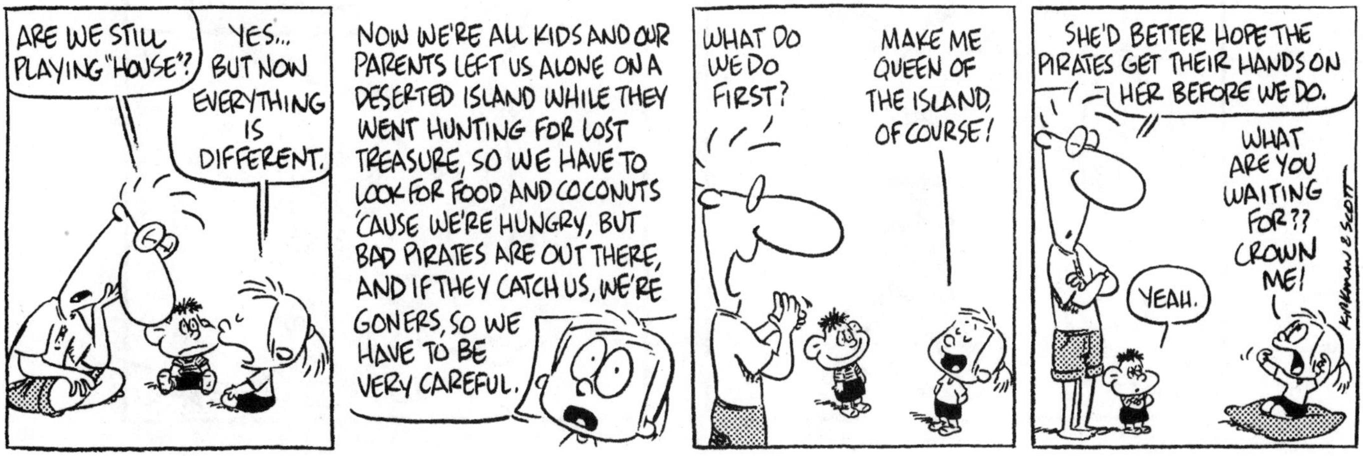
ARE WE STILL PLAYING "HOUSE"?
YES... BUT NOW EVERYTHING IS DIFFERENT.
NOW WE'RE ALL KIDS AND OUR PARENTS LEFT US ALONE ON A DESERTED ISLAND WHILE THEY WENT HUNTING FOR LOST TREASURE, SO WE HAVE TO LOOK FOR FOOD AND COCONUTS 'CAUSE WE'RE HUNGRY, BUT BAD PIRATES ARE OUT THERE, AND IF THEY CATCH US, WE'RE GONERS, SO WE HAVE TO BE VERY CAREFUL.
WHAT DO WE DO FIRST?
MAKE ME QUEEN OF THE ISLAND, OF COURSE!
SHE'D BETTER HOPE THE PIRATES GET THEIR HANDS ON HER BEFORE WE DO.
WHAT ARE YOU WAITING FOR?? CROWN ME!
YEAH.
KIRKMAN & SCOTT

WOW! IT SEEMS LIKE EVERYBODY HAS A NANNY THESE DAYS!
IF WE COULD AFFORD IT, WOULD YOU WANT TO HAVE SOMEBODY TO HELP WITH THE KIDS?
NAAAAW...
...NANNIES ARE FOR WIMPS.
KIRKMAN & SCOTT

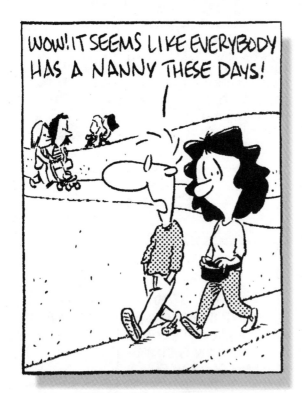

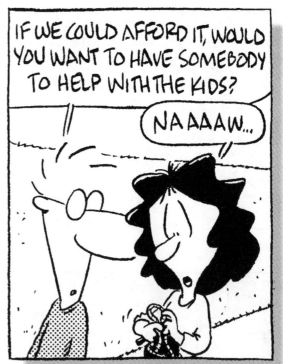

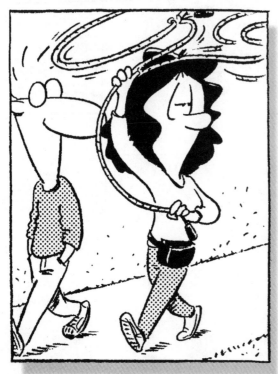

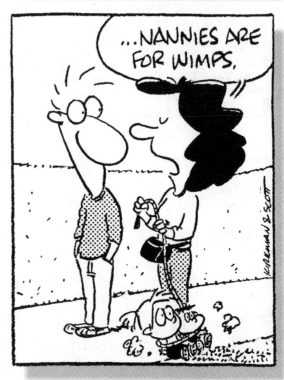

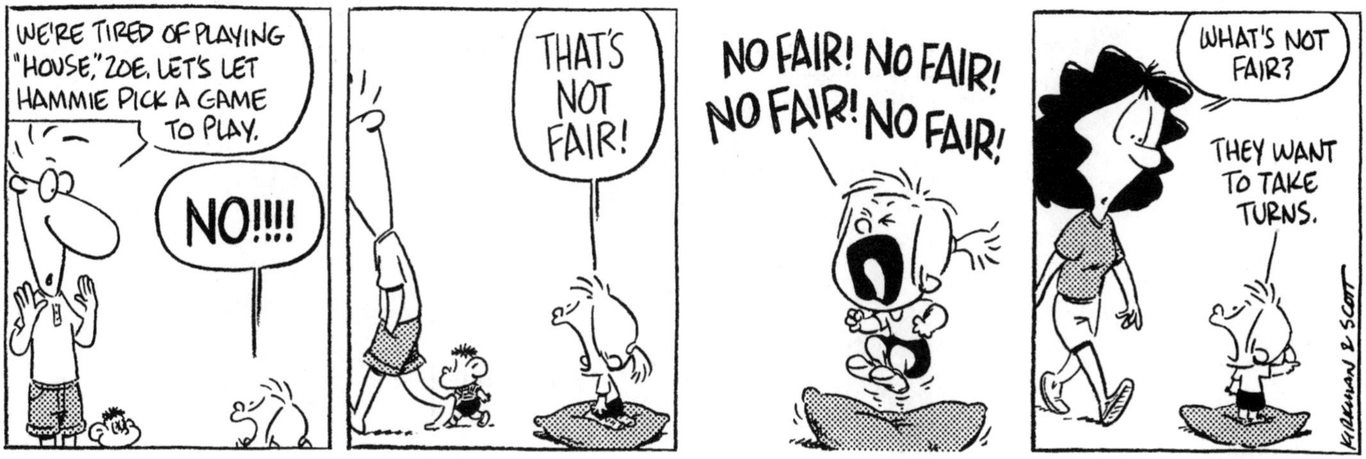
WE'RE TIRED OF PLAYING "HOUSE," ZOE. LET'S LET HAMMIE PICK A GAME TO PLAY.
NO!!!!
THAT'S NOT FAIR!
NO FAIR! NO FAIR! NO FAIR! NO FAIR!
WHAT'S NOT FAIR?
THEY WANT TO TAKE TURNS.
KIRKMAN & SCOTT

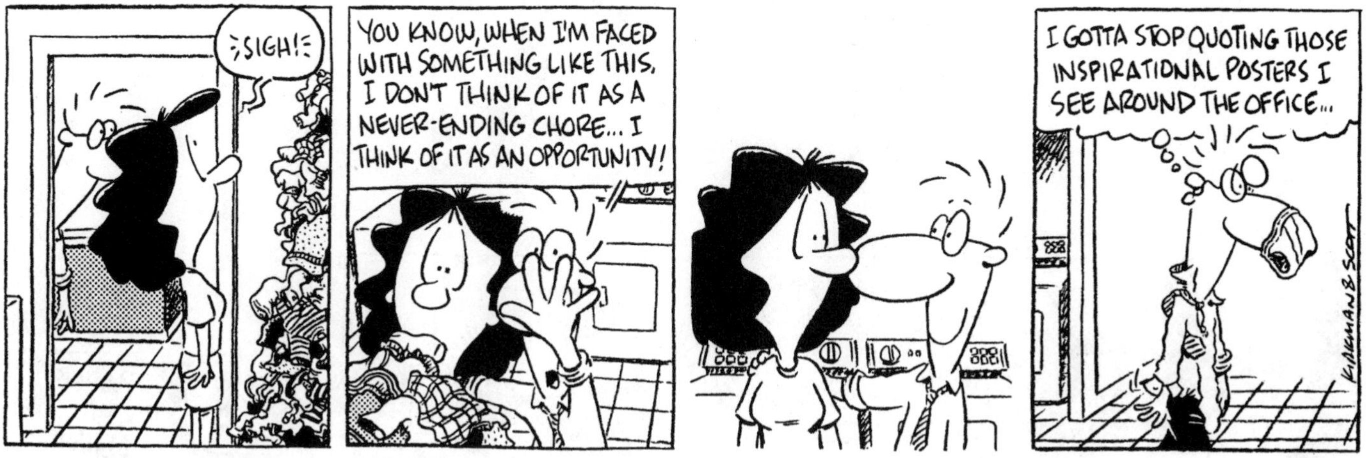
SIGH!
YOU KNOW, WHEN I'M FACED WITH SOMETHING LIKE THIS, I DON'T THINK OF IT AS A NEVER-ENDING CHORE... I THINK OF IT AS AN OPPORTUNITY!
I GOTTA STOP QUOTING THOSE INSPIRATIONAL POSTERS I SEE AROUND THE OFFICE...
KIRKMAN & SCOTT

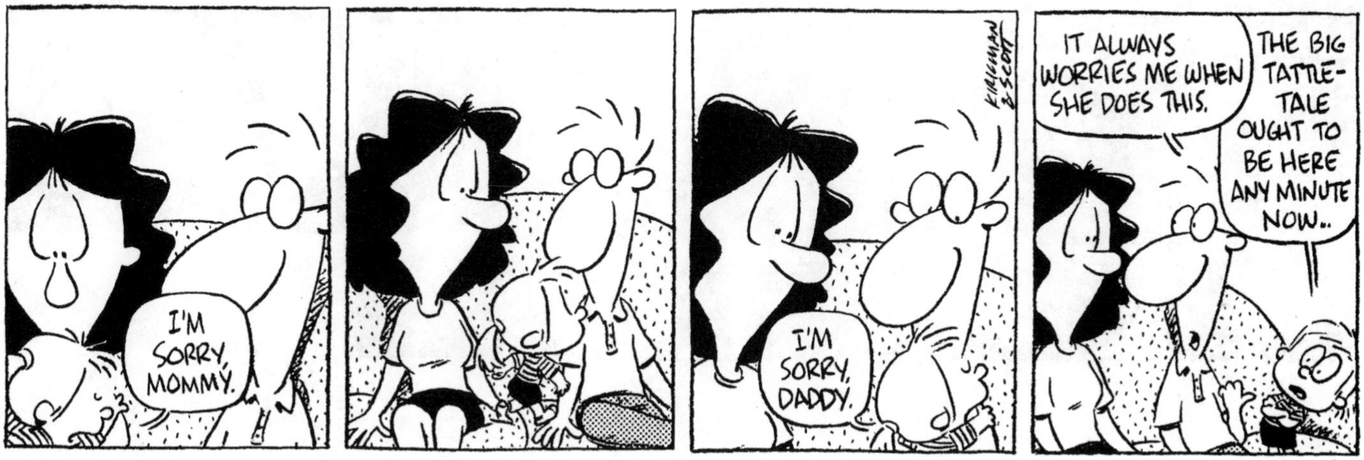
I'M SORRY, MOMMY.
I'M SORRY, DADDY.
KIRKMAN & SCOTT
IT ALWAYS WORRIES ME WHEN SHE DOES THIS.
THE BIG TATTLE-TALE OUGHT TO BE HERE ANY MINUTE NOW..

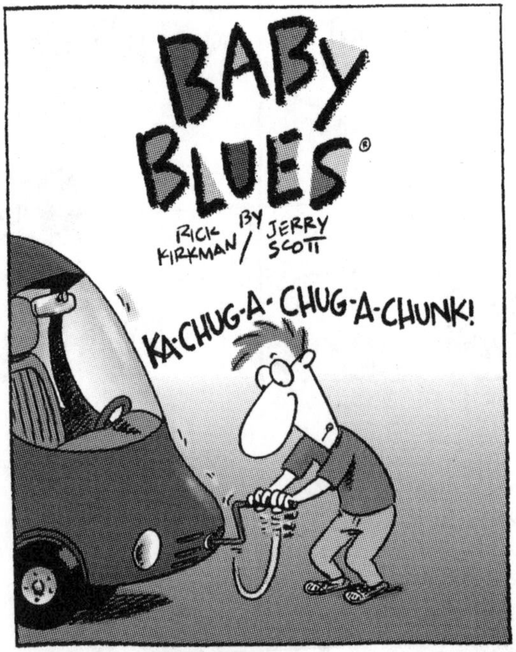
BABY BLUES®
BY RICK KIRKMAN / JERRY SCOTT
KA-CHUG-A-CHUG-A-CHUNK!

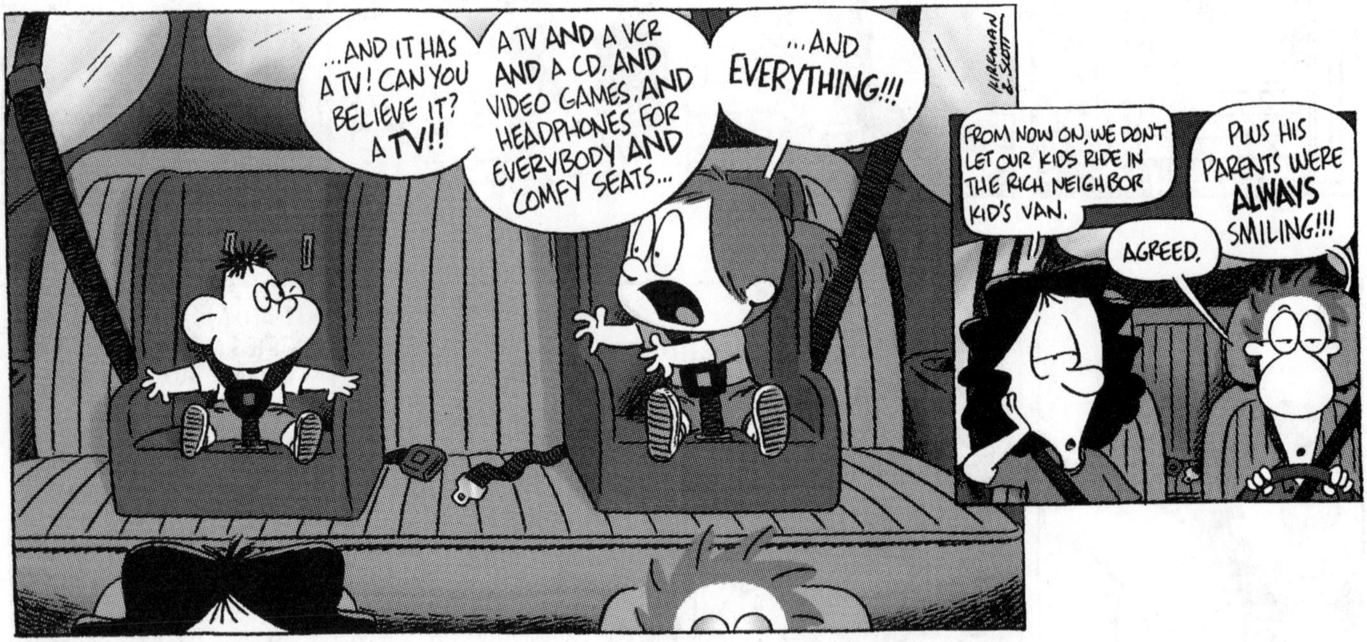
...AND IT HAS A TV! CAN YOU BELIEVE IT? A TV!!
A TV AND A VCR AND A CD, AND VIDEO GAMES, AND HEADPHONES FOR EVERYBODY AND COMFY SEATS...
...AND EVERYTHING!!!
KIRKMAN & SCOTT
FROM NOW ON, WE DON'T LET OUR KIDS RIDE IN THE RICH NEIGHBOR KID'S VAN.
AGREED.
PLUS HIS PARENTS WERE ALWAYS SMILING!!!

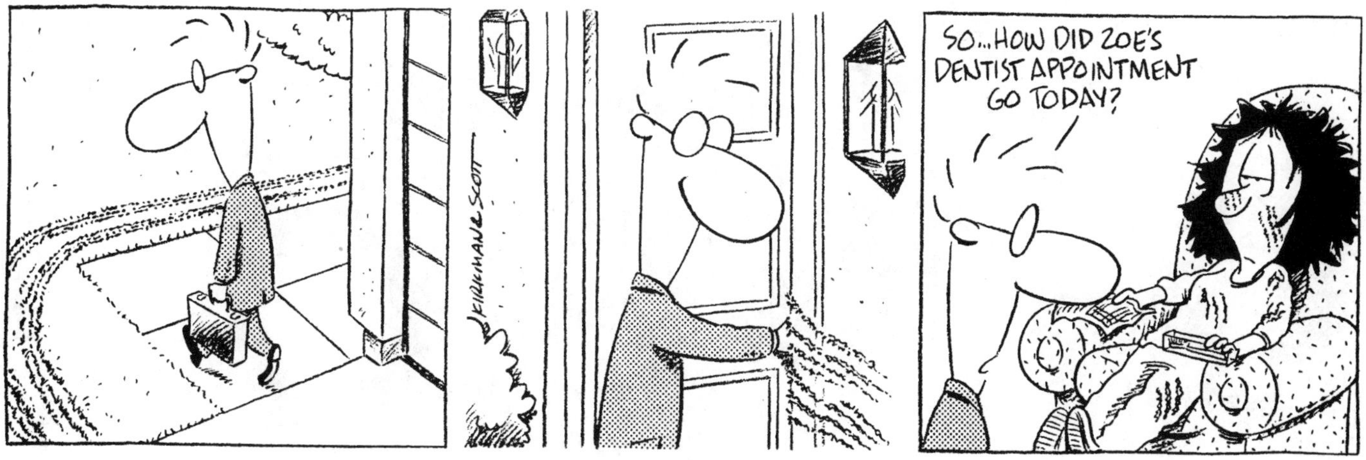
KIRKMAN & SCOTT
SO...HOW DID ZOE'S DENTIST APPOINTMENT GO TODAY?

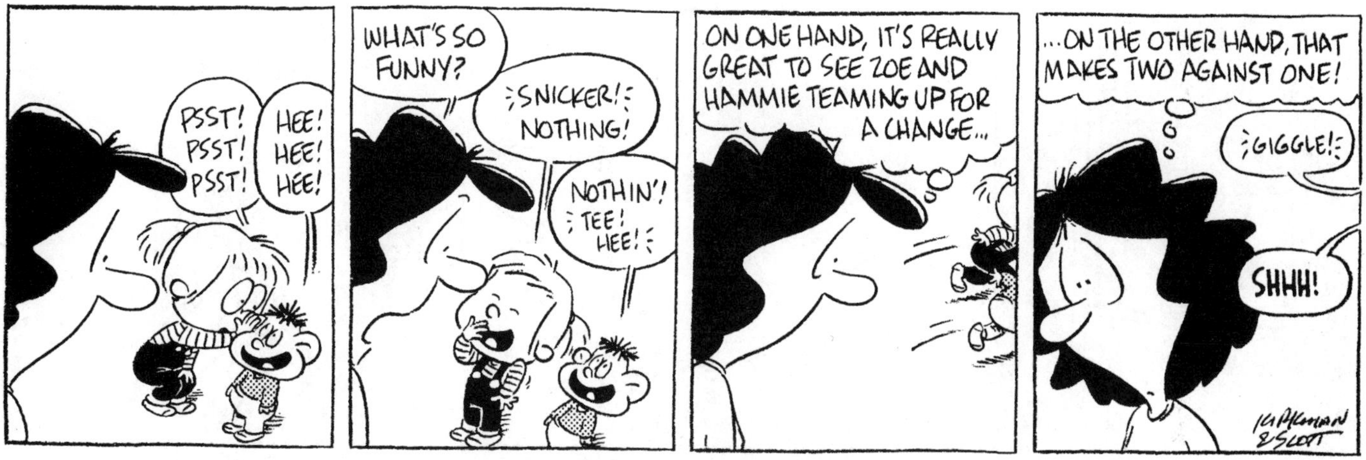
PSST! PSST! PSST!
HEE! HEE! HEE!
WHAT'S SO FUNNY?
SNICKER! NOTHING!
NOTHIN'! TEE! HEE!
ON ONE HAND, IT'S REALLY GREAT TO SEE ZOE AND HAMMIE TEAMING UP FOR A CHANGE...
...ON THE OTHER HAND, THAT MAKES TWO AGAINST ONE!
GIGGLE!
SHHH!
KIRKMAN & SCOTT

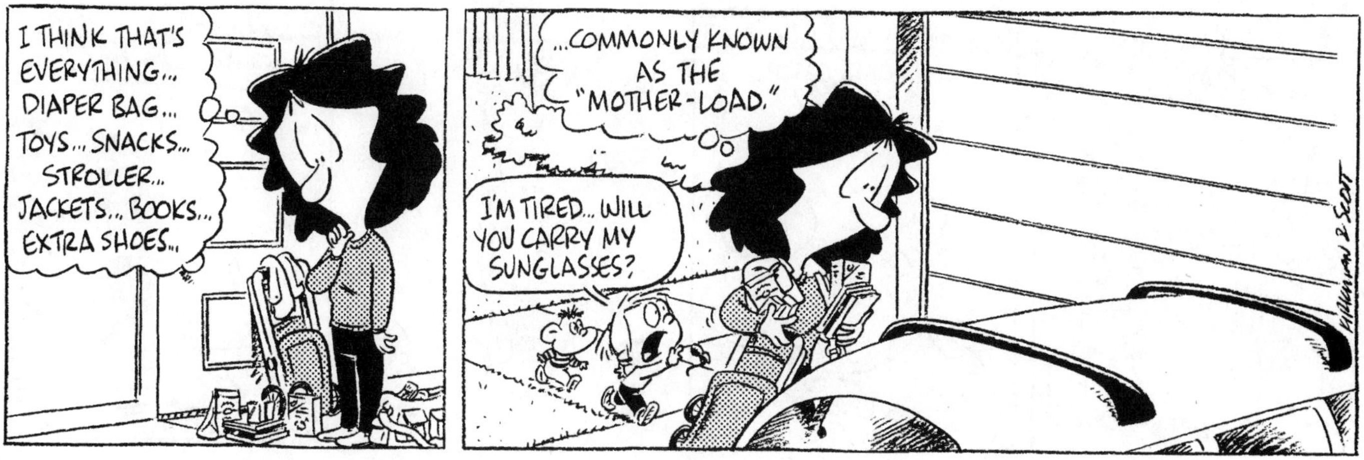
I THINK THAT'S EVERYTHING... DIAPER BAG... TOYS... SNACKS... STROLLER... JACKETS... BOOKS... EXTRA SHOES...
...COMMONLY KNOWN AS THE "MOTHER-LOAD."
I'M TIRED... WILL YOU CARRY MY SUNGLASSES?
KIRKMAN & SCOTT

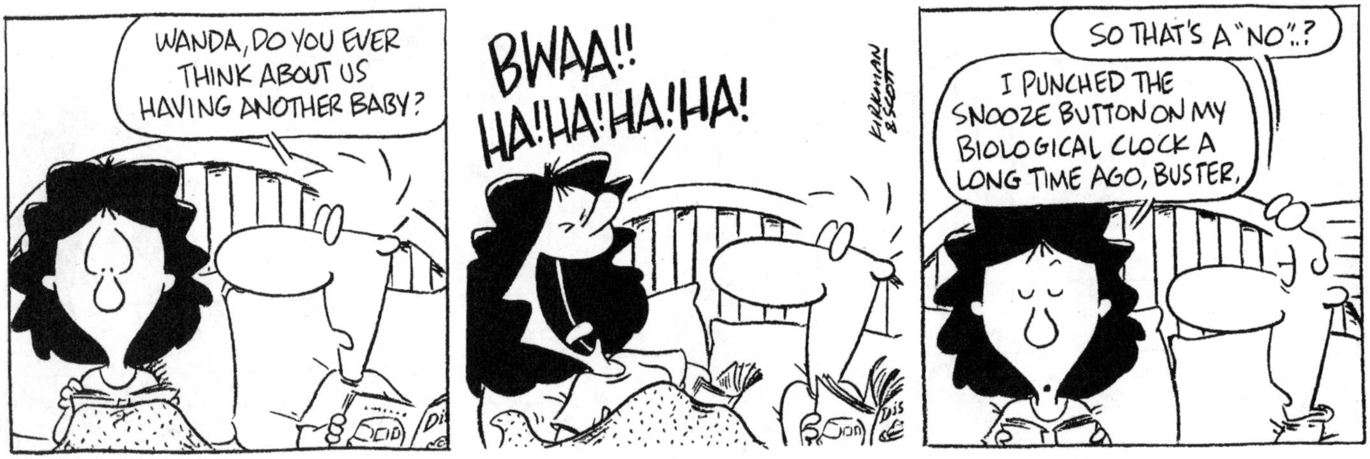
WANDA, DO YOU EVER THINK ABOUT US HAVING ANOTHER BABY?
BWAA!! HA!HA!HA!HA!
KIRKMAN & SCOTT
I PUNCHED THE SNOOZE BUTTON ON MY BIOLOGICAL CLOCK A LONG TIME AGO, BUSTER.
SO THAT'S A "NO"..?

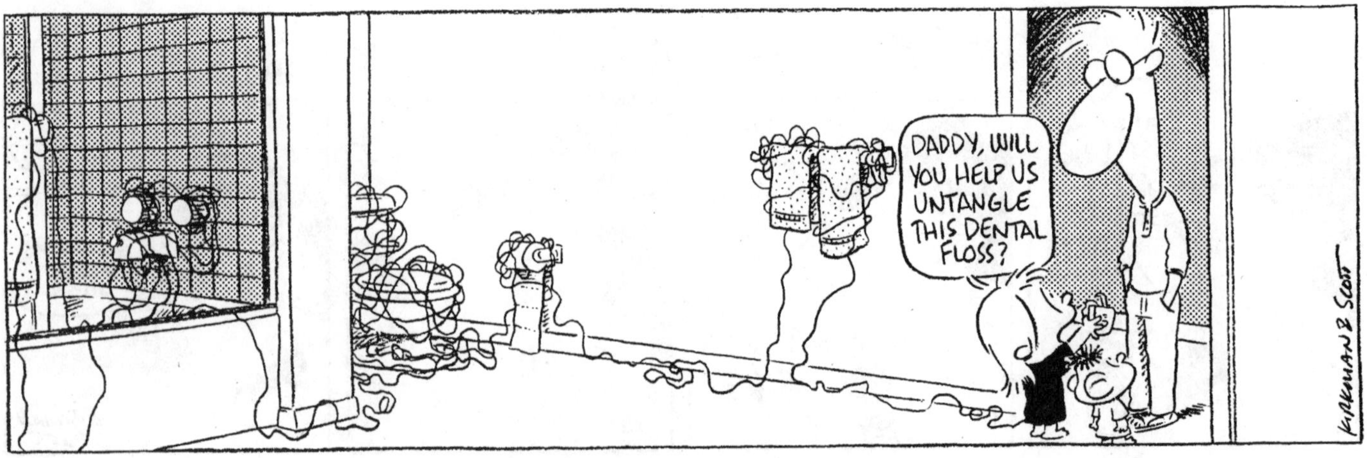
DADDY, WILL YOU HELP US UNTANGLE THIS DENTAL FLOSS?
KIRKMAN & SCOTT

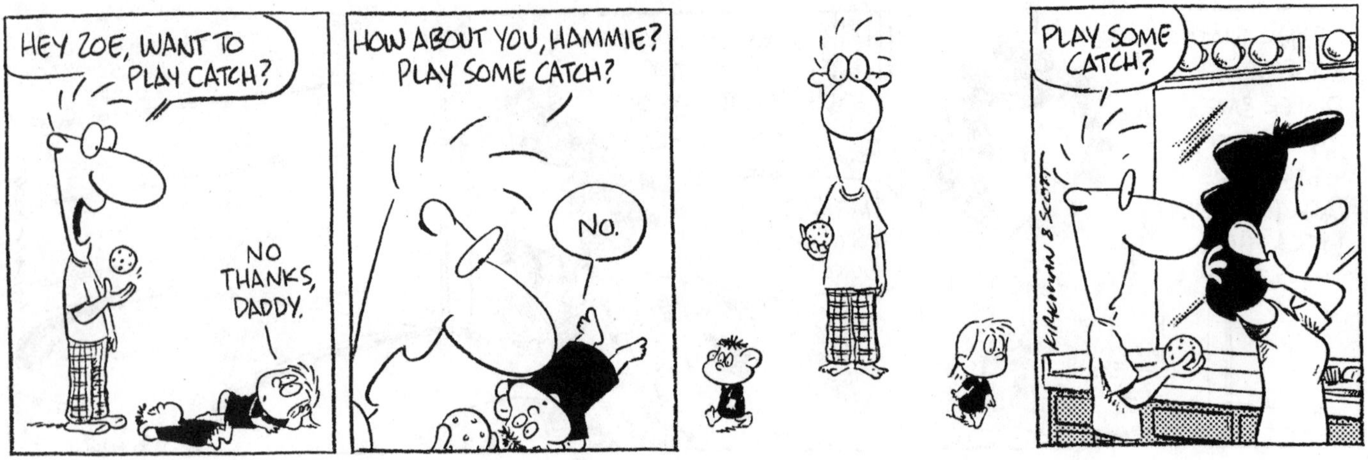
HEY ZOE, WANT TO PLAY CATCH?
NO THANKS, DADDY.
HOW ABOUT YOU, HAMMIE? PLAY SOME CATCH?
NO.
PLAY SOME CATCH?
KIRKMAN & SCOTT

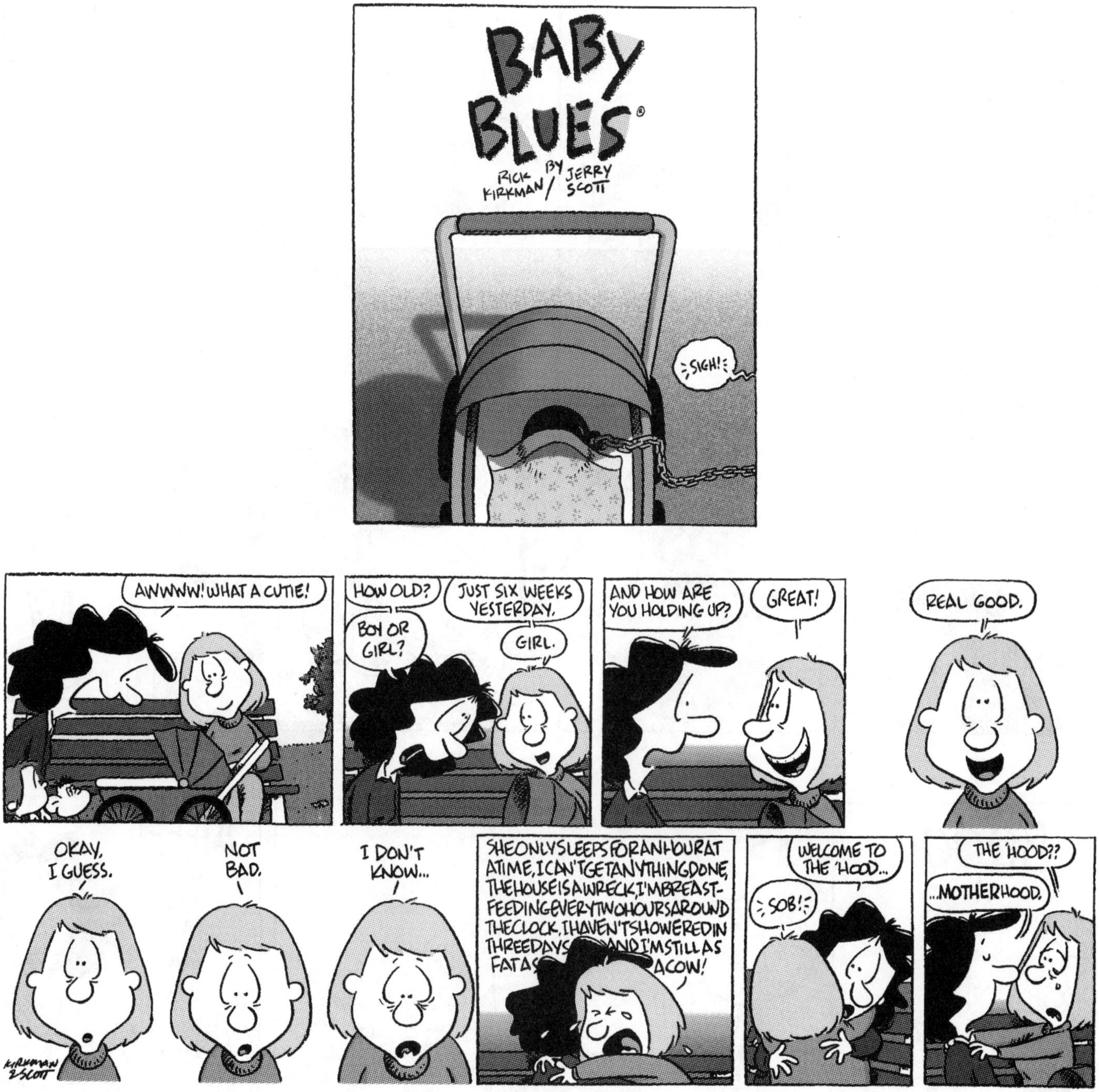
BABY BLUES®
BY RICK KIRKMAN / JERRY SCOTT
SIGH!
AWWWW! WHAT A CUTIE!
HOW OLD?
JUST SIX WEEKS YESTERDAY.
BOY OR GIRL?
GIRL.
AND HOW ARE YOU HOLDING UP?
GREAT!
REAL GOOD.
OKAY, I GUESS.
NOT BAD.
I DON'T KNOW...
SHE ONLY SLEEPS FOR AN HOUR AT A TIME, I CAN'T GET ANYTHING DONE, THE HOUSE IS A WRECK, I'M BREAST-FEEDING EVERY TWO HOURS AROUND THE CLOCK, I HAVEN'T SHOWERED IN THREE DAYS AND I'M STILL AS FAT AS A COW!
WELCOME TO THE 'HOOD...
SOB!
THE 'HOOD??
...MOTHERHOOD.
KIRKMAN & SCOTT

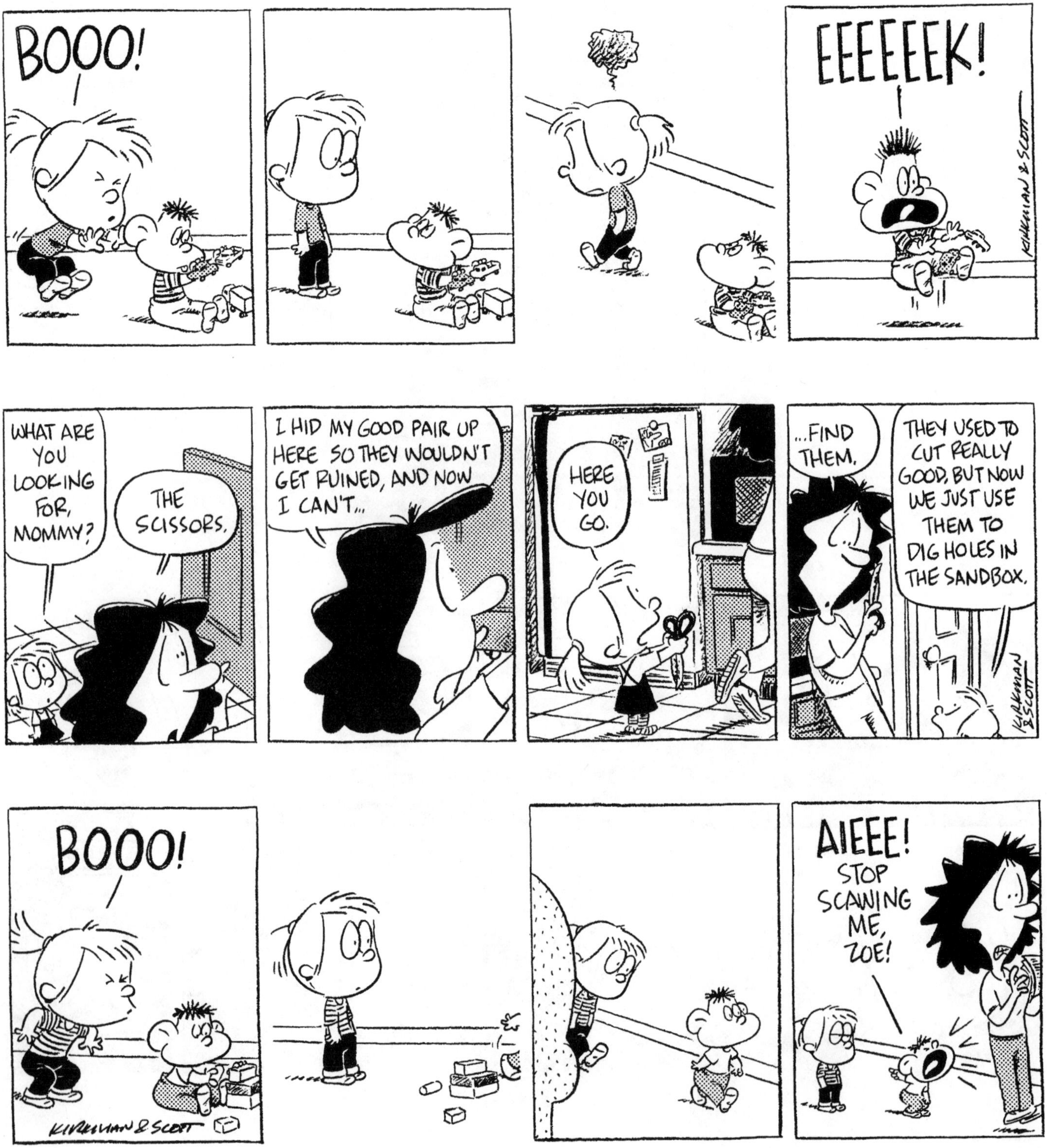
BOOO!
EEEEEEK!
KIRKMAN & SCOTT
WHAT ARE YOU LOOKING FOR, MOMMY?
THE SCISSORS.
I HID MY GOOD PAIR UP HERE SO THEY WOULDN'T GET RUINED, AND NOW I CAN'T...
HERE YOU GO.
...FIND THEM.
THEY USED TO CUT REALLY GOOD, BUT NOW WE JUST USE THEM TO DIG HOLES IN THE SANDBOX.
KIRKMAN & SCOTT
BOOO!
KIRKMAN & SCOTT
AIEEE!
STOP SCAWING ME, ZOE!

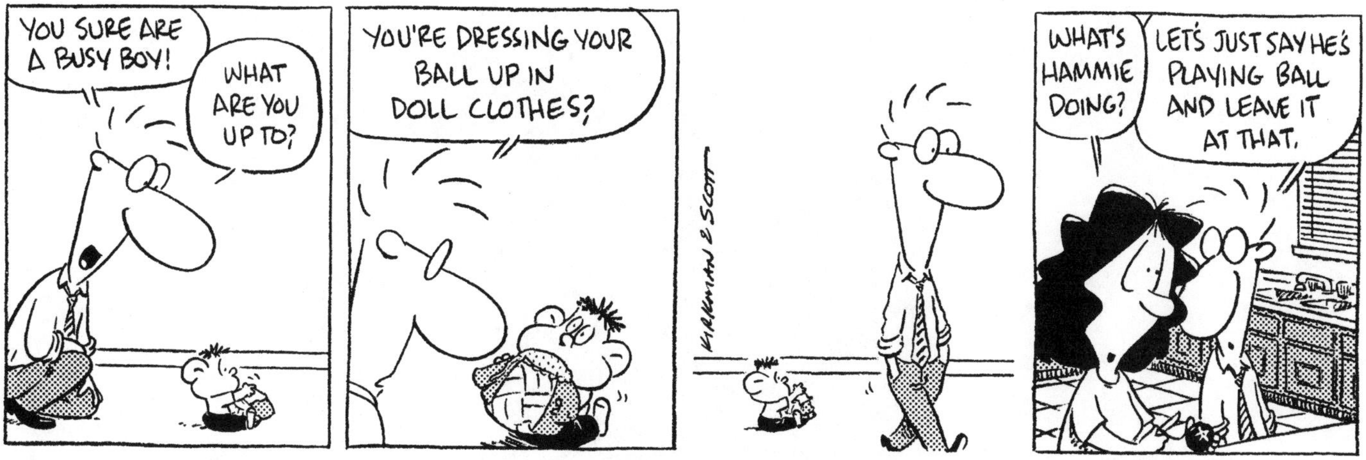
YOU SURE ARE A BUSY BOY!
WHAT ARE YOU UP TO?
YOU'RE DRESSING YOUR BALL UP IN DOLL CLOTHES?
KIRKMAN & SCOTT
WHAT'S HAMMIE DOING?
LET'S JUST SAY HE'S PLAYING BALL AND LEAVE IT AT THAT.

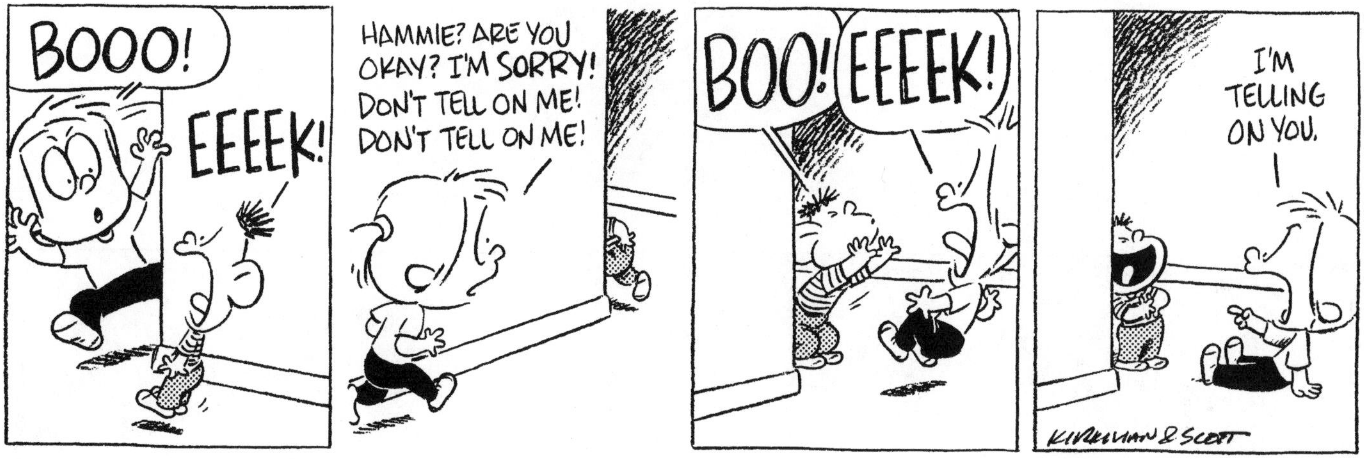
BOOO!
EEEEK!
HAMMIE? ARE YOU OKAY? I'M SORRY! DON'T TELL ON ME! DON'T TELL ON ME!
BOO!
EEEEK!
I'M TELLING ON YOU.
KIRKMAN & SCOTT

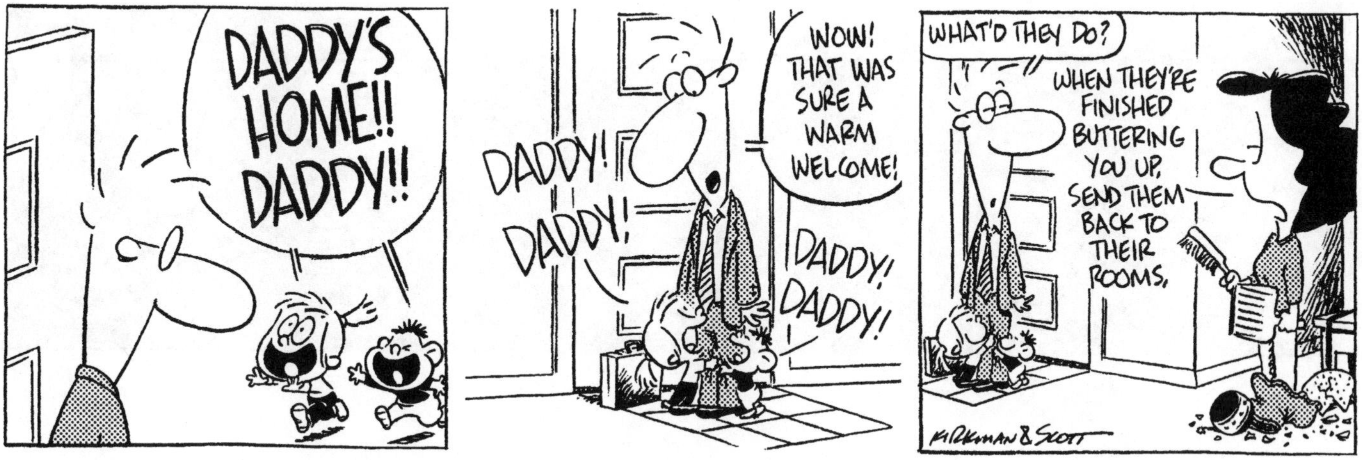
DADDY'S HOME!! DADDY!!
DADDY! DADDY!
WOW! THAT WAS SURE A WARM WELCOME!
DADDY! DADDY!
WHAT'D THEY DO?
WHEN THEY'RE FINISHED BUTTERING YOU UP, SEND THEM BACK TO THEIR ROOMS.
KIRKMAN & SCOTT

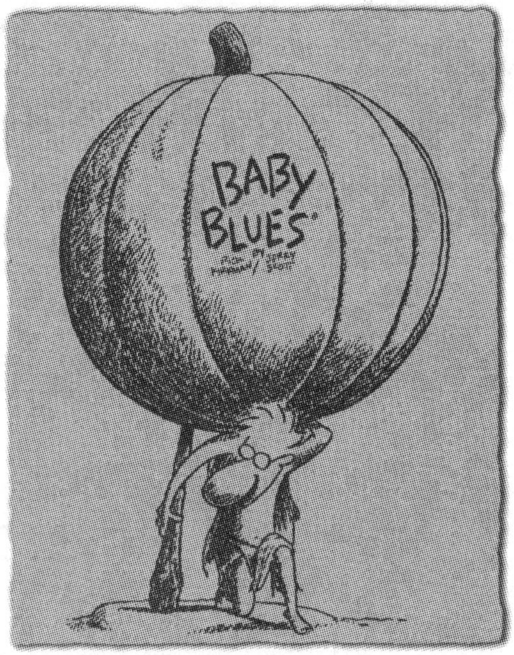
BABY BLUES

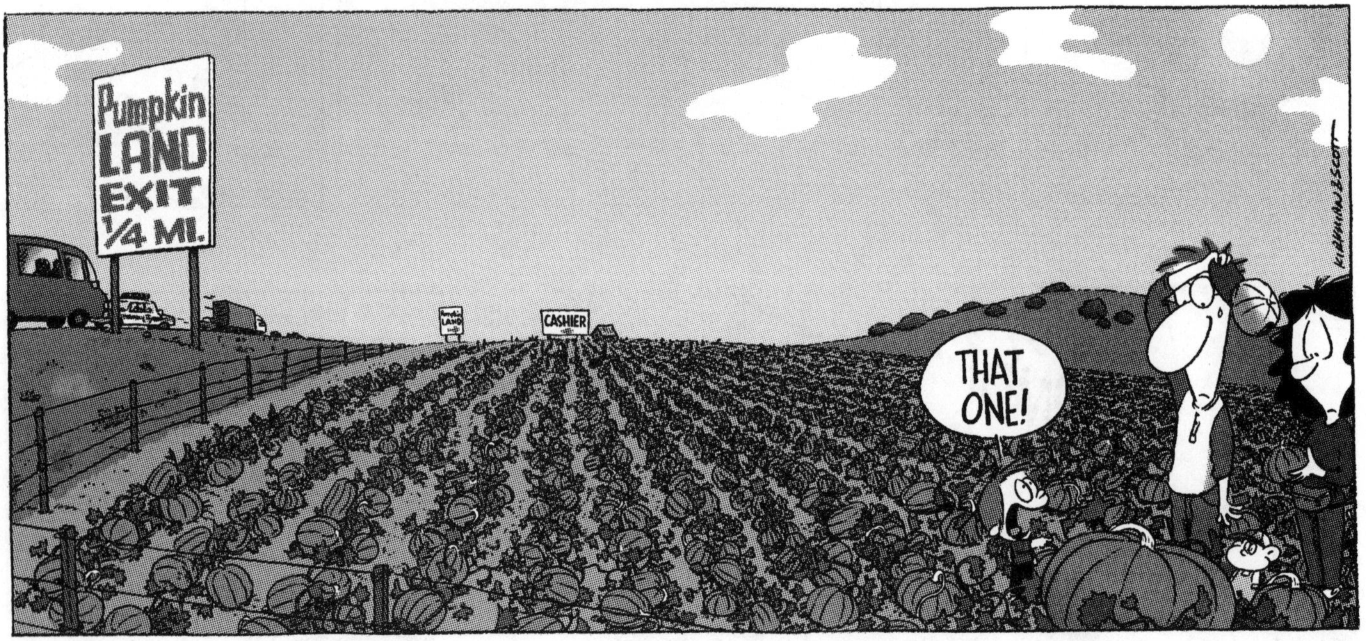
Pumpkin LAND EXIT 1/4 MI.
CASHIER
THAT ONE!
KIRKMAN & SCOTT

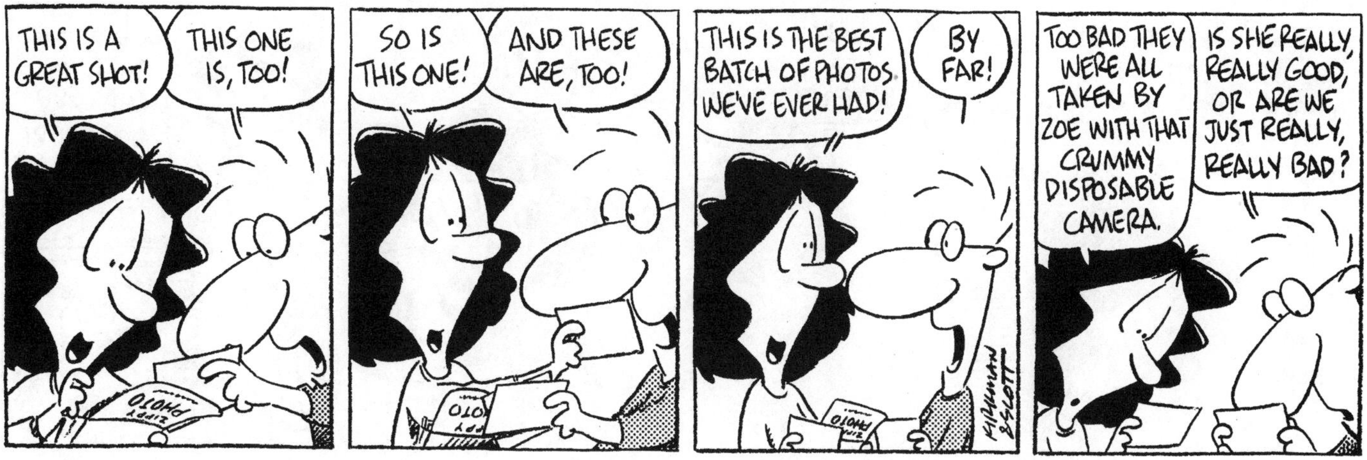
THIS IS A GREAT SHOT!
THIS ONE IS, TOO!
SO IS THIS ONE!
AND THESE ARE, TOO!
THIS IS THE BEST BATCH OF PHOTOS WE'VE EVER HAD!
BY FAR!
KIRKMAN & SCOTT
TOO BAD THEY WERE ALL TAKEN BY ZOE WITH THAT CRUMMY DISPOSABLE CAMERA.
IS SHE REALLY, REALLY GOOD, OR ARE WE JUST REALLY, REALLY BAD?

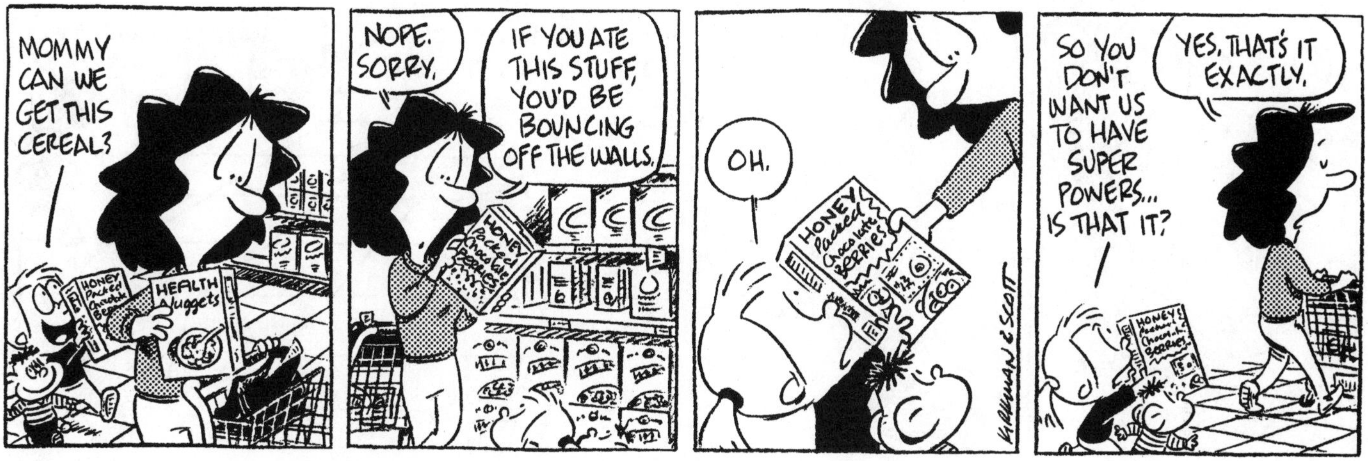
MOMMY CAN WE GET THIS CEREAL?
HEALTH Nuggets
NOPE. SORRY.
IF YOU ATE THIS STUFF, YOU'D BE BOUNCING OFF THE WALLS.
OH.
HONEY Packed Chocolate BERRIES
KIRKMAN & SCOTT
SO YOU DON'T WANT US TO HAVE SUPER POWERS... IS THAT IT?
YES, THAT'S IT EXACTLY.

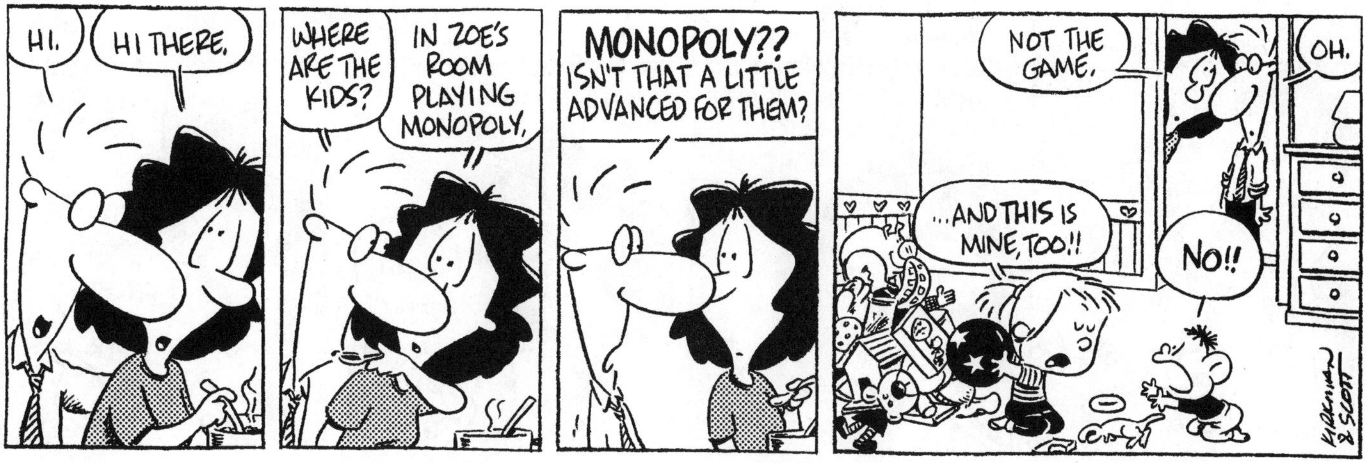
HI.
HI THERE.
WHERE ARE THE KIDS?
IN ZOE'S ROOM PLAYING MONOPOLY.
MONOPOLY?? ISN'T THAT A LITTLE ADVANCED FOR THEM?
NOT THE GAME.
OH.
...AND THIS IS MINE, TOO!!
NO!!
KIRKMAN & SCOTT

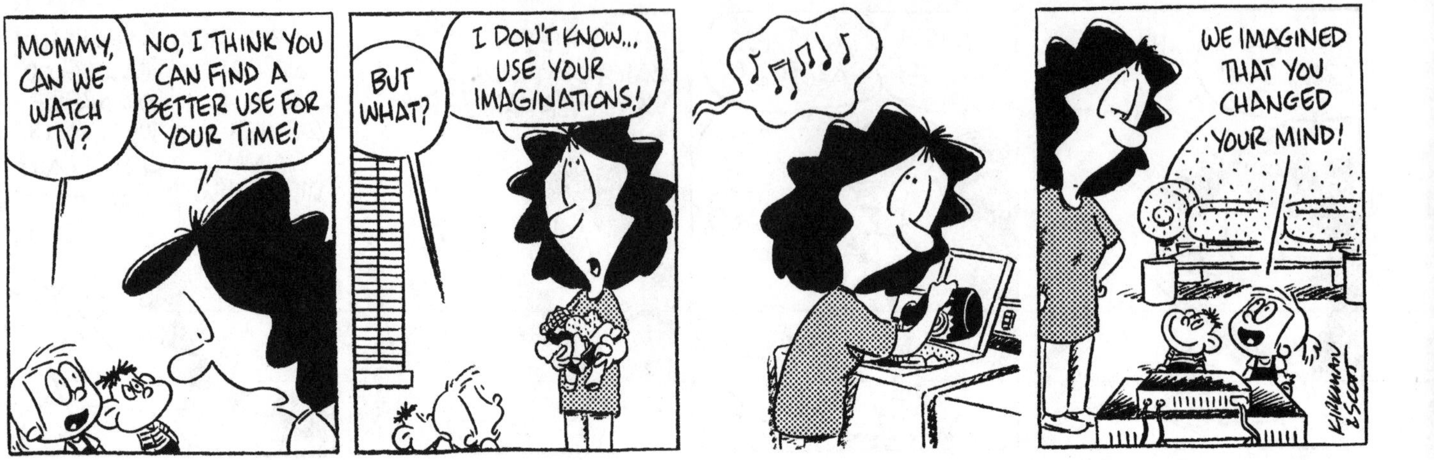
MOMMY, CAN WE WATCH TV?
NO, I THINK YOU CAN FIND A BETTER USE FOR YOUR TIME!
BUT WHAT?
I DON'T KNOW... USE YOUR IMAGINATIONS!
WE IMAGINED THAT YOU CHANGED YOUR MIND!
KIRKMAN & SCOTT

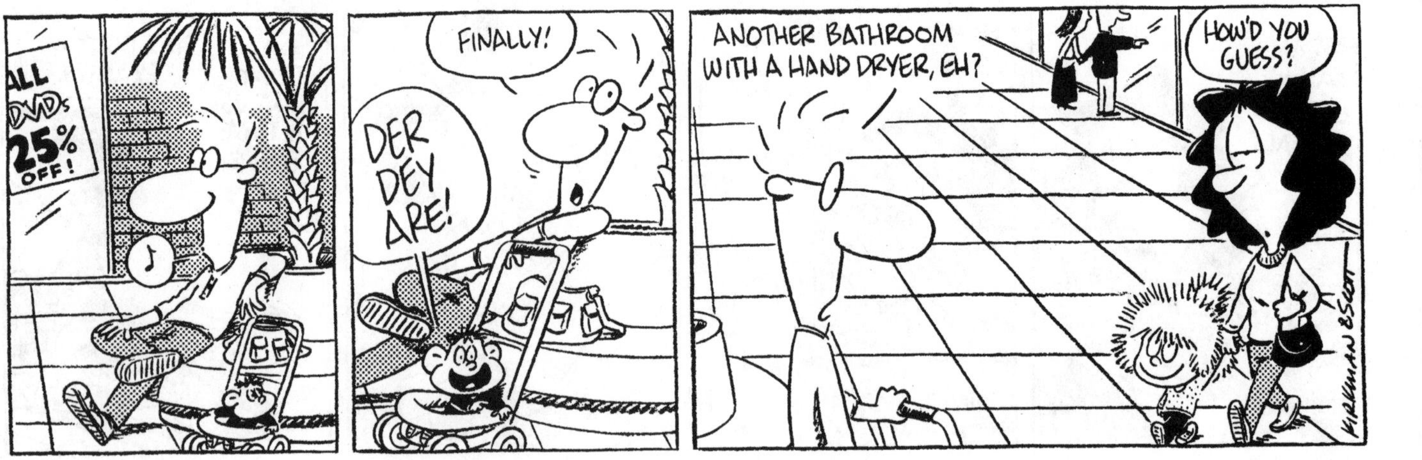
ALL DVDs 25% OFF!
FINALLY!
DER DEY ARE!
ANOTHER BATHROOM WITH A HAND DRYER, EH?
HOW'D YOU GUESS?
KIRKMAN & SCOTT

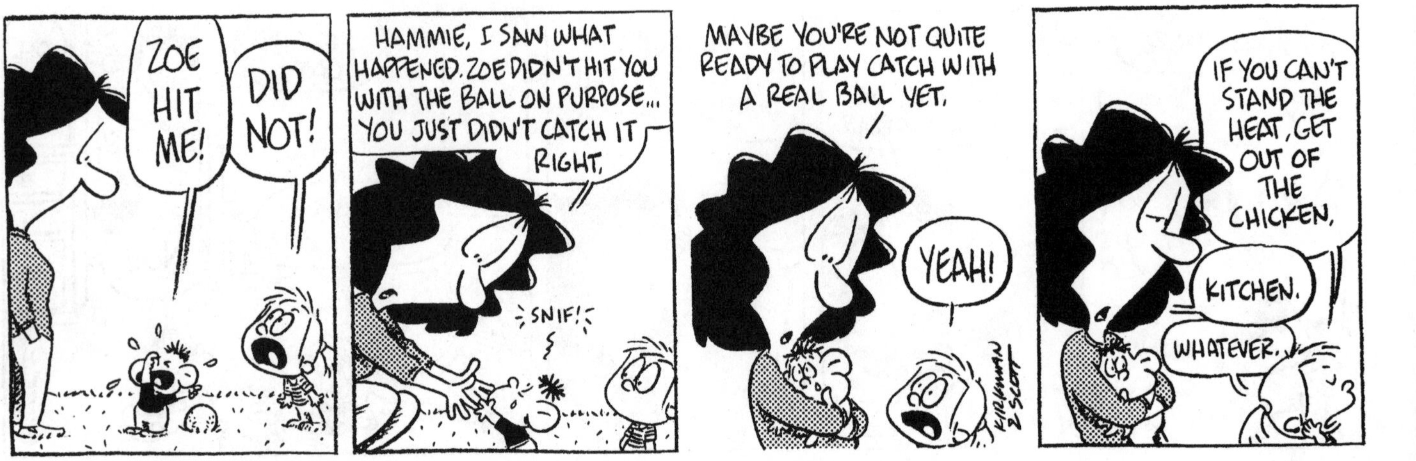
ZOE HIT ME!
DID NOT!
HAMMIE, I SAW WHAT HAPPENED. ZOE DIDN'T HIT YOU WITH THE BALL ON PURPOSE... YOU JUST DIDN'T CATCH IT RIGHT.
SNIF!
MAYBE YOU'RE NOT QUITE READY TO PLAY CATCH WITH A REAL BALL YET.
YEAH!
KIRKMAN & SCOTT
IF YOU CAN'T STAND THE HEAT, GET OUT OF THE CHICKEN.
KITCHEN.
WHATEVER.

BABY BLUES®
BY RICK KIRKMAN / JERRY SCOTT

SPLAT!
WOW! THAT LOOKS LIKE A HOUSE!
SPLAT!
NOW IT'S A CAR!
OR A TWEE...
SPLAT!
SPLAT!
LOOK! A BUNNY! AND A CROCODILE!
A BUNNY! A BUNNY!
SPLAT!
THAT ONE LOOKS LIKE DADDY!
SNICKER! YEAH!
HAHAHAHAHAHAHA!
WELL, I GUESS WE CAN ADD LOW-FAT MILK TO THE LIST OF FOODS THAT HAVE BECOME ART SUPPLIES.
WHICH ONE LOOKS LIKE DADDY??
AN AIRPWANE!
SPLAT!

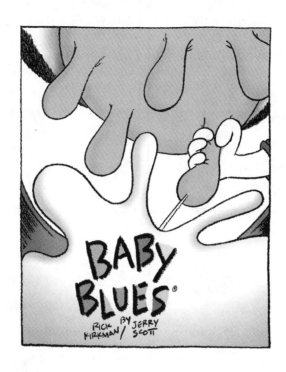

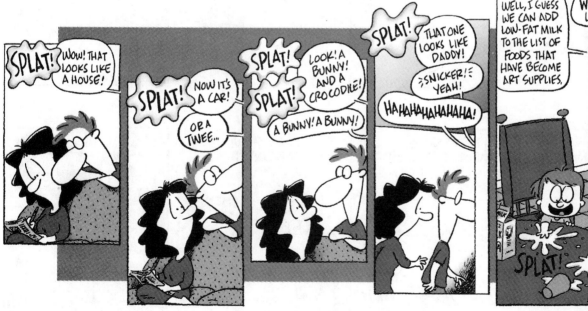

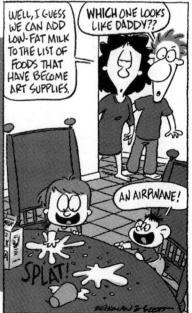

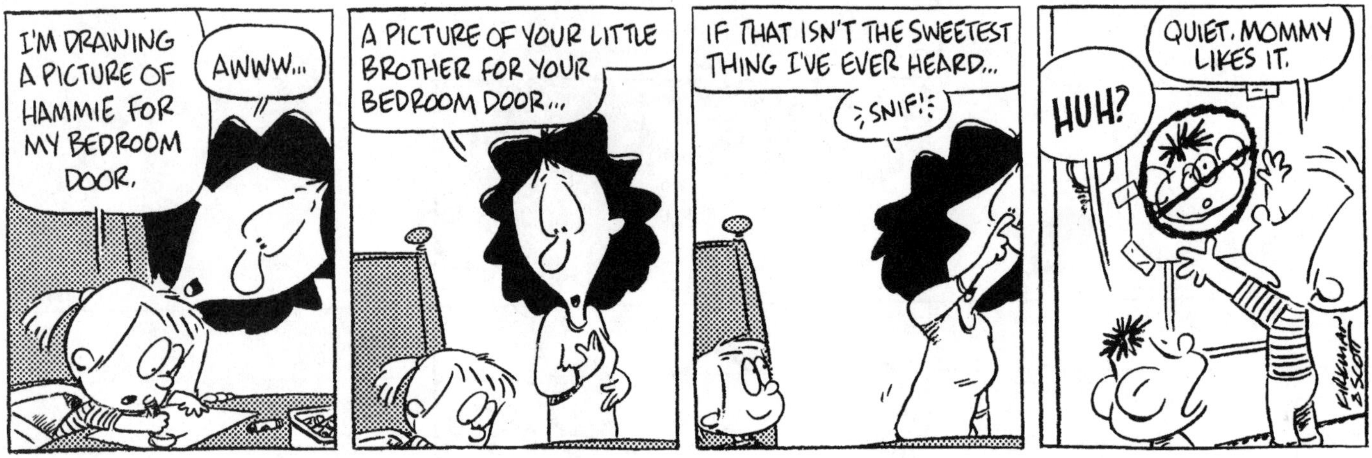
I'M DRAWING A PICTURE OF HAMMIE FOR MY BEDROOM DOOR.
AWWW...
A PICTURE OF YOUR LITTLE BROTHER FOR YOUR BEDROOM DOOR...
IF THAT ISN'T THE SWEETEST THING I'VE EVER HEARD...
SNIF!
HUH?
QUIET. MOMMY LIKES IT.
KIRKMAN & SCOTT

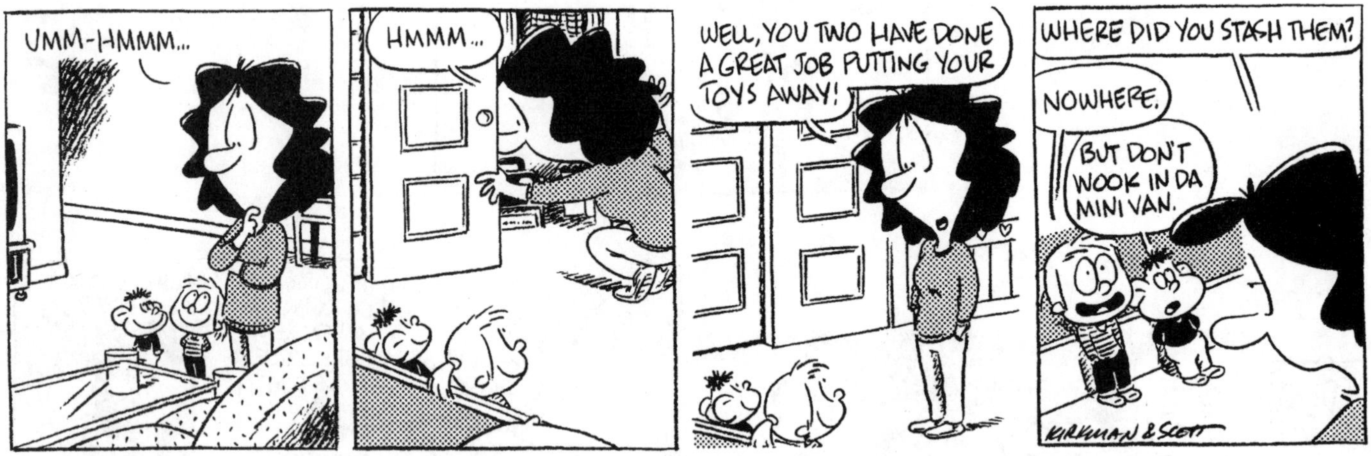
UMM-HMMM...
HMMM...
WELL, YOU TWO HAVE DONE A GREAT JOB PUTTING YOUR TOYS AWAY!
WHERE DID YOU STASH THEM?
NOWHERE.
BUT DON'T WOOK IN DA MINI VAN.
KIRKMAN & SCOTT

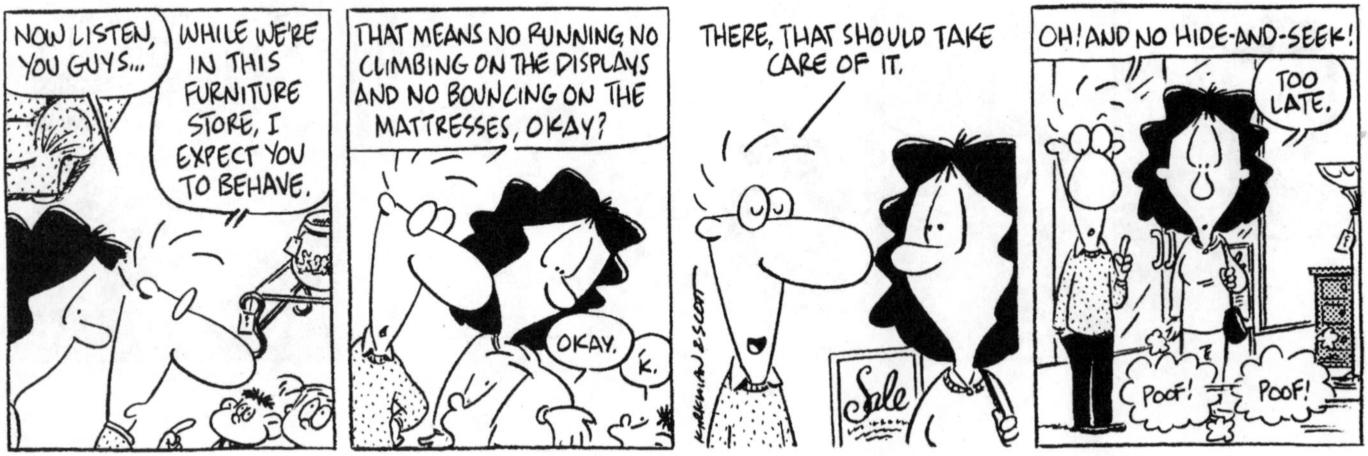
NOW LISTEN, YOU GUYS...
WHILE WE'RE IN THIS FURNITURE STORE, I EXPECT YOU TO BEHAVE.
THAT MEANS NO RUNNING, NO CLIMBING ON THE DISPLAYS AND NO BOUNCING ON THE MATTRESSES, OKAY?
OKAY.
K.
THERE, THAT SHOULD TAKE CARE OF IT.
KIRKMAN & SCOTT
Sale
OH! AND NO HIDE-AND-SEEK!
TOO LATE.
POOF!
POOF!

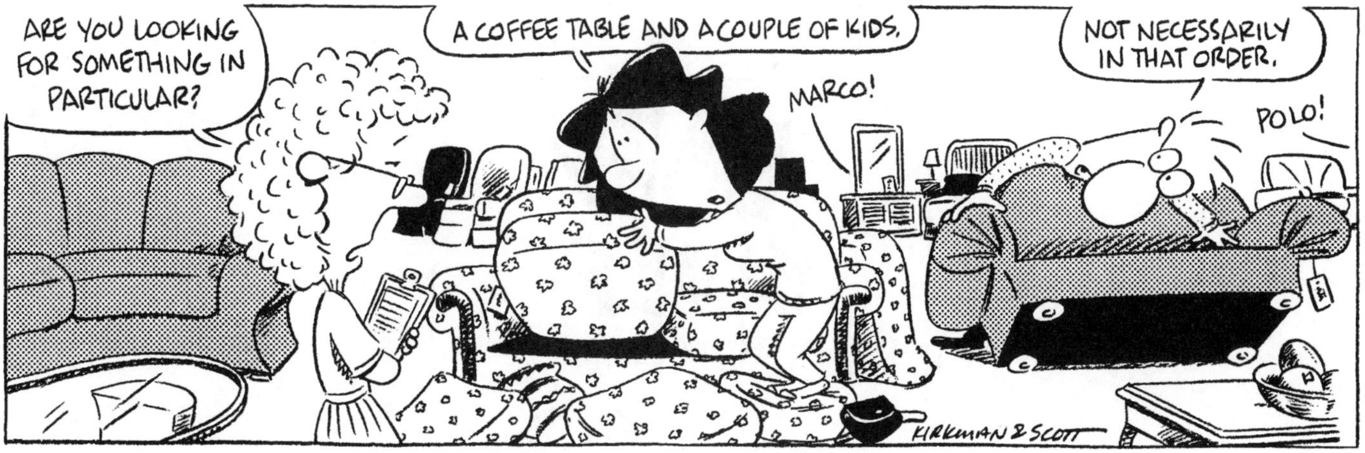
ARE YOU LOOKING FOR SOMETHING IN PARTICULAR?
A COFFEE TABLE AND A COUPLE OF KIDS.
MARCO!
NOT NECESSARILY IN THAT ORDER.
POLO!
KIRKMAN & SCOTT

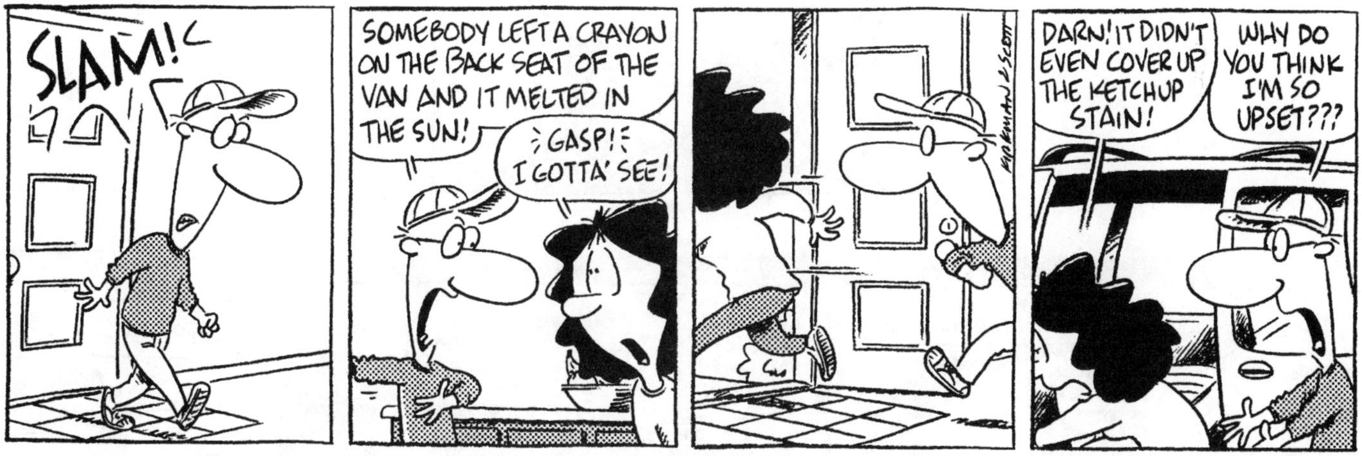
SLAM!
SOMEBODY LEFT A CRAYON ON THE BACK SEAT OF THE VAN AND IT MELTED IN THE SUN!
GASP! I GOTTA' SEE!
KIRKMAN & SCOTT
DARN! IT DIDN'T EVEN COVER UP THE KETCHUP STAIN!
WHY DO YOU THINK I'M SO UPSET???

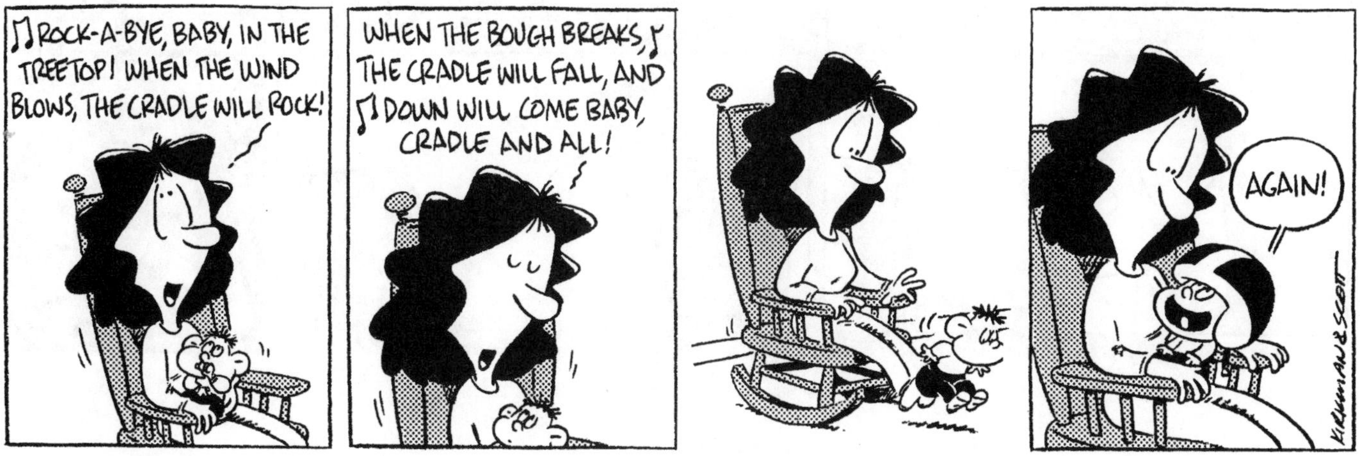
ROCK-A-BYE, BABY, IN THE TREETOP! WHEN THE WIND BLOWS, THE CRADLE WILL ROCK!
WHEN THE BOUGH BREAKS, THE CRADLE WILL FALL, AND DOWN WILL COME BABY, CRADLE AND ALL!
AGAIN!
KIRKMAN & SCOTT

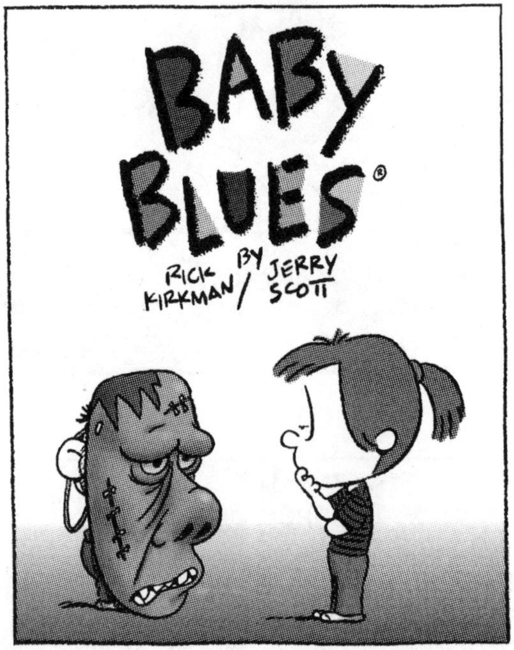
BABY BLUES®
BY RICK KIRKMAN / JERRY SCOTT

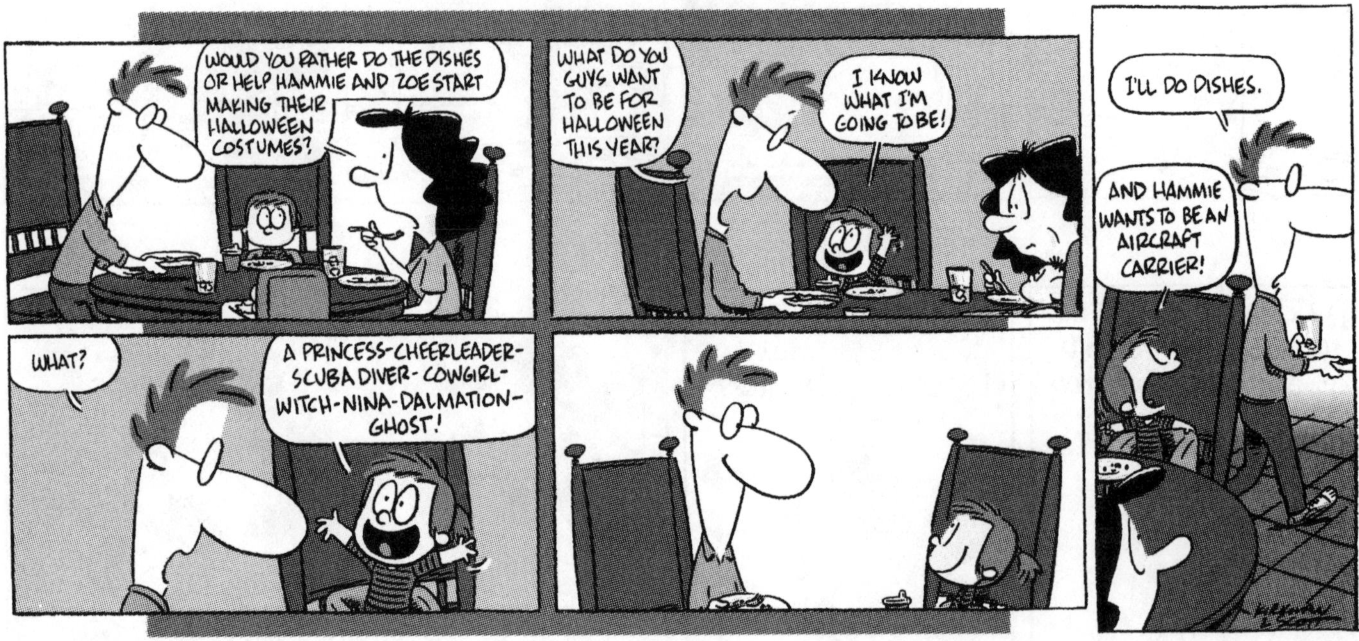
WOULD YOU RATHER DO THE DISHES OR HELP HAMMIE AND ZOE START MAKING THEIR HALLOWEEN COSTUMES?
WHAT DO YOU GUYS WANT TO BE FOR HALLOWEEN THIS YEAR?
I KNOW WHAT I'M GOING TO BE!
WHAT?
A PRINCESS-CHEERLEADER-SCUBA DIVER-COWGIRL-WITCH-NINA-DALMATION-GHOST!
I'LL DO DISHES.
AND HAMMIE WANTS TO BE AN AIRCRAFT CARRIER!

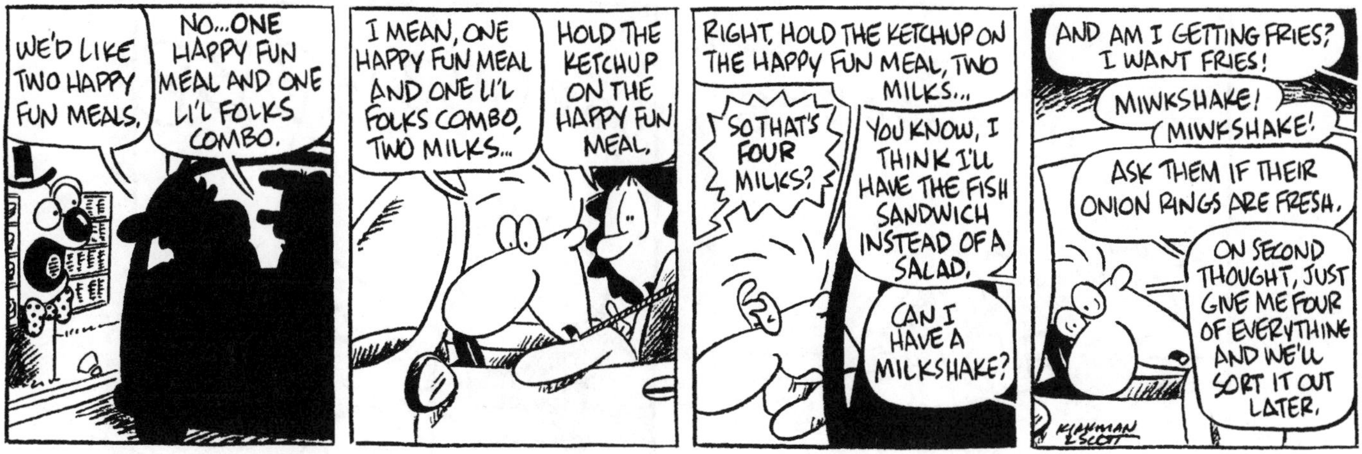
WE'D LIKE TWO HAPPY FUN MEALS.
NO...ONE HAPPY FUN MEAL AND ONE LI'L FOLKS COMBO.
I MEAN, ONE HAPPY FUN MEAL AND ONE LI'L FOLKS COMBO, TWO MILKS...
HOLD THE KETCHUP ON THE HAPPY FUN MEAL.
RIGHT. HOLD THE KETCHUP ON THE HAPPY FUN MEAL, TWO MILKS...
SO THAT'S FOUR MILKS?
YOU KNOW, I THINK I'LL HAVE THE FISH SANDWICH INSTEAD OF A SALAD.
CAN I HAVE A MILKSHAKE?
AND AM I GETTING FRIES? I WANT FRIES!
MIWKSHAKE!
MIWKSHAKE!
ASK THEM IF THEIR ONION RINGS ARE FRESH.
ON SECOND THOUGHT, JUST GIVE ME FOUR OF EVERYTHING AND WE'LL SORT IT OUT LATER.
KIRKMAN & SCOTT

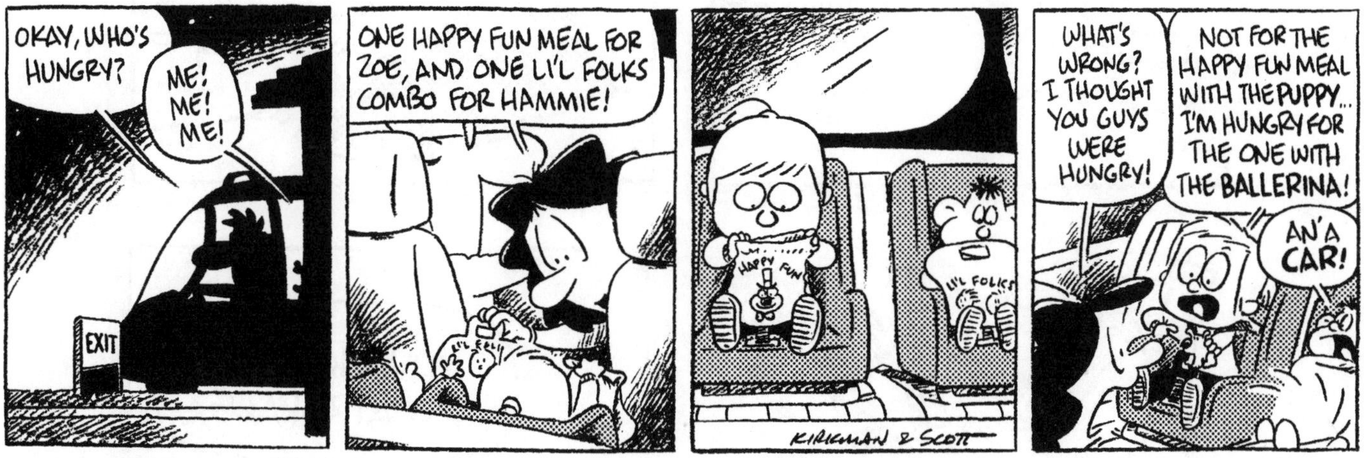
OKAY, WHO'S HUNGRY?
ME! ME! ME!
EXIT
ONE HAPPY FUN MEAL FOR ZOE, AND ONE LI'L FOLKS COMBO FOR HAMMIE!
HAPPY FUN
LI'L FOLKS
KIRKMAN & SCOTT
WHAT'S WRONG? I THOUGHT YOU GUYS WERE HUNGRY!
NOT FOR THE HAPPY FUN MEAL WITH THE PUPPY... I'M HUNGRY FOR THE ONE WITH THE BALLERINA!
AN'A CAR!

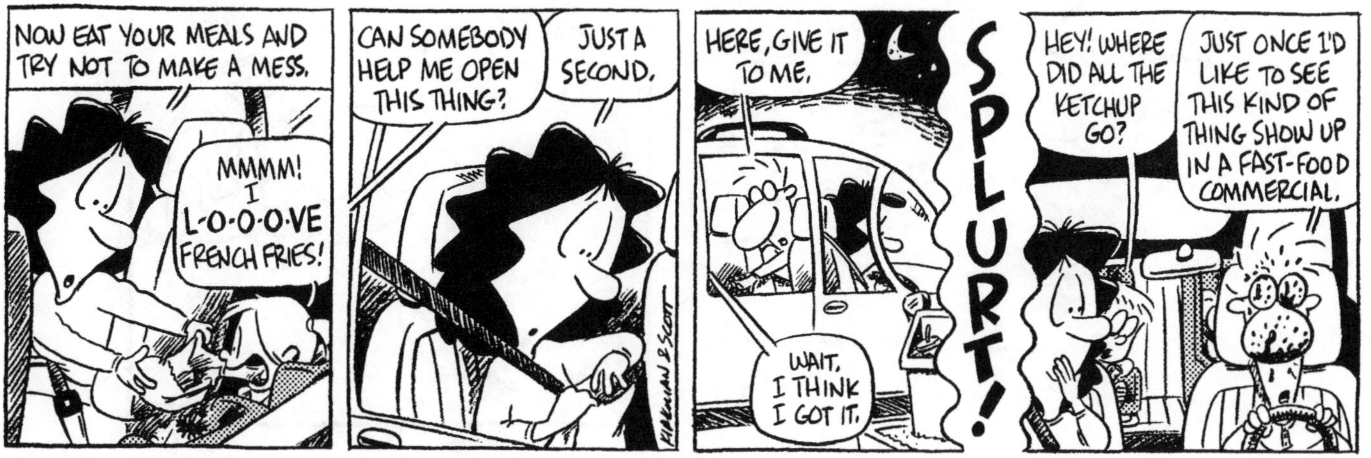
NOW EAT YOUR MEALS AND TRY NOT TO MAKE A MESS.
MMMM! I L-O-O-O-VE FRENCH FRIES!
CAN SOMEBODY HELP ME OPEN THIS THING?
JUST A SECOND.
KIRKMAN & SCOTT
HERE, GIVE IT TO ME.
WAIT, I THINK I GOT IT.
SPLURT!
HEY! WHERE DID ALL THE KETCHUP GO?
JUST ONCE I'D LIKE TO SEE THIS KIND OF THING SHOW UP IN A FAST-FOOD COMMERCIAL.

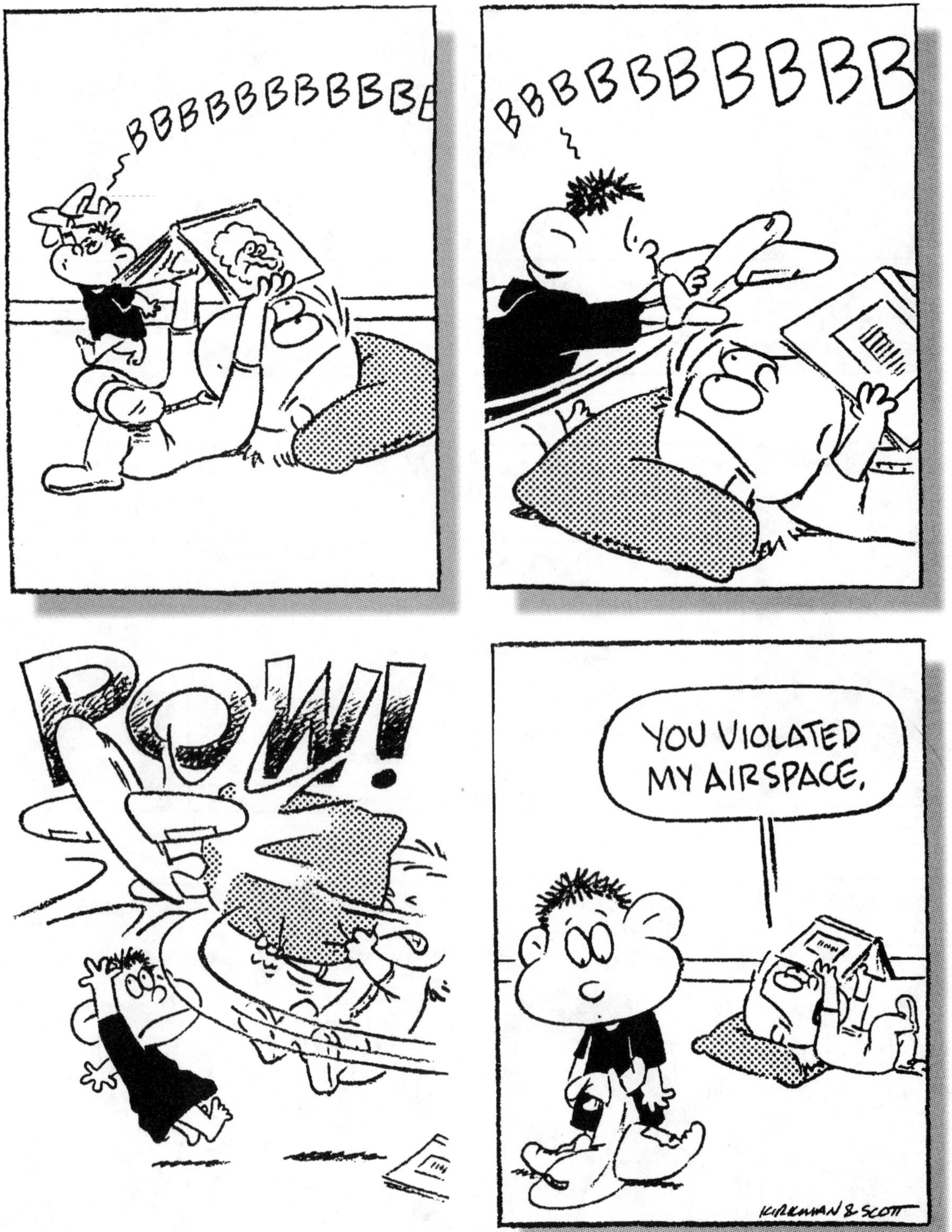
BBBBBBBBBBB
BBBBBBBBBB
POW!
YOU VIOLATED MY AIRSPACE.
KIRKMAN & SCOTT

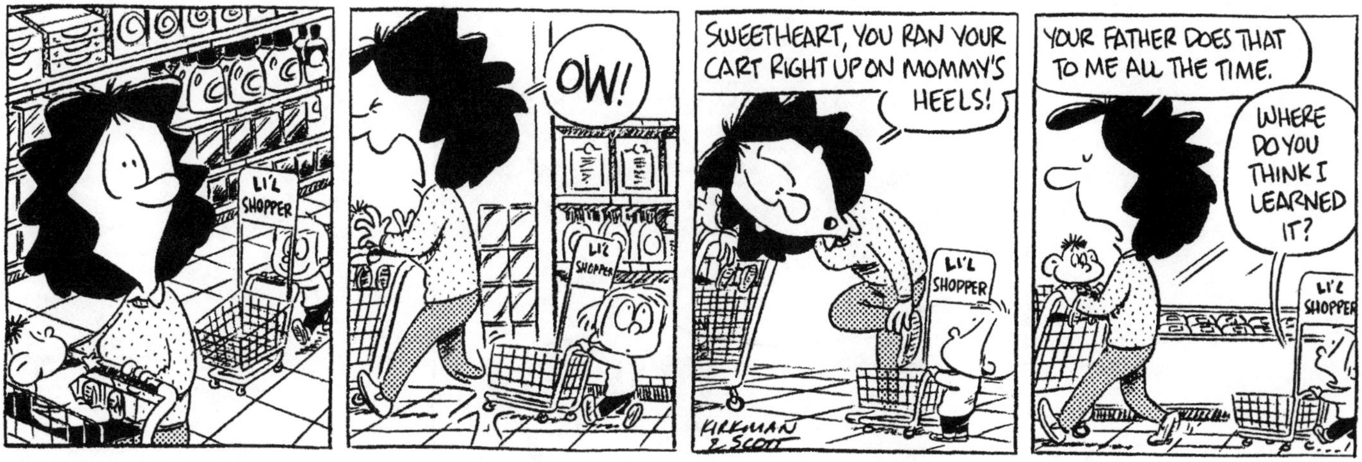
OW!
SWEETHEART, YOU RAN YOUR CART RIGHT UP ON MOMMY'S HEELS!
YOUR FATHER DOES THAT TO ME ALL THE TIME.
WHERE DO YOU THINK I LEARNED IT?
LI'L SHOPPER
KIRKMAN & SCOTT

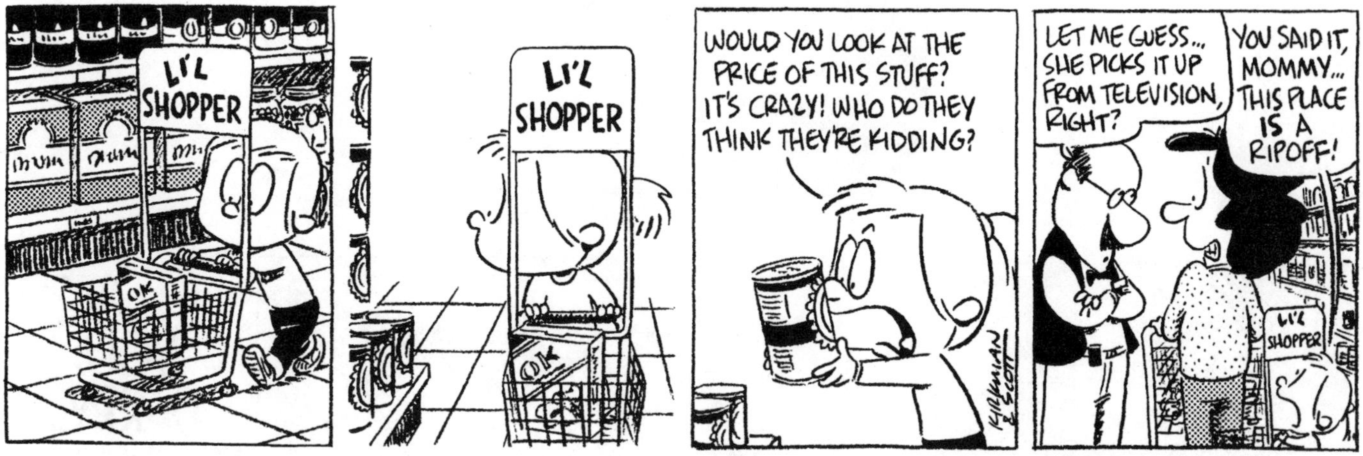
LI'L SHOPPER
WOULD YOU LOOK AT THE PRICE OF THIS STUFF? IT'S CRAZY! WHO DO THEY THINK THEY'RE KIDDING?
LET ME GUESS... SHE PICKS IT UP FROM TELEVISION, RIGHT?
YOU SAID IT, MOMMY... THIS PLACE IS A RIPOFF!
KIRKMAN & SCOTT

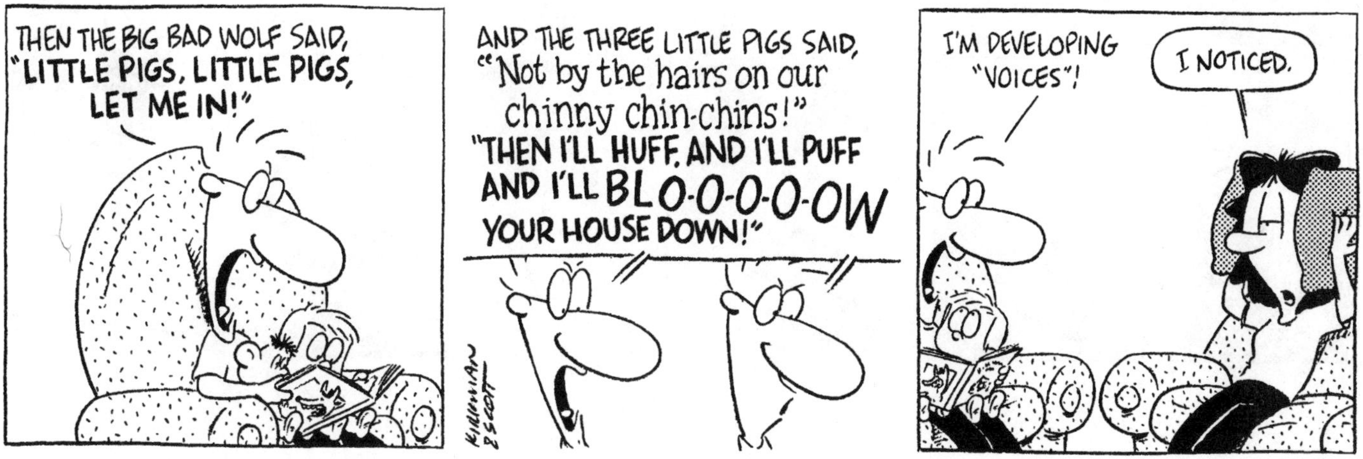
THEN THE BIG BAD WOLF SAID, "LITTLE PIGS, LITTLE PIGS, LET ME IN!"
AND THE THREE LITTLE PIGS SAID, "Not by the hairs on our chinny chin-chins!"
"THEN I'LL HUFF, AND I'LL PUFF AND I'LL BLO-O-O-O-OW YOUR HOUSE DOWN!"
I'M DEVELOPING "VOICES"!
I NOTICED.
KIRKMAN & SCOTT

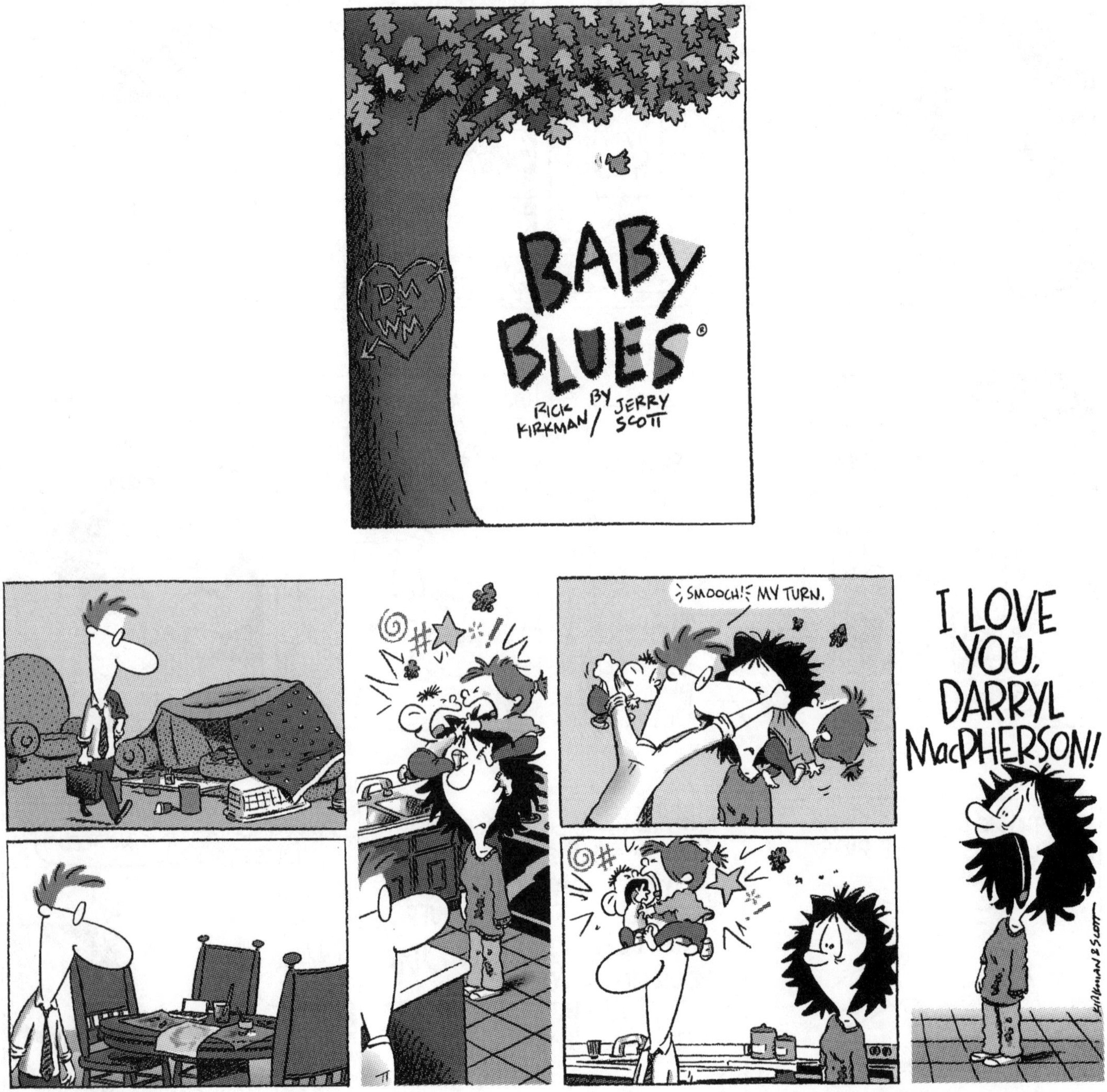
DM + WM
BABY BLUES®
BY RICK KIRKMAN / JERRY SCOTT
SMOOCH!
MY TURN.
I LOVE YOU, DARRYL MacPHERSON!
KIRKMAN & SCOTT

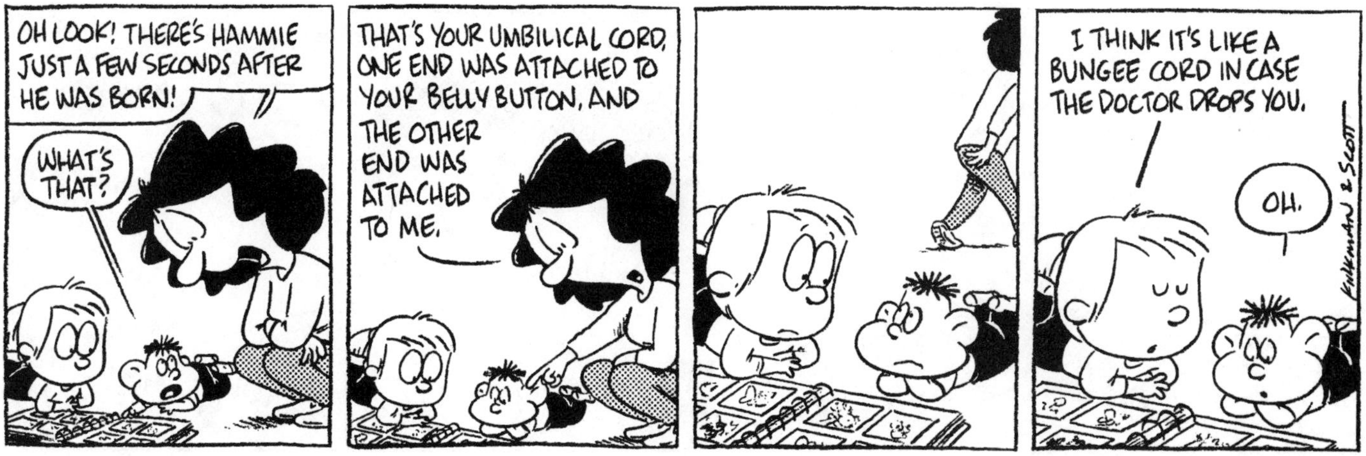
OH LOOK! THERE'S HAMMIE JUST A FEW SECONDS AFTER HE WAS BORN!
WHAT'S THAT?
THAT'S YOUR UMBILICAL CORD. ONE END WAS ATTACHED TO YOUR BELLY BUTTON, AND THE OTHER END WAS ATTACHED TO ME.
I THINK IT'S LIKE A BUNGEE CORD IN CASE THE DOCTOR DROPS YOU.
OH.
KIRKMAN & SCOTT

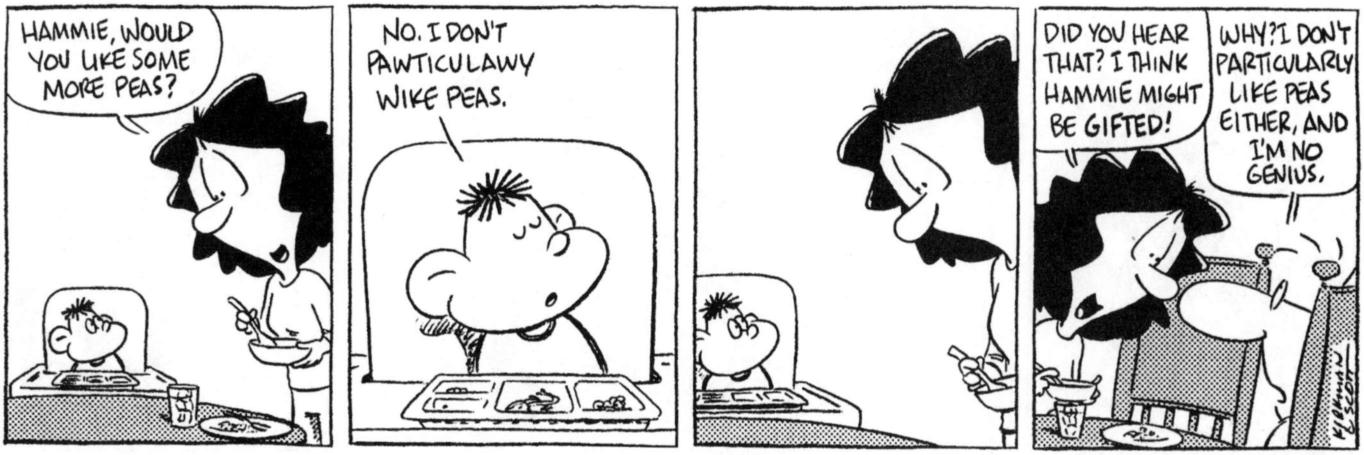
HAMMIE, WOULD YOU LIKE SOME MORE PEAS?
NO. I DON'T PAWTICULAWY WIKE PEAS.
DID YOU HEAR THAT? I THINK HAMMIE MIGHT BE GIFTED!
WHY? I DON'T PARTICULARLY LIKE PEAS EITHER, AND I'M NO GENIUS.

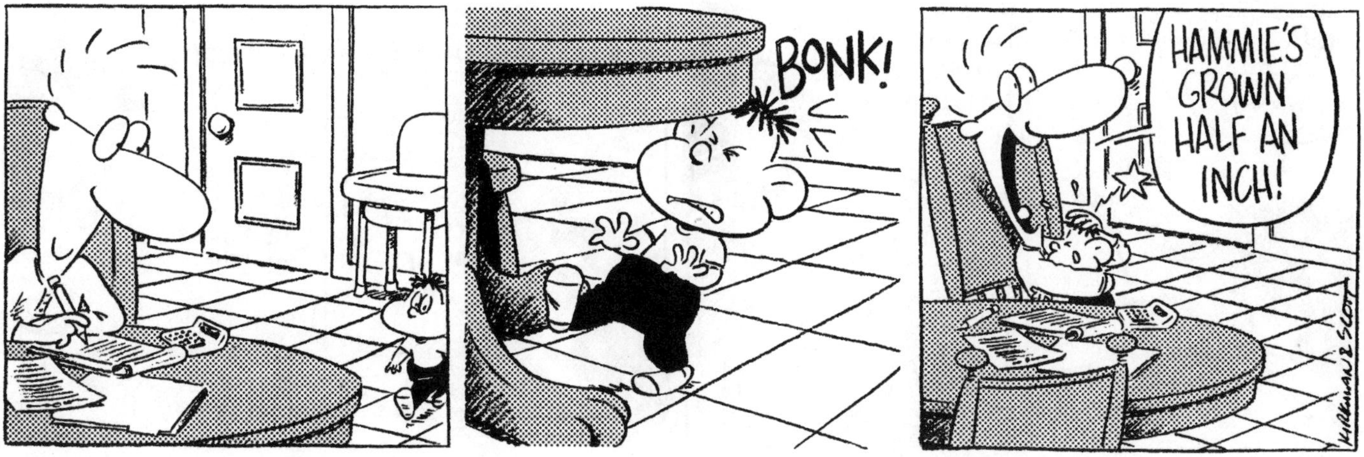
BONK!
HAMMIE'S GROWN HALF AN INCH!
KIRKMAN & SCOTT

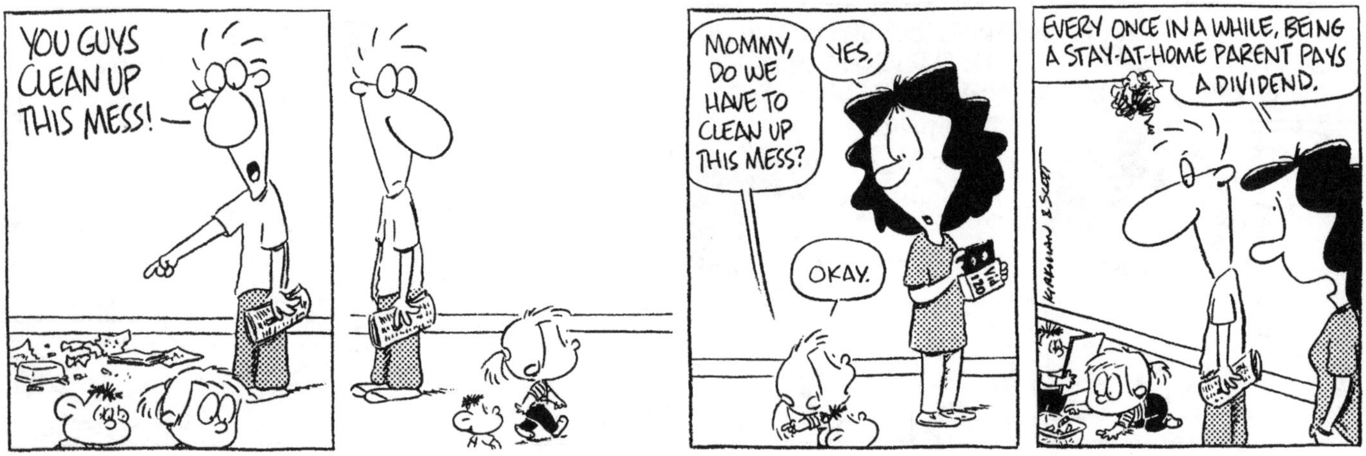
YOU GUYS CLEAN UP THIS MESS!
MOMMY, DO WE HAVE TO CLEAN UP THIS MESS?
YES.
OKAY.
EVERY ONCE IN A WHILE, BEING A STAY-AT-HOME PARENT PAYS A DIVIDEND.
KIRKMAN & SCOTT

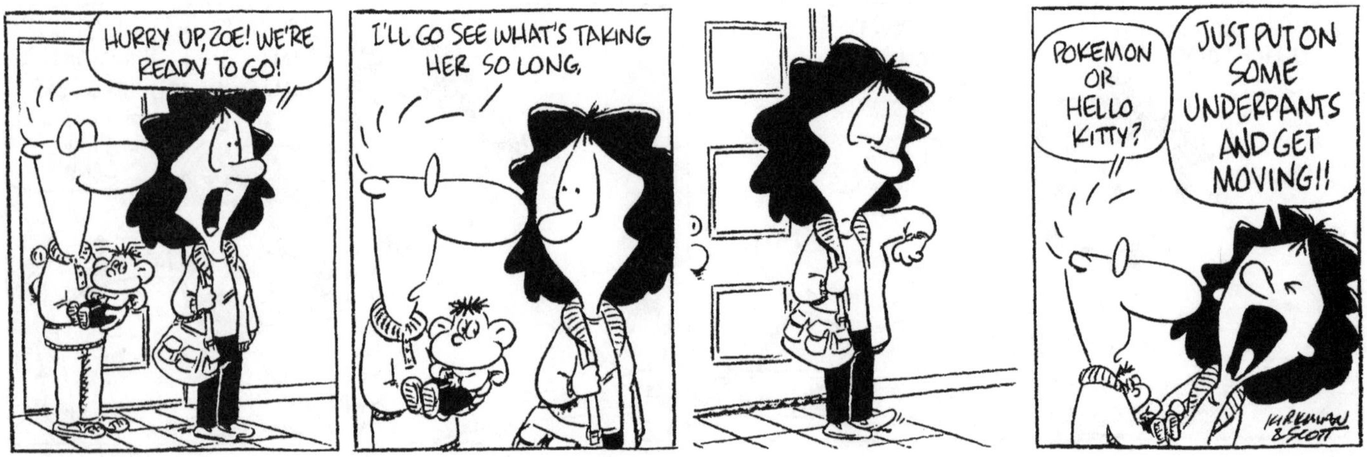
HURRY UP, ZOE! WE'RE READY TO GO!
I'LL GO SEE WHAT'S TAKING HER SO LONG.
POKEMON OR HELLO KITTY?
JUST PUT ON SOME UNDERPANTS AND GET MOVING!!
KIRKMAN & SCOTT

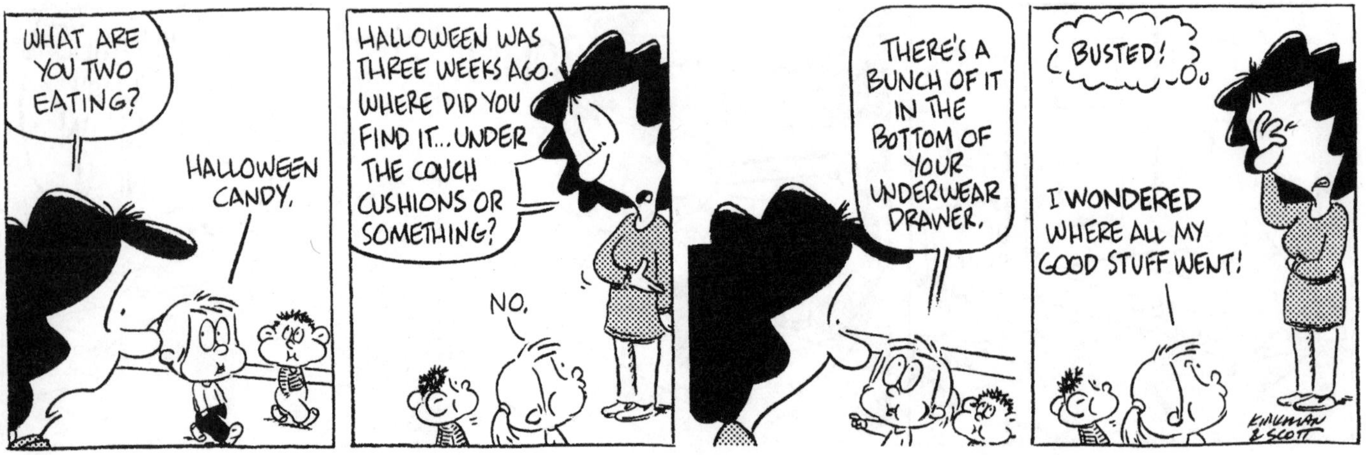
WHAT ARE YOU TWO EATING?
HALLOWEEN CANDY.
HALLOWEEN WAS THREE WEEKS AGO. WHERE DID YOU FIND IT... UNDER THE COUCH CUSHIONS OR SOMETHING?
NO.
THERE'S A BUNCH OF IT IN THE BOTTOM OF YOUR UNDERWEAR DRAWER.
BUSTED!
I WONDERED WHERE ALL MY GOOD STUFF WENT!
KIRKMAN & SCOTT

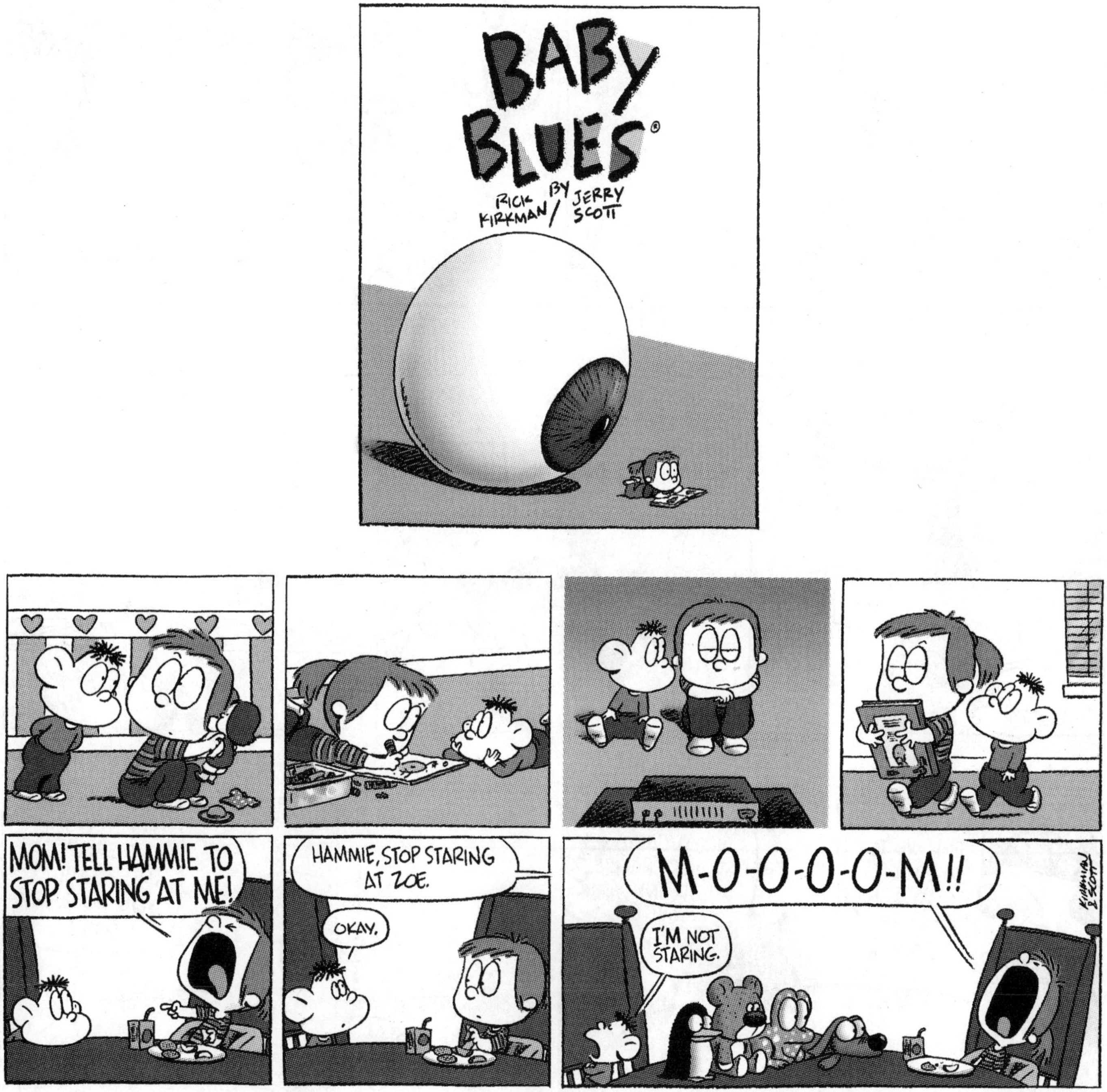
BABY BLUES®
BY RICK KIRKMAN / JERRY SCOTT
MOM! TELL HAMMIE TO STOP STARING AT ME!
HAMMIE, STOP STARING AT ZOE.
OKAY.
M-O-O-O-O-M!!
I'M NOT STARING.
KIRKMAN & SCOTT

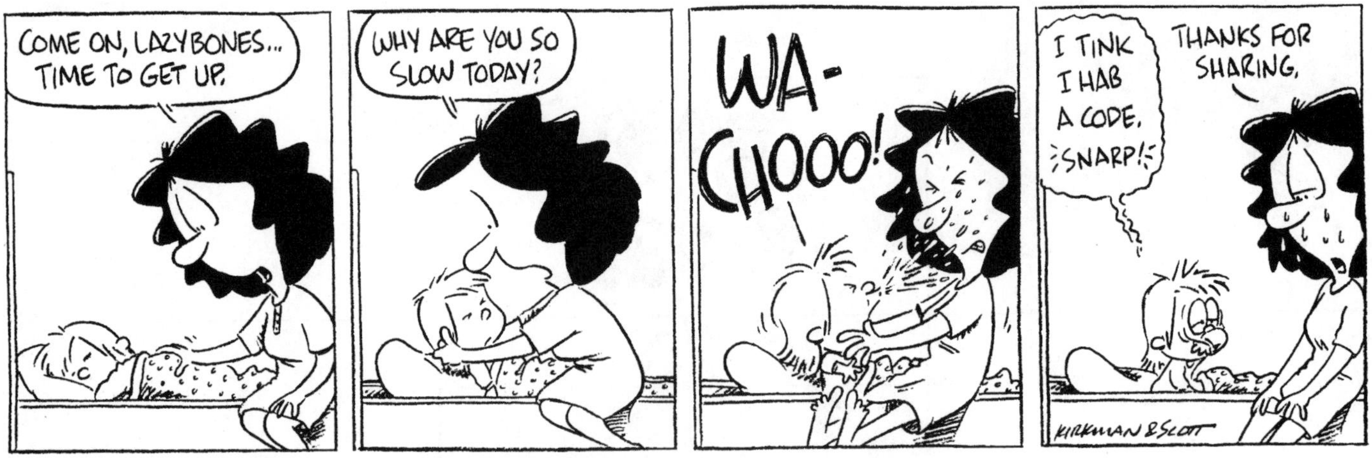
COME ON, LAZYBONES... TIME TO GET UP.
WHY ARE YOU SO SLOW TODAY?
WA-CHOOO!
I TINK I HAB A CODE. SNARP!
THANKS FOR SHARING.
KIRKMAN & SCOTT

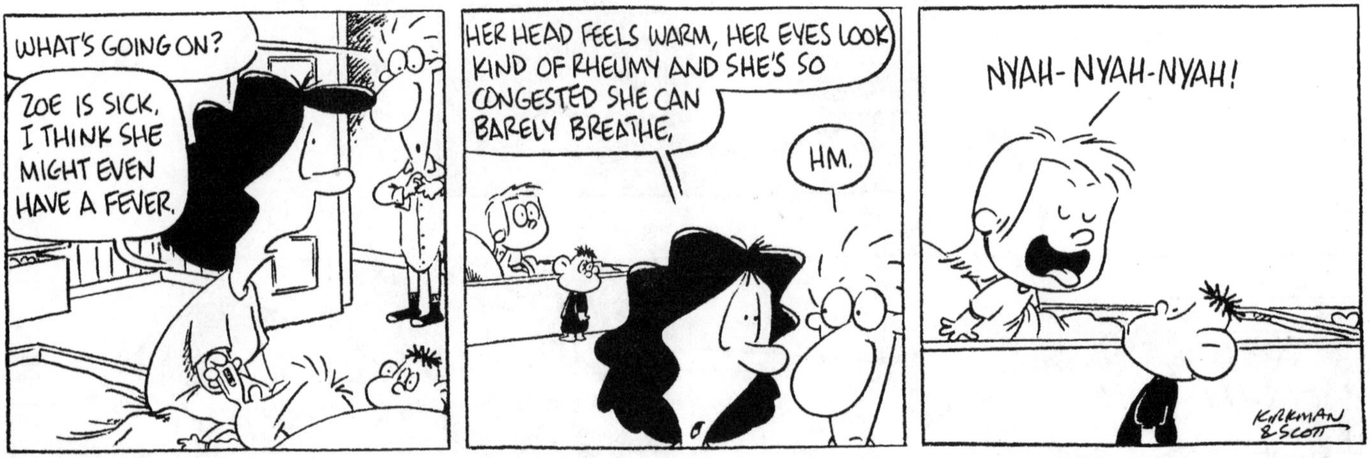
WHAT'S GOING ON?
ZOE IS SICK. I THINK SHE MIGHT EVEN HAVE A FEVER.
HER HEAD FEELS WARM, HER EYES LOOK KIND OF RHEUMY AND SHE'S SO CONGESTED SHE CAN BARELY BREATHE.
HM.
NYAH-NYAH-NYAH!
KIRKMAN & SCOTT

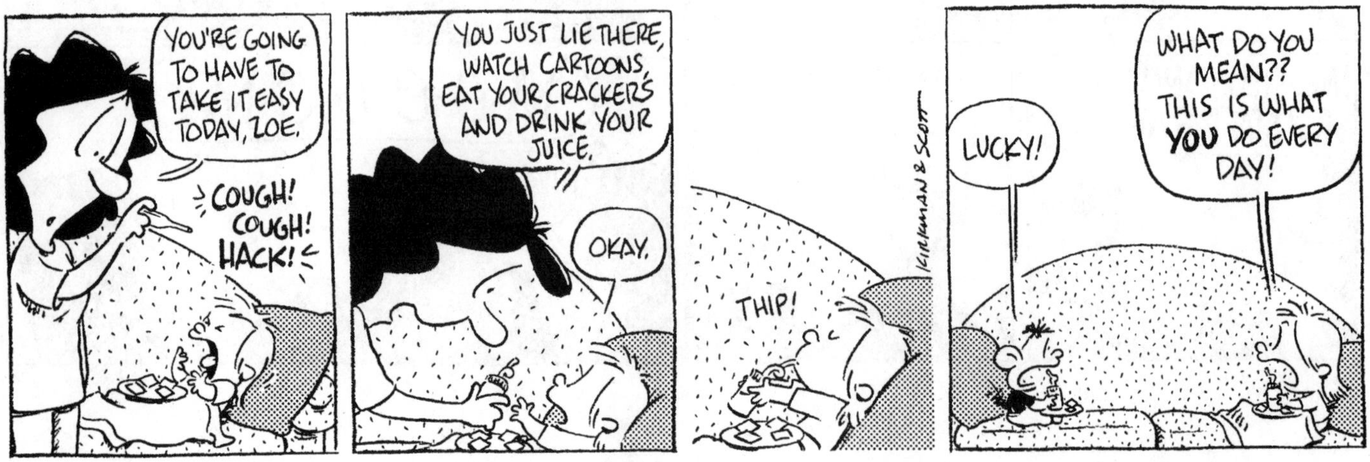
YOU'RE GOING TO HAVE TO TAKE IT EASY TODAY, ZOE.
COUGH! COUGH! HACK!
YOU JUST LIE THERE, WATCH CARTOONS, EAT YOUR CRACKERS AND DRINK YOUR JUICE.
OKAY.
THIP!
KIRKMAN & SCOTT
LUCKY!
WHAT DO YOU MEAN?? THIS IS WHAT YOU DO EVERY DAY!

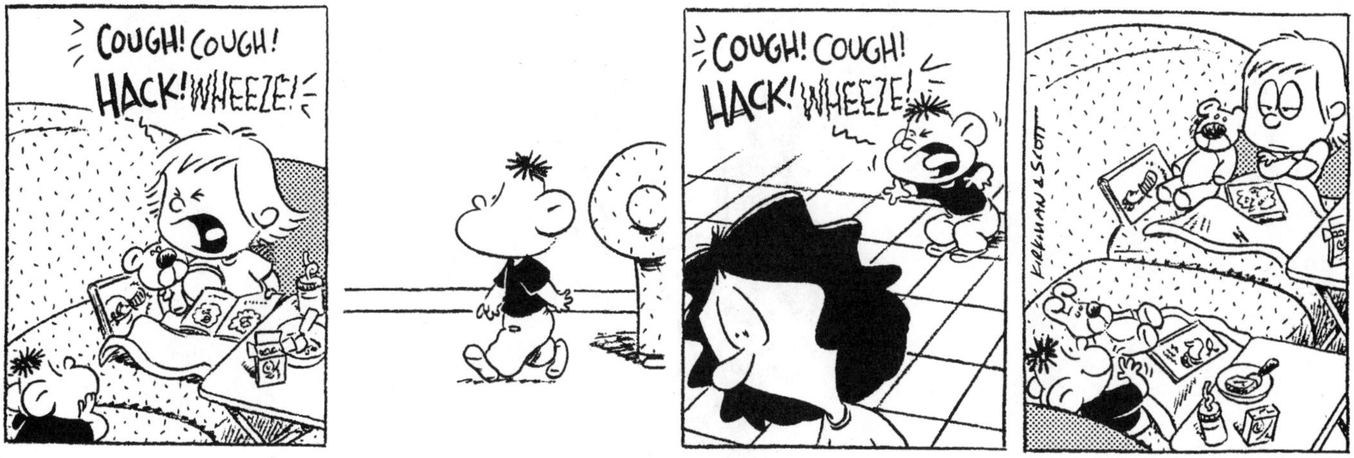
COUGH! COUGH!
HACK! WHEEZE!
COUGH! COUGH!
HACK! WHEEZE!
KIRKMAN & SCOTT

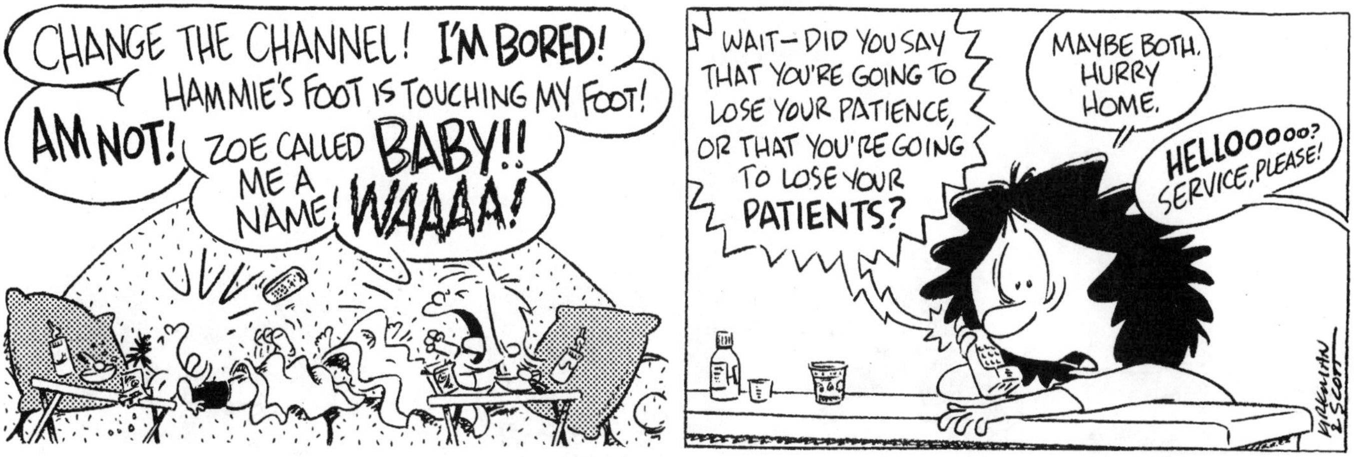
CHANGE THE CHANNEL! I'M BORED!
HAMMIE'S FOOT IS TOUCHING MY FOOT!
AM NOT!
ZOE CALLED ME A NAME!
BABY!!
WAAAA!
WAIT— DID YOU SAY THAT YOU'RE GOING TO LOSE YOUR PATIENCE, OR THAT YOU'RE GOING TO LOSE YOUR PATIENTS?
MAYBE BOTH. HURRY HOME.
HELLOOooo? SERVICE, PLEASE!
KIRKMAN & SCOTT

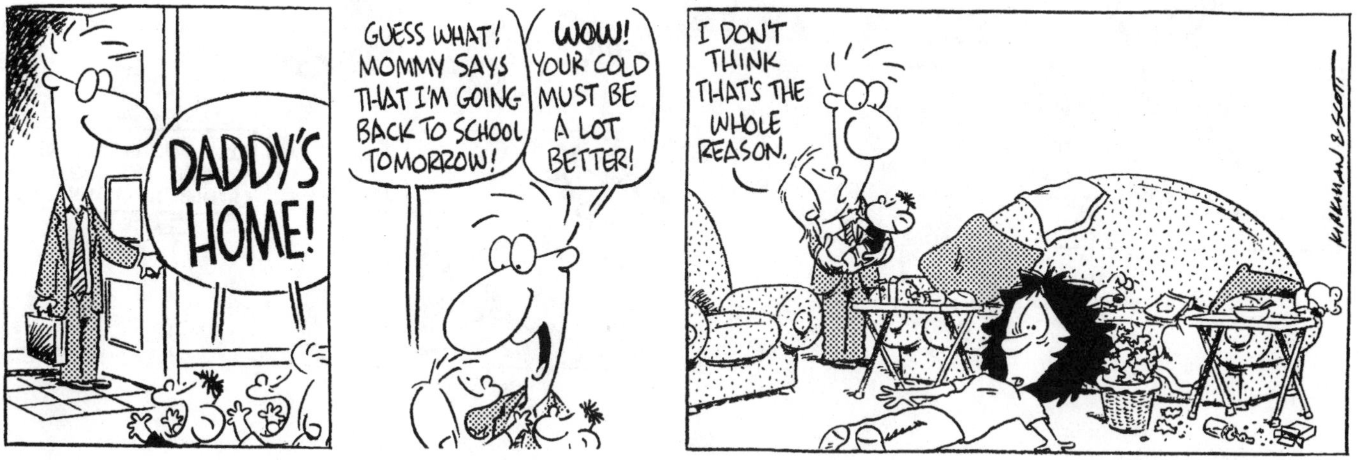
DADDY'S HOME!
GUESS WHAT! MOMMY SAYS THAT I'M GOING BACK TO SCHOOL TOMORROW!
WOW! YOUR COLD MUST BE A LOT BETTER!
I DON'T THINK THAT'S THE WHOLE REASON.
KIRKMAN & SCOTT

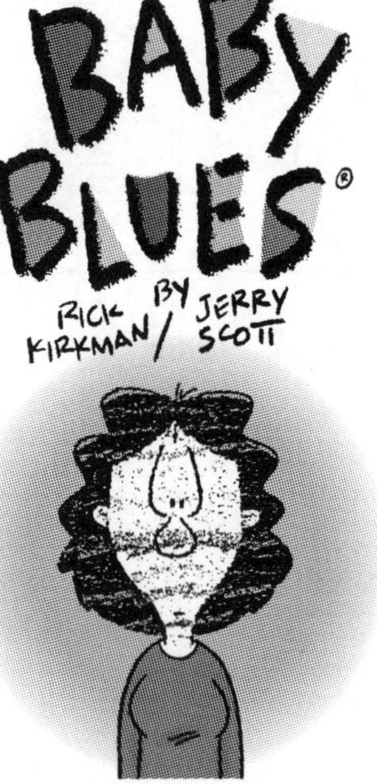
BABY BLUES®
RICK KIRKMAN / BY / JERRY SCOTT

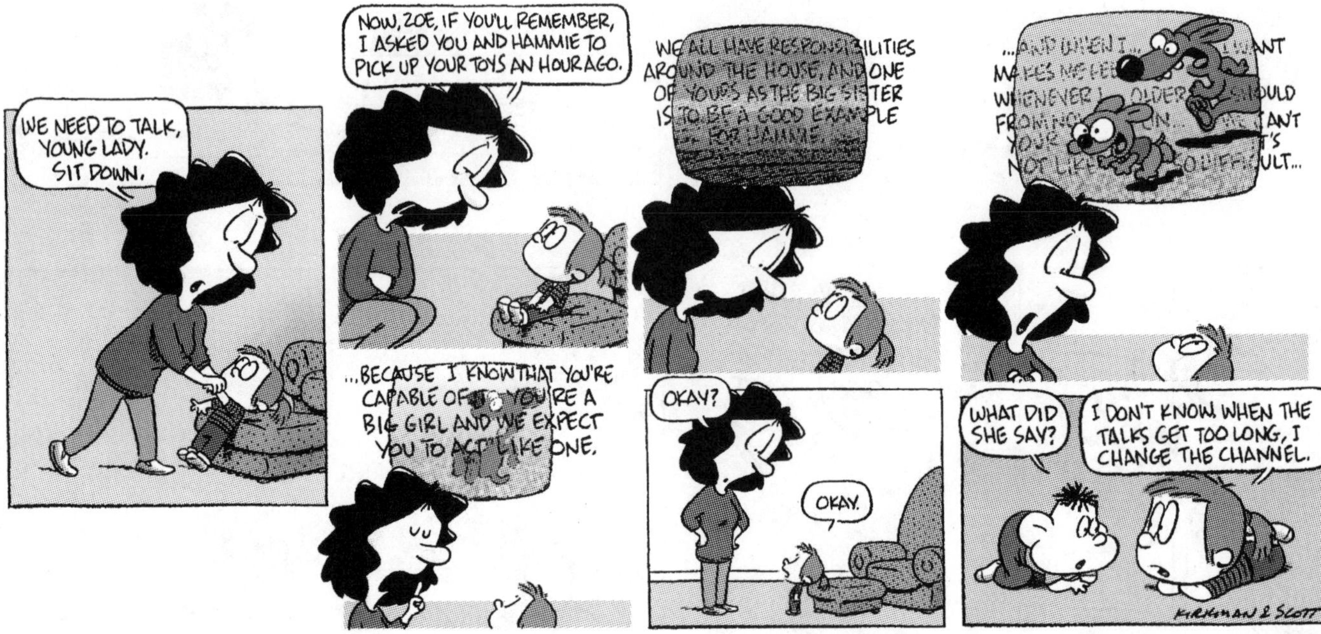
WE NEED TO TALK, YOUNG LADY. SIT DOWN.
NOW, ZOE, IF YOU'LL REMEMBER, I ASKED YOU AND HAMMIE TO PICK UP YOUR TOYS AN HOUR AGO.
WE ALL HAVE RESPONSIBILITIES AROUND THE HOUSE, AND ONE OF YOURS AS THE BIG SISTER IS TO BE A GOOD EXAMPLE FOR HAMMIE.
...BECAUSE I KNOW THAT YOU'RE CAPABLE OF YOU'RE A BIG GIRL AND WE EXPECT YOU TO ACT LIKE ONE.
OKAY?
OKAY.
WHAT DID SHE SAY?
I DON'T KNOW. WHEN THE TALKS GET TOO LONG, I CHANGE THE CHANNEL.
KIRKMAN & SCOTT

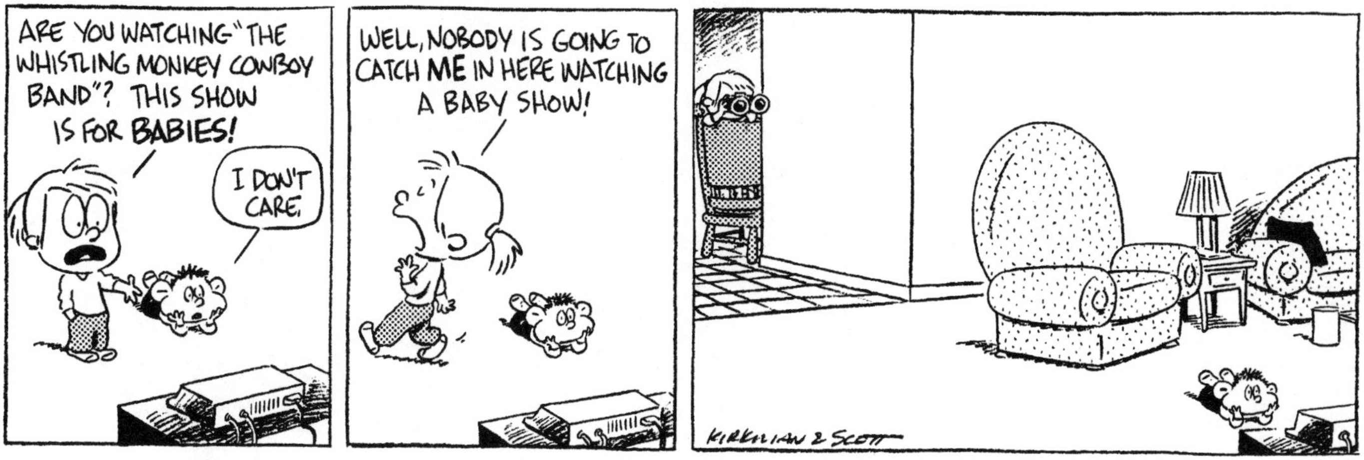
ARE YOU WATCHING "THE WHISTLING MONKEY COWBOY BAND"? THIS SHOW IS FOR BABIES!
I DON'T CARE.
WELL, NOBODY IS GOING TO CATCH ME IN HERE WATCHING A BABY SHOW!
KIRKMAN & SCOTT

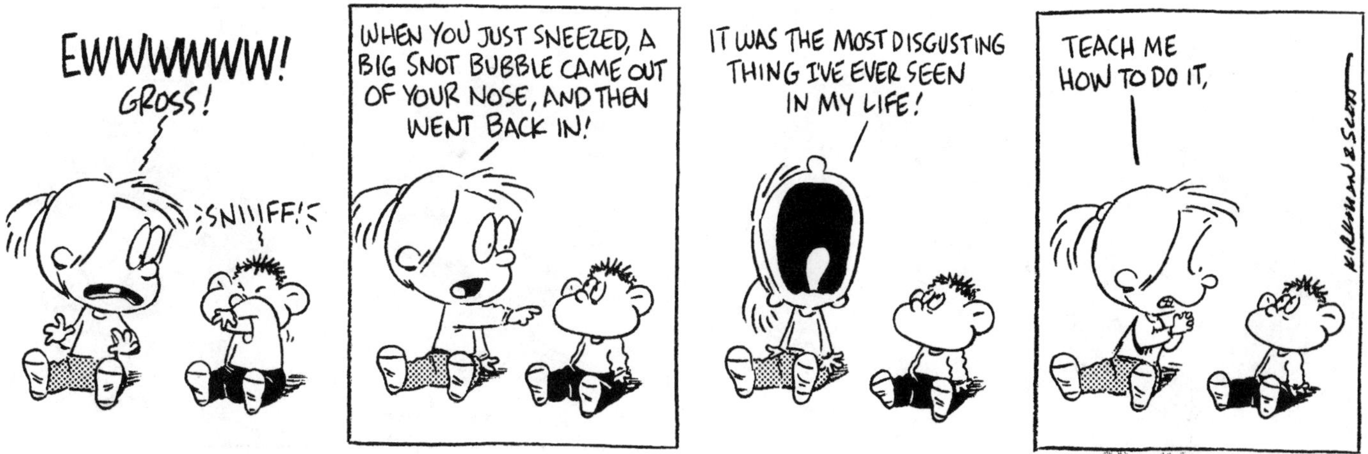
EWWWWWW! GROSS!
SNIIIFF!
WHEN YOU JUST SNEEZED, A BIG SNOT BUBBLE CAME OUT OF YOUR NOSE, AND THEN WENT BACK IN!
IT WAS THE MOST DISGUSTING THING I'VE EVER SEEN IN MY LIFE!
TEACH ME HOW TO DO IT.
KIRKMAN & SCOTT

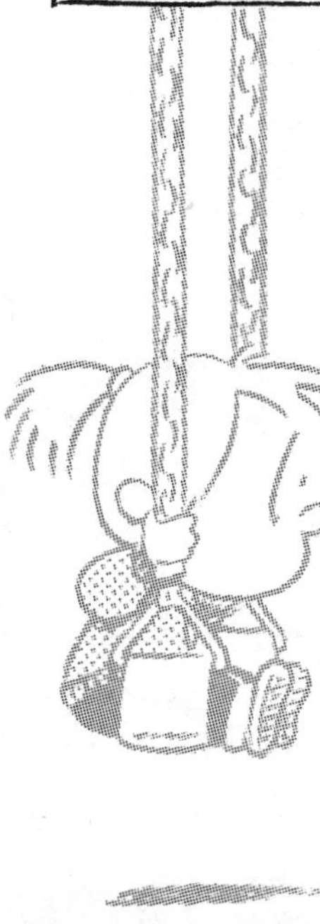

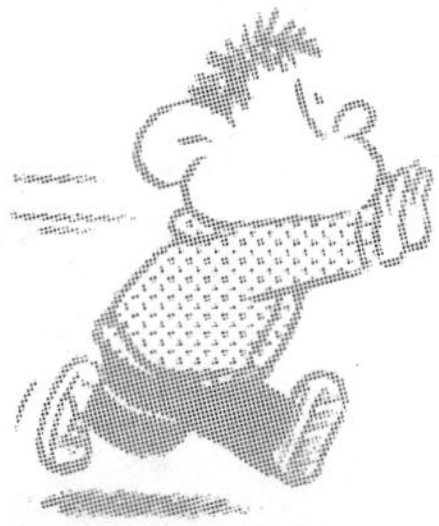

Panel 1:
NO! DON'T TOUCH THAT! STOP IT! DON'T YOU DARE! NO! DID YOU **HEAR** ME? I SAID **NO!**

Panel 2:
WHIRRRR! CLICK! CLICK!

Panel 3:

KIRKMAN & SCOTT

Panel 4:
ARE YOU READY TO GO INTO THE ANTIQUE STORE?

ALL SET!

Panel 5:
⸘ SNIFF! ⸘ ⸘ CHOKE! ⸘ WANDA, COME SEE THIS.

Panel 6:
A MULTI-MILLIONAIRE PROFESSIONAL GOLFER WHO OWNS HIS OWN JET KNOCKS A GOLF BALL INTO A HOLE AND GETS A CHECK FOR TEN TIMES WHAT OUR HOUSE IS WORTH?

UH... WELL, YEAH.

Panel 7:
BAWWWWWWW!

Panel 8:
WANDA AND I BOTH GET EMOTIONAL ABOUT SPORTS... JUST FOR DIFFERENT REASONS.

KIRKMAN & SCOTT

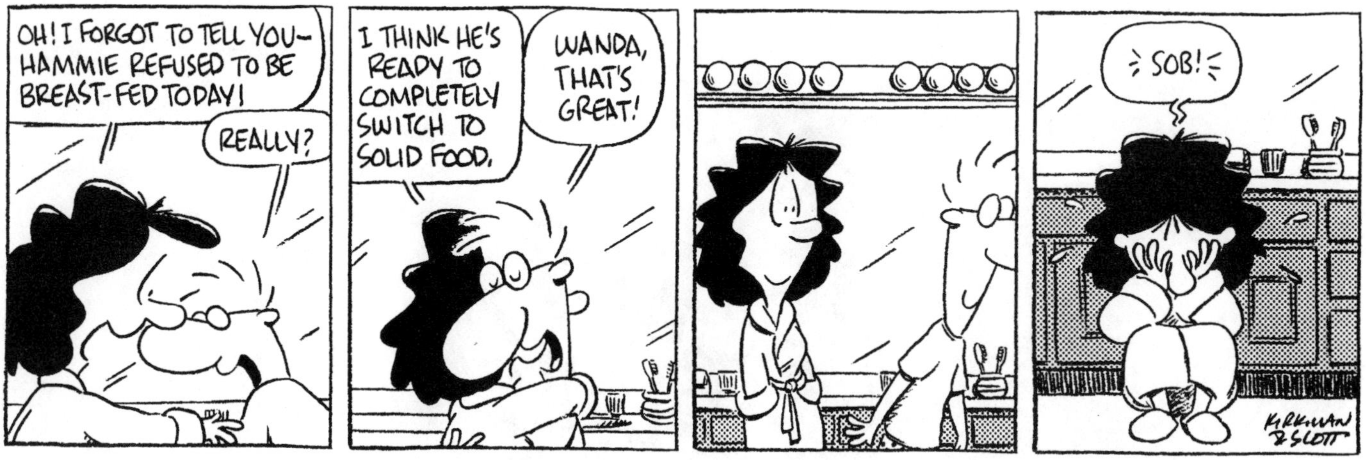
OH! I FORGOT TO TELL YOU- HAMMIE REFUSED TO BE BREAST-FED TODAY!
REALLY?
I THINK HE'S READY TO COMPLETELY SWITCH TO SOLID FOOD.
WANDA, THAT'S GREAT!
SOB!
KIRKMAN & SCOTT

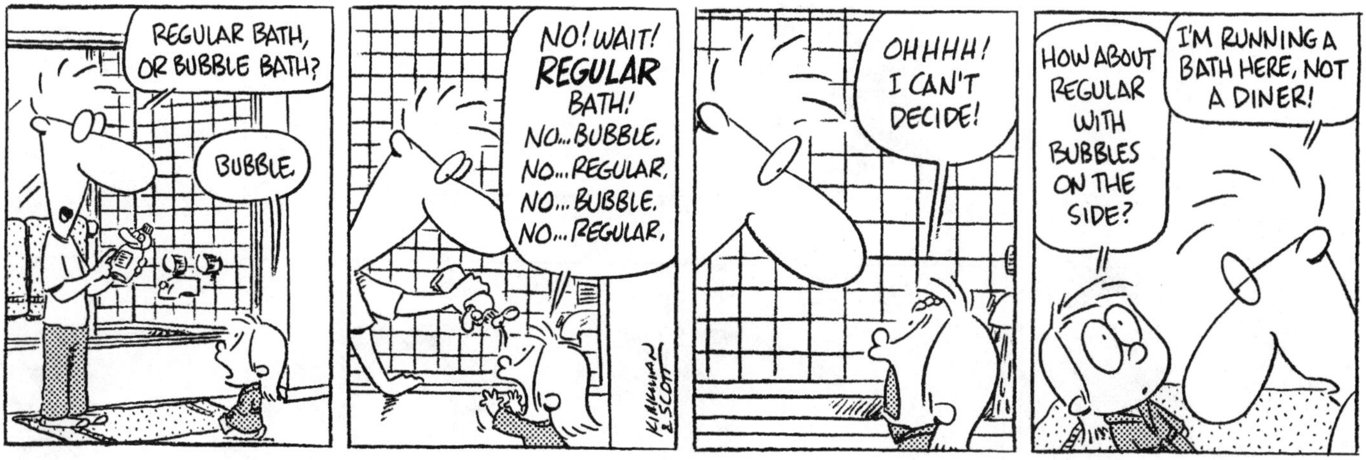
REGULAR BATH, OR BUBBLE BATH?
BUBBLE.
NO! WAIT! **REGULAR** BATH! NO...BUBBLE. NO...REGULAR. NO...BUBBLE. NO...REGULAR.
KIRKMAN & SCOTT
OHHHH! I CAN'T DECIDE!
HOW ABOUT REGULAR WITH BUBBLES ON THE SIDE?
I'M RUNNING A BATH HERE, NOT A DINER!

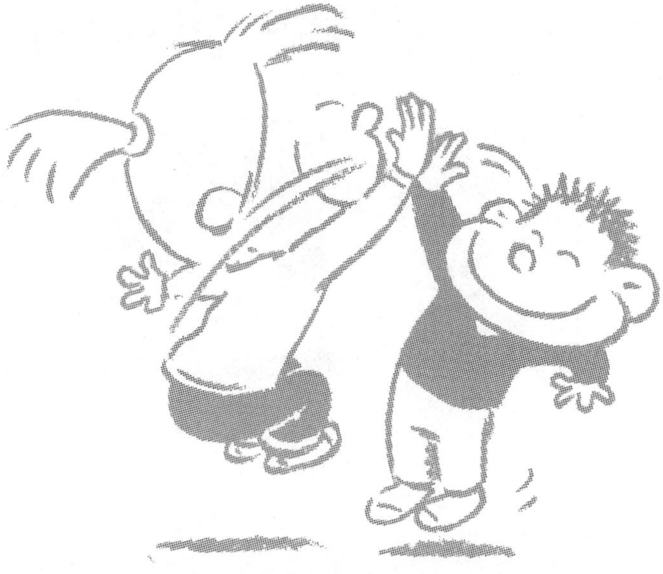

BABY BLUES®
BY
RICK KIRKMAN / JERRY SCOTT

NAME?
WANDA MacPHERSON
MAIDEN NAME?
WIZOWSKI.
OCCUPATION?
OCCUPATION??
COORDINATOR.
CHEF. SANITARY ENGINEER. CHAUFFEUR. REFEREE. EDUCATOR. WRANGLER. PERSONAL SHOPPER. COP. ACCOUNTANT. INVESTMENT ANALYST. ENTERTAINER. ORGANIZER. MEDIATOR. INVESTIGATOR. DIETICIAN. LIFEGUARD. PSYCHOLOGIST. NURSE. PLUMBER...
THERE'S ONLY ONE LINE.
IN THAT CASE, JUST PUT "MOM."

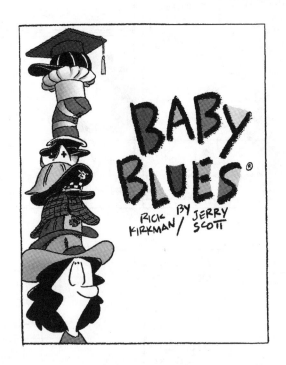

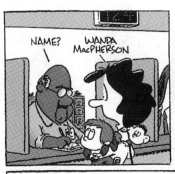

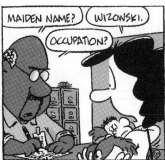

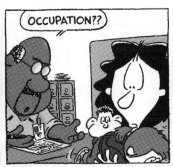

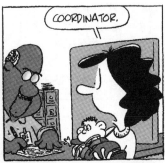

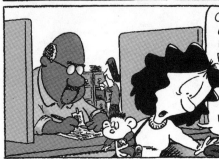

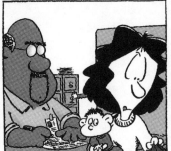

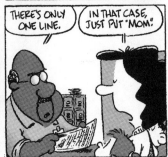

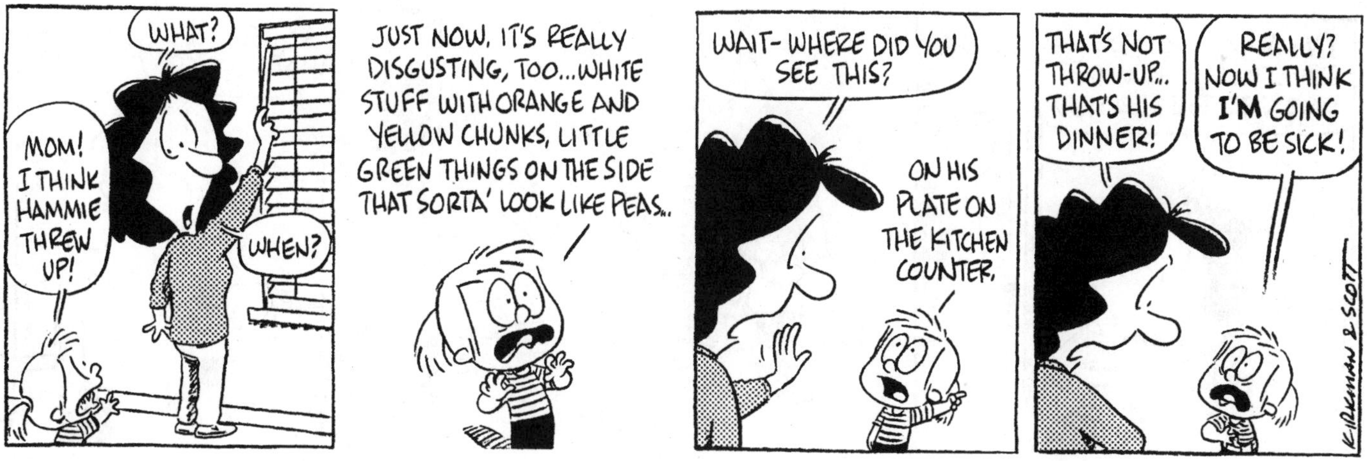
MOM! I THINK HAMMIE THREW UP!
WHAT?
WHEN?
JUST NOW. IT'S REALLY DISGUSTING, TOO...WHITE STUFF WITH ORANGE AND YELLOW CHUNKS, LITTLE GREEN THINGS ON THE SIDE THAT SORTA' LOOK LIKE PEAS...
WAIT- WHERE DID YOU SEE THIS?
ON HIS PLATE ON THE KITCHEN COUNTER.
THAT'S NOT THROW-UP... THAT'S HIS DINNER!
REALLY? NOW I THINK **I'M** GOING TO BE SICK!
KIRKMAN & SCOTT

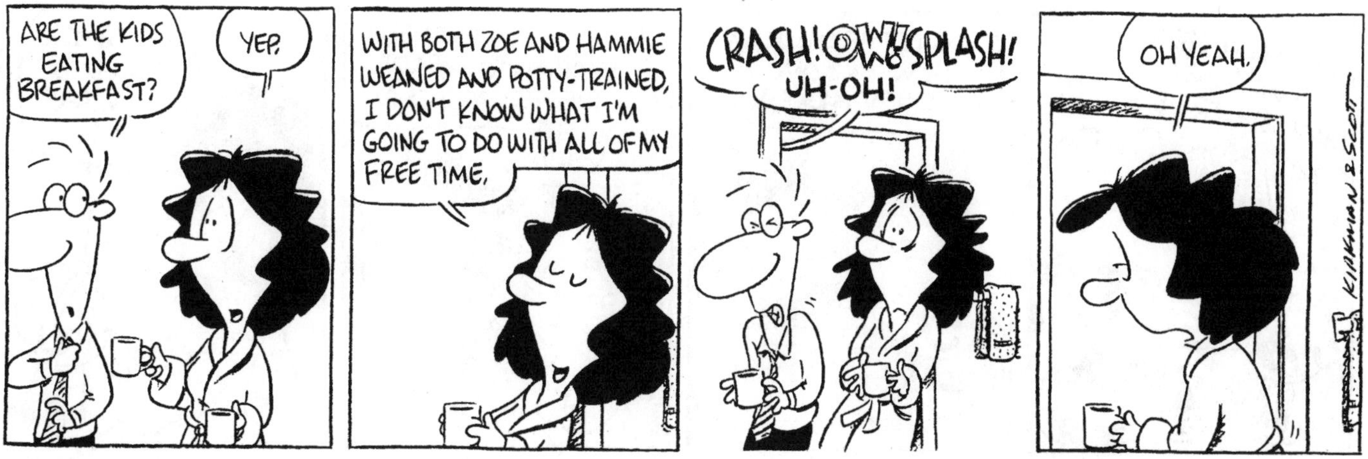
ARE THE KIDS EATING BREAKFAST?
YEP.
WITH BOTH ZOE AND HAMMIE WEANED AND POTTY-TRAINED, I DON'T KNOW WHAT I'M GOING TO DO WITH ALL OF MY FREE TIME.
CRASH! OW! SPLASH!
UH-OH!
OH YEAH.
KIRKMAN & SCOTT

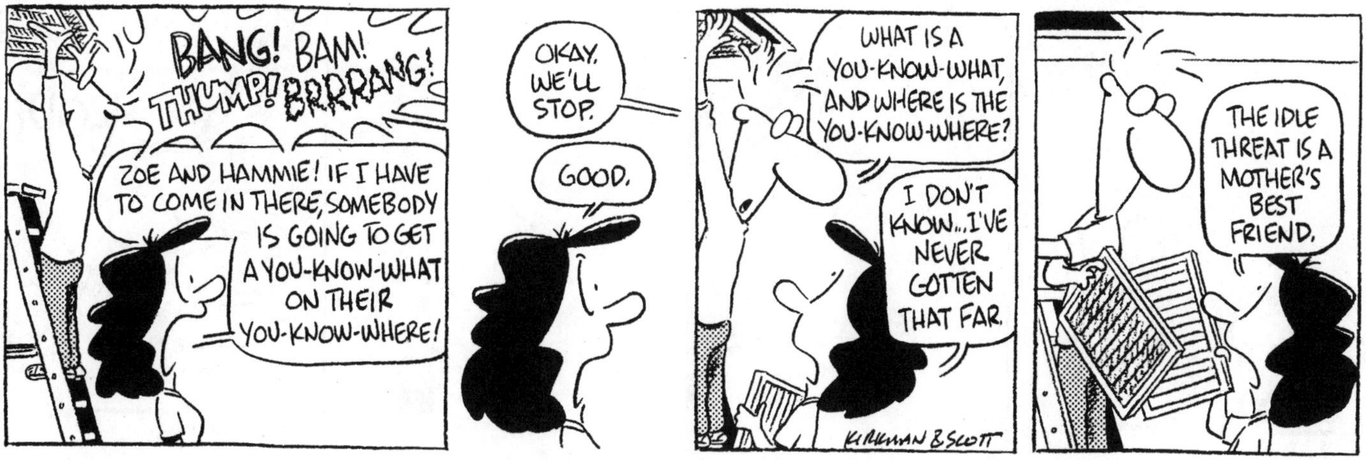
BANG! BAM! THUMP! BRRRANG!
ZOE AND HAMMIE! IF I HAVE TO COME IN THERE, SOMEBODY IS GOING TO GET A YOU-KNOW-WHAT ON THEIR YOU-KNOW-WHERE!
OKAY. WE'LL STOP.
GOOD.
WHAT IS A YOU-KNOW-WHAT, AND WHERE IS THE YOU-KNOW-WHERE?
I DON'T KNOW...I'VE NEVER GOTTEN THAT FAR.
THE IDLE THREAT IS A MOTHER'S BEST FRIEND.
KIRKMAN & SCOTT

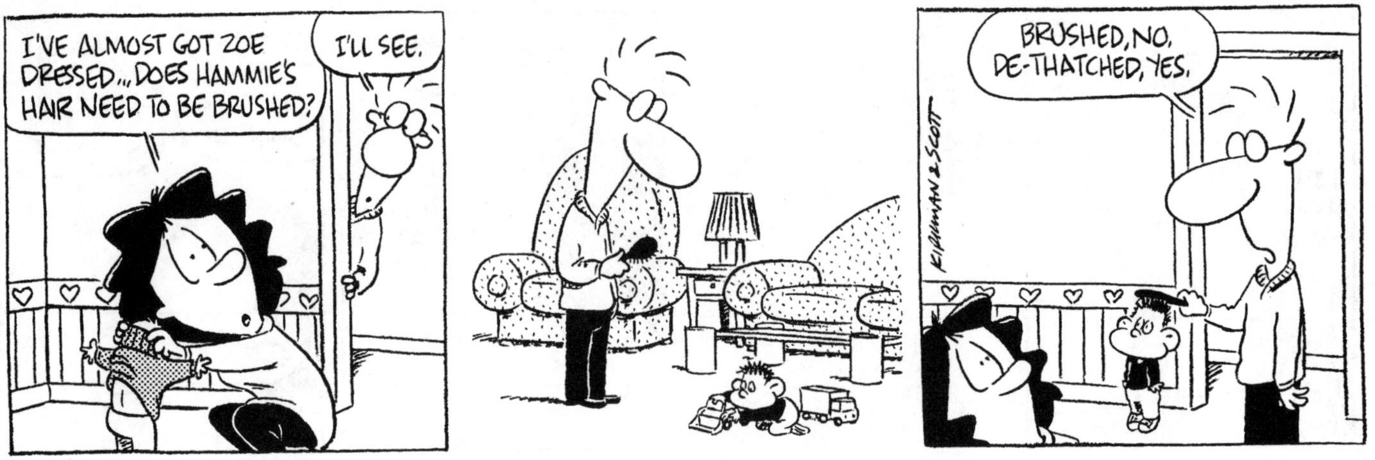
I'VE ALMOST GOT ZOE DRESSED... DOES HAMMIE'S HAIR NEED TO BE BRUSHED?
I'LL SEE.
KIRKMAN & SCOTT
BRUSHED, NO. DE-THATCHED, YES.

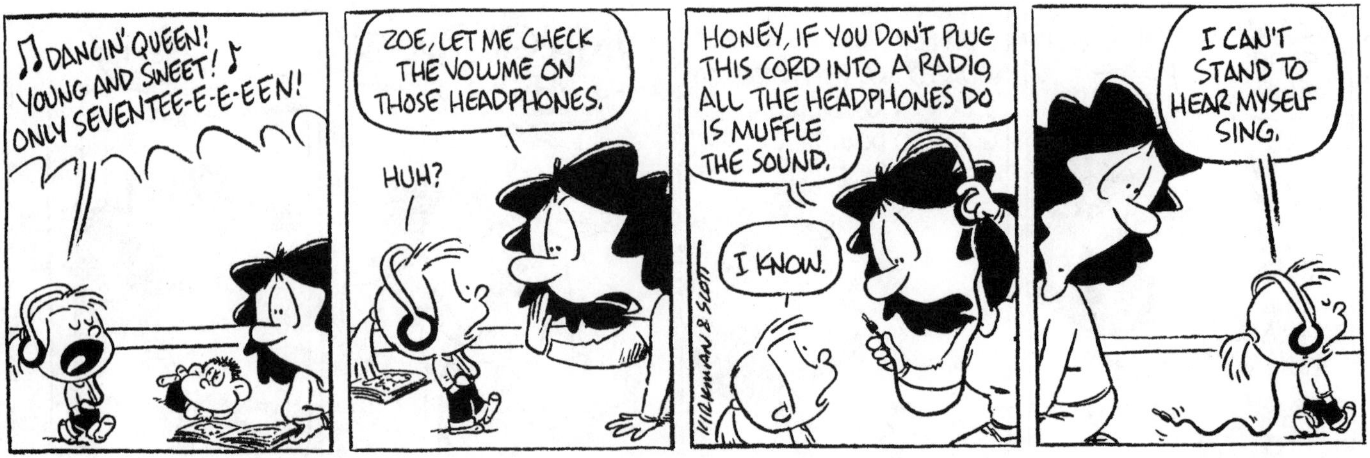
♫ DANCIN' QUEEN! YOUNG AND SWEET! ♪ ONLY SEVENTEE-E-E-EEN!
ZOE, LET ME CHECK THE VOLUME ON THOSE HEADPHONES.
HUH?
KIRKMAN & SCOTT
HONEY, IF YOU DON'T PLUG THIS CORD INTO A RADIO, ALL THE HEADPHONES DO IS MUFFLE THE SOUND.
I KNOW.
I CAN'T STAND TO HEAR MYSELF SING.

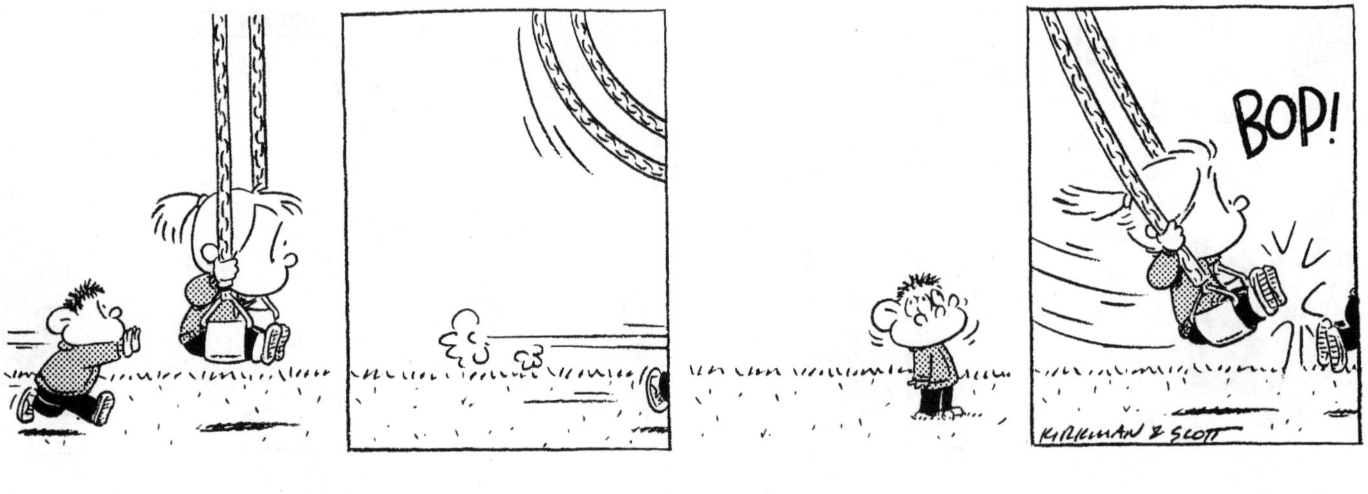
BOP!
KIRKMAN & SCOTT

BABY BLUES ®
BY RICK KIRKMAN / JERRY SCOTT

DID YOU CALL ME?

YES, CLOSE THE DOOR.

I WANT TO SHOW YOU THE SPECIAL KEEPSAKE ORNAMENTS I BOUGHT FOR THE KIDS TO HANG ON THE CHRISTMAS TREE.

THIS IS ZOE'S.

WOW.

IT'S HAND-BLOWN GLASS WITH A 14-KARAT HALO, SATIN DRESS, ANTIQUE LACE AND A REAL PEARL NECKLACE.

IT'S SO DELICATE!

I KNOW, BUT I THINK ZOE IS THE KIND OF CHILD WE CAN TRUST TO HANDLE SOMETHING AS FRAGILE AS THIS.

PROBABLY SO.

SO, WHAT'S HAMMIE'S ORNAMENT MADE OF?

KEVLAR.

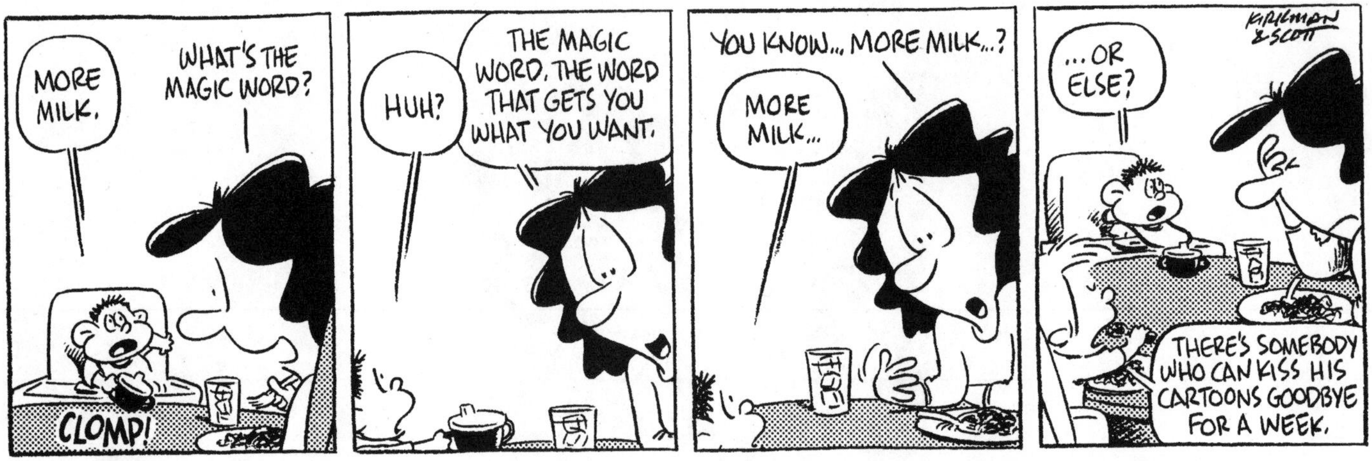
MORE MILK.
WHAT'S THE MAGIC WORD?
CLOMP!
HUH?
THE MAGIC WORD. THE WORD THAT GETS YOU WHAT YOU WANT.
YOU KNOW... MORE MILK...?
MORE MILK...
KIRKMAN & SCOTT
...OR ELSE?
THERE'S SOMEBODY WHO CAN KISS HIS CARTOONS GOODBYE FOR A WEEK.

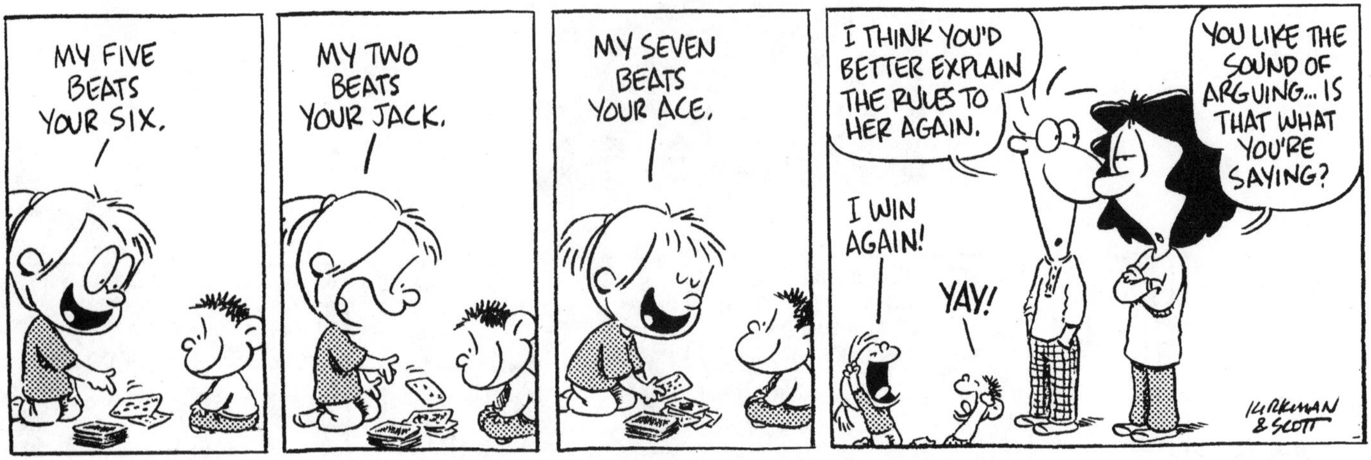
MY FIVE BEATS YOUR SIX.
MY TWO BEATS YOUR JACK.
MY SEVEN BEATS YOUR ACE.
I THINK YOU'D BETTER EXPLAIN THE RULES TO HER AGAIN.
YOU LIKE THE SOUND OF ARGUING... IS THAT WHAT YOU'RE SAYING?
I WIN AGAIN!
YAY!
KIRKMAN & SCOTT

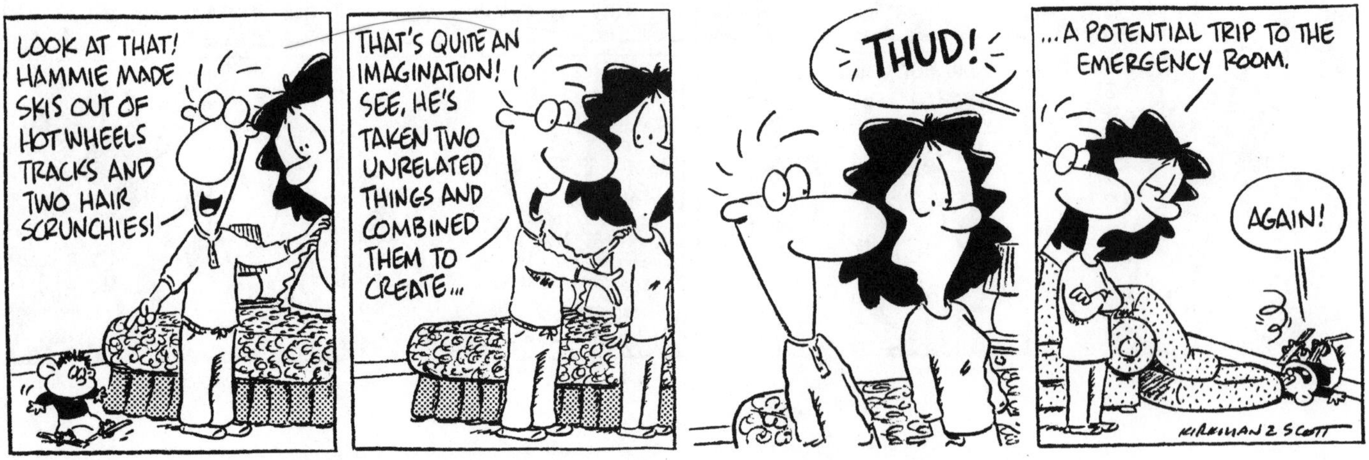
LOOK AT THAT! HAMMIE MADE SKIS OUT OF HOT WHEELS TRACKS AND TWO HAIR SCRUNCHIES!
THAT'S QUITE AN IMAGINATION! SEE, HE'S TAKEN TWO UNRELATED THINGS AND COMBINED THEM TO CREATE...
THUD!
...A POTENTIAL TRIP TO THE EMERGENCY ROOM.
AGAIN!
KIRKMAN & SCOTT

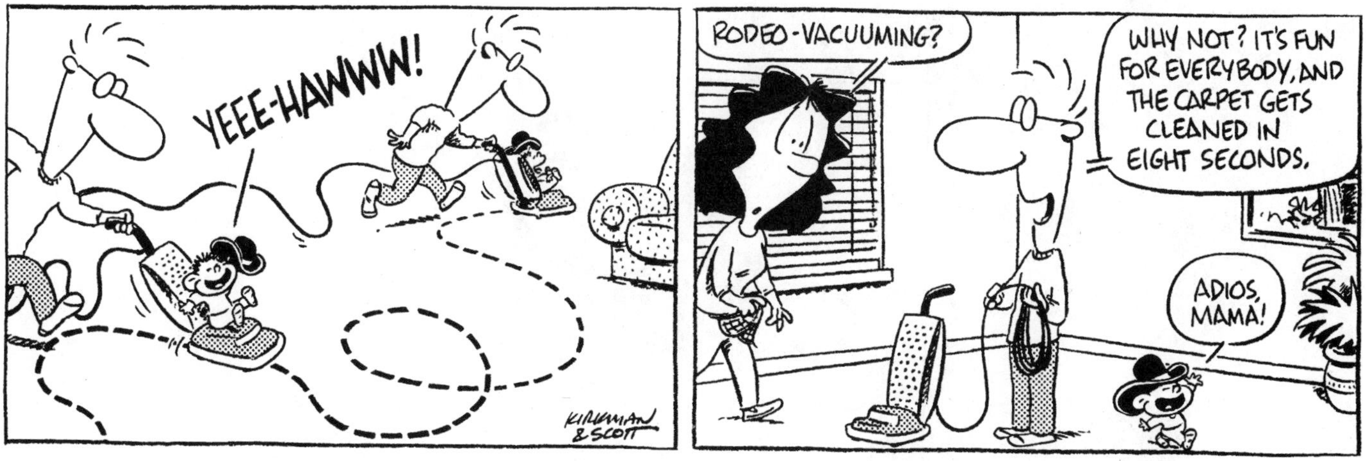
YEEE-HAWWW!
KIRKMAN & SCOTT
RODEO-VACUUMING?
WHY NOT? IT'S FUN FOR EVERYBODY, AND THE CARPET GETS CLEANED IN EIGHT SECONDS.
ADIOS, MAMA!

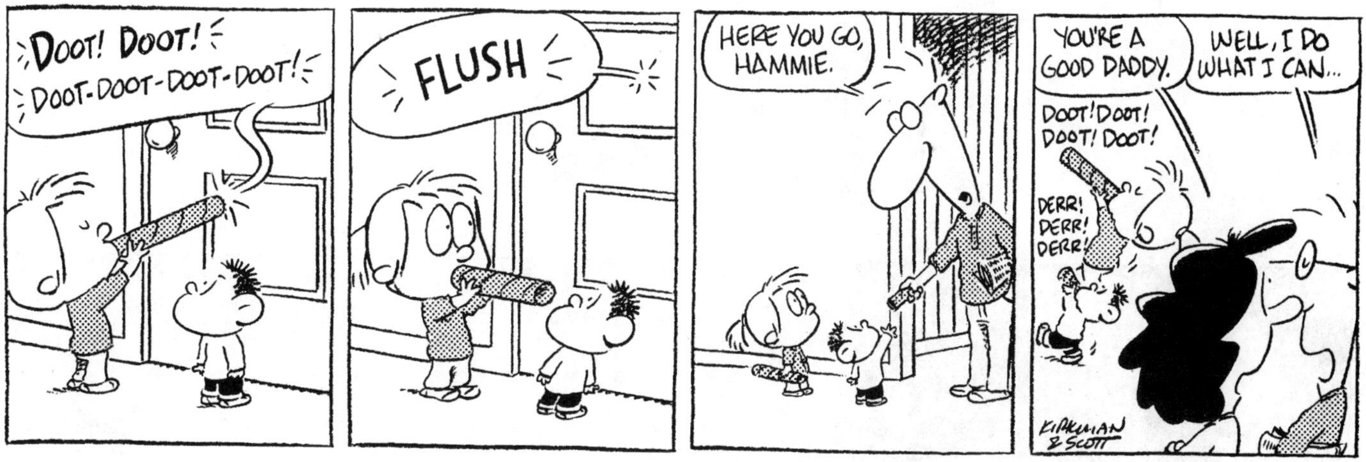
DOOT! DOOT! DOOT-DOOT-DOOT-DOOT!
FLUSH
HERE YOU GO, HAMMIE.
YOU'RE A GOOD DADDY.
WELL, I DO WHAT I CAN...
DOOT! DOOT! DOOT! DOOT!
DERR! DERR! DERR!
KIRKMAN & SCOTT

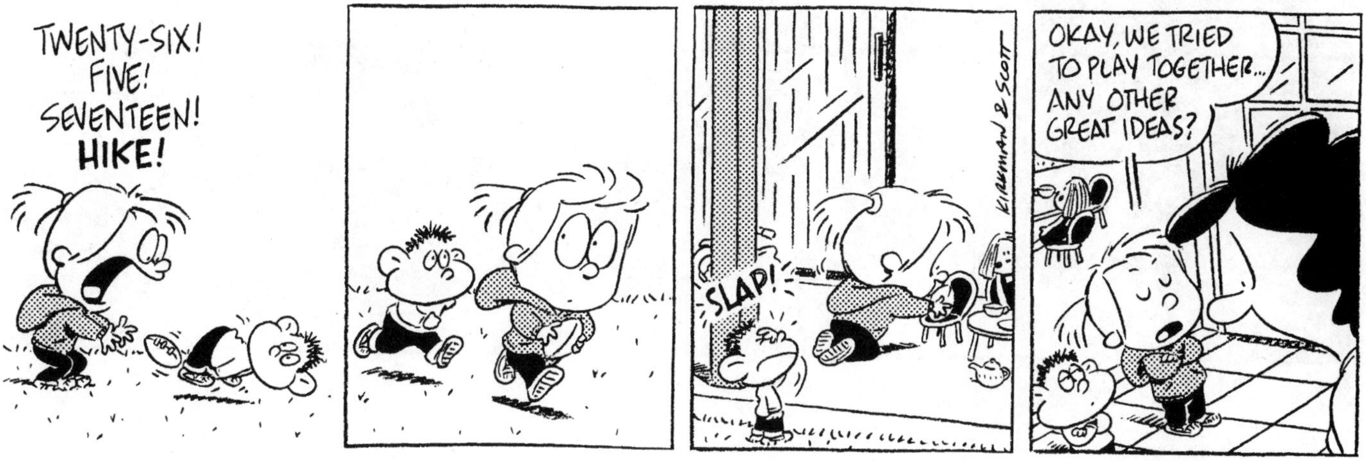
TWENTY-SIX! FIVE! SEVENTEEN! HIKE!
SLAP!
KIRKMAN & SCOTT
OKAY, WE TRIED TO PLAY TOGETHER... ANY OTHER GREAT IDEAS?

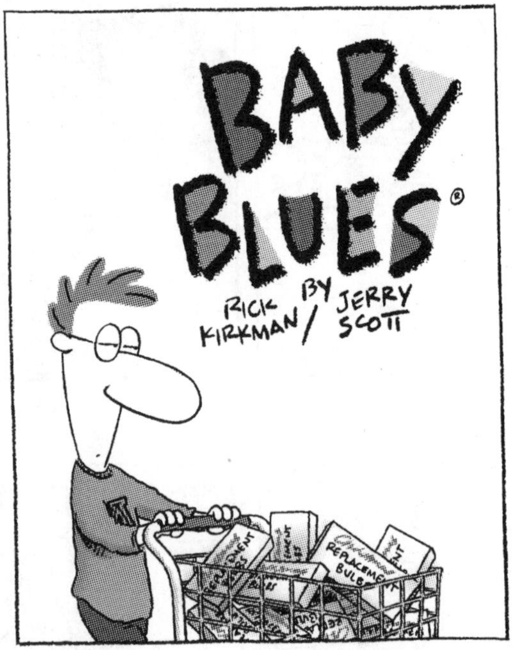
BABY BLUES®
BY RICK KIRKMAN / JERRY SCOTT
REPLACEMENT BULBS

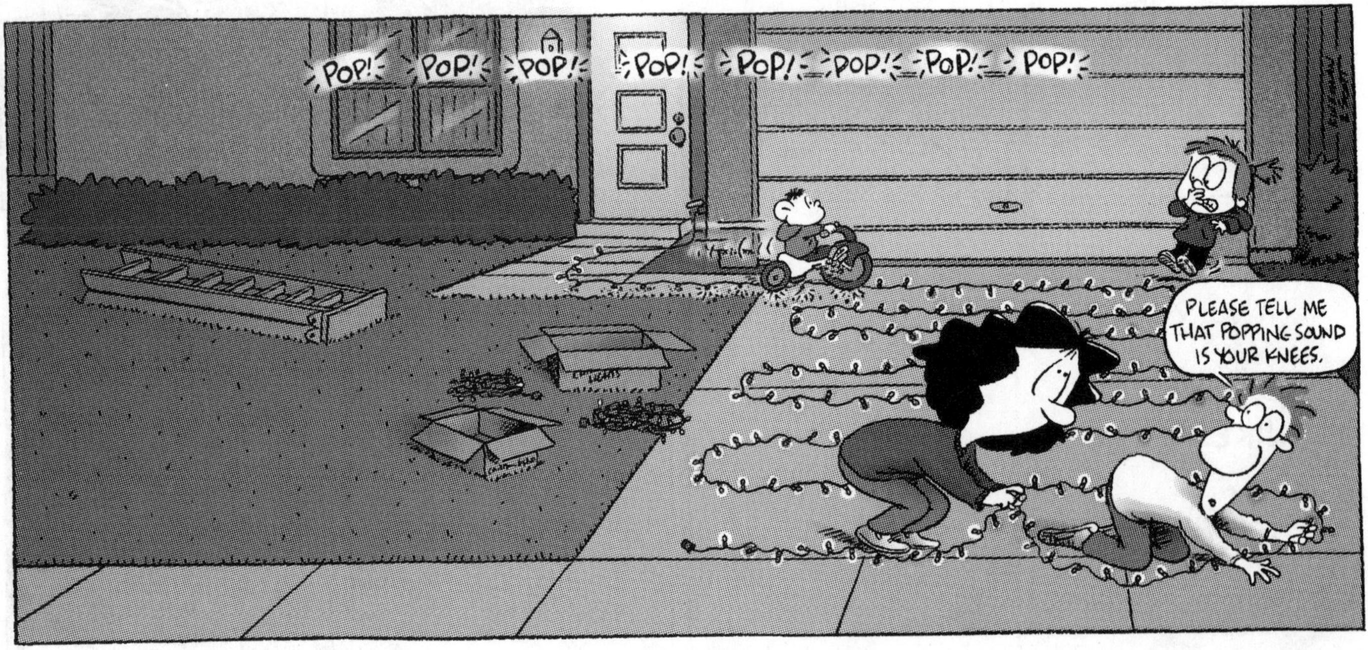
POP! POP! POP! POP! POP! POP! POP! POP!
PLEASE TELL ME THAT POPPING SOUND IS YOUR KNEES.

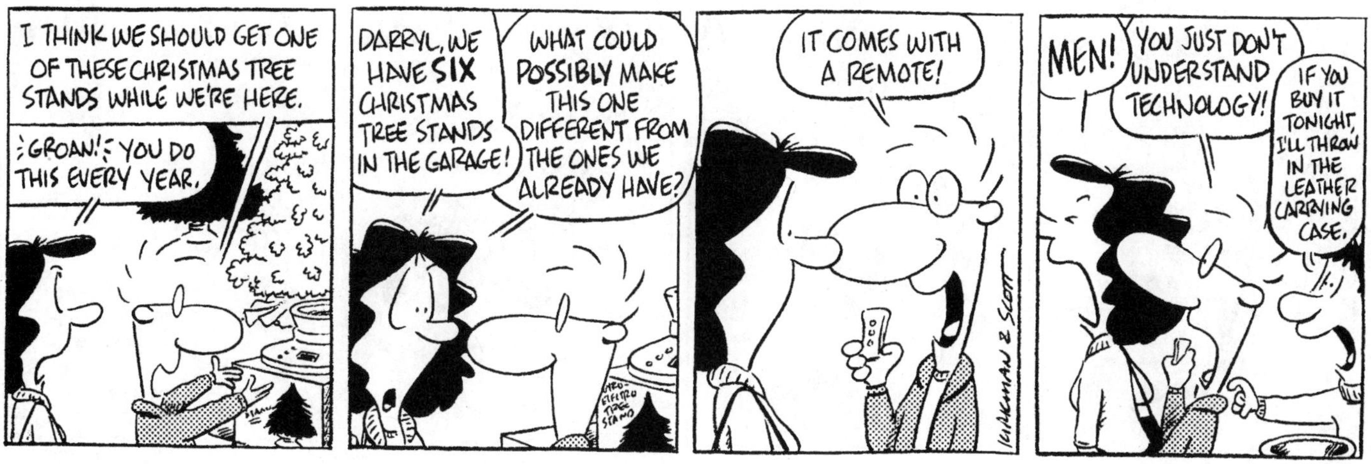
I THINK WE SHOULD GET ONE OF THESE CHRISTMAS TREE STANDS WHILE WE'RE HERE.
;GROAN!; YOU DO THIS EVERY YEAR.
DARRYL, WE HAVE SIX CHRISTMAS TREE STANDS IN THE GARAGE!
WHAT COULD POSSIBLY MAKE THIS ONE DIFFERENT FROM THE ONES WE ALREADY HAVE?
IT COMES WITH A REMOTE!
KIRKMAN & SCOTT
MEN!
YOU JUST DON'T UNDERSTAND TECHNOLOGY!
IF YOU BUY IT TONIGHT, I'LL THROW IN THE LEATHER CARRYING CASE.

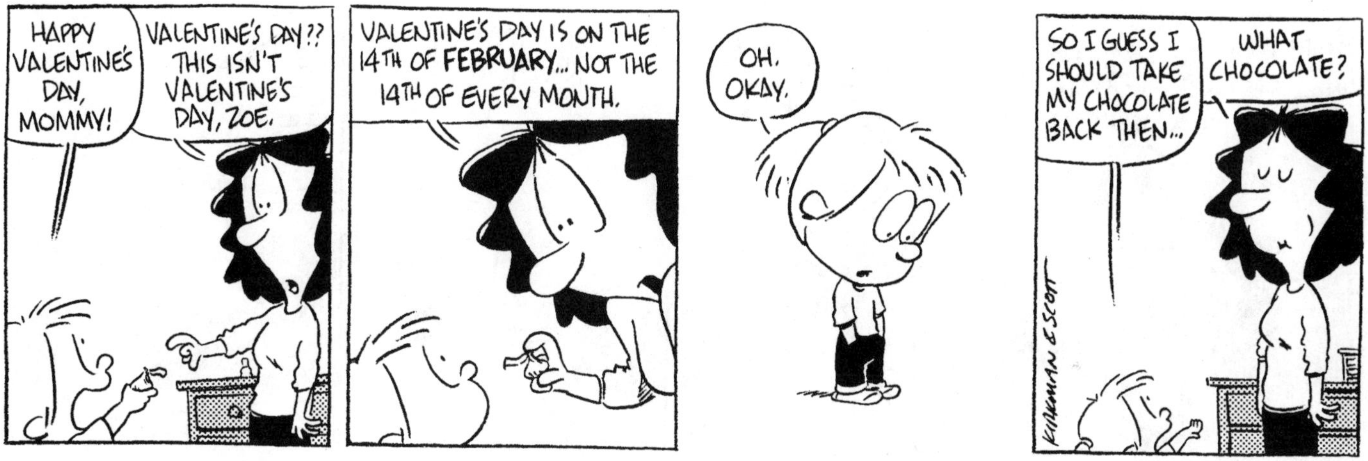
HAPPY VALENTINE'S DAY, MOMMY!
VALENTINE'S DAY?? THIS ISN'T VALENTINE'S DAY, ZOE.
VALENTINE'S DAY IS ON THE 14TH OF FEBRUARY... NOT THE 14TH OF EVERY MONTH.
OH. OKAY.
KIRKMAN & SCOTT
SO I GUESS I SHOULD TAKE MY CHOCOLATE BACK THEN...
WHAT CHOCOLATE?

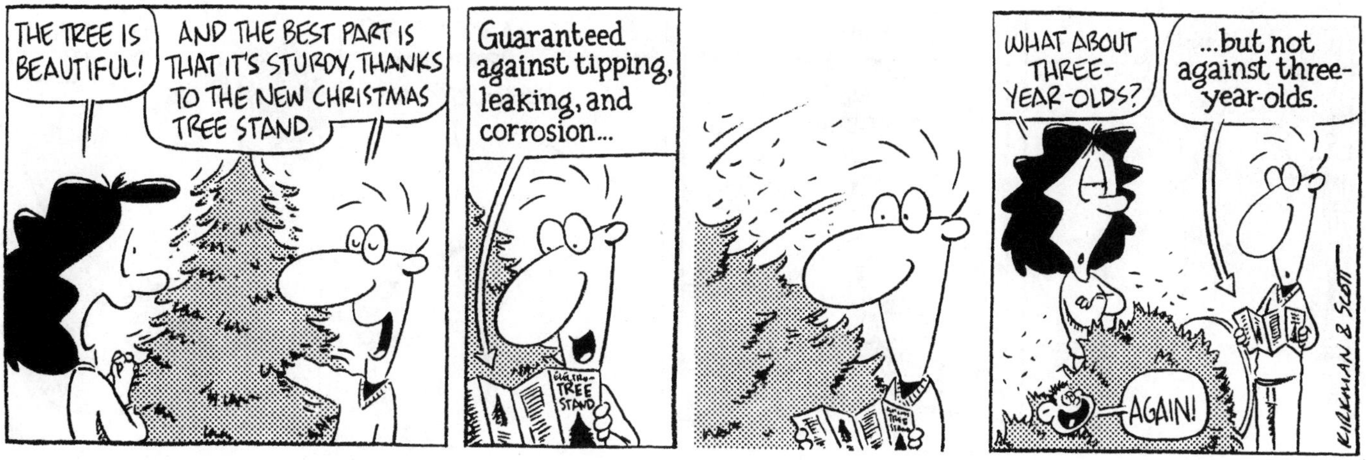
THE TREE IS BEAUTIFUL!
AND THE BEST PART IS THAT IT'S STURDY, THANKS TO THE NEW CHRISTMAS TREE STAND.
Guaranteed against tipping, leaking, and corrosion...
TREE STAND
WHAT ABOUT THREE-YEAR-OLDS?
...but not against three-year-olds.
AGAIN!
KIRKMAN & SCOTT

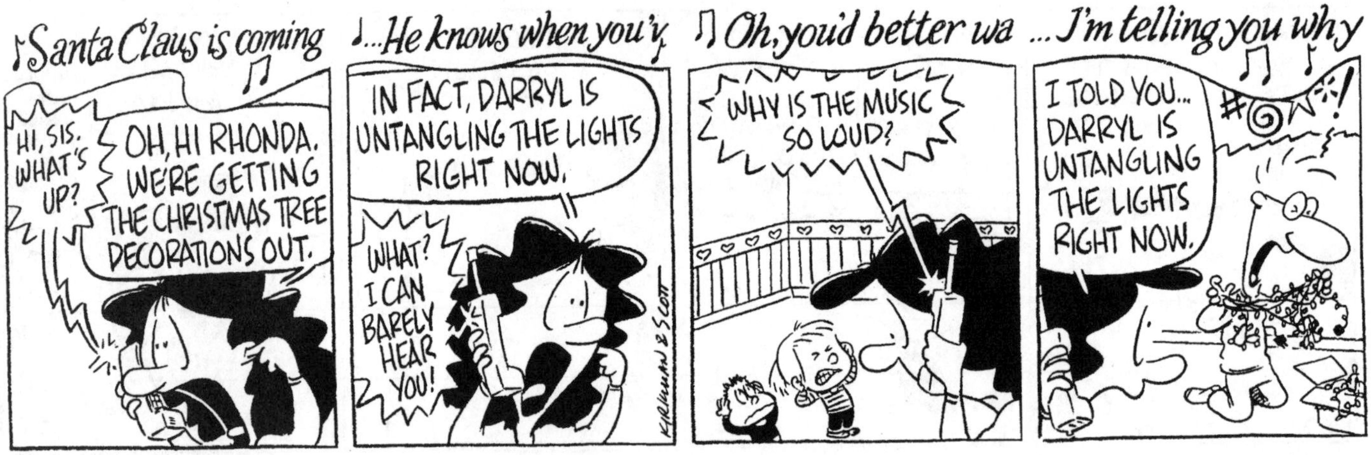
Santa Claus is coming
HI, SIS. WHAT'S UP?
OH, HI RHONDA. WE'RE GETTING THE CHRISTMAS TREE DECORATIONS OUT.
...He knows when you'v
IN FACT, DARRYL IS UNTANGLING THE LIGHTS RIGHT NOW.
WHAT? I CAN BARELY HEAR YOU!
KIRKMAN & SCOTT
Oh, you'd better wa
WHY IS THE MUSIC SO LOUD?
... I'm telling you why
I TOLD YOU... DARRYL IS UNTANGLING THE LIGHTS RIGHT NOW.

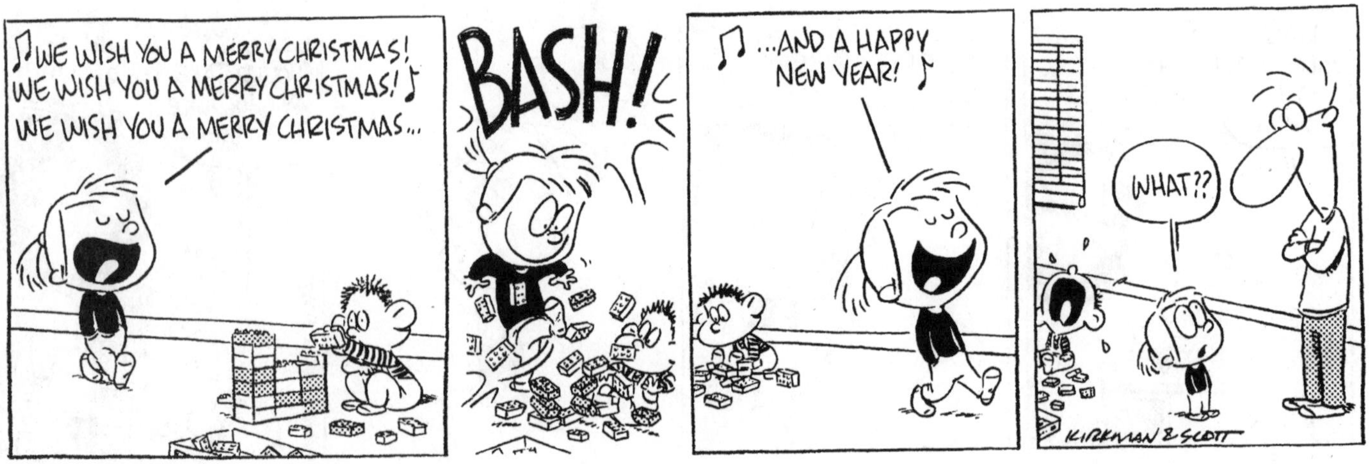
WE WISH YOU A MERRY CHRISTMAS! WE WISH YOU A MERRY CHRISTMAS! WE WISH YOU A MERRY CHRISTMAS...
BASH!
...AND A HAPPY NEW YEAR!
WHAT??
KIRKMAN & SCOTT

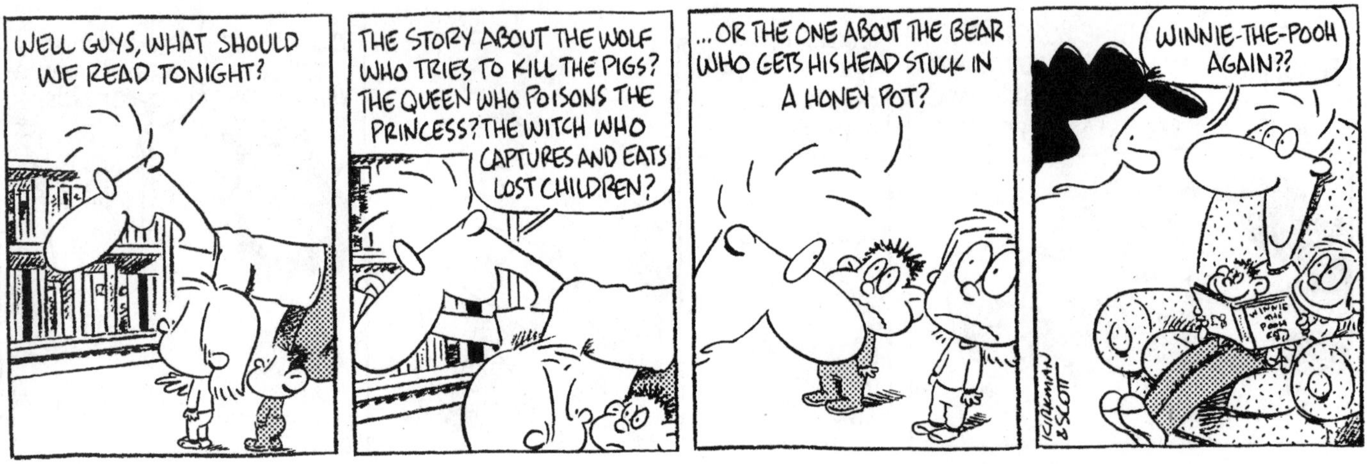
WELL GUYS, WHAT SHOULD WE READ TONIGHT?
THE STORY ABOUT THE WOLF WHO TRIES TO KILL THE PIGS? THE QUEEN WHO POISONS THE PRINCESS? THE WITCH WHO CAPTURES AND EATS LOST CHILDREN?
...OR THE ONE ABOUT THE BEAR WHO GETS HIS HEAD STUCK IN A HONEY POT?
KIRKMAN & SCOTT
WINNIE-THE-POOH AGAIN??

BABY BLUES®
BY RICK KIRKMAN / JERRY SCOTT
POWER
VOL
CHAN
YIKES!

VOLUME
SCREECH! HEY! COME BACK HERE! WHY YOU...
VOLUME
CLICK!
#@!&*%!!!
MUTE
VOLUME
VOLUME
*&#%# #@@!!! $★!
CLICK!
MUTE
WATCHING MOVIES WOULD BE A LOT MORE FUN IF THE KIDS' BEDROOMS WERE ON THE OTHER SIDE OF THE HOUSE.
KIRKMAN & SCOTT

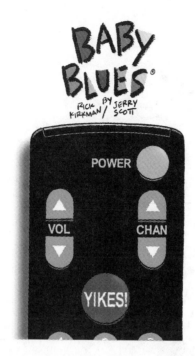

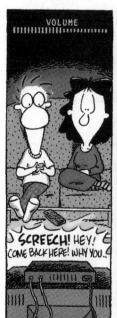

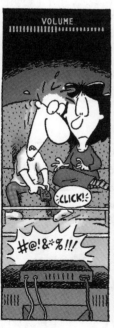

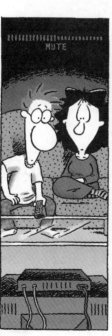

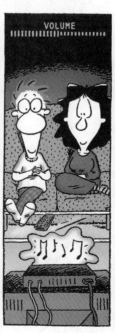

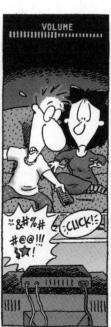

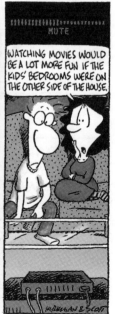

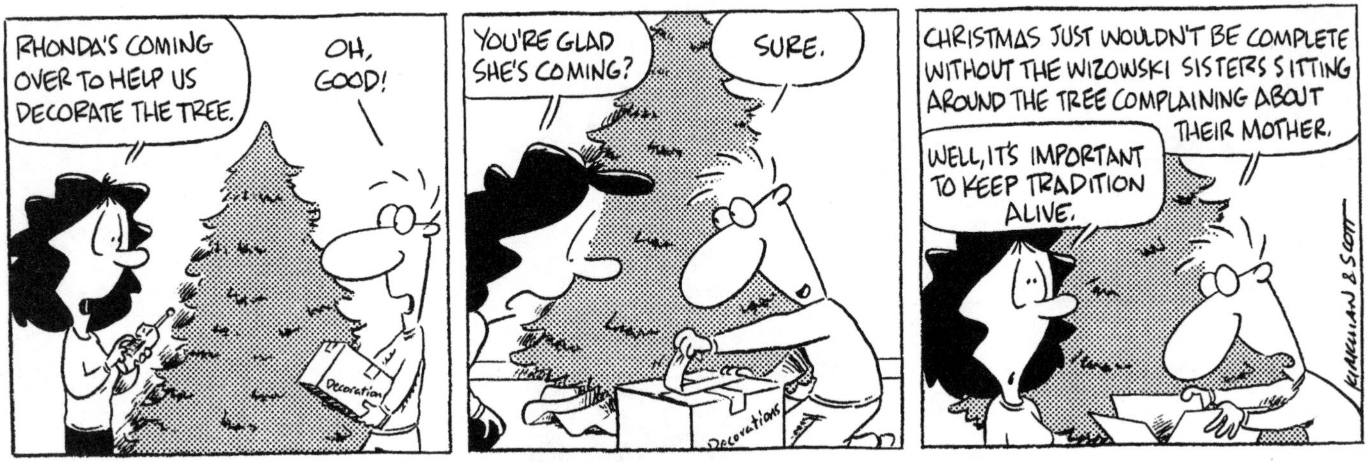

RHONDA'S COMING OVER TO HELP US DECORATE THE TREE.
OH, GOOD!
Decoration
YOU'RE GLAD SHE'S COMING?
SURE.
Decorations
CHRISTMAS JUST WOULDN'T BE COMPLETE WITHOUT THE WIZOWSKI SISTERS SITTING AROUND THE TREE COMPLAINING ABOUT THEIR MOTHER.
WELL, IT'S IMPORTANT TO KEEP TRADITION ALIVE.
KIRKMAN & SCOTT

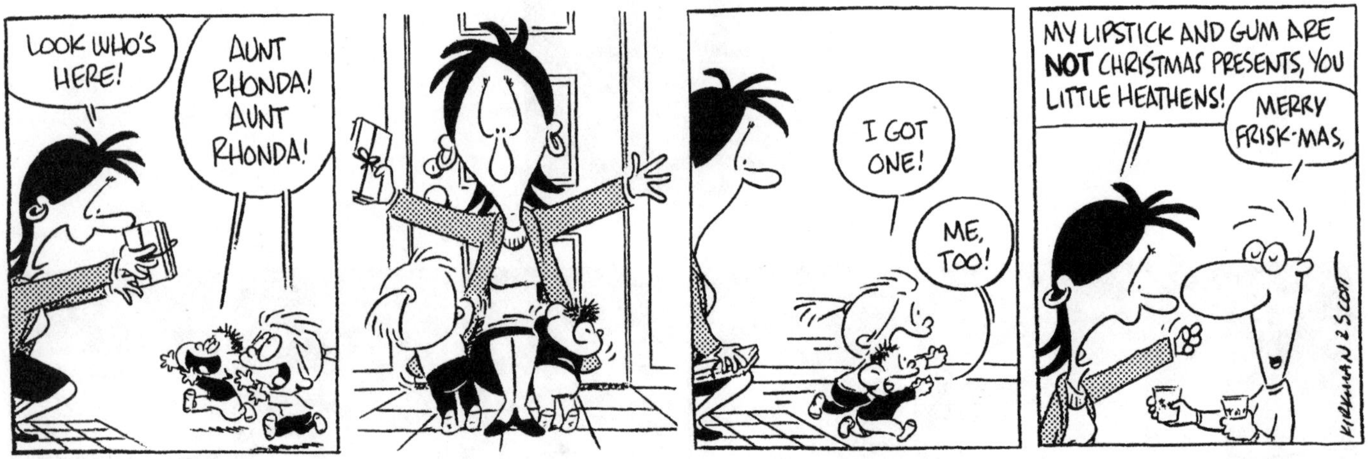

LOOK WHO'S HERE!
AUNT RHONDA! AUNT RHONDA!
I GOT ONE!
ME, TOO!
MY LIPSTICK AND GUM ARE **NOT** CHRISTMAS PRESENTS, YOU LITTLE HEATHENS!
MERRY FRISK-MAS,
KIRKMAN & SCOTT

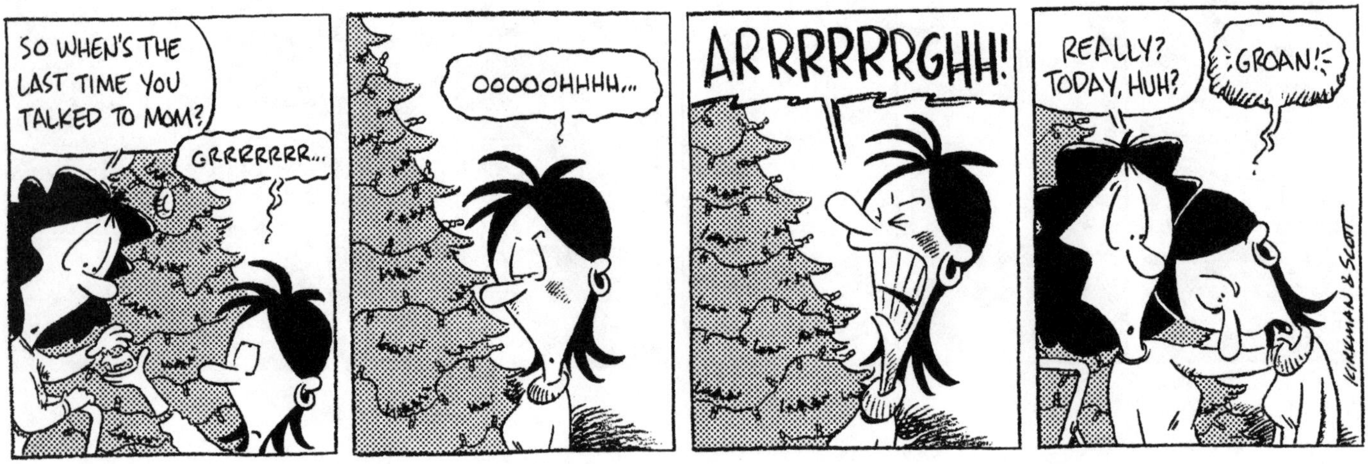

SO WHEN'S THE LAST TIME YOU TALKED TO MOM?
GRRRRRRR...
OOOOOHHHH...
ARRRRRRGHH!
REALLY? TODAY, HUH?
GROAN!
KIRKMAN & SCOTT

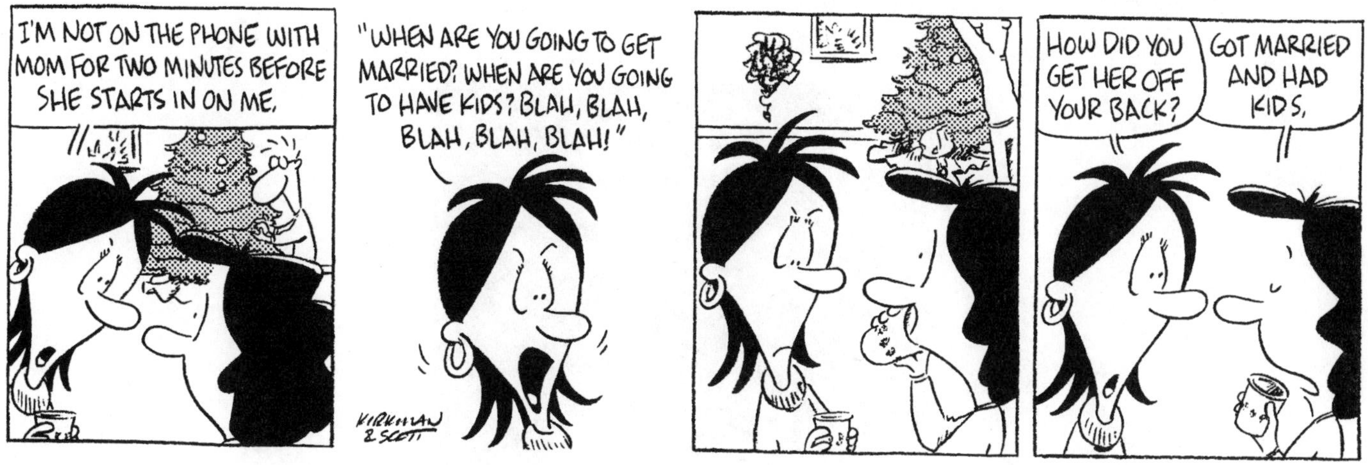
I'M NOT ON THE PHONE WITH MOM FOR TWO MINUTES BEFORE SHE STARTS IN ON ME.
"WHEN ARE YOU GOING TO GET MARRIED? WHEN ARE YOU GOING TO HAVE KIDS? BLAH, BLAH, BLAH, BLAH, BLAH!"
KIRKMAN & SCOTT
HOW DID YOU GET HER OFF YOUR BACK?
GOT MARRIED AND HAD KIDS.

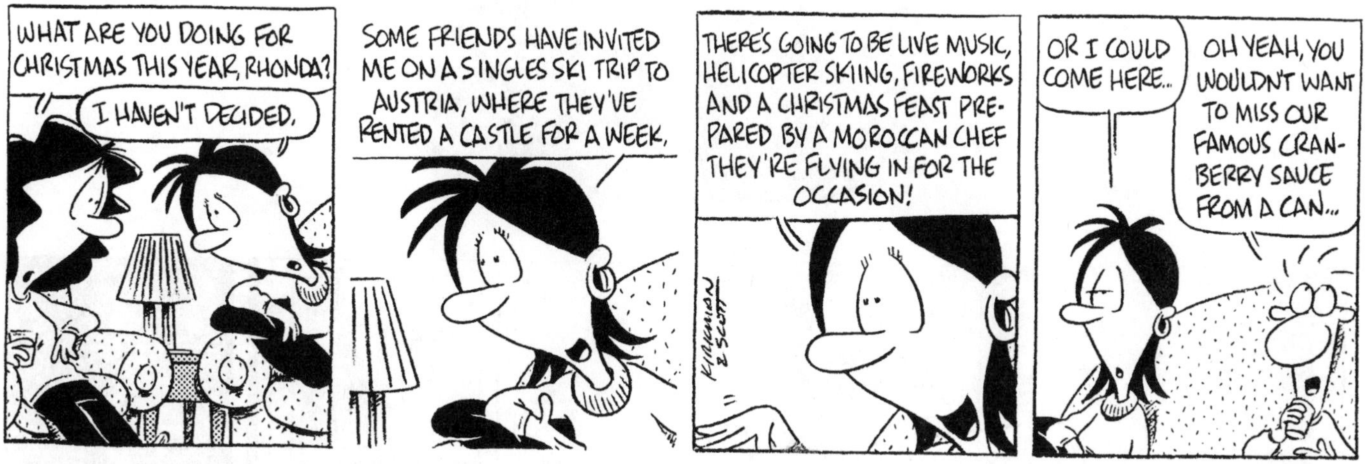
WHAT ARE YOU DOING FOR CHRISTMAS THIS YEAR, RHONDA?
I HAVEN'T DECIDED.
SOME FRIENDS HAVE INVITED ME ON A SINGLES SKI TRIP TO AUSTRIA, WHERE THEY'VE RENTED A CASTLE FOR A WEEK.
THERE'S GOING TO BE LIVE MUSIC, HELICOPTER SKIING, FIREWORKS AND A CHRISTMAS FEAST PREPARED BY A MOROCCAN CHEF THEY'RE FLYING IN FOR THE OCCASION!
KIRKMAN & SCOTT
OR I COULD COME HERE...
OH YEAH, YOU WOULDN'T WANT TO MISS OUR FAMOUS CRANBERRY SAUCE FROM A CAN...

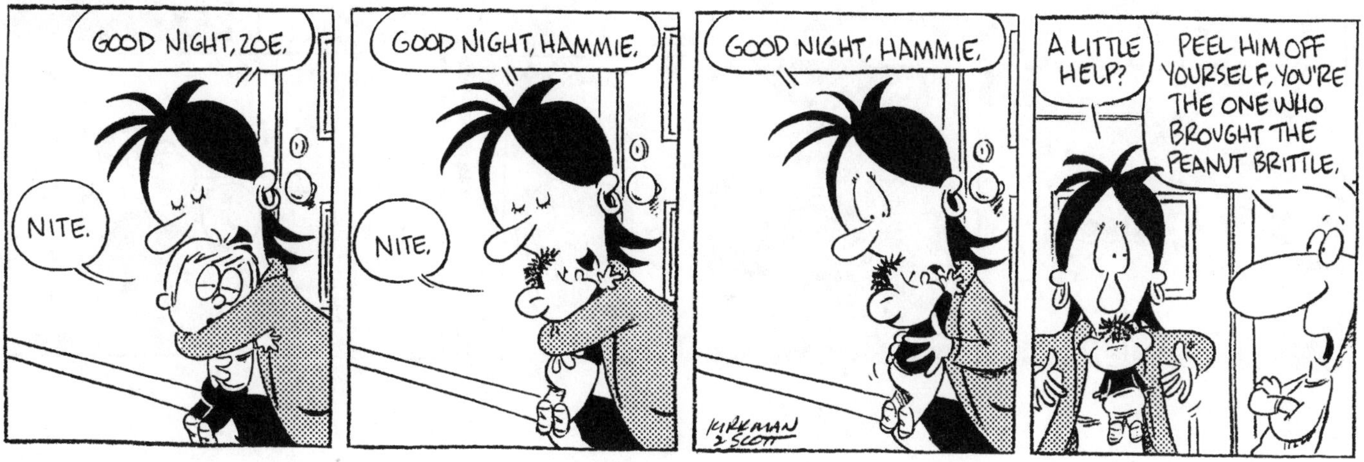
GOOD NIGHT, ZOE.
NITE.
GOOD NIGHT, HAMMIE.
NITE.
GOOD NIGHT, HAMMIE.
KIRKMAN & SCOTT
A LITTLE HELP?
PEEL HIM OFF YOURSELF, YOU'RE THE ONE WHO BROUGHT THE PEANUT BRITTLE.

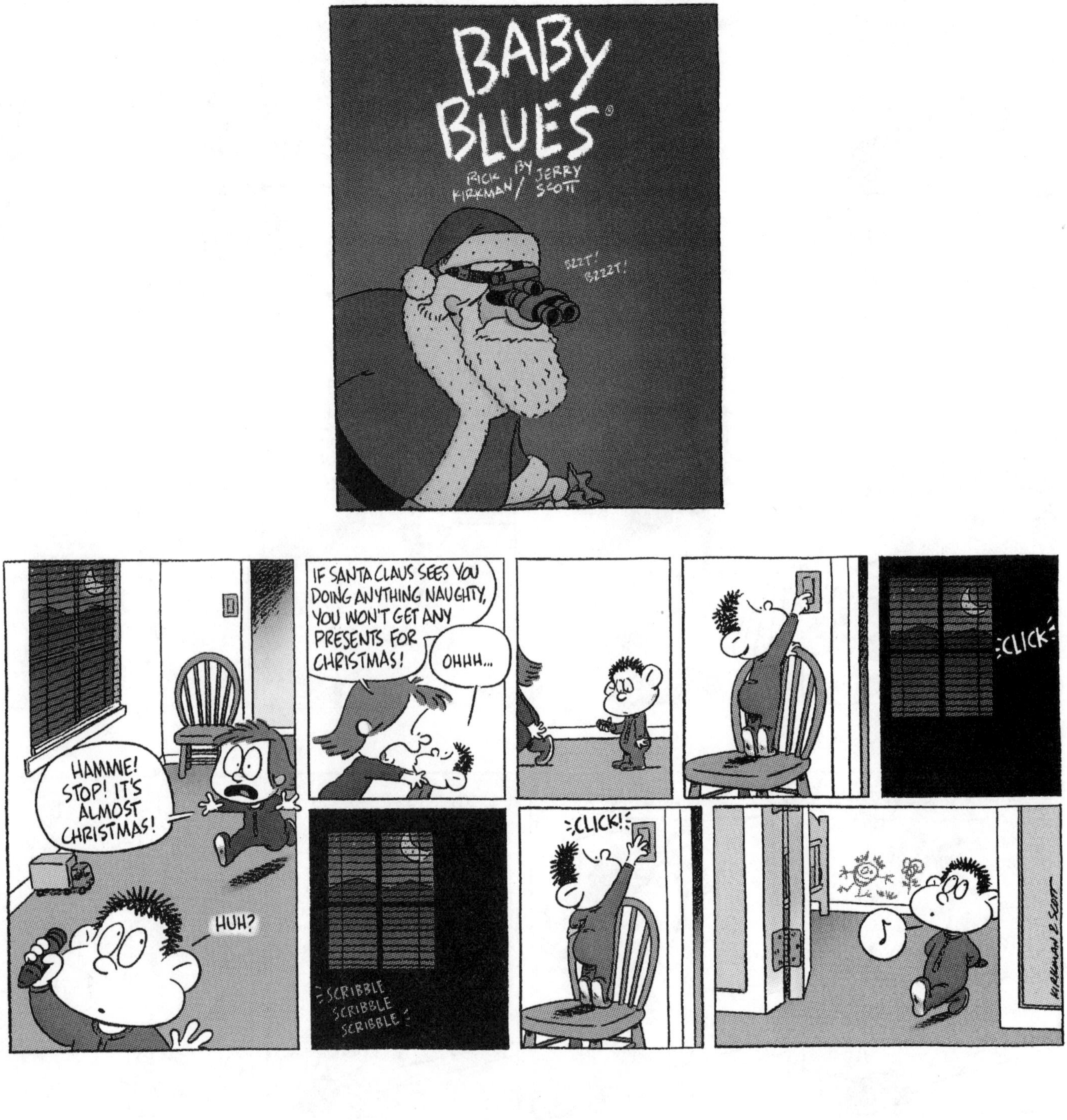
BABY BLUES®
BY RICK KIRKMAN / JERRY SCOTT
BZZT! BZZZT!
HAMMIE! STOP! IT'S ALMOST CHRISTMAS!
HUH?
IF SANTA CLAUS SEES YOU DOING ANYTHING NAUGHTY, YOU WON'T GET ANY PRESENTS FOR CHRISTMAS!
OHHH...
CLICK
SCRIBBLE SCRIBBLE SCRIBBLE
CLICK!
♪
KIRKMAN & SCOTT

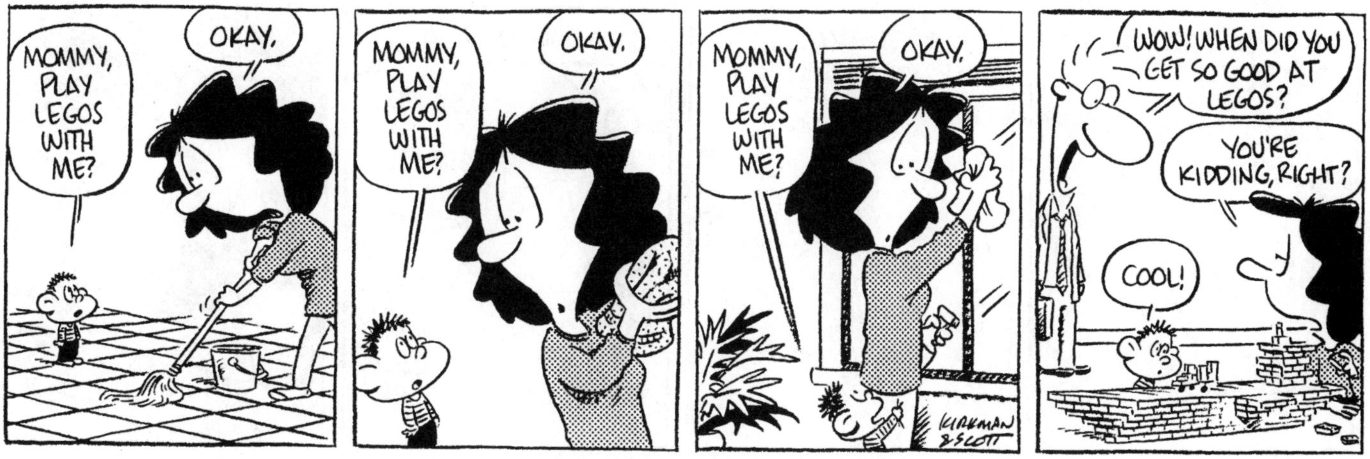
MOMMY, PLAY LEGOS WITH ME?
OKAY.
MOMMY, PLAY LEGOS WITH ME?
OKAY.
MOMMY, PLAY LEGOS WITH ME?
OKAY.
KIRKMAN & SCOTT
WOW! WHEN DID YOU GET SO GOOD AT LEGOS?
YOU'RE KIDDING, RIGHT?
COOL!

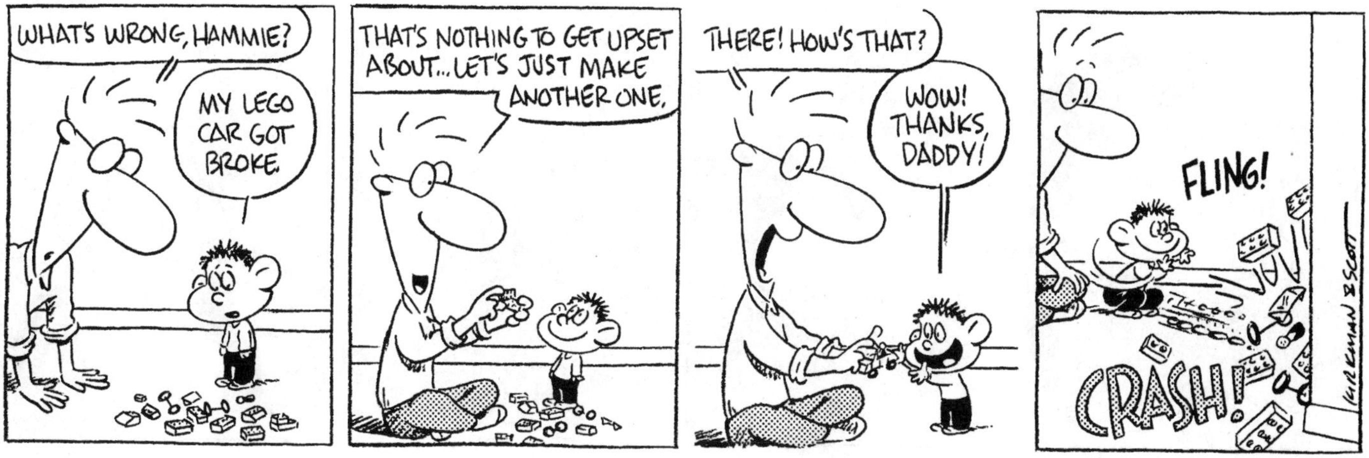
WHAT'S WRONG, HAMMIE?
MY LEGO CAR GOT BROKE.
THAT'S NOTHING TO GET UPSET ABOUT... LET'S JUST MAKE ANOTHER ONE.
THERE! HOW'S THAT?
WOW! THANKS, DADDY!
FLING!
CRASH!
KIRKMAN & SCOTT

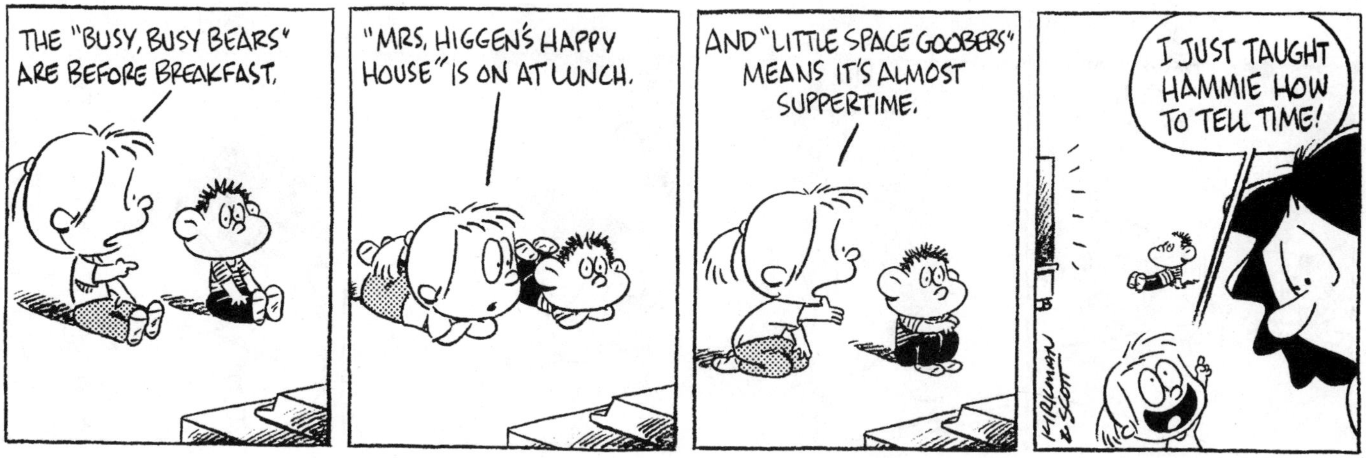
THE "BUSY, BUSY BEARS" ARE BEFORE BREAKFAST.
"MRS. HIGGEN'S HAPPY HOUSE" IS ON AT LUNCH.
AND "LITTLE SPACE GOOBERS" MEANS IT'S ALMOST SUPPERTIME.
KIRKMAN & SCOTT
I JUST TAUGHT HAMMIE HOW TO TELL TIME!

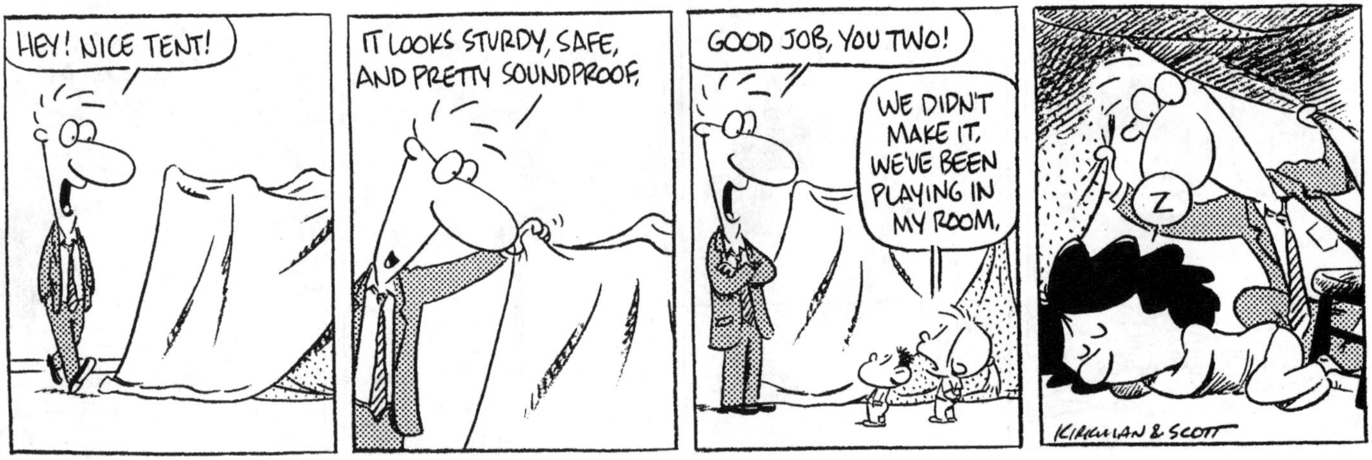
HEY! NICE TENT!
IT LOOKS STURDY, SAFE, AND PRETTY SOUNDPROOF.
GOOD JOB, YOU TWO!
WE DIDN'T MAKE IT. WE'VE BEEN PLAYING IN MY ROOM.
Z
KIRKMAN & SCOTT

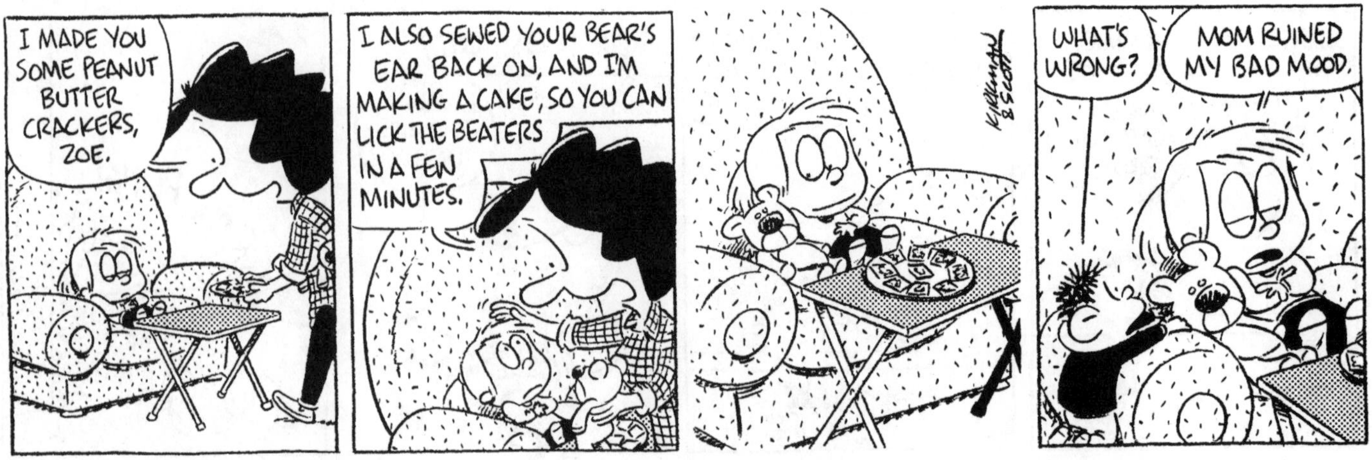
I MADE YOU SOME PEANUT BUTTER CRACKERS, ZOE.
I ALSO SEWED YOUR BEAR'S EAR BACK ON, AND I'M MAKING A CAKE, SO YOU CAN LICK THE BEATERS IN A FEW MINUTES.
KIRKMAN & SCOTT
WHAT'S WRONG?
MOM RUINED MY BAD MOOD.

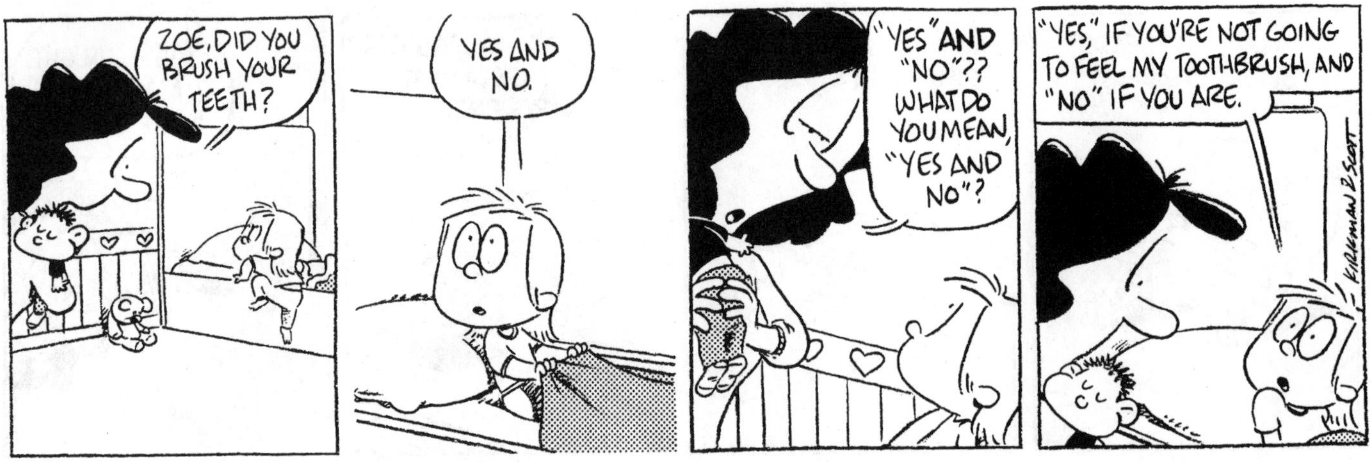
ZOE, DID YOU BRUSH YOUR TEETH?
YES AND NO.
"YES" AND "NO"?? WHAT DO YOU MEAN, "YES AND NO"?
"YES," IF YOU'RE NOT GOING TO FEEL MY TOOTHBRUSH, AND "NO" IF YOU ARE.
KIRKMAN & SCOTT

BABY BLUES®
BY
RICK KIRKMAN / JERRY SCOTT
2000
2001

...THREE!...
...THREE!...
...TWO!...
...TWO!...
...ONE!...
...ONE!...
HAPPY NEW YEAR!
HONK! TWEET! BLATT! YAY! WHEEE!
WE DID IT! WE STAYED UP UNTIL MIDNIGHT!!
YAY!
Z
Z
SHOULD WE WAKE UP MOM AND DAD TO TELL 'EM?

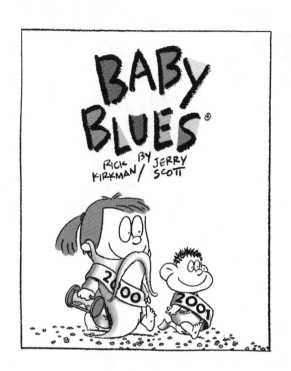

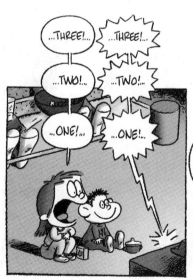

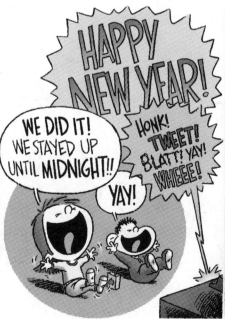

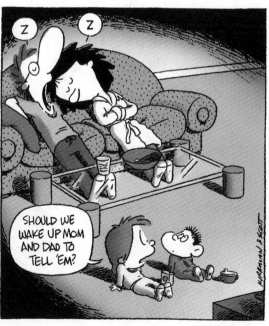

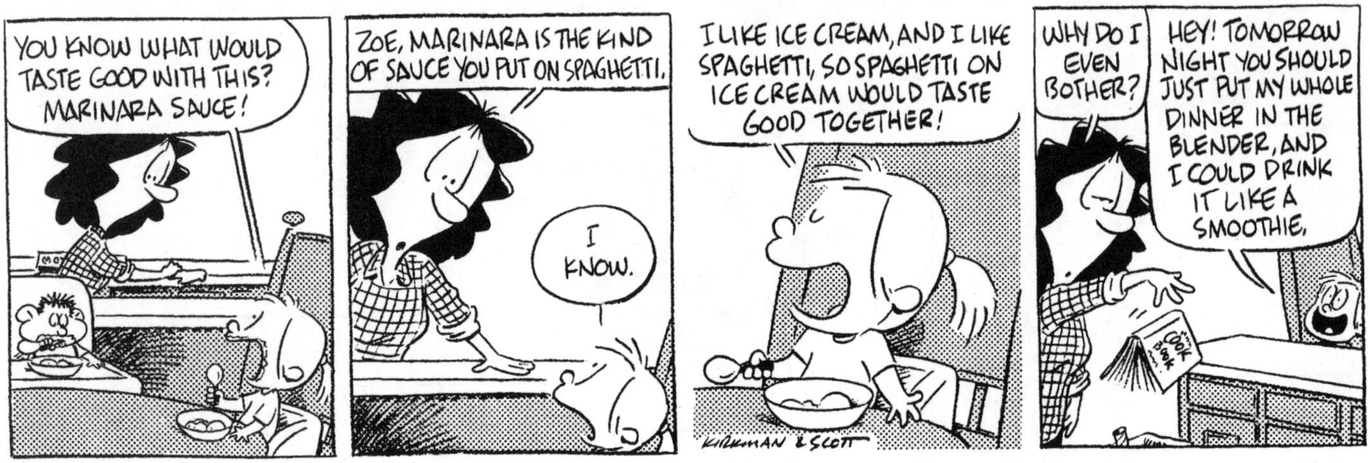
YOU KNOW WHAT WOULD TASTE GOOD WITH THIS? MARINARA SAUCE!
ZOE, MARINARA IS THE KIND OF SAUCE YOU PUT ON SPAGHETTI.
I KNOW.
I LIKE ICE CREAM, AND I LIKE SPAGHETTI, SO SPAGHETTI ON ICE CREAM WOULD TASTE GOOD TOGETHER!
KIRKMAN & SCOTT
WHY DO I EVEN BOTHER?
HEY! TOMORROW NIGHT YOU SHOULD JUST PUT MY WHOLE DINNER IN THE BLENDER, AND I COULD DRINK IT LIKE A SMOOTHIE.
COOK BOOK

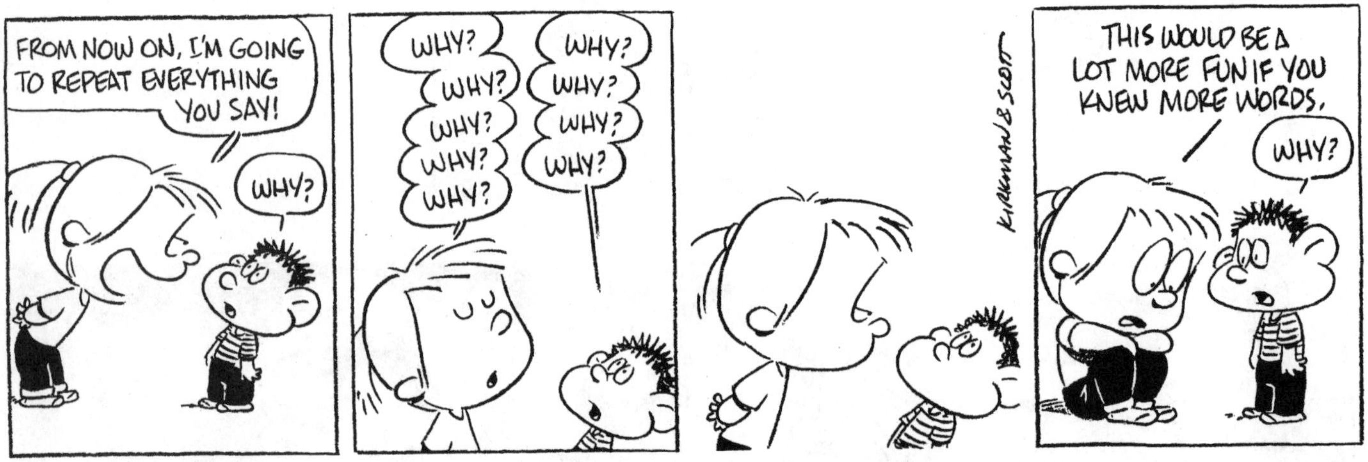
FROM NOW ON, I'M GOING TO REPEAT EVERYTHING YOU SAY!
WHY?
WHY? WHY? WHY? WHY? WHY?
WHY? WHY? WHY? WHY?
KIRKMAN & SCOTT
THIS WOULD BE A LOT MORE FUN IF YOU KNEW MORE WORDS.
WHY?

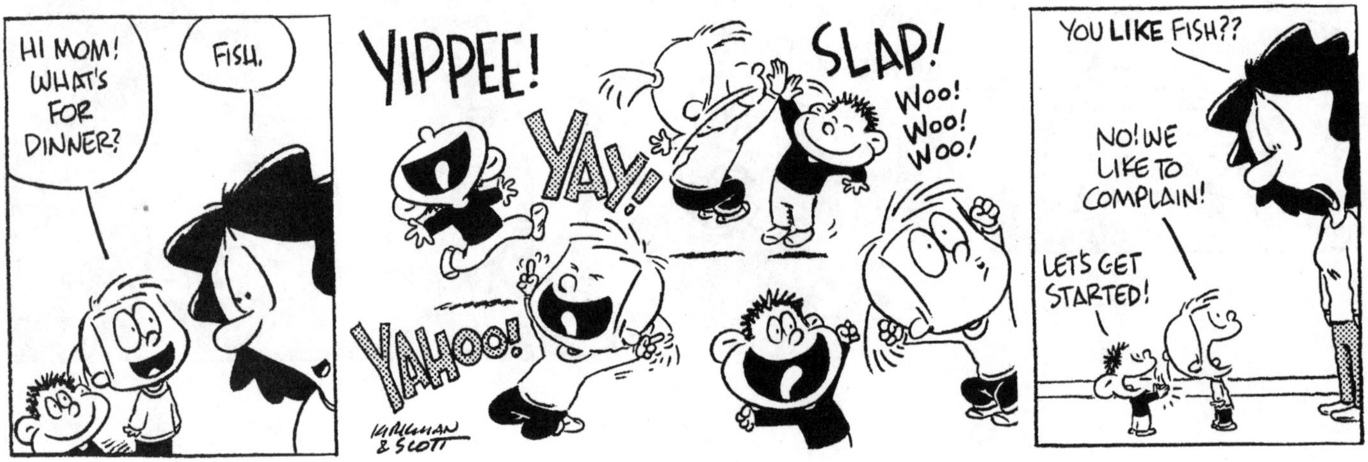
HI MOM! WHAT'S FOR DINNER?
FISH.
YIPPEE!
YAY!
SLAP!
Woo! Woo! Woo!
YAHOO!
KIRKMAN & SCOTT
YOU **LIKE** FISH??
NO! WE LIKE TO COMPLAIN!
LET'S GET STARTED!

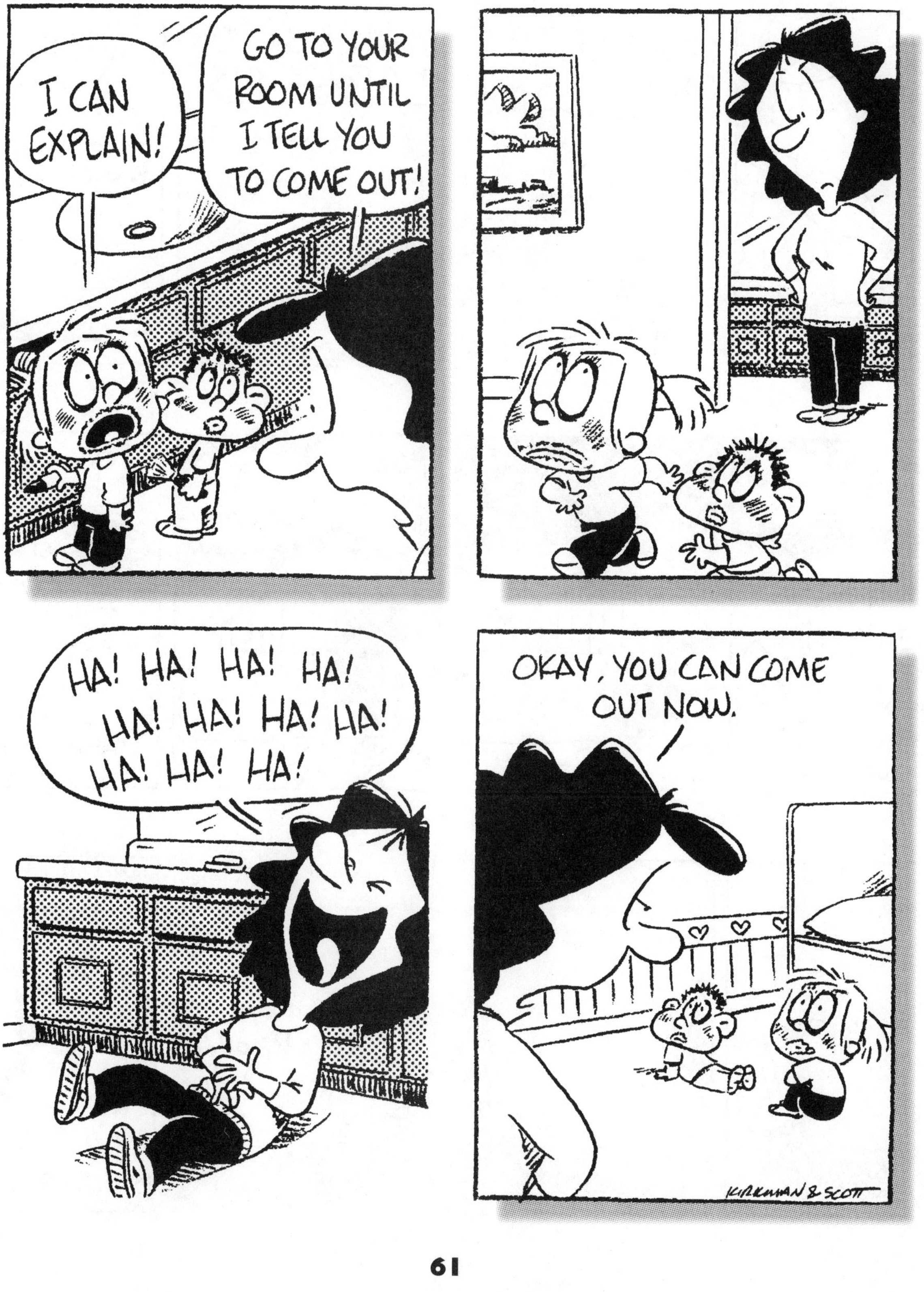
I CAN EXPLAIN!
GO TO YOUR ROOM UNTIL I TELL YOU TO COME OUT!
HA! HA! HA! HA! HA! HA! HA! HA! HA! HA! HA!
OKAY, YOU CAN COME OUT NOW.
KIRKMAN & SCOTT

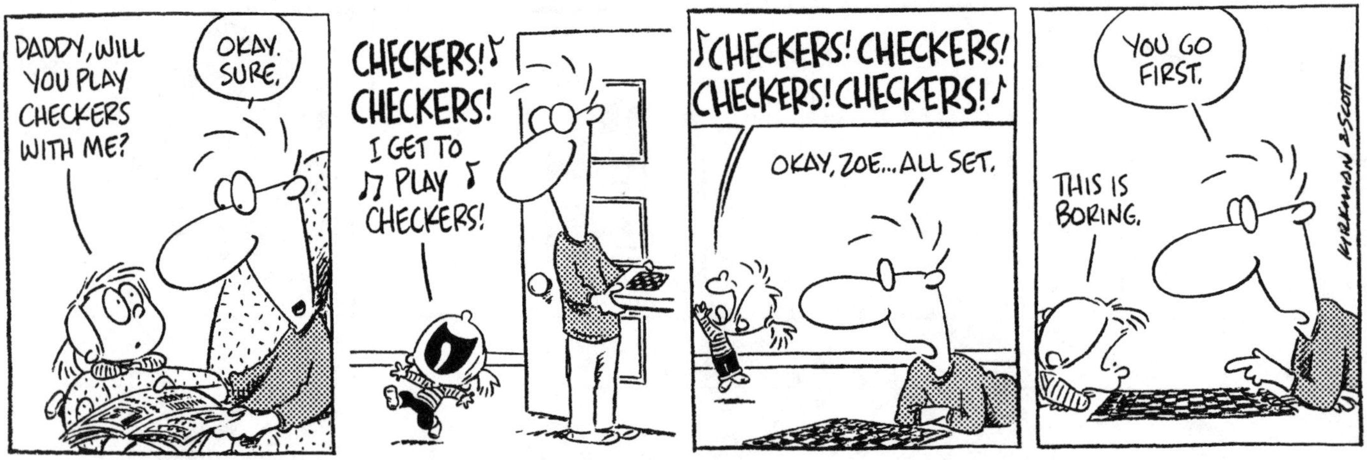
DADDY, WILL YOU PLAY CHECKERS WITH ME?
OKAY. SURE.
CHECKERS! CHECKERS! I GET TO PLAY CHECKERS!
CHECKERS! CHECKERS! CHECKERS! CHECKERS!
OKAY, ZOE... ALL SET.
YOU GO FIRST.
THIS IS BORING.
KIRKMAN & SCOTT

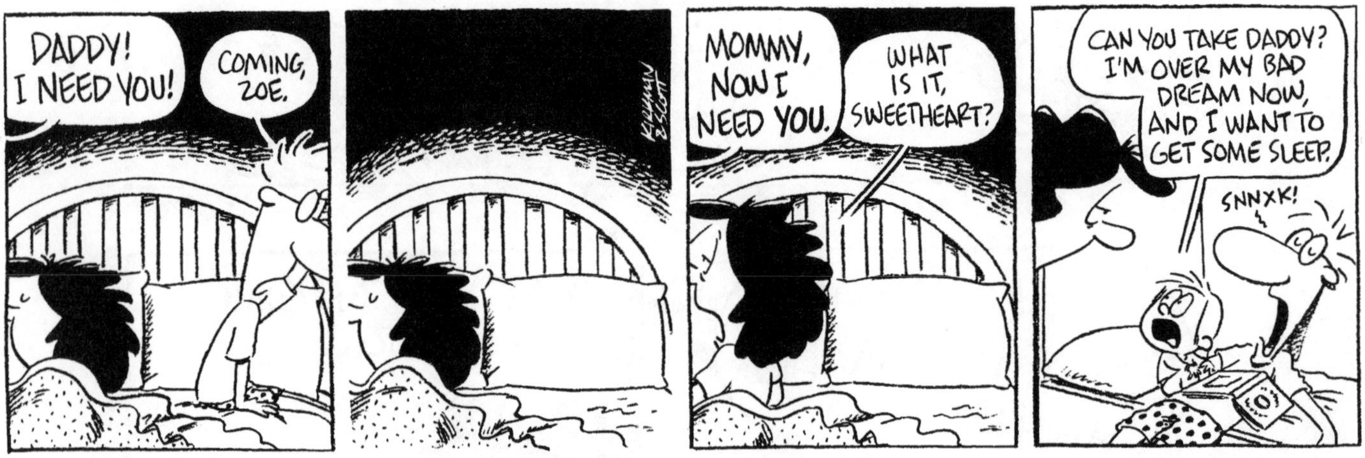
DADDY! I NEED YOU!
COMING, ZOE.
KIRKMAN & SCOTT
MOMMY, NOW I NEED YOU.
WHAT IS IT, SWEETHEART?
CAN YOU TAKE DADDY? I'M OVER MY BAD DREAM NOW, AND I WANT TO GET SOME SLEEP.
SNNXK!

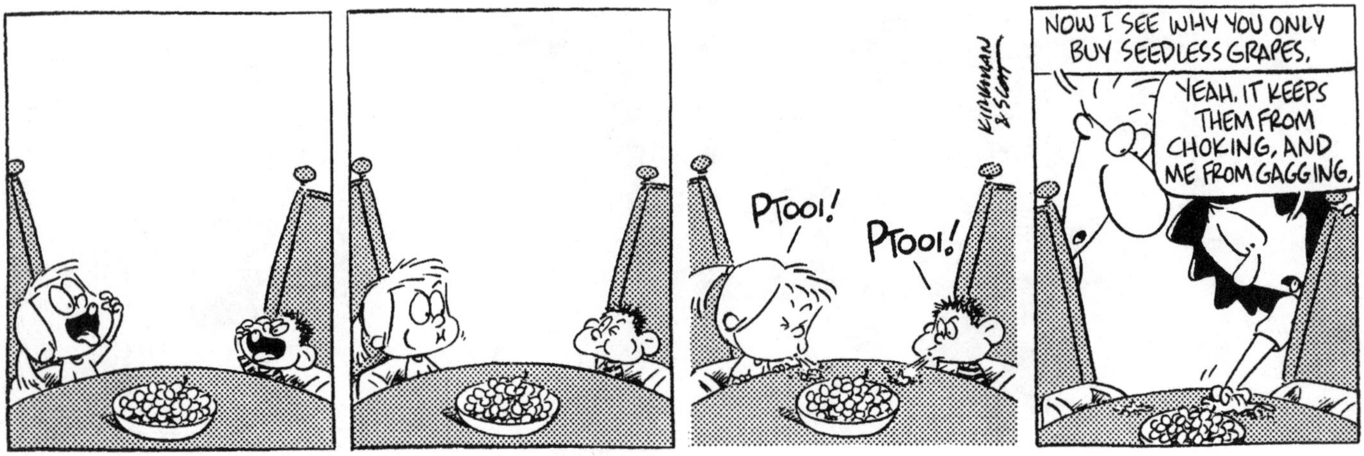
KIRKMAN & SCOTT
PTOOI!
PTOOI!
NOW I SEE WHY YOU ONLY BUY SEEDLESS GRAPES.
YEAH. IT KEEPS THEM FROM CHOKING, AND ME FROM GAGGING.

BABY BLUES®
BY RICK KIRKMAN / JERRY SCOTT

ZOE AND HAMISH MacPHERSON!
THAT DOES IT!!!
MMFG!
GRRFF!
KIRKMAN & SCOTT
I'VE TOLD YOU TEN TIMES TO STOP THAT, AND YOU HAVEN'T LISTENED TO ME!
ANYBODY WHO PUTS TINSEL IN HIS MOUTH IS NOT GROWN UP ENOUGH TO HELP TAKE DOWN THE CHRISTMAS TREE. NOW GO!
AWWW!
AWWW!
FORGET IT... YOU CAN'T BE FIRED. YOU'RE MANAGEMENT.
AWWW!

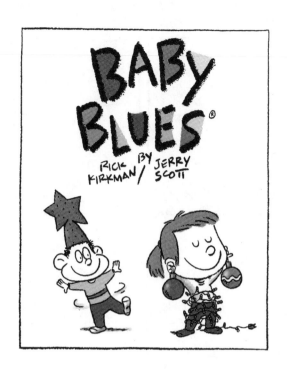

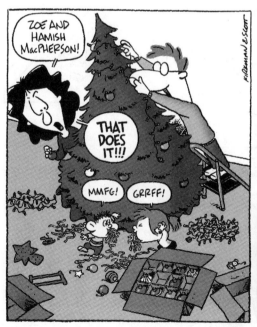

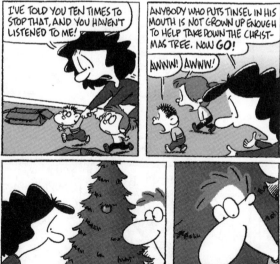

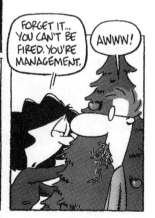

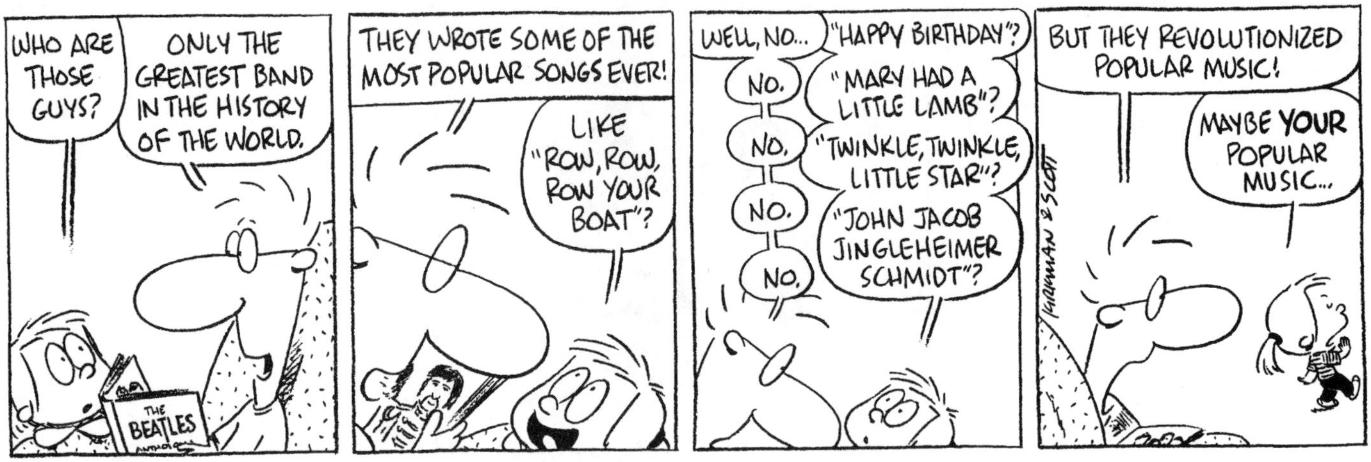
WHO ARE THOSE GUYS?
ONLY THE GREATEST BAND IN THE HISTORY OF THE WORLD.
THE BEATLES
THEY WROTE SOME OF THE MOST POPULAR SONGS EVER!
LIKE "ROW, ROW, ROW YOUR BOAT"?
WELL, NO...
"HAPPY BIRTHDAY"?
NO.
"MARY HAD A LITTLE LAMB"?
NO.
"TWINKLE, TWINKLE, LITTLE STAR"?
NO.
"JOHN JACOB JINGLEHEIMER SCHMIDT"?
NO.
KIRKMAN & SCOTT
BUT THEY REVOLUTIONIZED POPULAR MUSIC!
MAYBE **YOUR** POPULAR MUSIC...

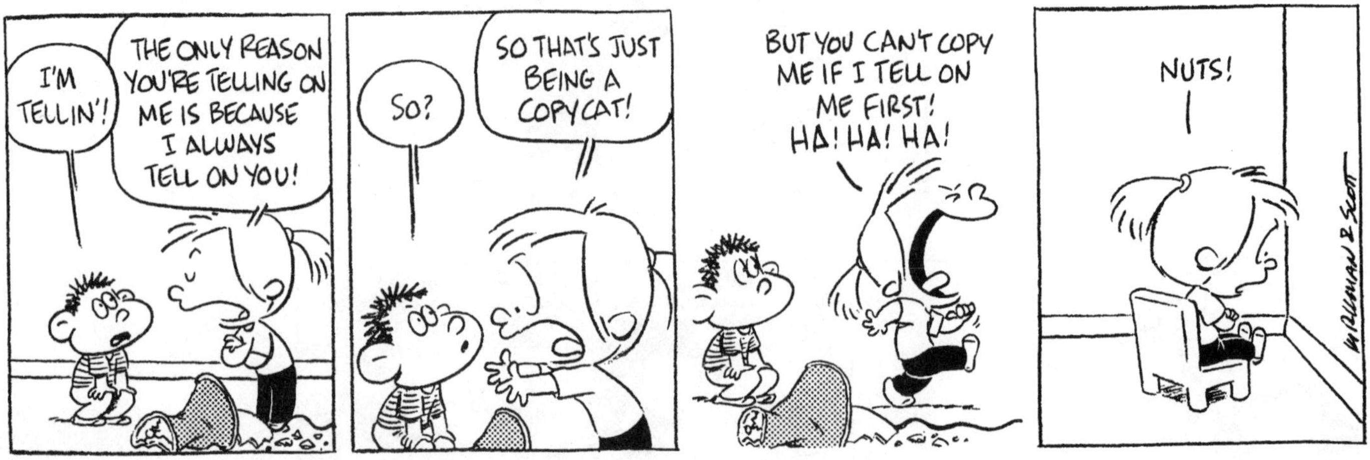
I'M TELLIN'!
THE ONLY REASON YOU'RE TELLING ON ME IS BECAUSE I ALWAYS TELL ON YOU!
SO?
SO THAT'S JUST BEING A COPYCAT!
BUT YOU CAN'T COPY ME IF I TELL ON ME FIRST! HA! HA! HA!
NUTS!
KIRKMAN & SCOTT

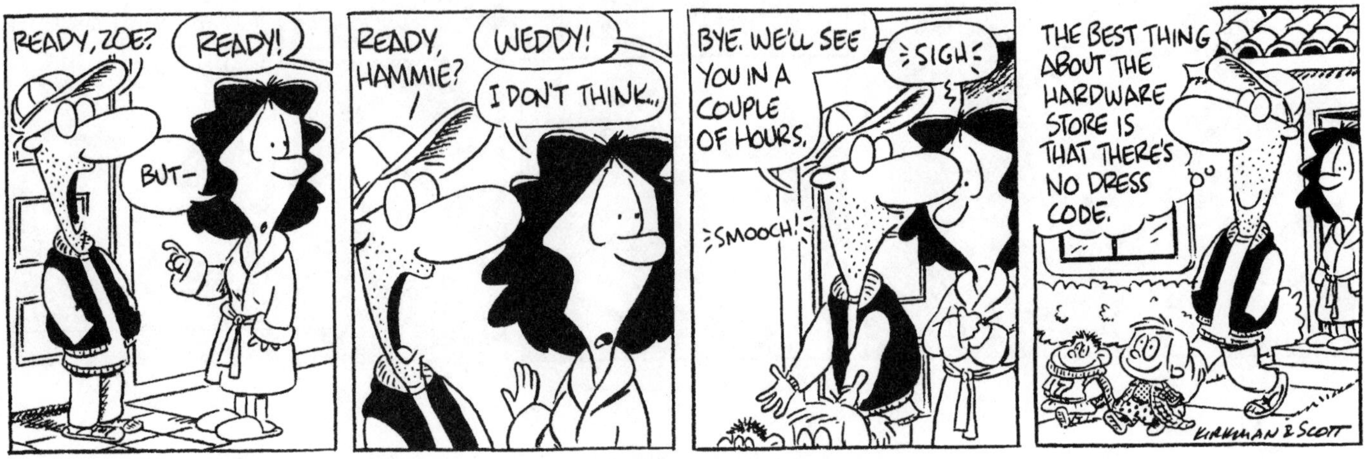
READY, ZOE?
READY!
BUT-
READY, HAMMIE?
WEDDY!
I DON'T THINK...
BYE. WE'LL SEE YOU IN A COUPLE OF HOURS.
SIGH
SMOOCH!
THE BEST THING ABOUT THE HARDWARE STORE IS THAT THERE'S NO DRESS CODE.
KIRKMAN & SCOTT

BABY BLUES®
BY RICK KIRKMAN / JERRY SCOTT
DUNCE
THAT DOES IT.
I WARNED YOU THREE TIMES THAT IF YOU DIDN'T PICK UP THESE TOYS, I WAS GOING TO TAKE THEM AWAY.
WELL, YOU DIDN'T PICK THEM UP, SO HERE THEY GO!
FUMP!
NOW MAYBE YOU'LL LEARN THAT WHEN I TELL YOU TO DO SOMETHING, AND YOU DON'T LISTEN, THERE WILL BE...
...CONSEQUENCES.
WHAT THE HECK WAS SANTA CLAUS THINKING??

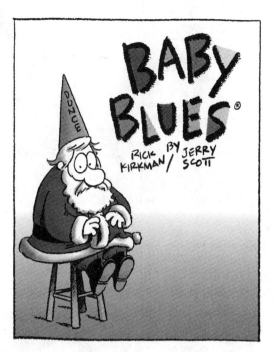

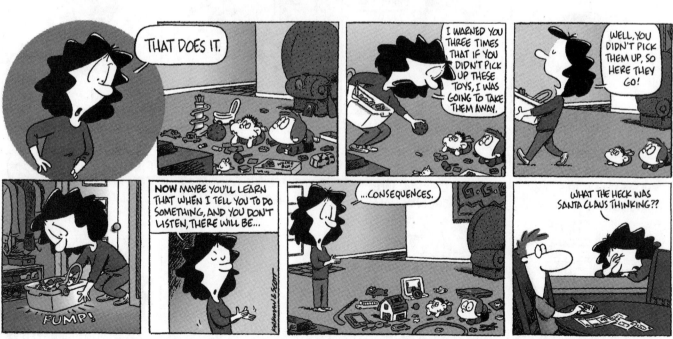

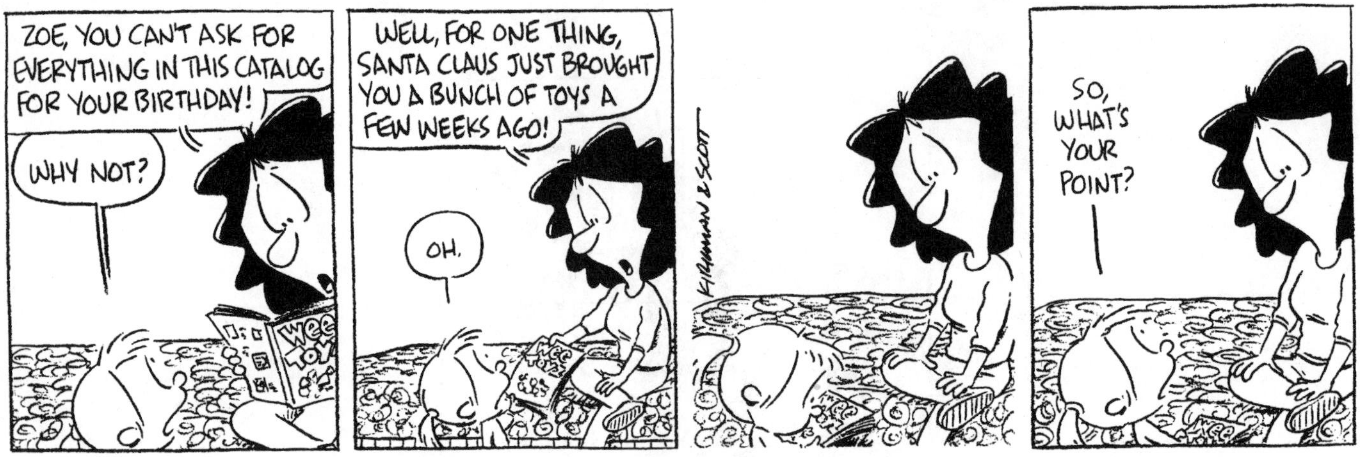
ZOE, YOU CAN'T ASK FOR EVERYTHING IN THIS CATALOG FOR YOUR BIRTHDAY!
WHY NOT?
WELL, FOR ONE THING, SANTA CLAUS JUST BROUGHT YOU A BUNCH OF TOYS A FEW WEEKS AGO!
OH.
KIRKMAN & SCOTT
SO, WHAT'S YOUR POINT?

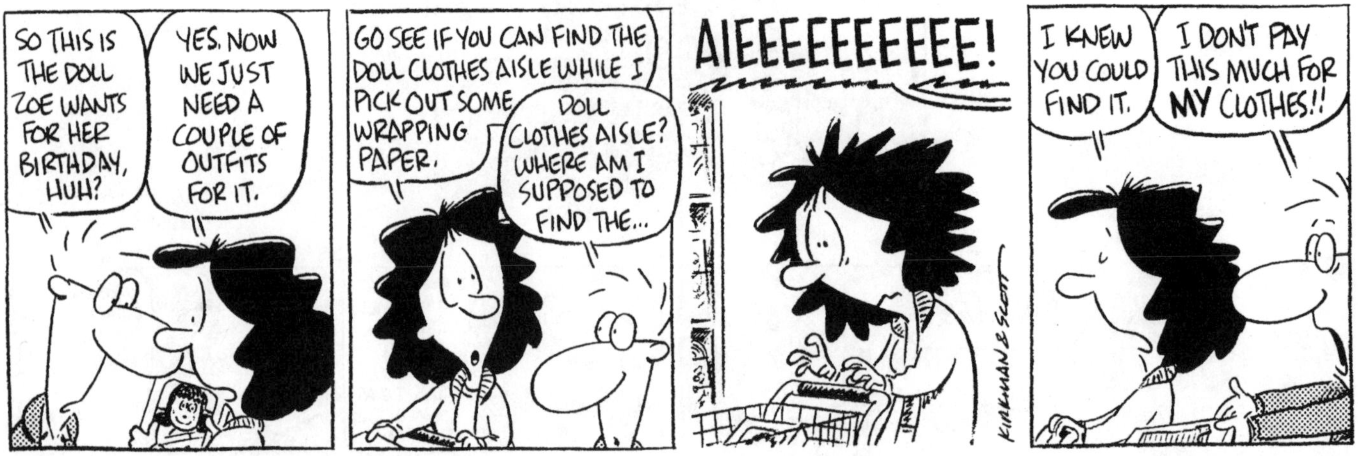
SO THIS IS THE DOLL ZOE WANTS FOR HER BIRTHDAY, HUH?
YES. NOW WE JUST NEED A COUPLE OF OUTFITS FOR IT.
GO SEE IF YOU CAN FIND THE DOLL CLOTHES AISLE WHILE I PICK OUT SOME WRAPPING PAPER.
DOLL CLOTHES AISLE? WHERE AM I SUPPOSED TO FIND THE...
AIEEEEEEEEEEE!
KIRKMAN & SCOTT
I KNEW YOU COULD FIND IT.
I DON'T PAY THIS MUCH FOR MY CLOTHES!!

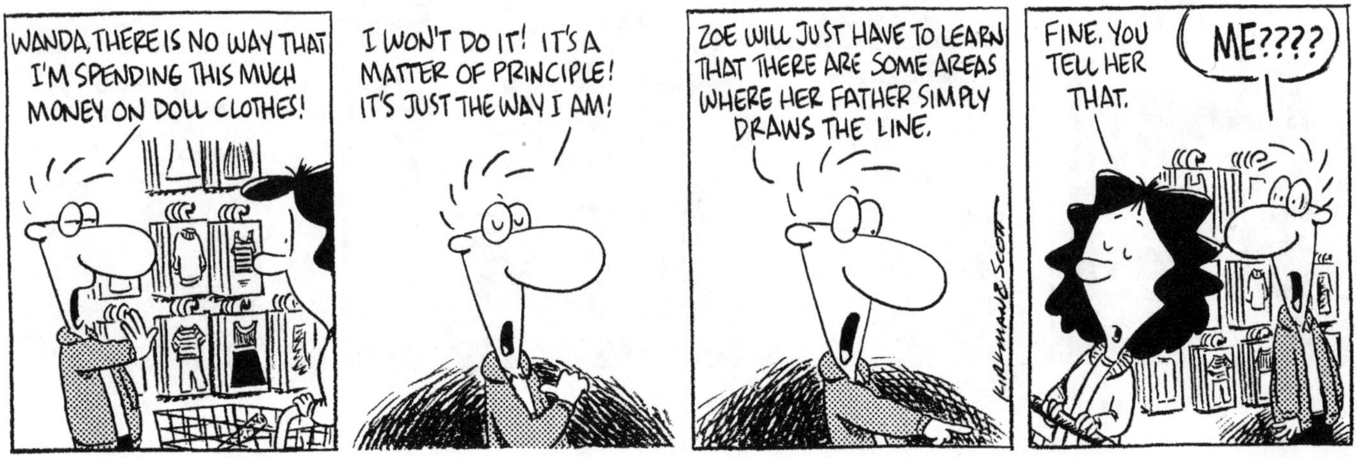
WANDA, THERE IS NO WAY THAT I'M SPENDING THIS MUCH MONEY ON DOLL CLOTHES!
I WON'T DO IT! IT'S A MATTER OF PRINCIPLE! IT'S JUST THE WAY I AM!
ZOE WILL JUST HAVE TO LEARN THAT THERE ARE SOME AREAS WHERE HER FATHER SIMPLY DRAWS THE LINE.
KIRKMAN & SCOTT
FINE. YOU TELL HER THAT.
ME????

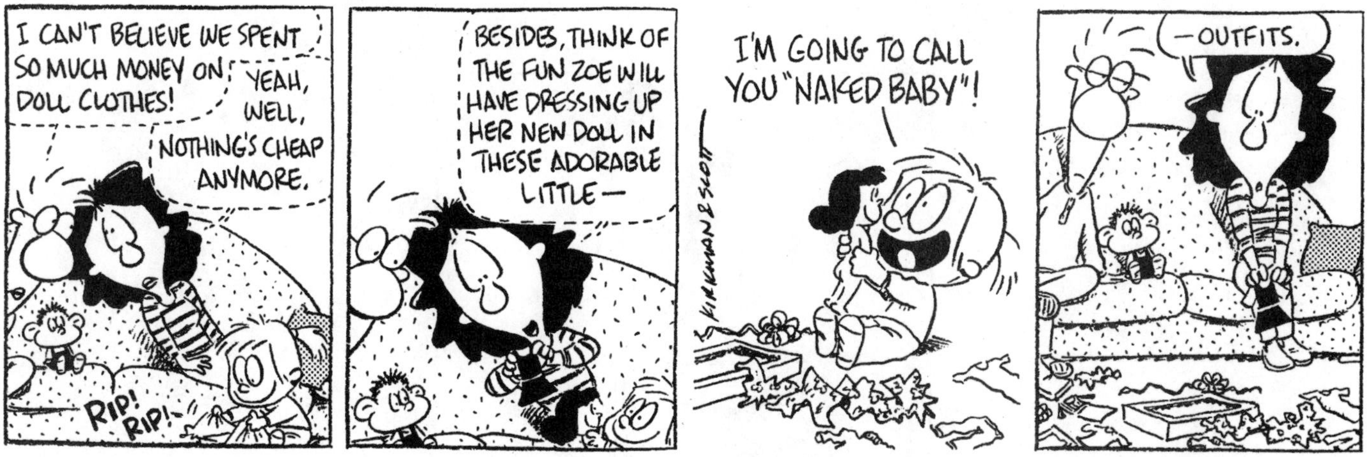
I CAN'T BELIEVE WE SPENT SO MUCH MONEY ON DOLL CLOTHES!
YEAH, WELL, NOTHING'S CHEAP ANYMORE.
RIP! RIP!
BESIDES, THINK OF THE FUN ZOE WILL HAVE DRESSING UP HER NEW DOLL IN THESE ADORABLE LITTLE—
I'M GOING TO CALL YOU "NAKED BABY"!
—OUTFITS.

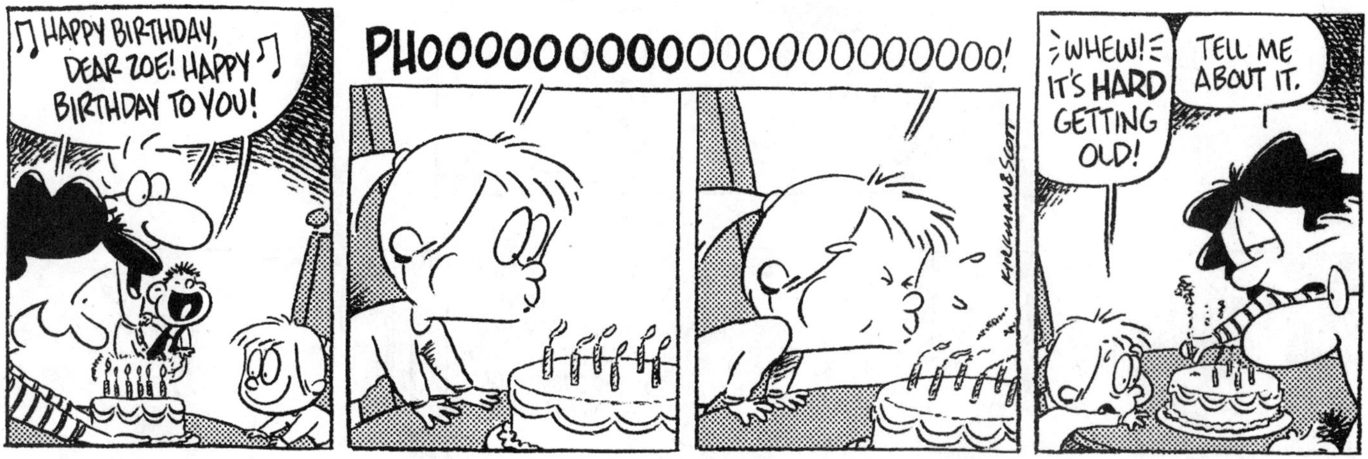
♫ HAPPY BIRTHDAY, DEAR ZOE! HAPPY BIRTHDAY TO YOU! ♫
PHOOOOOOOOOOOOOOOOOOOOOOO!
WHEW! IT'S **HARD** GETTING OLD!
TELL ME ABOUT IT.

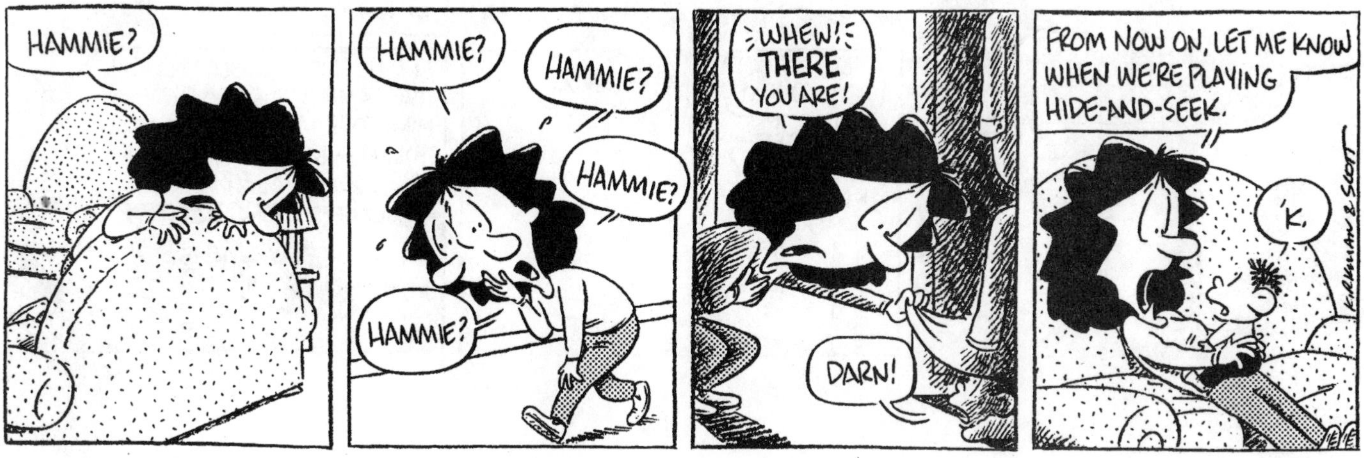
HAMMIE?
HAMMIE?
HAMMIE?
HAMMIE?
HAMMIE?
WHEW! **THERE** YOU ARE!
DARN!
FROM NOW ON, LET ME KNOW WHEN WE'RE PLAYING HIDE-AND-SEEK.
'K.

BABY BLUES®
BY RICK KIRKMAN / JERRY SCOTT
TROUBLE Bath
KNOCK! KNOCK!
MOM?
YES?
HAMMIE HAS TO GO POTTY, THE PHONE IS RINGING, SOMEBODY IS AT THE DOOR AND THE OVEN TIMER IS BEEPING!
I'M IN THE BATH TUB! GO TELL DADDY!
OKAY!
ALL RIGHT. I TOLD HIM.
AND...?
KNOCK! KNOCK!
KIRKMAN & SCOTT
AND HE SAID I SHOULD TELL YOU THAT HAMMIE WON'T GO POTTY FOR HIM, YOUR MOM IS ON THE PHONE, YOLANDA NEEDS A RECIPE AND THE COOKIES ARE BURNING.
SIGH!

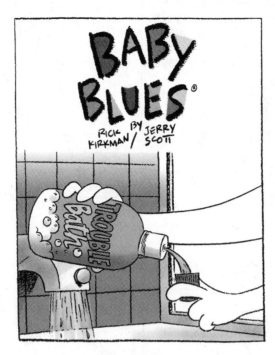

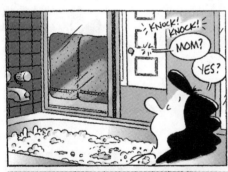

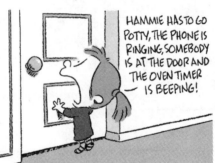

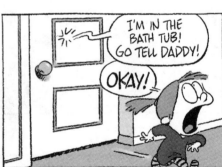

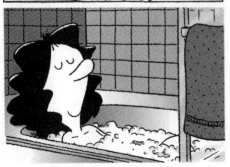

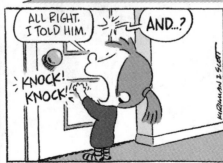

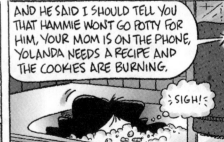

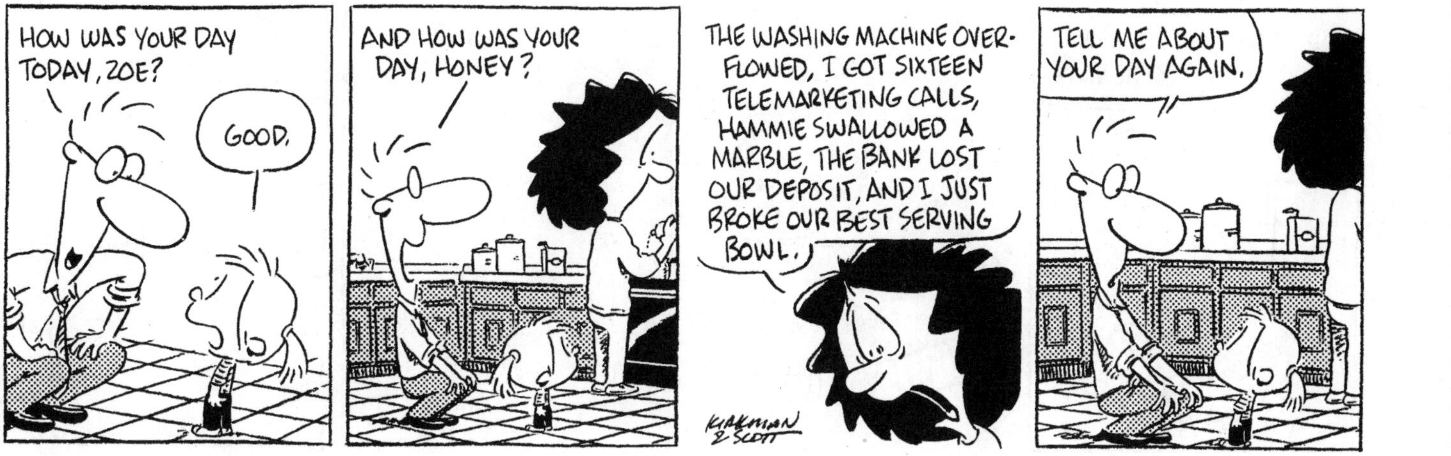
HOW WAS YOUR DAY TODAY, ZOE?
GOOD.
AND HOW WAS YOUR DAY, HONEY?
THE WASHING MACHINE OVER-FLOWED, I GOT SIXTEEN TELEMARKETING CALLS, HAMMIE SWALLOWED A MARBLE, THE BANK LOST OUR DEPOSIT, AND I JUST BROKE OUR BEST SERVING BOWL.
KIRKMAN & SCOTT
TELL ME ABOUT YOUR DAY AGAIN.

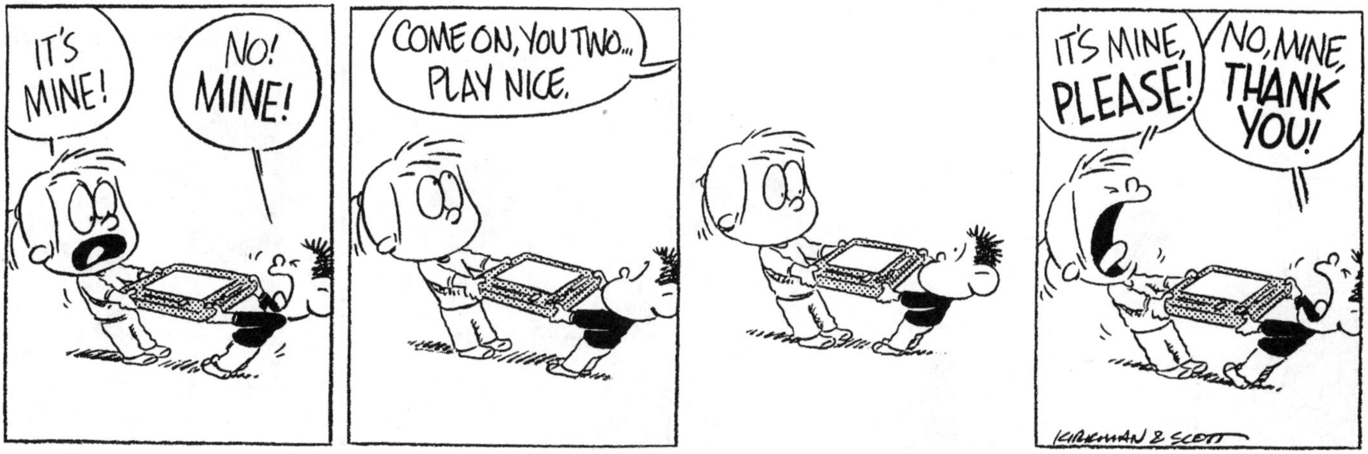
IT'S MINE!
NO! MINE!
COME ON, YOU TWO... PLAY NICE.
IT'S MINE, PLEASE!
NO, MINE, THANK YOU!
KIRKMAN & SCOTT

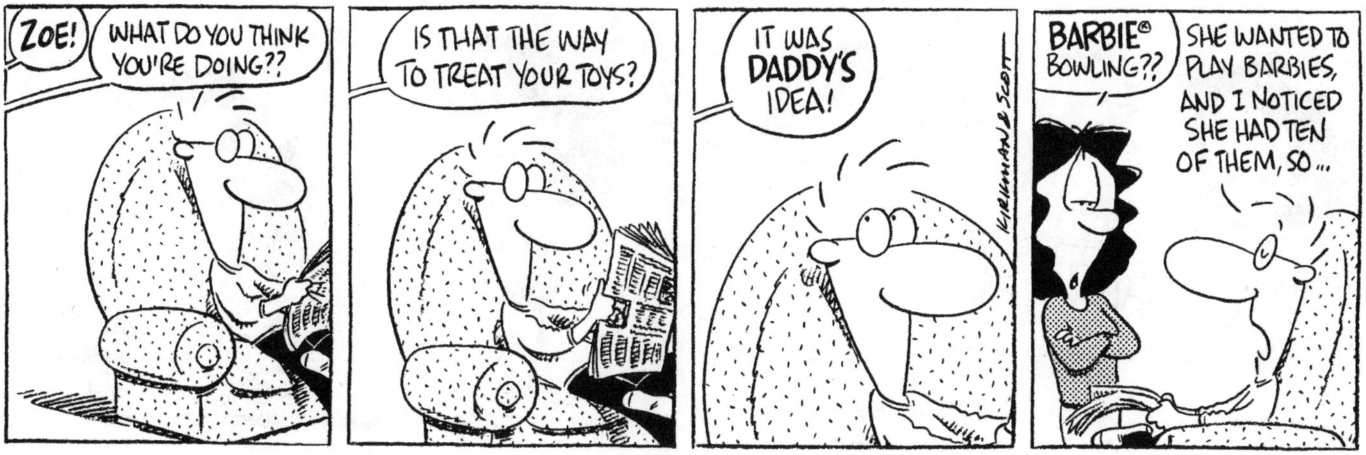
ZOE!
WHAT DO YOU THINK YOU'RE DOING??
IS THAT THE WAY TO TREAT YOUR TOYS?
IT WAS DADDY'S IDEA!
KIRKMAN & SCOTT
BARBIE® BOWLING??
SHE WANTED TO PLAY BARBIES, AND I NOTICED SHE HAD TEN OF THEM, SO...

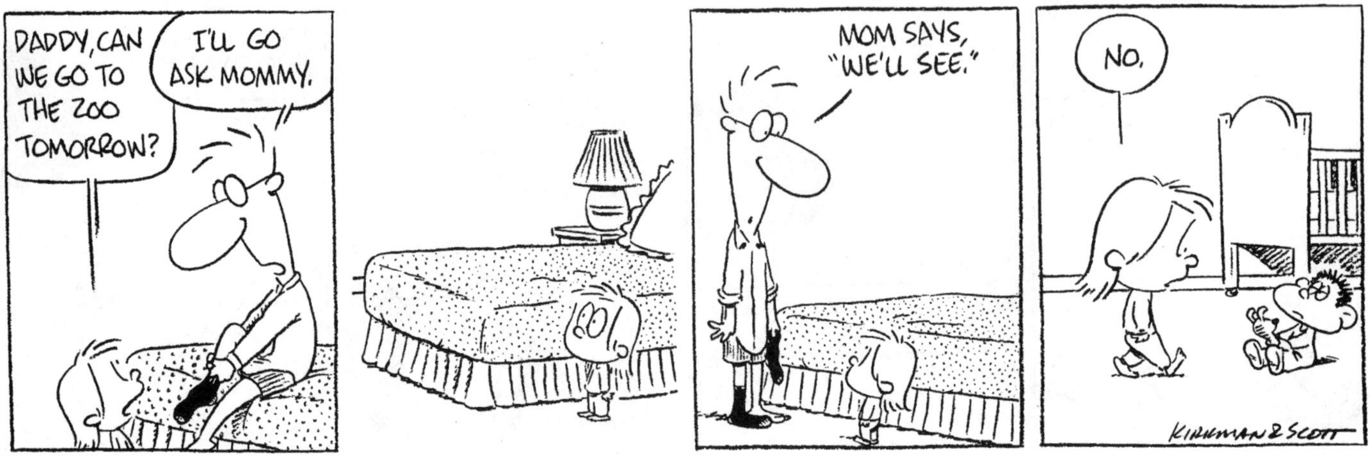
DADDY, CAN WE GO TO THE ZOO TOMORROW?
I'LL GO ASK MOMMY.
MOM SAYS, "WE'LL SEE."
NO.
KIRKMAN & SCOTT

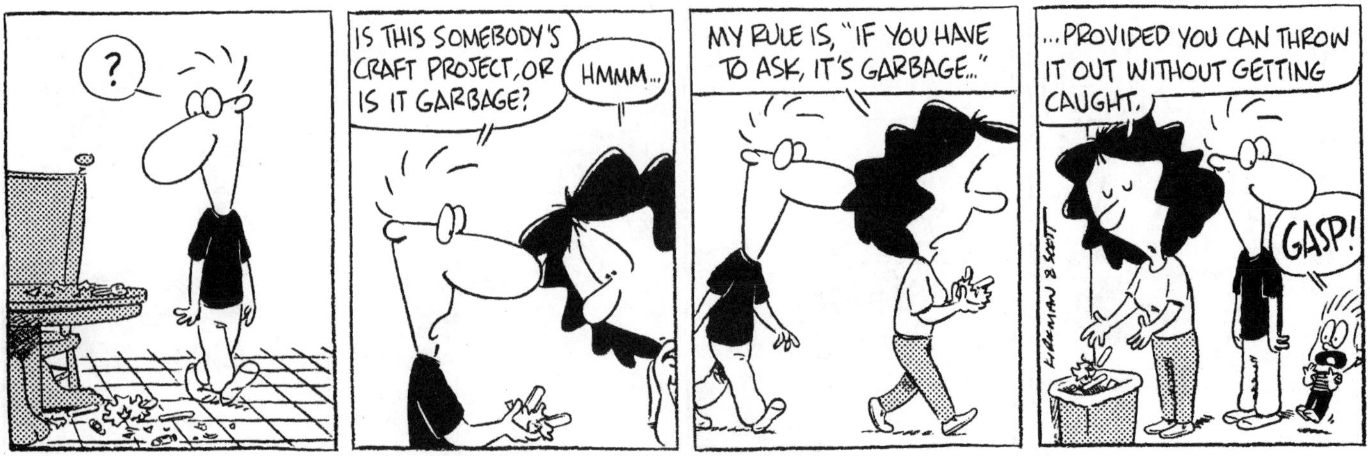
?
IS THIS SOMEBODY'S CRAFT PROJECT, OR IS IT GARBAGE?
HMMM...
MY RULE IS, "IF YOU HAVE TO ASK, IT'S GARBAGE..."
...PROVIDED YOU CAN THROW IT OUT WITHOUT GETTING CAUGHT.
KIRKMAN & SCOTT
GASP!

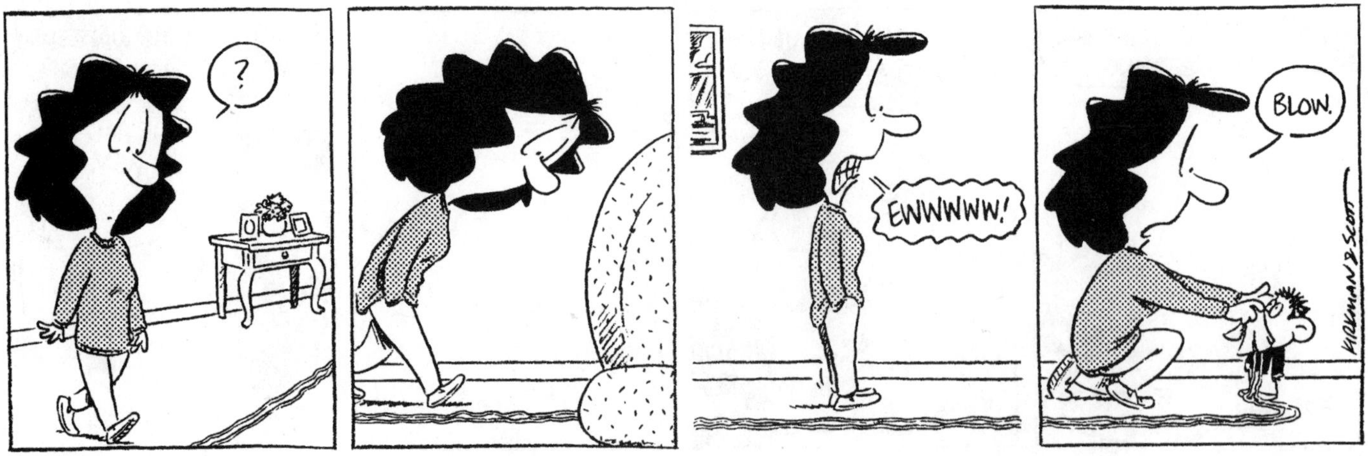
?
EWWWWW!
BLOW.
KIRKMAN & SCOTT

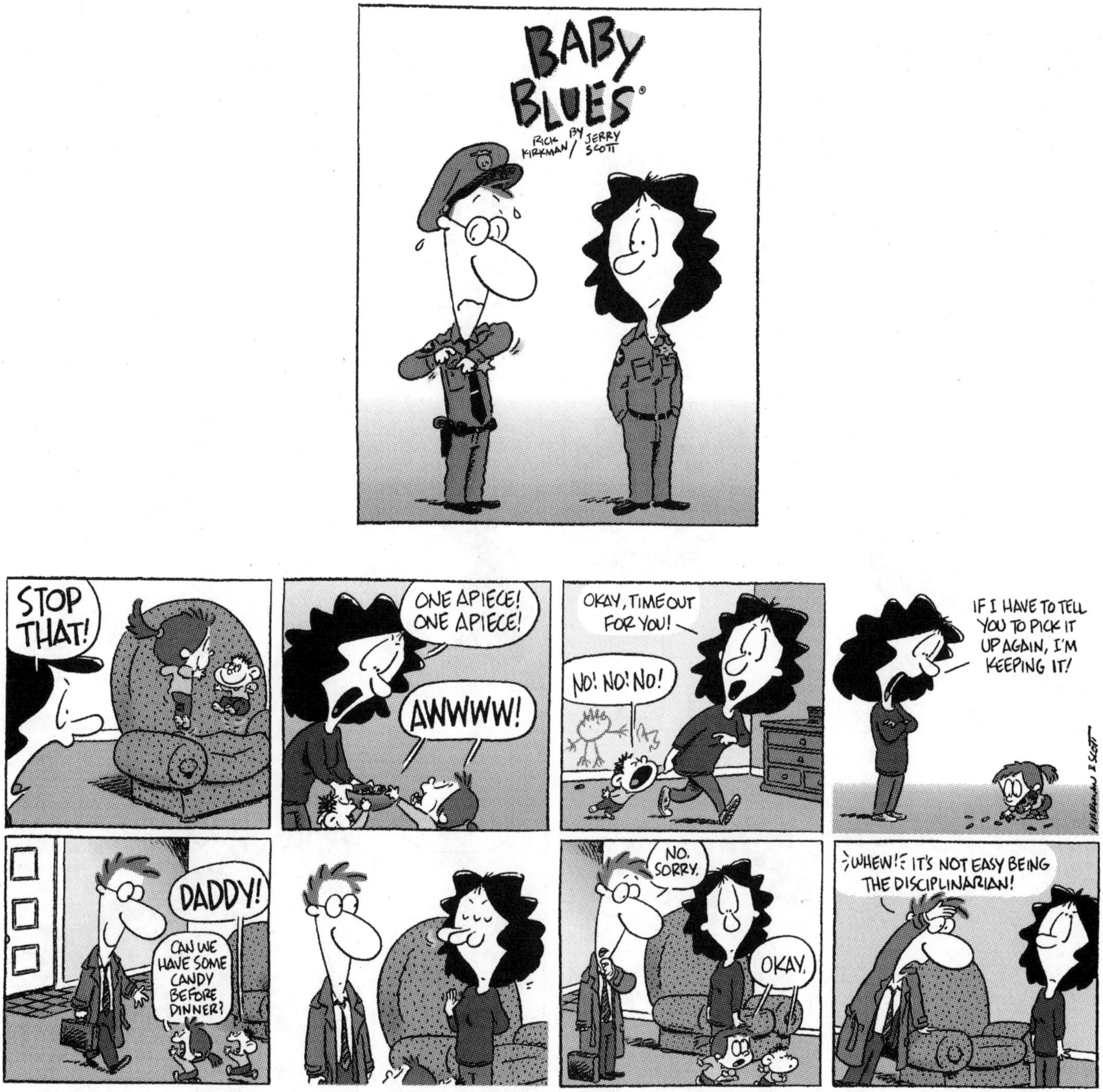
BABY BLUES®
BY RICK KIRKMAN / JERRY SCOTT
STOP THAT!
ONE APIECE! ONE APIECE!
AWWWW!
OKAY, TIME OUT FOR YOU!
NO! NO! NO!
IF I HAVE TO TELL YOU TO PICK IT UP AGAIN, I'M KEEPING IT!
DADDY!
CAN WE HAVE SOME CANDY BEFORE DINNER?
NO. SORRY.
OKAY.
WHEW! IT'S NOT EASY BEING THE DISCIPLINARIAN!

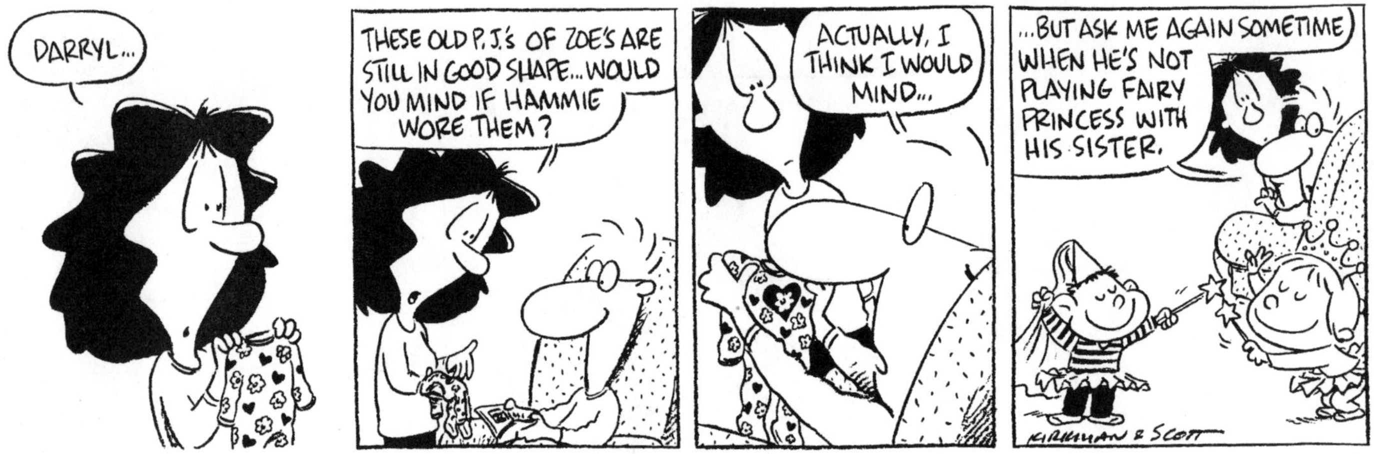
DARRYL...
THESE OLD P.J.'S OF ZOE'S ARE STILL IN GOOD SHAPE... WOULD YOU MIND IF HAMMIE WORE THEM?
ACTUALLY, I THINK I WOULD MIND...
...BUT ASK ME AGAIN SOMETIME WHEN HE'S NOT PLAYING FAIRY PRINCESS WITH HIS SISTER.
KIRKMAN & SCOTT

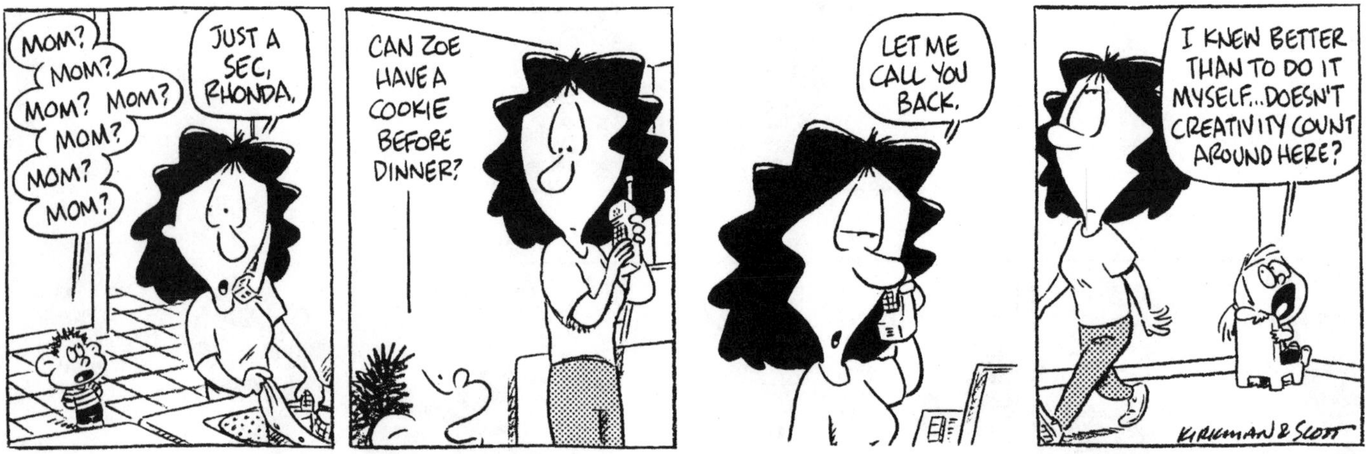
MOM? MOM? MOM? MOM? MOM? MOM? MOM?
JUST A SEC, RHONDA.
CAN ZOE HAVE A COOKIE BEFORE DINNER?
LET ME CALL YOU BACK.
I KNEW BETTER THAN TO DO IT MYSELF... DOESN'T CREATIVITY COUNT AROUND HERE?
KIRKMAN & SCOTT

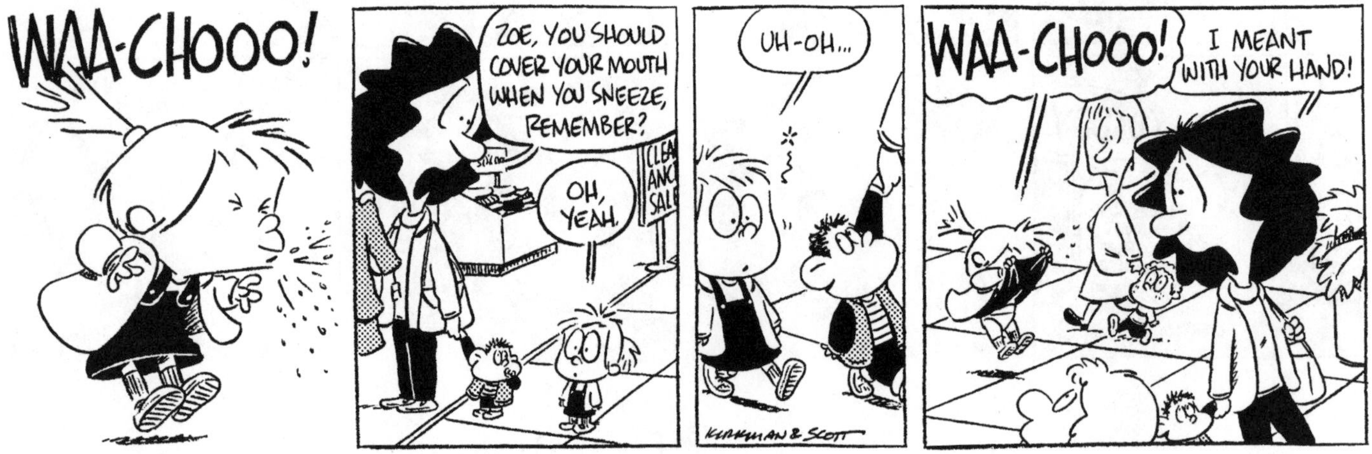
WAA-CHOOO!
ZOE, YOU SHOULD COVER YOUR MOUTH WHEN YOU SNEEZE, REMEMBER?
OH, YEAH.
UH-OH...
KIRKMAN & SCOTT
WAA-CHOOO!
I MEANT WITH YOUR HAND!

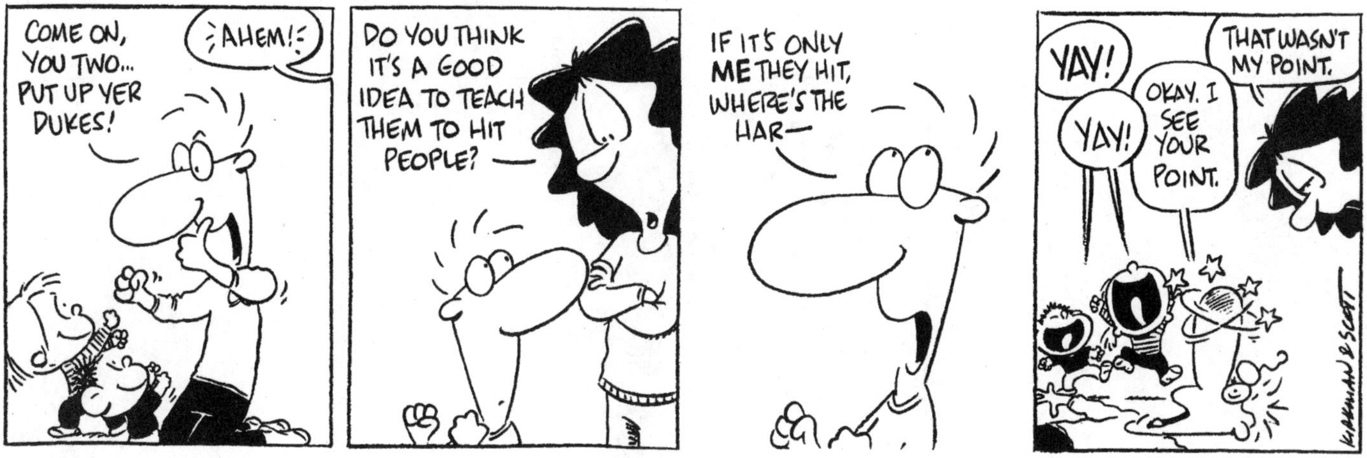
COME ON, YOU TWO... PUT UP YER DUKES!
AHEM!
DO YOU THINK IT'S A GOOD IDEA TO TEACH THEM TO HIT PEOPLE?
IF IT'S ONLY **ME** THEY HIT, WHERE'S THE HAR—
YAY!
YAY!
OKAY. I SEE YOUR POINT.
THAT WASN'T MY POINT.
KIRKMAN & SCOTT

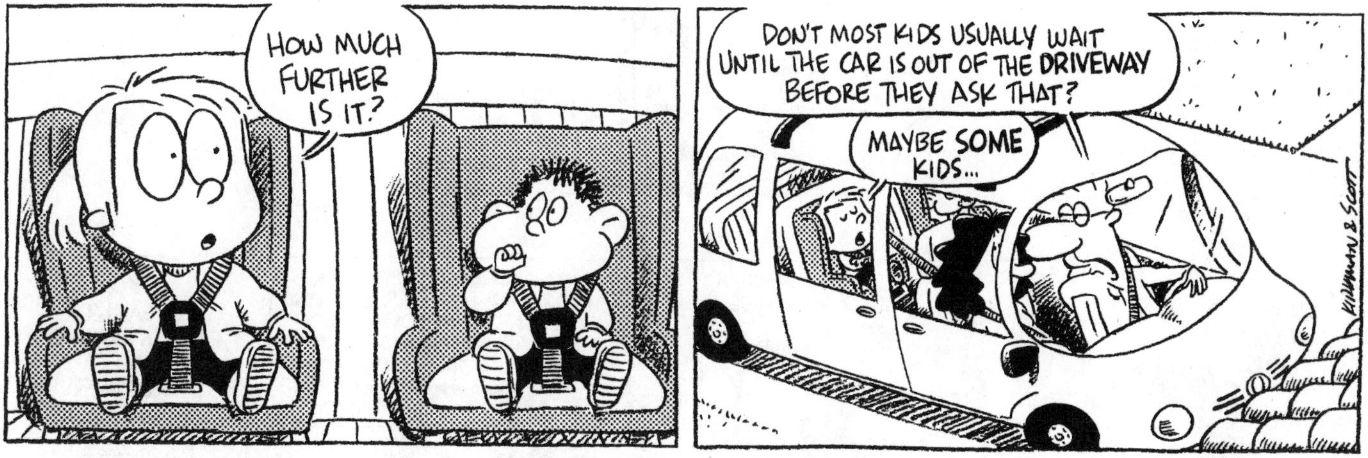
HOW MUCH FURTHER IS IT?
DON'T MOST KIDS USUALLY WAIT UNTIL THE CAR IS OUT OF THE **DRIVEWAY** BEFORE THEY ASK THAT?
MAYBE **SOME** KIDS...
KIRKMAN & SCOTT

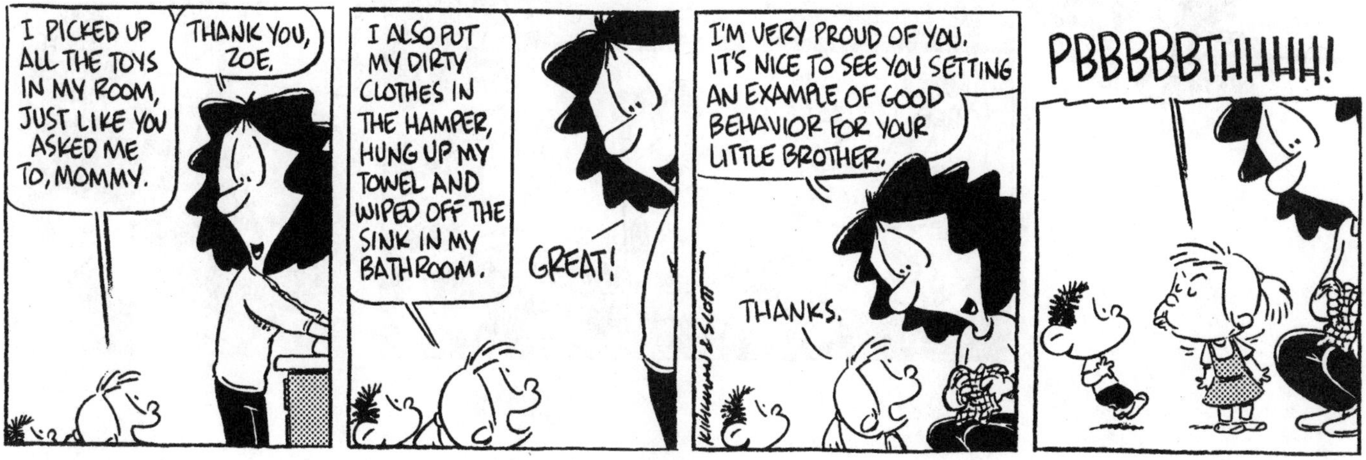
I PICKED UP ALL THE TOYS IN MY ROOM, JUST LIKE YOU ASKED ME TO, MOMMY.
THANK YOU, ZOE.
I ALSO PUT MY DIRTY CLOTHES IN THE HAMPER, HUNG UP MY TOWEL AND WIPED OFF THE SINK IN MY BATHROOM.
GREAT!
KIRKMAN & SCOTT
I'M VERY PROUD OF YOU. IT'S NICE TO SEE YOU SETTING AN EXAMPLE OF GOOD BEHAVIOR FOR YOUR LITTLE BROTHER.
THANKS.
PBBBBBTHHHH!

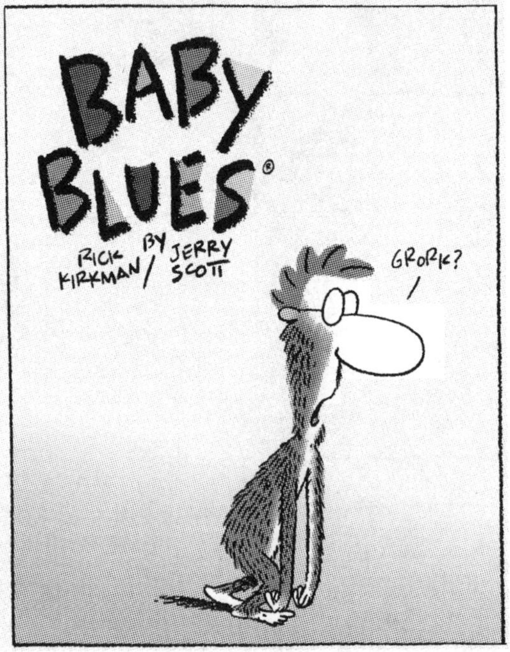
BABY BLUES®
BY RICK KIRKMAN / JERRY SCOTT
GRORK?

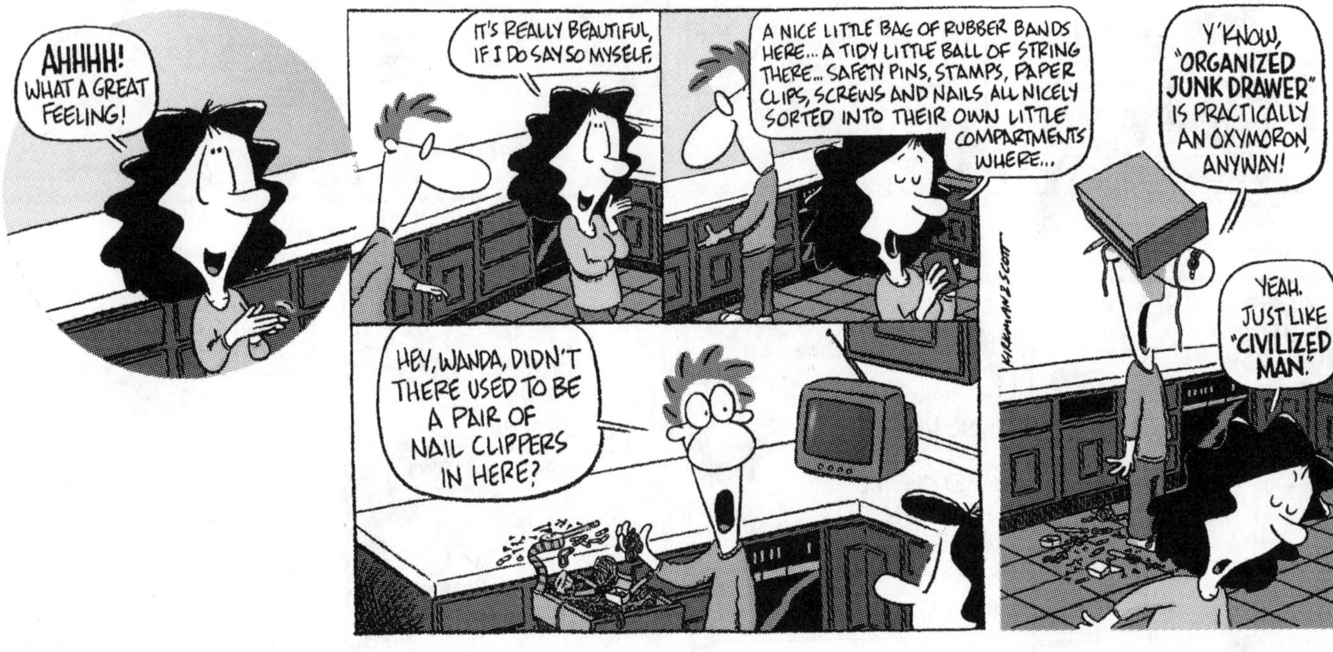
AHHHH! WHAT A GREAT FEELING!
IT'S REALLY BEAUTIFUL, IF I DO SAY SO MYSELF.
A NICE LITTLE BAG OF RUBBER BANDS HERE... A TIDY LITTLE BALL OF STRING THERE... SAFETY PINS, STAMPS, PAPER CLIPS, SCREWS AND NAILS ALL NICELY SORTED INTO THEIR OWN LITTLE COMPARTMENTS WHERE...
HEY, WANDA, DIDN'T THERE USED TO BE A PAIR OF NAIL CLIPPERS IN HERE?
Y'KNOW, "ORGANIZED JUNK DRAWER" IS PRACTICALLY AN OXYMORON, ANYWAY!
YEAH. JUST LIKE "CIVILIZED MAN."
KIRKMAN & SCOTT

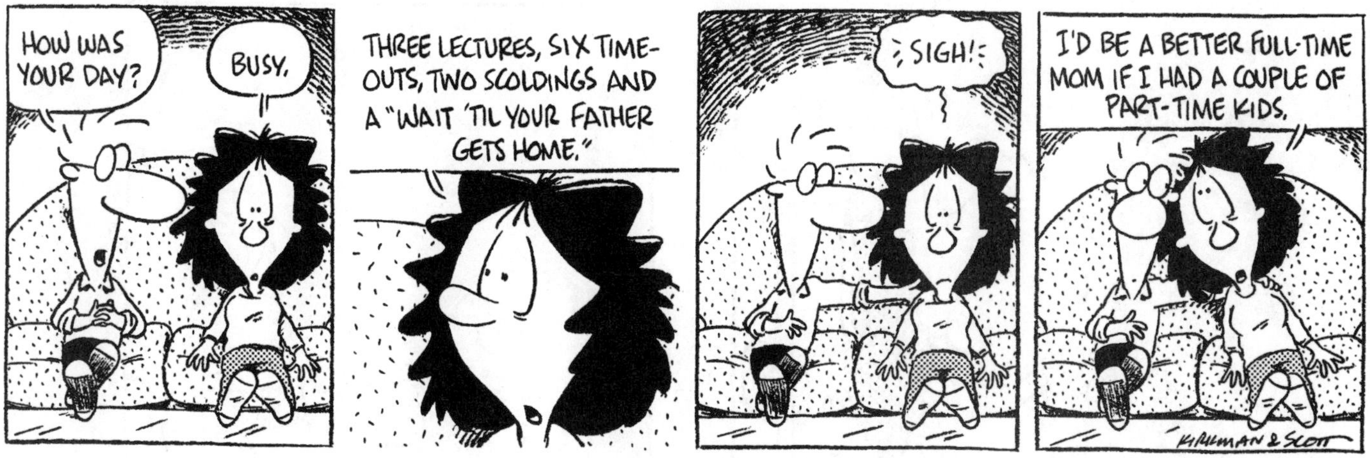
HOW WAS YOUR DAY?
BUSY.
THREE LECTURES, SIX TIME-OUTS, TWO SCOLDINGS AND A "WAIT 'TIL YOUR FATHER GETS HOME."
SIGH!
I'D BE A BETTER FULL-TIME MOM IF I HAD A COUPLE OF PART-TIME KIDS.
KIRKMAN & SCOTT

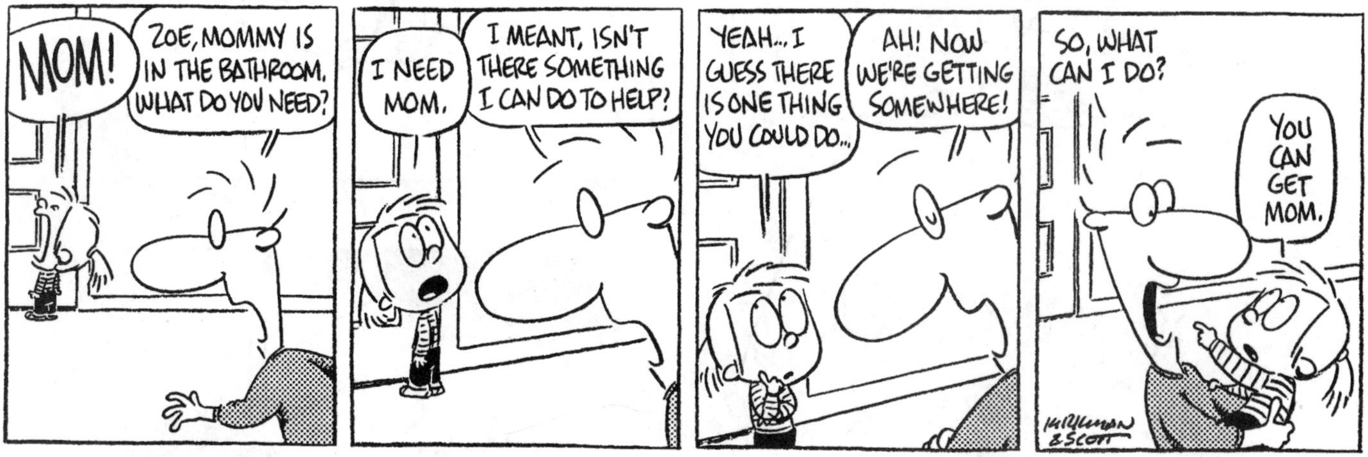
MOM!
ZOE, MOMMY IS IN THE BATHROOM. WHAT DO YOU NEED?
I NEED MOM.
I MEANT, ISN'T THERE SOMETHING I CAN DO TO HELP?
YEAH... I GUESS THERE IS ONE THING YOU COULD DO...
AH! NOW WE'RE GETTING SOMEWHERE!
SO, WHAT CAN I DO?
YOU CAN GET MOM.
KIRKMAN & SCOTT

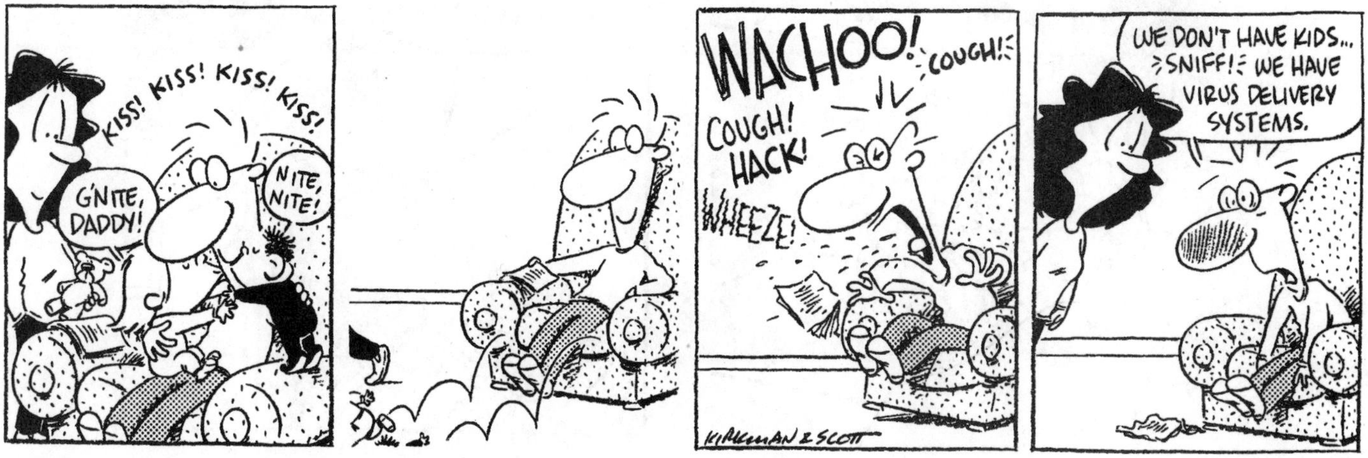
KISS! KISS! KISS! KISS!
G'NITE, DADDY!
NITE, NITE!
WACHOO!
COUGH!
COUGH! HACK!
WHEEZE!
KIRKMAN & SCOTT
WE DON'T HAVE KIDS... SNIFF! WE HAVE VIRUS DELIVERY SYSTEMS.

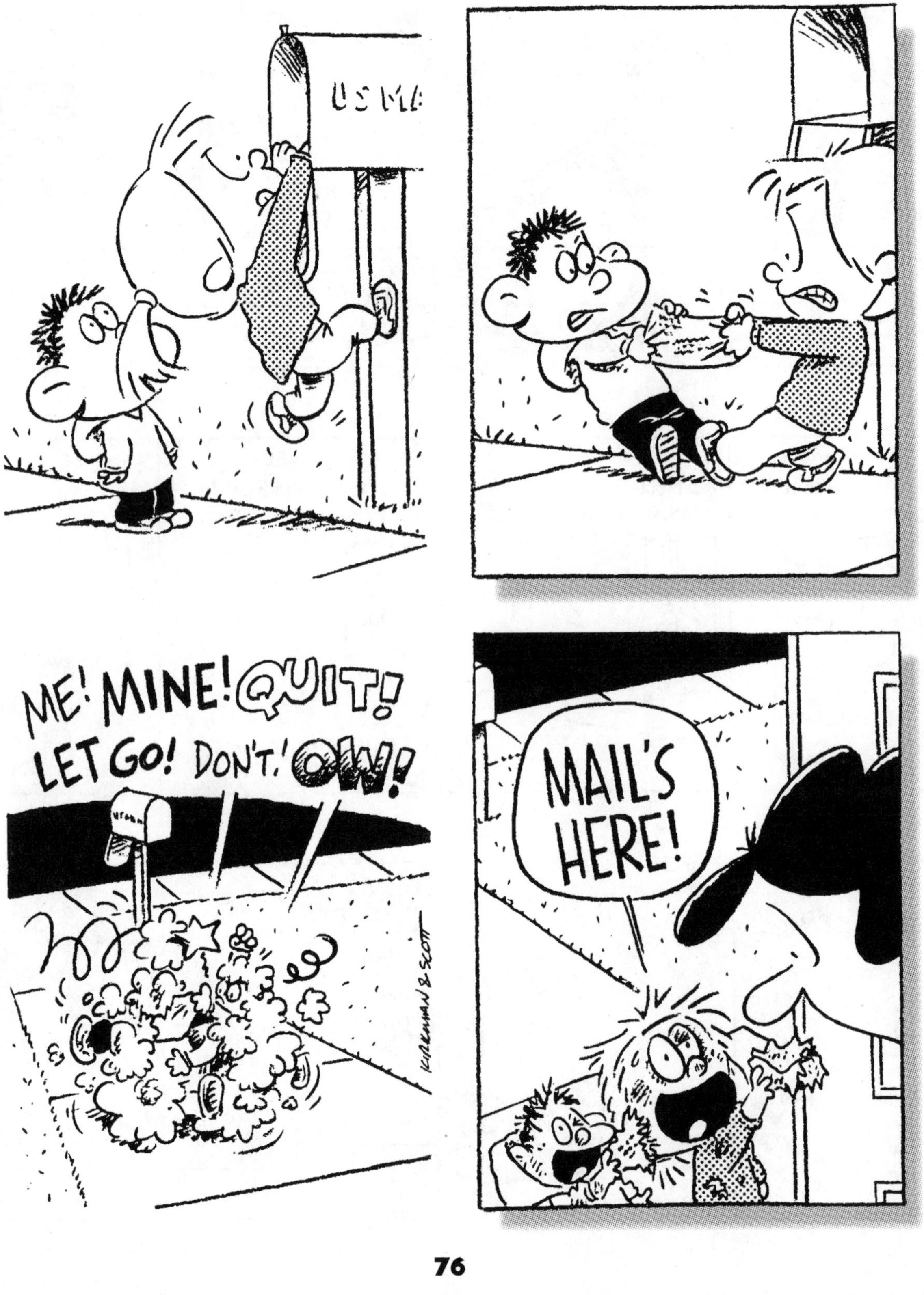
US MA
ME! MINE! QUIT!
LET GO! DON'T! OW!
KIRKMAN & SCOTT
MAIL'S HERE!

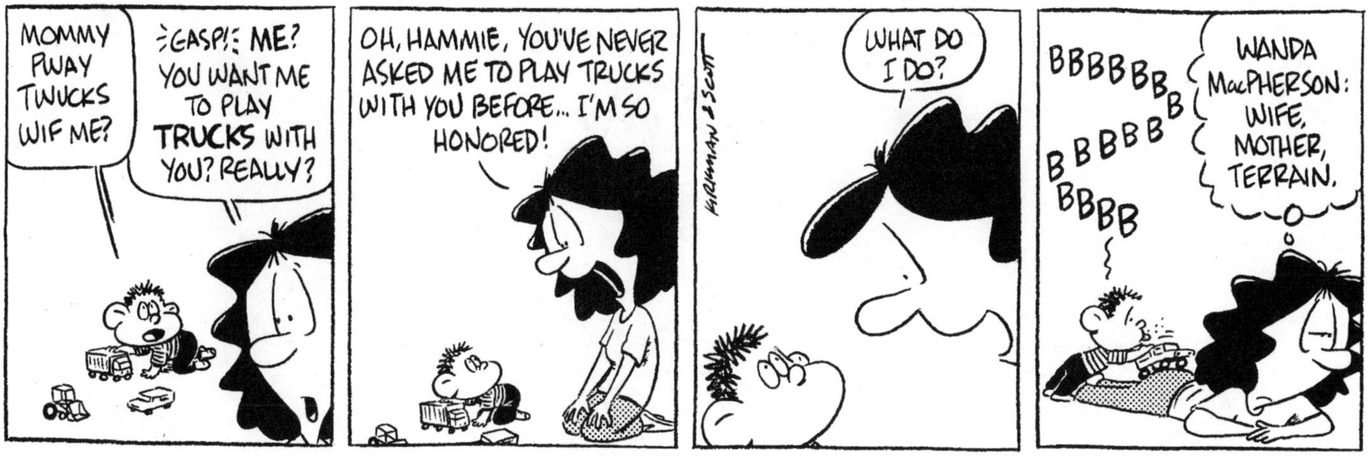

MOMMY PWAY TWUCKS WIF ME?
GASP! ME? YOU WANT ME TO PLAY TRUCKS WITH YOU? REALLY?
OH, HAMMIE, YOU'VE NEVER ASKED ME TO PLAY TRUCKS WITH YOU BEFORE... I'M SO HONORED!
WHAT DO I DO?
BBBBBBBB BBBBBB BBBB
WANDA MacPHERSON: WIFE, MOTHER, TERRAIN.
KIRKMAN & SCOTT

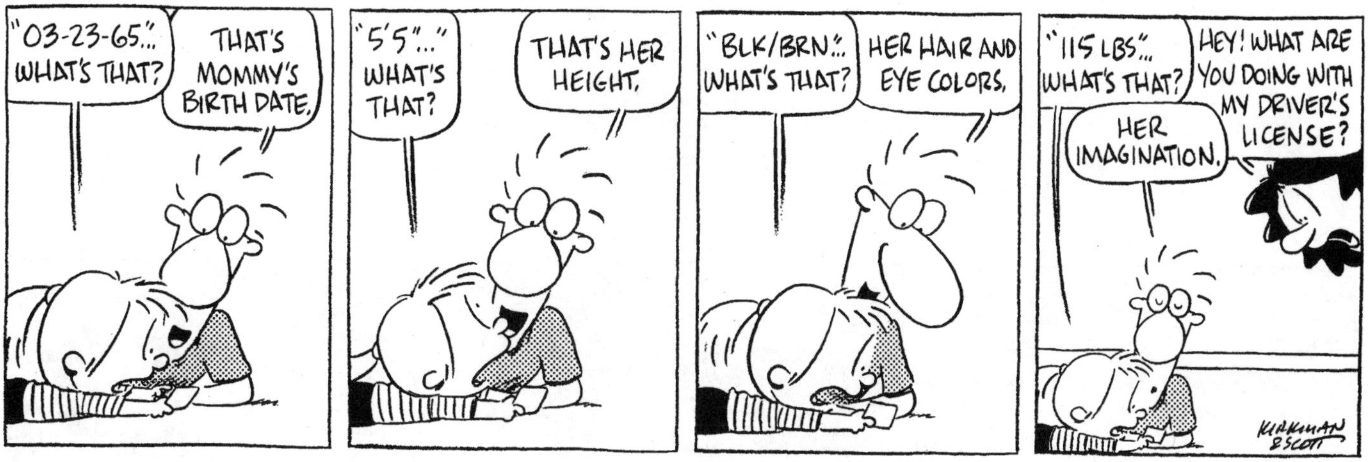

"03-23-65."... WHAT'S THAT?
THAT'S MOMMY'S BIRTH DATE.
"5'5"..." WHAT'S THAT?
THAT'S HER HEIGHT.
"BLK/BRN."... WHAT'S THAT?
HER HAIR AND EYE COLORS.
"115 LBS."... WHAT'S THAT?
HER IMAGINATION.
HEY! WHAT ARE YOU DOING WITH MY DRIVER'S LICENSE?
KIRKMAN & SCOTT

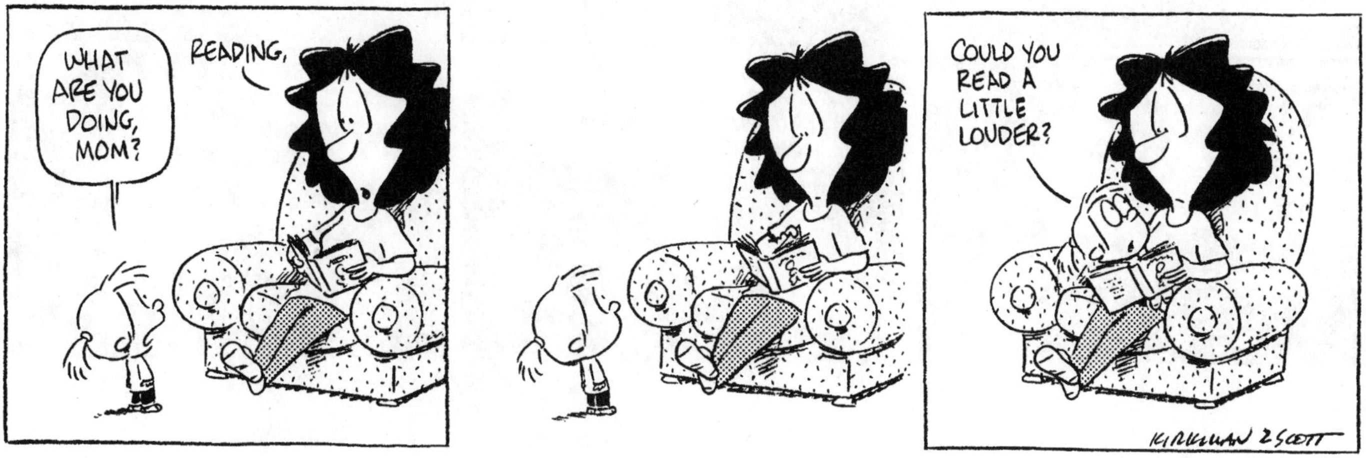

WHAT ARE YOU DOING, MOM?
READING.
COULD YOU READ A LITTLE LOUDER?
KIRKMAN & SCOTT

BABY BLUES®

by Rick Kirkman / Jerry Scott

BABY

GROAN! FINALLY! I THOUGHT THAT MOVIE WOULD NEVER END.
EXIT
WHY DO WE COME HERE? THESE ARE THE WORST SEATS IN TOWN!
MINE WAS OKAY.
MY BACK HURTS... MY LEGS ACHE... AND I DON'T KNOW IF I'LL **EVER** GET THE FEELING BACK IN MY REAR-END!
TAKE SOME ASPIRIN WHEN WE GET HOME.
ASPIRIN? **HA!**
WANDA, YOU DON'T KNOW THE MEANING OF DISCOMFORT UNTIL YOU'VE SPENT TWO AND A HALF HOURS IN A ROTTEN MOVIE THEATER SEAT!
TRY BEING **PREGNANT** FOR NINE MONTHS.
TWICE.

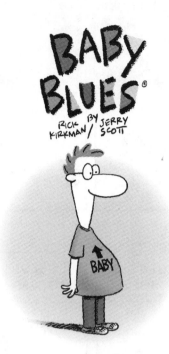

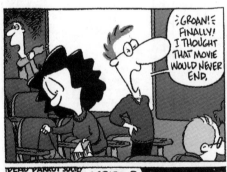

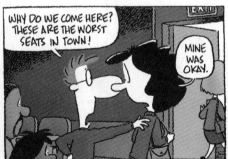

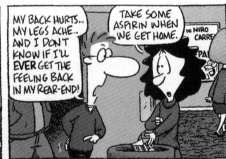

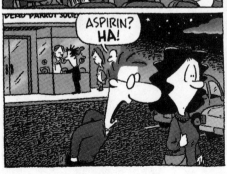

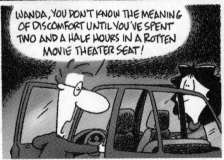

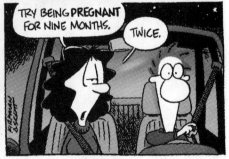

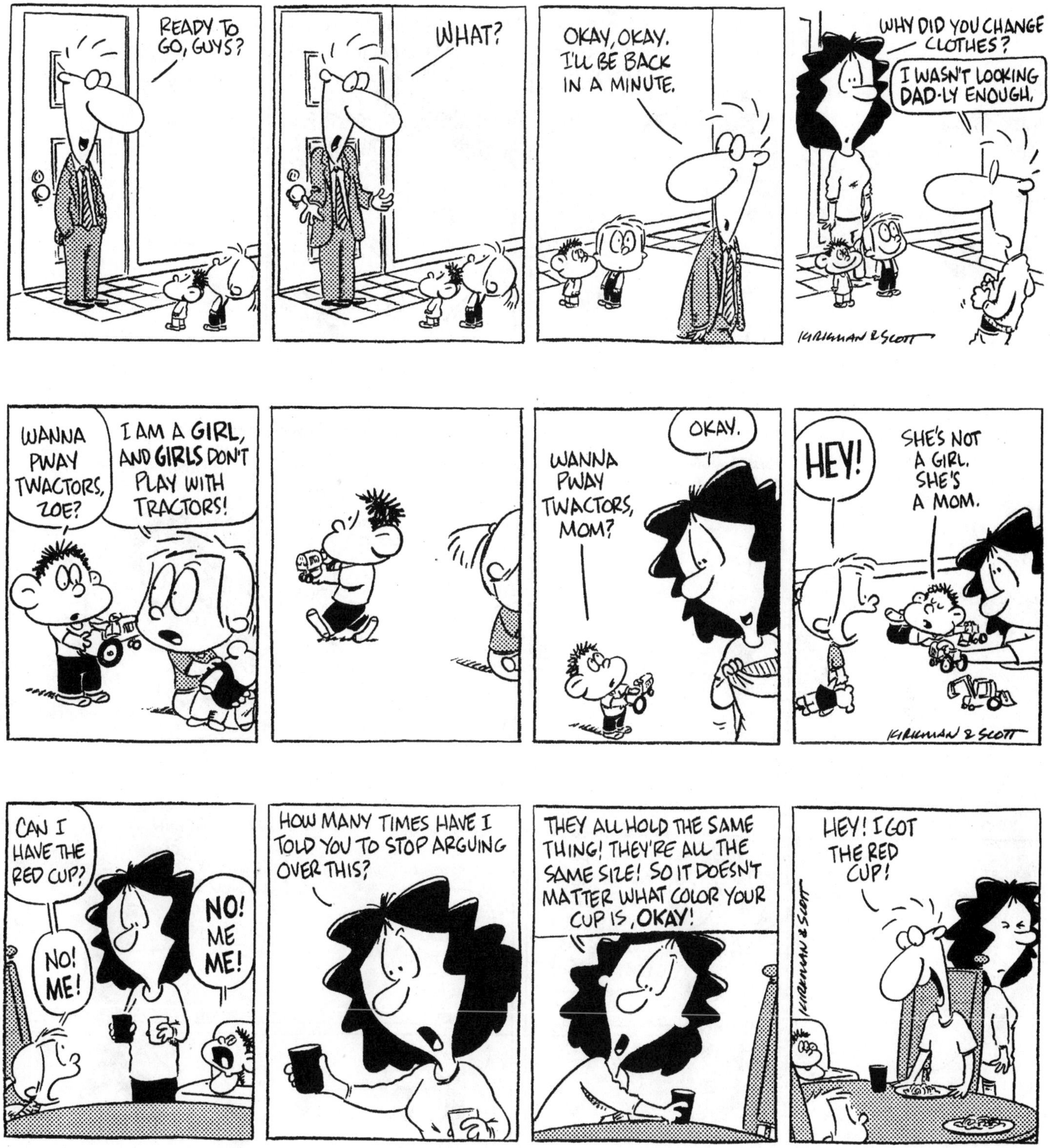
READY TO GO, GUYS?
WHAT?
OKAY, OKAY. I'LL BE BACK IN A MINUTE.
WHY DID YOU CHANGE CLOTHES?
I WASN'T LOOKING DAD-LY ENOUGH.
KIRKMAN & SCOTT
WANNA PWAY TWACTORS, ZOE?
I AM A GIRL, AND GIRLS DON'T PLAY WITH TRACTORS!
WANNA PWAY TWACTORS, MOM?
OKAY.
HEY!
SHE'S NOT A GIRL. SHE'S A MOM.
KIRKMAN & SCOTT
CAN I HAVE THE RED CUP?
NO! ME!
NO! ME ME!
HOW MANY TIMES HAVE I TOLD YOU TO STOP ARGUING OVER THIS?
THEY ALL HOLD THE SAME THING! THEY'RE ALL THE SAME SIZE! SO IT DOESN'T MATTER WHAT COLOR YOUR CUP IS, OKAY!
KIRKMAN & SCOTT
HEY! I GOT THE RED CUP!

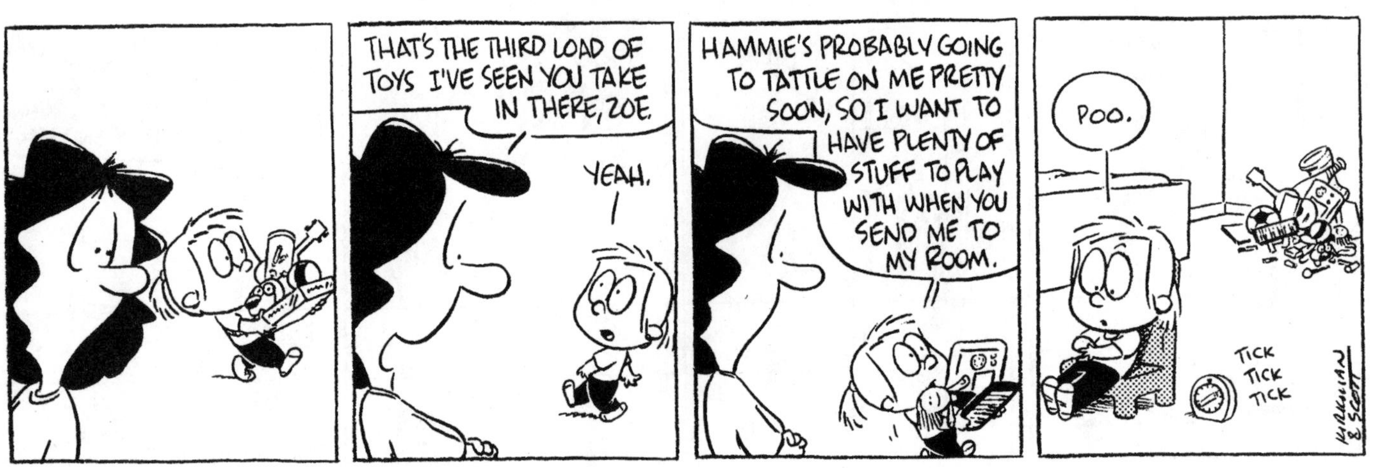
THAT'S THE THIRD LOAD OF TOYS I'VE SEEN YOU TAKE IN THERE, ZOE.
YEAH.
HAMMIE'S PROBABLY GOING TO TATTLE ON ME PRETTY SOON, SO I WANT TO HAVE PLENTY OF STUFF TO PLAY WITH WHEN YOU SEND ME TO MY ROOM.
POO.
TICK TICK TICK
KIRKMAN & SCOTT

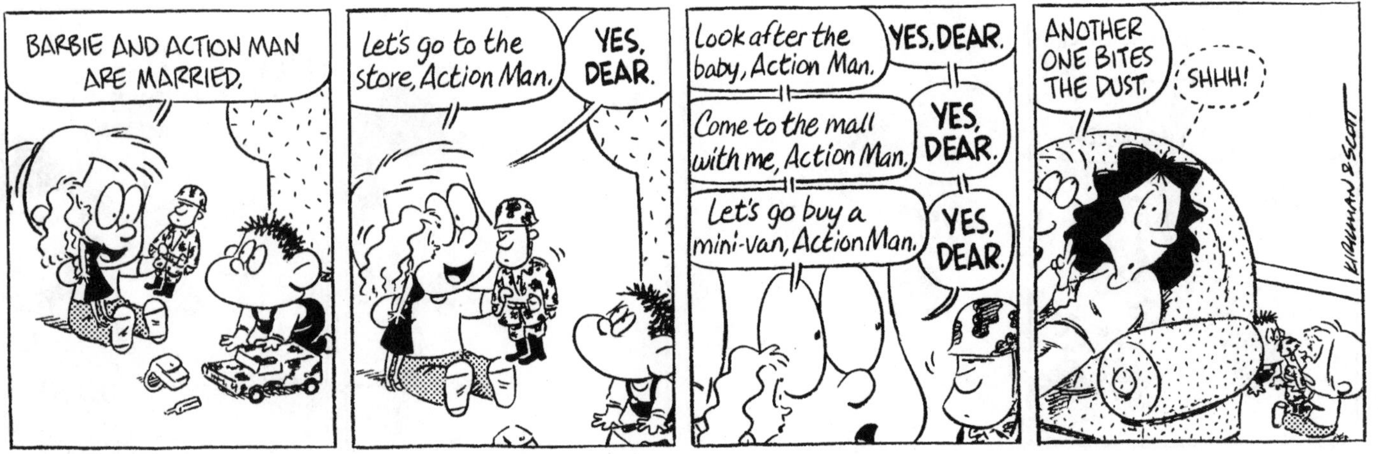
BARBIE AND ACTION MAN ARE MARRIED.
Let's go to the store, Action Man.
YES, DEAR.
Look after the baby, Action Man.
YES, DEAR.
Come to the mall with me, Action Man.
YES, DEAR.
Let's go buy a mini-van, Action Man.
YES, DEAR.
ANOTHER ONE BITES THE DUST.
SHHH!
KIRKMAN & SCOTT

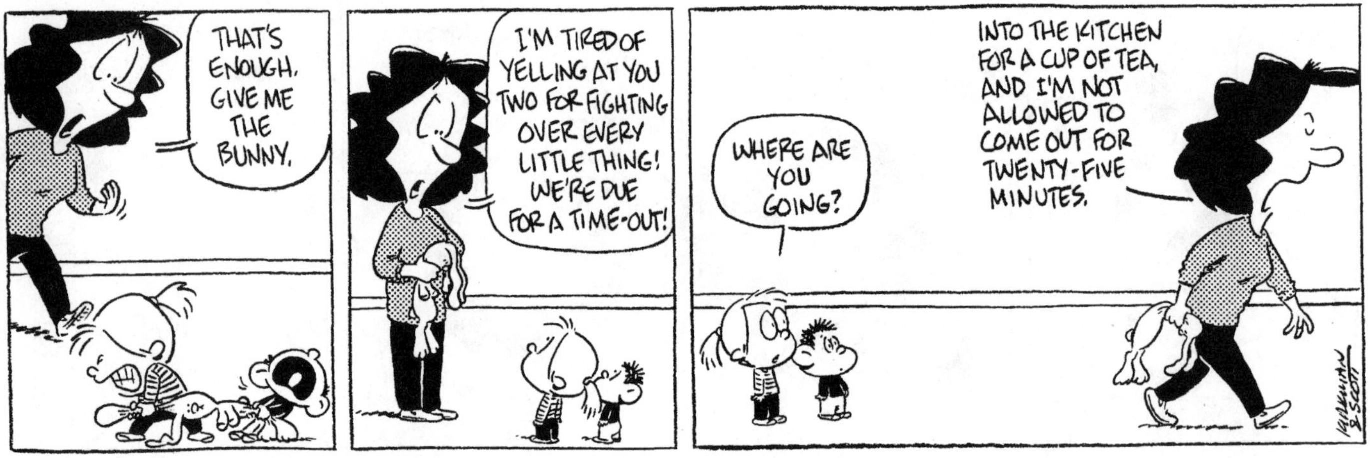
THAT'S ENOUGH. GIVE ME THE BUNNY.
I'M TIRED OF YELLING AT YOU TWO FOR FIGHTING OVER EVERY LITTLE THING! WE'RE DUE FOR A TIME-OUT!
WHERE ARE YOU GOING?
INTO THE KITCHEN FOR A CUP OF TEA, AND I'M NOT ALLOWED TO COME OUT FOR TWENTY-FIVE MINUTES.
KIRKMAN & SCOTT

BABY BLUES®

BY RICK KIRKMAN / JERRY SCOTT

Hammie and Me

WHEREVER I AM, THERE'S ALWAYS HAM, BUT WE ALL JUST CALL HIM "HAMMIE." WHATEVER I DO, HE WANTS TO, TOO, EVEN WHEN I TELL HIM TO "SCRAMMIE!"

"WHERE ARE YOU GOING? WHAT SHOULD WE DO?" HE WANTS TO KNOW ONE OR THE OTHER. "LEAVE ME ALONE," I WEARILY GROAN, IT AIN'T EASY HAVING A BROTHER.

HE WANTS TO PLAY TRUCKS OR CARS OR TRAINS (IT IS CONSTANTLY SOMETHING WITH WHEELS). HE WON'T DRESS-UP WITH ME ANYMORE EVEN THOUGH HE LOOKS GREAT IN HIGH HEELS.

ONE TIME GRAPE JUICE GOT SPILLED ON THE COUCH, WHEN MOM SAW IT I KNEW SHE WOULD SNAP. I HAD NO DOUBT I'D GET A TIME-OUT, BUT HEROICALLY, HAM TOOK THE RAP.

SO WHEREVER I AM, THERE'S ALWAYS HAM, AND SOMETIMES I THINK I MIGHT SMOTHER. BUT ORNERY, STINKY AND CLINGY ASIDE, THER'RE WORSE THINGS THAN HAVING A BROTHER.

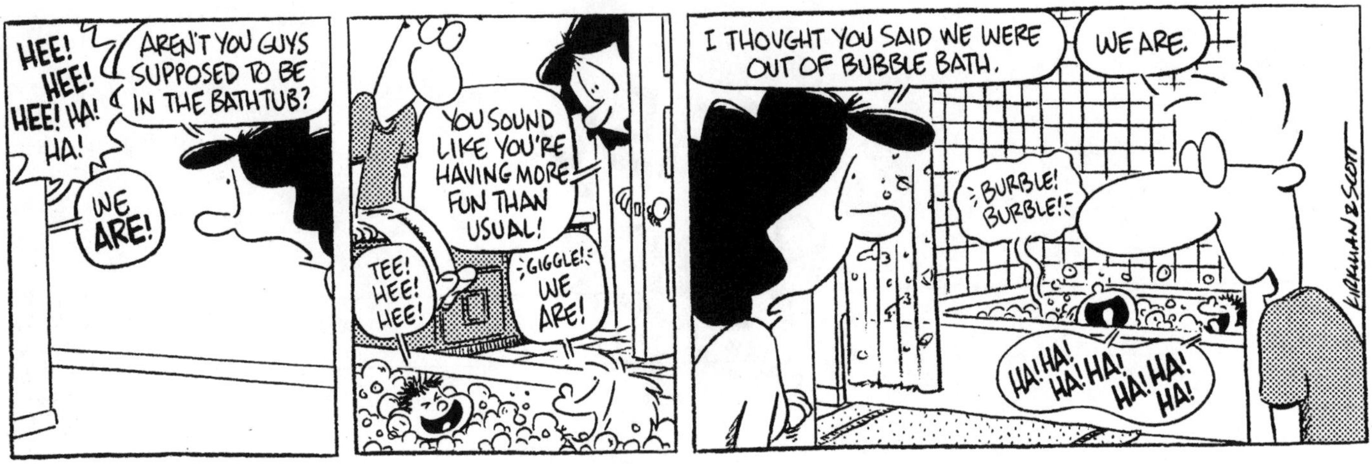
HEE! HEE! HEE! HA! HA!
AREN'T YOU GUYS SUPPOSED TO BE IN THE BATHTUB?
WE ARE!
YOU SOUND LIKE YOU'RE HAVING MORE FUN THAN USUAL!
TEE! HEE! HEE!
GIGGLE! WE ARE!
I THOUGHT YOU SAID WE WERE OUT OF BUBBLE BATH.
WE ARE.
BURBLE! BURBLE!
HA! HA! HA! HA! HA! HA! HA!
KIRKMAN & SCOTT

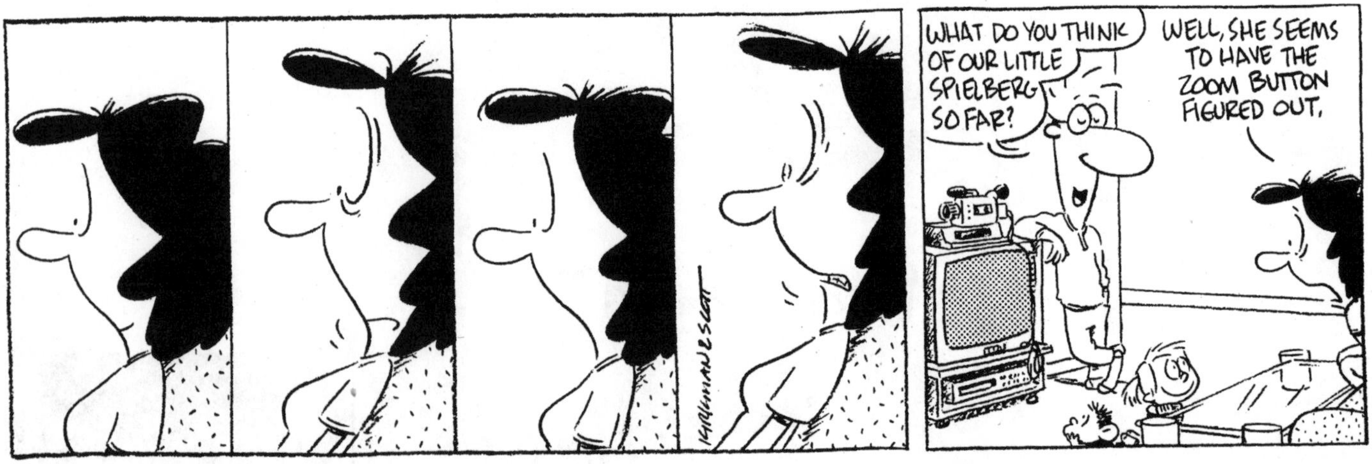
KIRKMAN & SCOTT
WHAT DO YOU THINK OF OUR LITTLE SPIELBERG SO FAR?
WELL, SHE SEEMS TO HAVE THE ZOOM BUTTON FIGURED OUT.

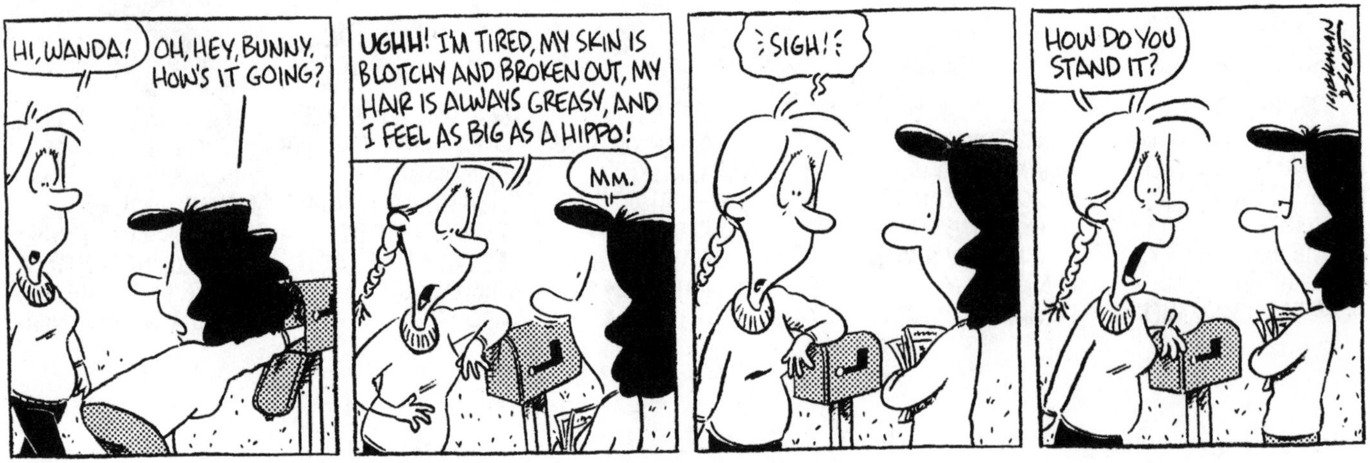
HI, WANDA!
OH, HEY, BUNNY. HOW'S IT GOING?
UGHH! I'M TIRED, MY SKIN IS BLOTCHY AND BROKEN OUT, MY HAIR IS ALWAYS GREASY, AND I FEEL AS BIG AS A HIPPO!
MM.
SIGH!
HOW DO YOU STAND IT?
KIRKMAN & SCOTT

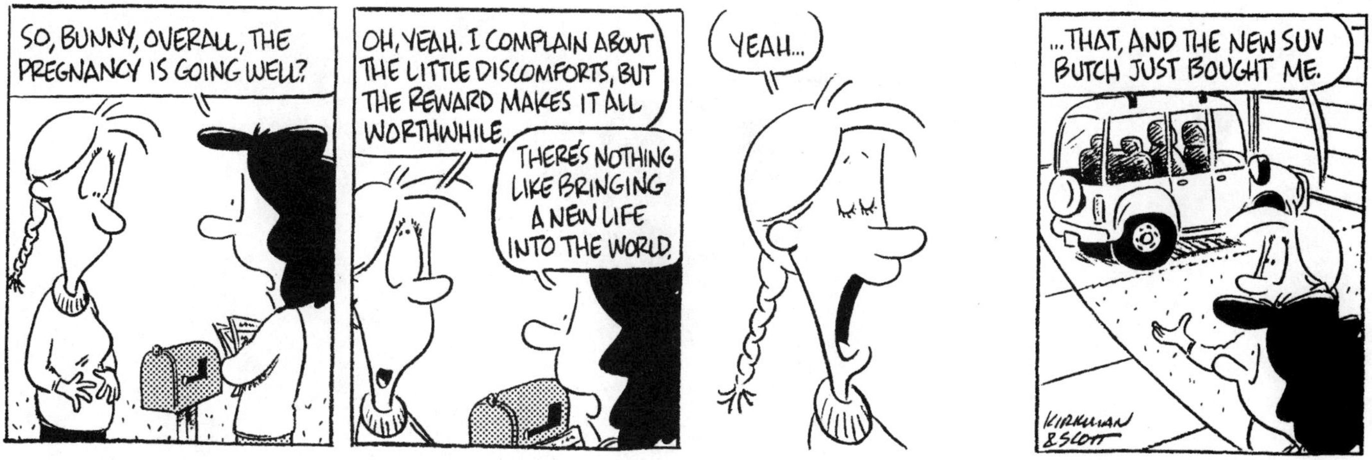
SO, BUNNY, OVERALL, THE PREGNANCY IS GOING WELL?
OH, YEAH. I COMPLAIN ABOUT THE LITTLE DISCOMFORTS, BUT THE REWARD MAKES IT ALL WORTHWHILE.
THERE'S NOTHING LIKE BRINGING A NEW LIFE INTO THE WORLD.
YEAH...
...THAT, AND THE NEW SUV BUTCH JUST BOUGHT ME.
KIRKMAN & SCOTT

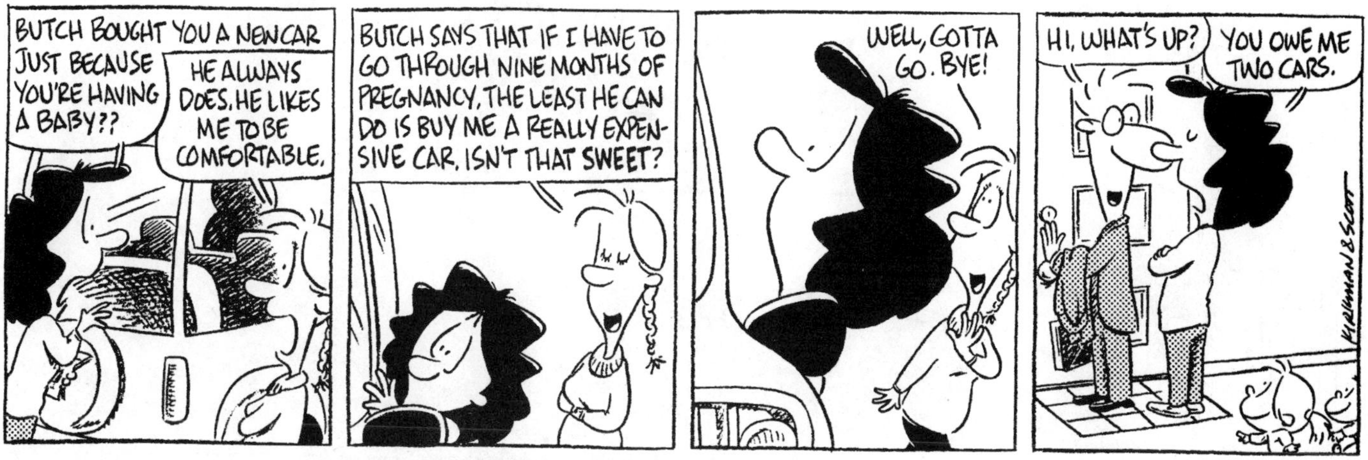
BUTCH BOUGHT YOU A NEW CAR JUST BECAUSE YOU'RE HAVING A BABY??
HE ALWAYS DOES. HE LIKES ME TO BE COMFORTABLE.
BUTCH SAYS THAT IF I HAVE TO GO THROUGH NINE MONTHS OF PREGNANCY, THE LEAST HE CAN DO IS BUY ME A REALLY EXPENSIVE CAR. ISN'T THAT SWEET?
WELL, GOTTA GO. BYE!
HI, WHAT'S UP?
YOU OWE ME TWO CARS.
KIRKMAN & SCOTT

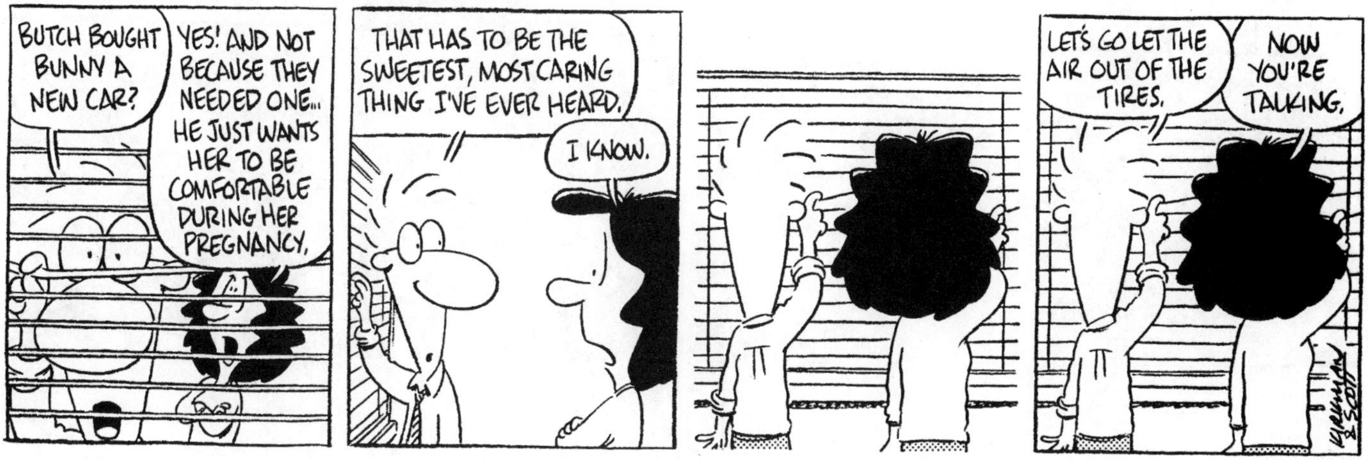
BUTCH BOUGHT BUNNY A NEW CAR?
YES! AND NOT BECAUSE THEY NEEDED ONE... HE JUST WANTS HER TO BE COMFORTABLE DURING HER PREGNANCY.
THAT HAS TO BE THE SWEETEST, MOST CARING THING I'VE EVER HEARD.
I KNOW.
LET'S GO LET THE AIR OUT OF THE TIRES.
NOW YOU'RE TALKING.
KIRKMAN & SCOTT

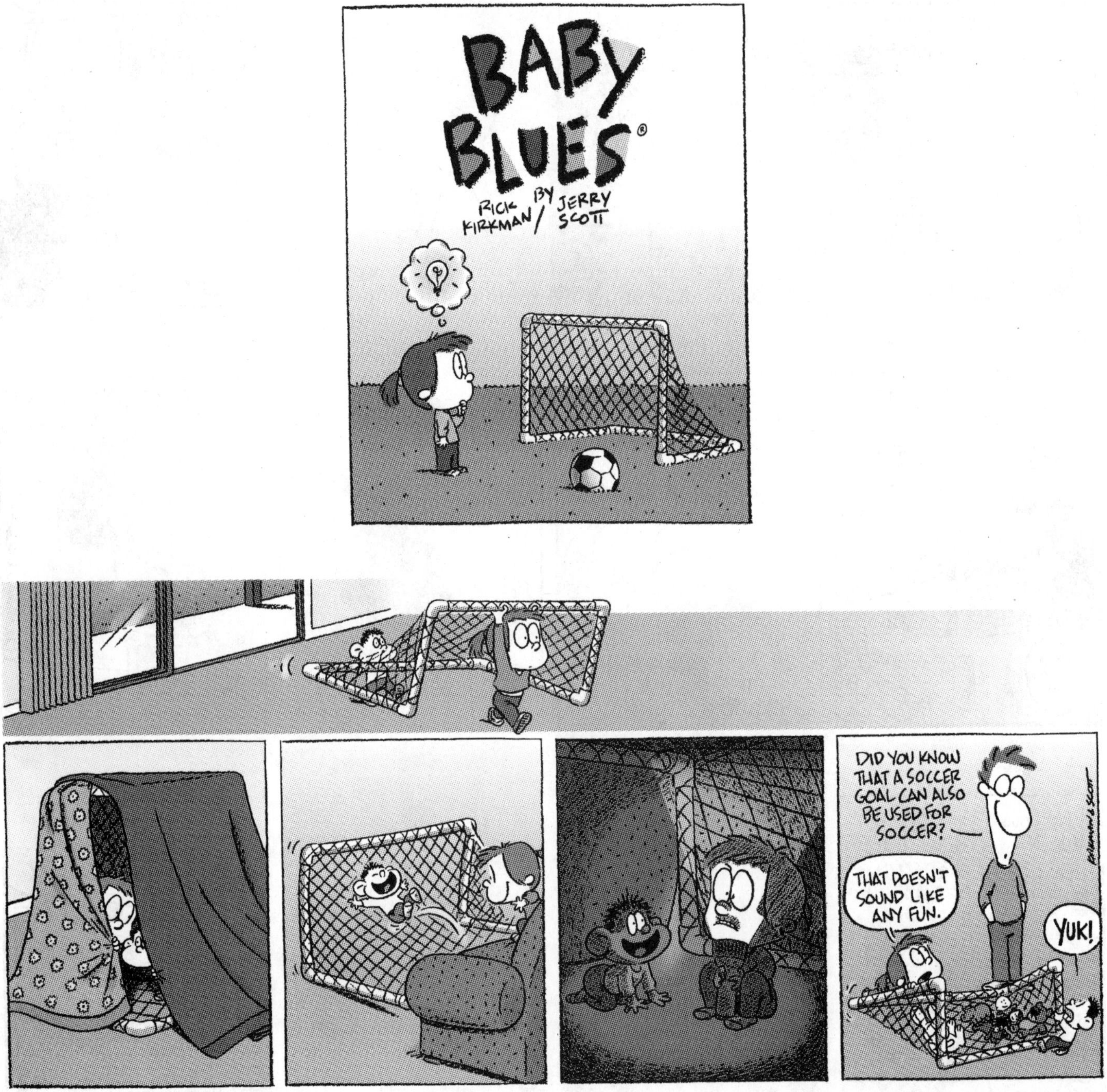
BABY BLUES®
BY RICK KIRKMAN / JERRY SCOTT
DID YOU KNOW THAT A SOCCER GOAL CAN ALSO BE USED FOR SOCCER?
THAT DOESN'T SOUND LIKE ANY FUN.
YUK!

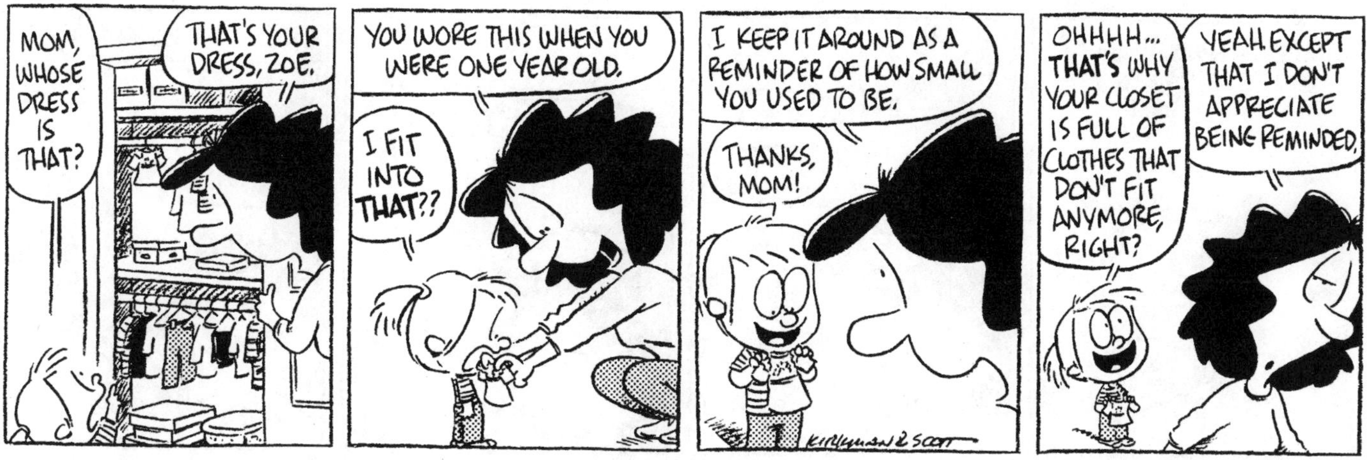
MOM, WHOSE DRESS IS THAT?
THAT'S YOUR DRESS, ZOE.
YOU WORE THIS WHEN YOU WERE ONE YEAR OLD.
I FIT INTO **THAT**??
I KEEP IT AROUND AS A REMINDER OF HOW SMALL YOU USED TO BE.
THANKS, MOM!
OHHHH... **THAT'S** WHY YOUR CLOSET IS FULL OF CLOTHES THAT DON'T FIT ANYMORE, RIGHT?
YEAH. EXCEPT THAT I DON'T APPRECIATE BEING REMINDED.

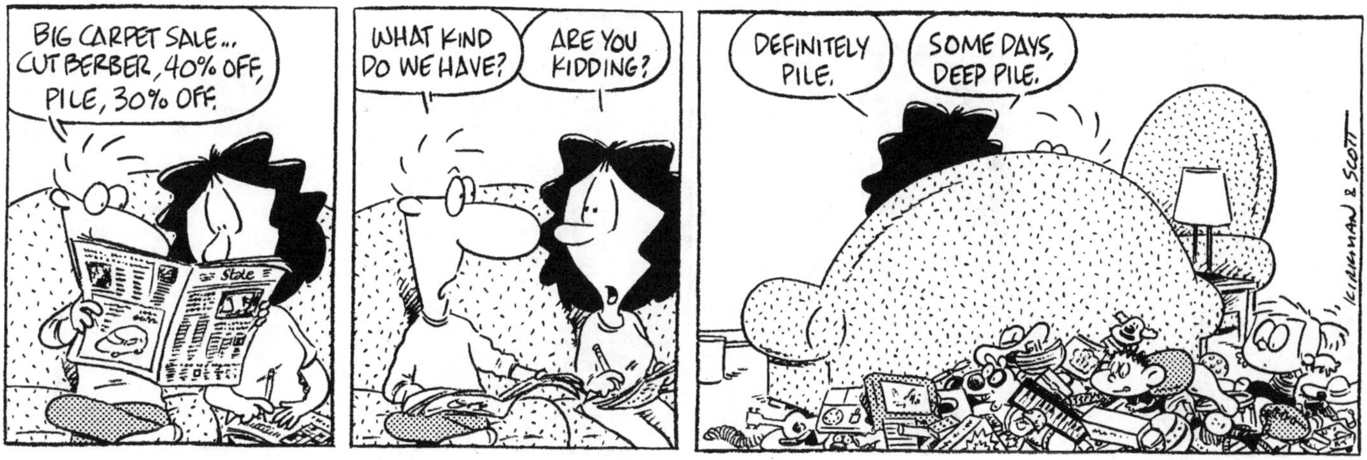
BIG CARPET SALE... CUT BERBER, 40% OFF, PILE, 30% OFF.
WHAT KIND DO WE HAVE?
ARE YOU KIDDING?
DEFINITELY PILE.
SOME DAYS, DEEP PILE.

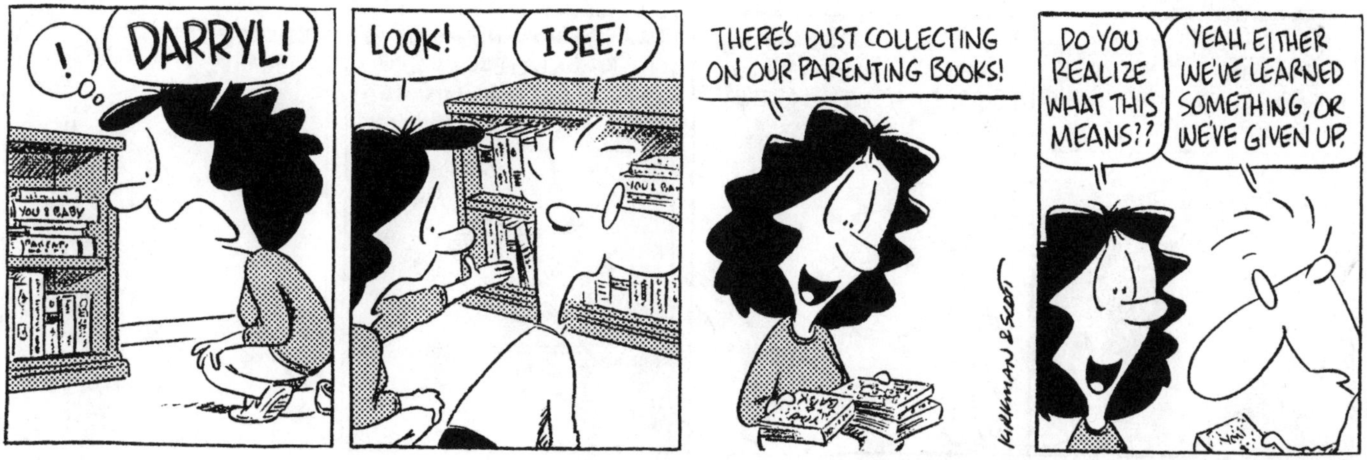
!
DARRYL!
LOOK!
I SEE!
THERE'S DUST COLLECTING ON OUR PARENTING BOOKS!
DO YOU REALIZE WHAT THIS MEANS??
YEAH. EITHER WE'VE LEARNED SOMETHING, OR WE'VE GIVEN UP.

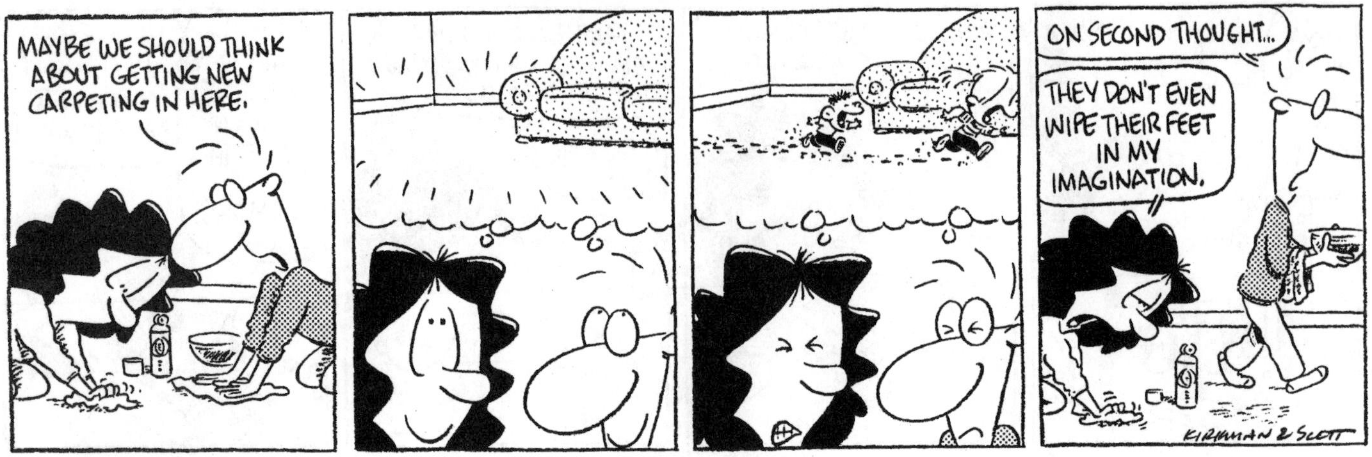
MAYBE WE SHOULD THINK ABOUT GETTING NEW CARPETING IN HERE.
ON SECOND THOUGHT...
THEY DON'T EVEN WIPE THEIR FEET IN MY IMAGINATION.
KIRKMAN & SCOTT

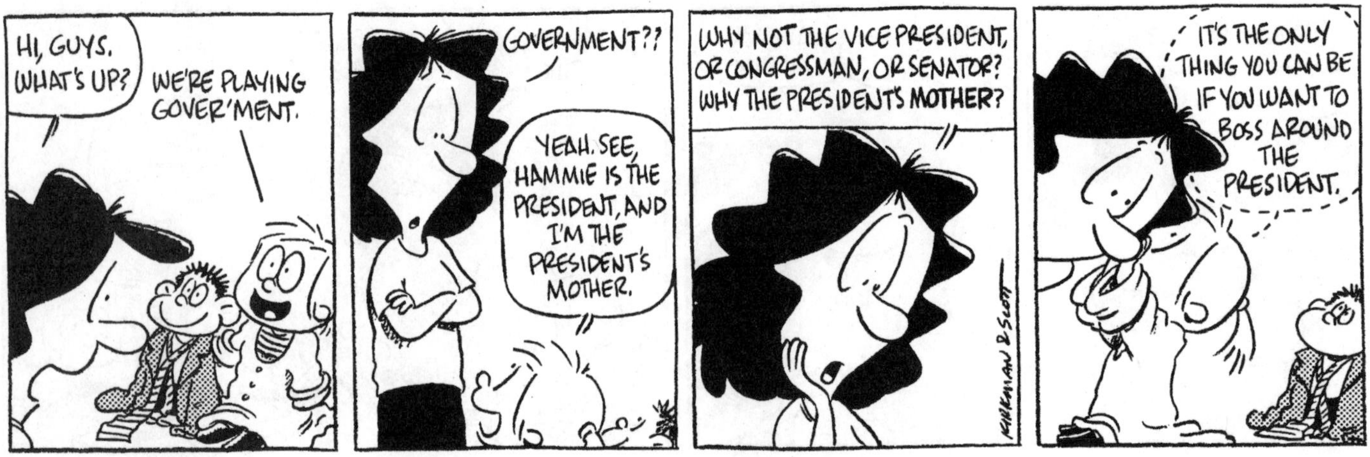
HI, GUYS. WHAT'S UP?
WE'RE PLAYING GOVER'MENT.
GOVERNMENT??
YEAH. SEE, HAMMIE IS THE PRESIDENT, AND I'M THE PRESIDENT'S MOTHER.
WHY NOT THE VICE PRESIDENT, OR CONGRESSMAN, OR SENATOR? WHY THE PRESIDENT'S MOTHER?
KIRKMAN & SCOTT
IT'S THE ONLY THING YOU CAN BE IF YOU WANT TO BOSS AROUND THE PRESIDENT.

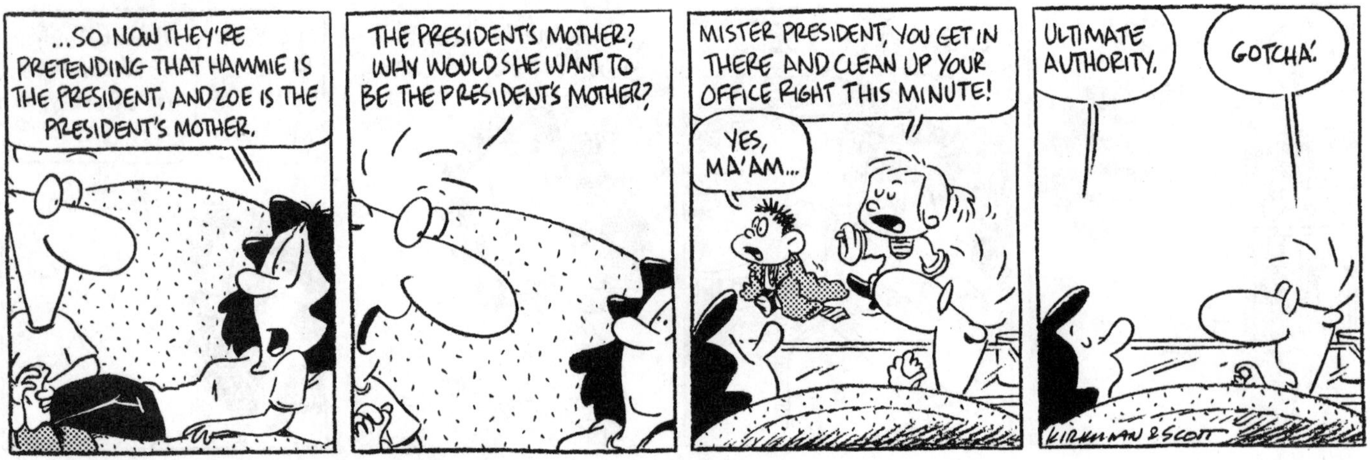
...SO NOW THEY'RE PRETENDING THAT HAMMIE IS THE PRESIDENT, AND ZOE IS THE PRESIDENT'S MOTHER.
THE PRESIDENT'S MOTHER? WHY WOULD SHE WANT TO BE THE PRESIDENT'S MOTHER?
MISTER PRESIDENT, YOU GET IN THERE AND CLEAN UP YOUR OFFICE RIGHT THIS MINUTE!
YES, MA'AM...
ULTIMATE AUTHORITY.
GOTCHA.
KIRKMAN & SCOTT

BABY BLUES®
BY RICK KIRKMAN / JERRY SCOTT

I THINK WHAT DARRYL IS SAYING IS THAT THEY'VE HAD DECADES TO FIX THE PROBLEM BUT THEY HAVEN'T!
RIGHT!
SO THE PROBLEM ISN'T THE LACK OF RESOURCES... IT'S THE ALLOCATION OF THE RESOURCES WE ALREADY HAVE.
EXACTLY. WE SIMPLY NEED TO GIVE TEACHERS MORE AUTHORITY.
MAKES SENSE
UH-HUH.
It's not what's poured into a child, but what is planted that counts.
THAT'S LOVELY, DARRYL! WAS THAT SHAKESPEARE?
ARISTOTLE?
TWAIN?
CHURCHILL?
VOLTAIRE?
CHUCKIE FINSTER. RUGRATS EPISODE #6,412.
WHAT?? IT WAS A GOOD SAYING!
YEAH, WELL, IF YOU WANT PEOPLE TO TAKE YOU SERIOUSLY, I WOULDN'T GO AROUND QUOTING CARTOON CHARACTERS.
KIRKMAN & SCOTT

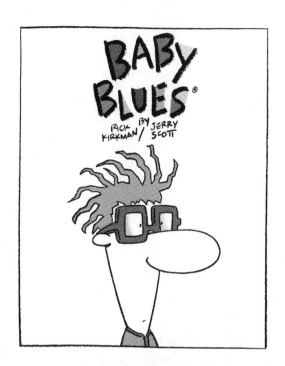

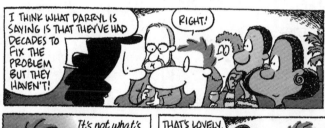

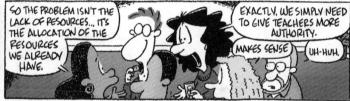

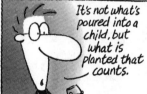

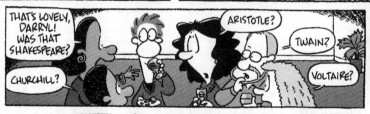

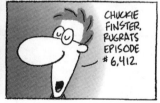

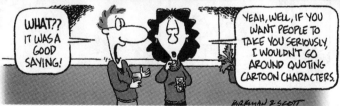

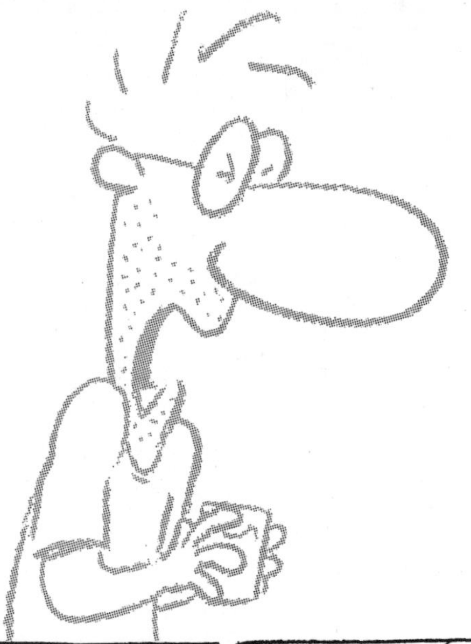

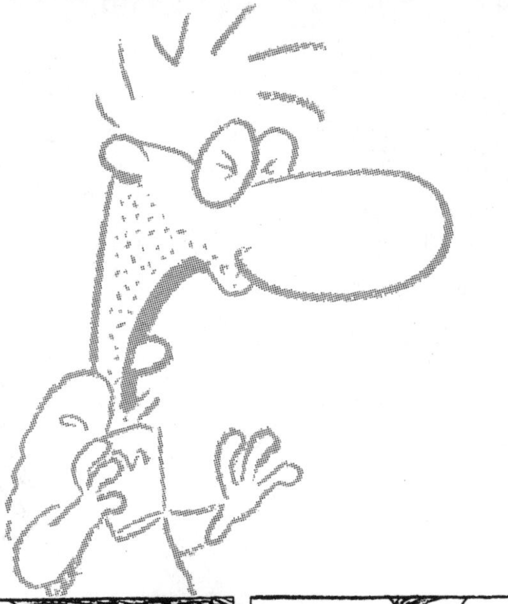

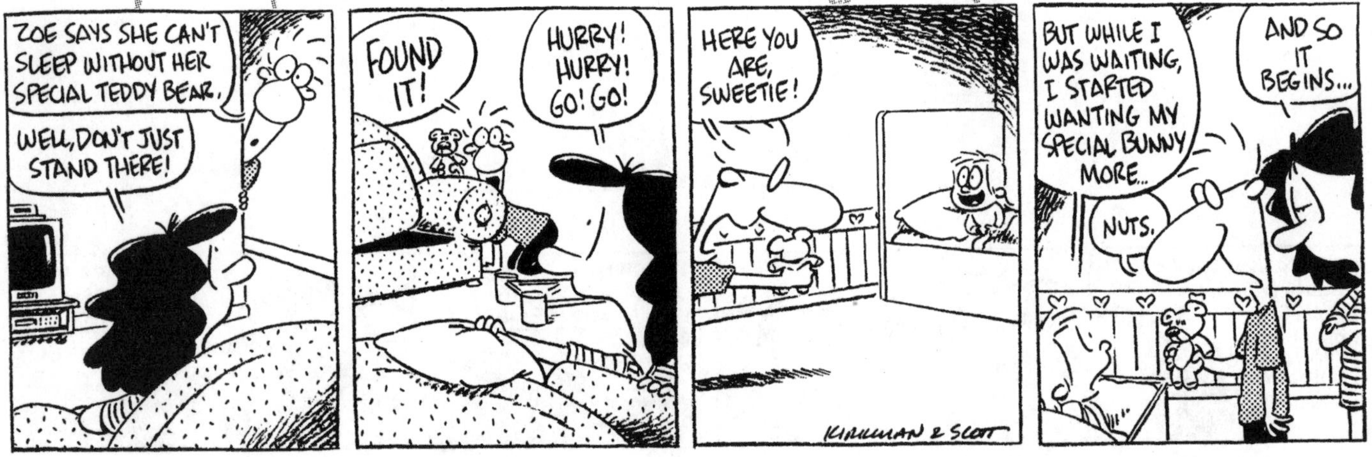
ZOE SAYS SHE CAN'T SLEEP WITHOUT HER SPECIAL TEDDY BEAR.
WELL, DON'T JUST STAND THERE!
FOUND IT!
HURRY! HURRY! GO! GO!
HERE YOU ARE, SWEETIE!
KIRKMAN & SCOTT
BUT WHILE I WAS WAITING, I STARTED WANTING MY SPECIAL BUNNY MORE...
AND SO IT BEGINS...
NUTS.

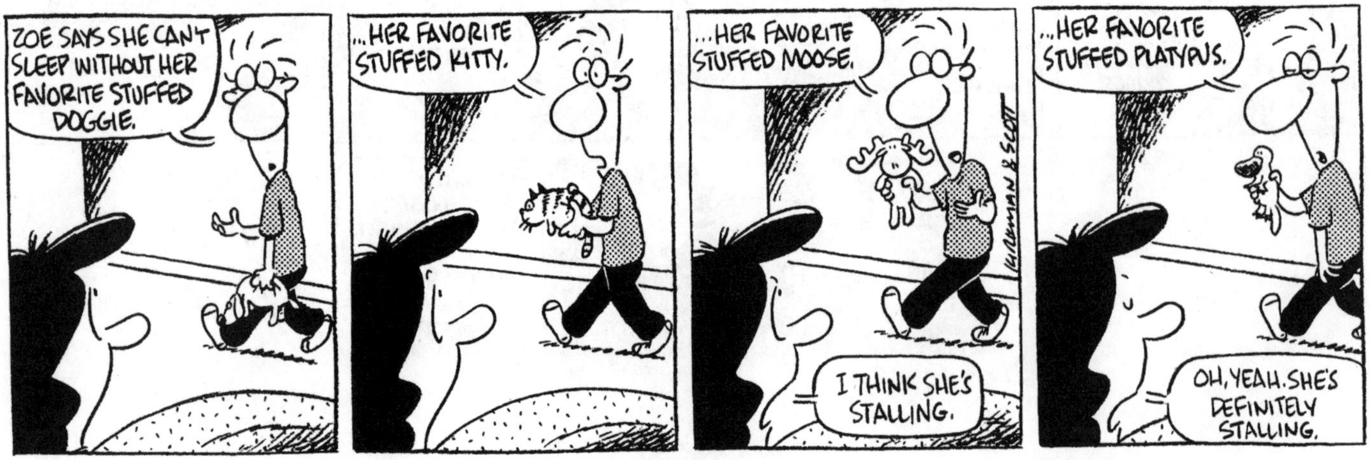
ZOE SAYS SHE CAN'T SLEEP WITHOUT HER FAVORITE STUFFED DOGGIE.
...HER FAVORITE STUFFED KITTY.
...HER FAVORITE STUFFED MOOSE.
KIRKMAN & SCOTT
I THINK SHE'S STALLING.
...HER FAVORITE STUFFED PLATYPUS.
OH, YEAH. SHE'S DEFINITELY STALLING.

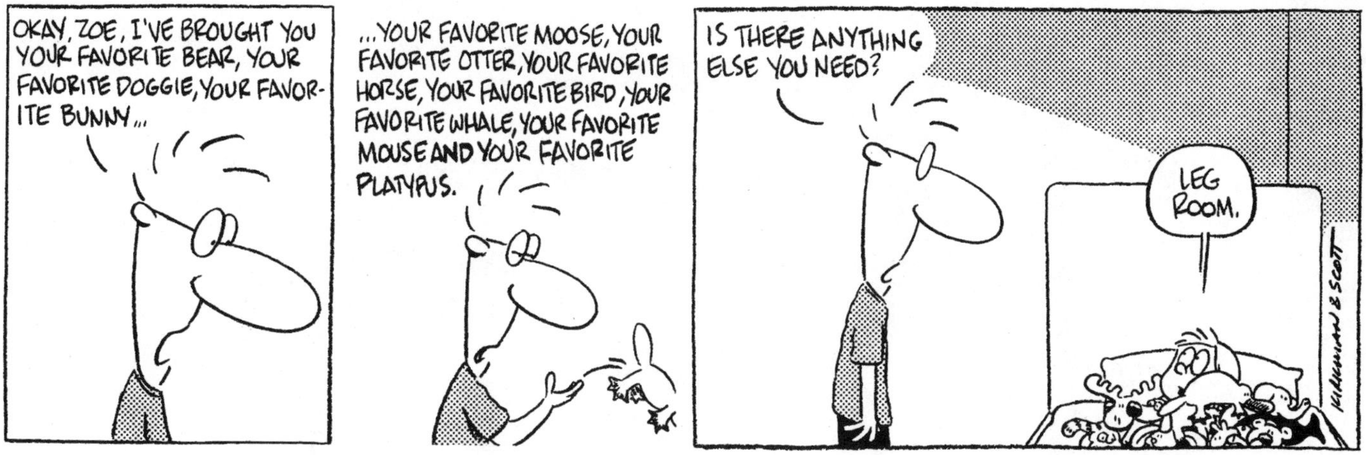
OKAY, ZOE, I'VE BROUGHT YOU YOUR FAVORITE BEAR, YOUR FAVORITE DOGGIE, YOUR FAVORITE BUNNY...
...YOUR FAVORITE MOOSE, YOUR FAVORITE OTTER, YOUR FAVORITE HORSE, YOUR FAVORITE BIRD, YOUR FAVORITE WHALE, YOUR FAVORITE MOUSE AND YOUR FAVORITE PLATYPUS.
IS THERE ANYTHING ELSE YOU NEED?
LEG ROOM.
KIRKMAN & SCOTT

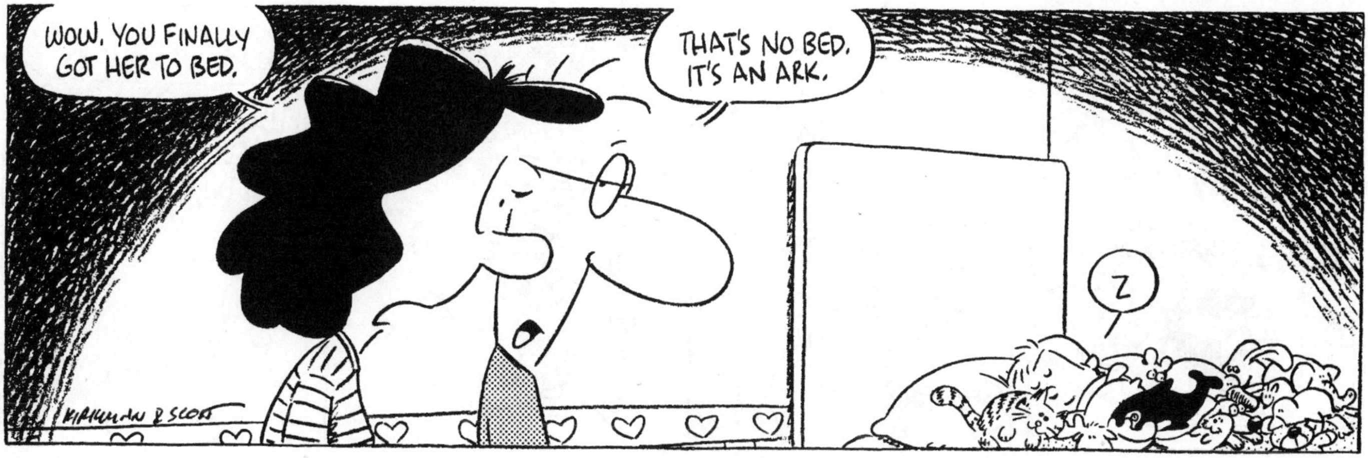
WOW. YOU FINALLY GOT HER TO BED.
THAT'S NO BED. IT'S AN ARK.
Z
KIRKMAN & SCOTT

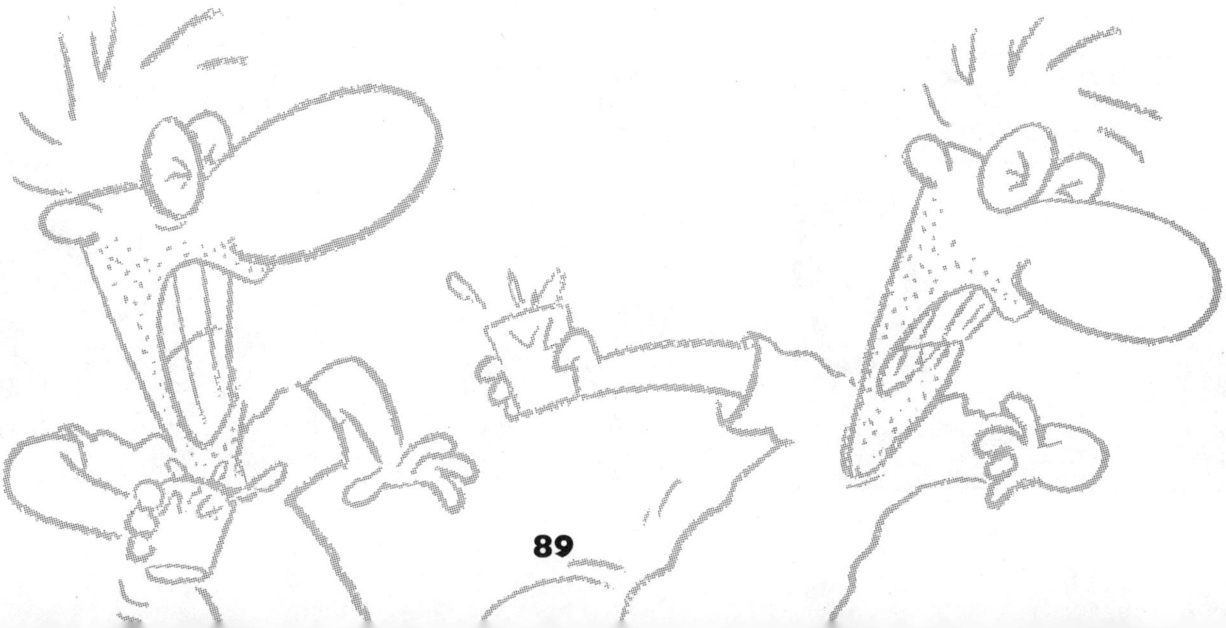

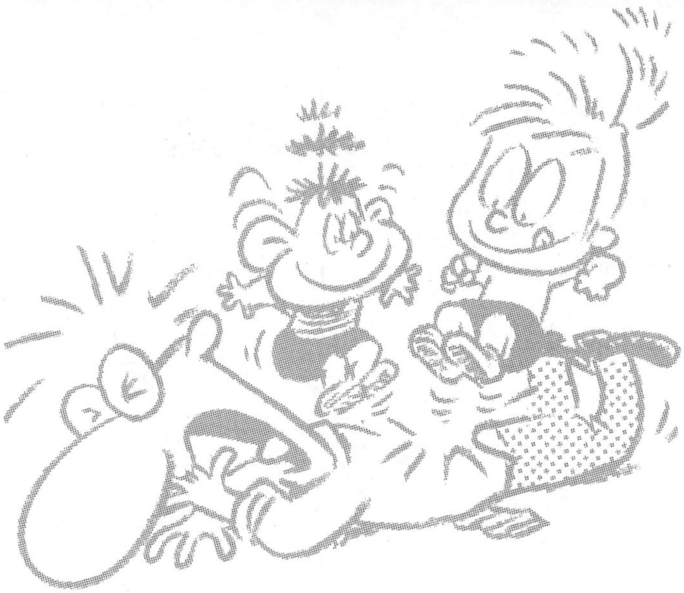

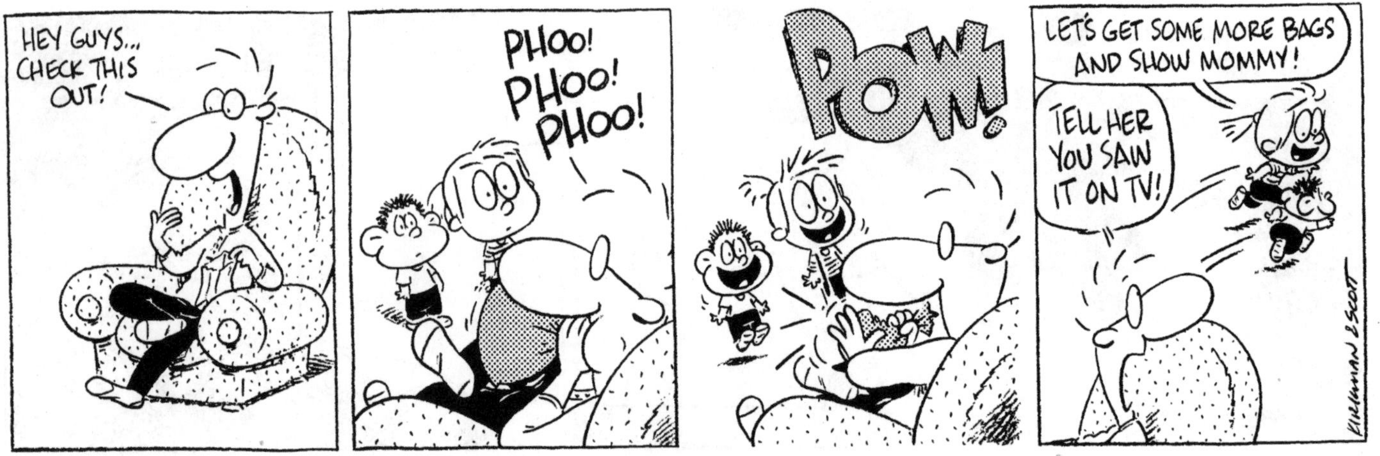
HEY GUYS...
CHECK THIS OUT!
PHOO! PHOO! PHOO!
POW!
LET'S GET SOME MORE BAGS AND SHOW MOMMY!
TELL HER YOU SAW IT ON TV!

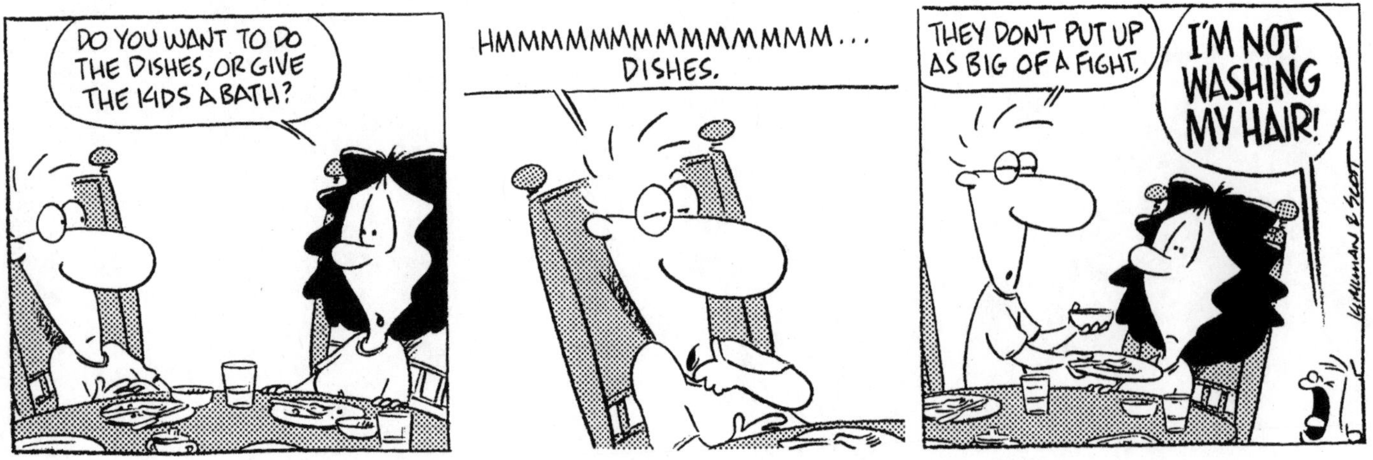
DO YOU WANT TO DO THE DISHES, OR GIVE THE KIDS A BATH?
HMMMMMMMMMMMMMMM...
DISHES.
THEY DON'T PUT UP AS BIG OF A FIGHT.
I'M NOT WASHING MY HAIR!

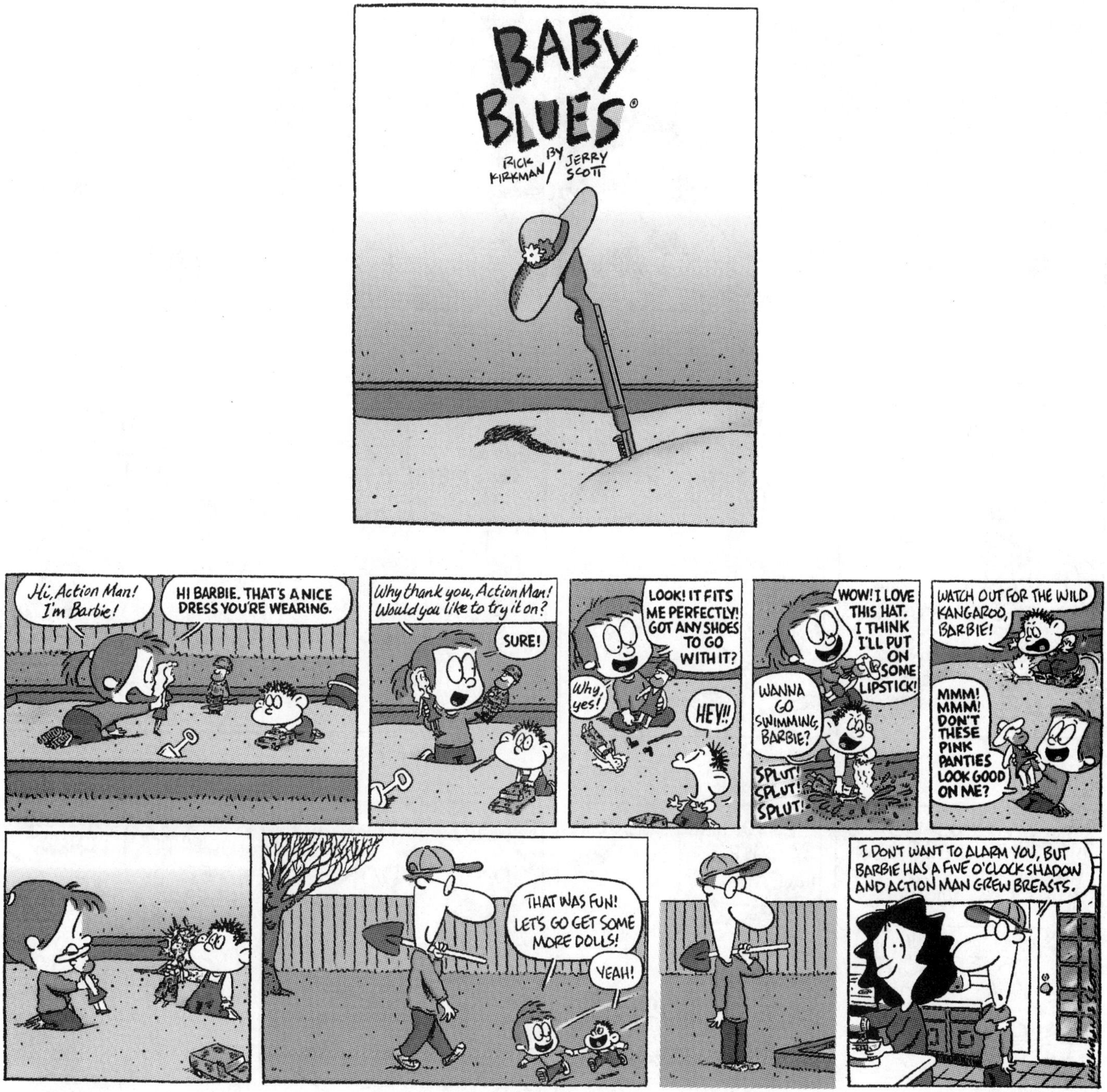
BABY BLUES®
BY RICK KIRKMAN / JERRY SCOTT
Hi, Action Man! I'm Barbie!
HI BARBIE. THAT'S A NICE DRESS YOU'RE WEARING.
Why thank you, Action Man! Would you like to try it on?
SURE!
LOOK! IT FITS ME PERFECTLY! GOT ANY SHOES TO GO WITH IT?
Why, yes!
HEY!!
WOW! I LOVE THIS HAT. I THINK I'LL PUT ON SOME LIPSTICK!
WANNA GO SWIMMING, BARBIE?
SPLUT! SPLUT! SPLUT!
WATCH OUT FOR THE WILD KANGAROO, BARBIE!
MMM! MMM! DON'T THESE PINK PANTIES LOOK GOOD ON ME?
THAT WAS FUN! LET'S GO GET SOME MORE DOLLS!
YEAH!
I DON'T WANT TO ALARM YOU, BUT BARBIE HAS A FIVE O'CLOCK SHADOW AND ACTION MAN GREW BREASTS.

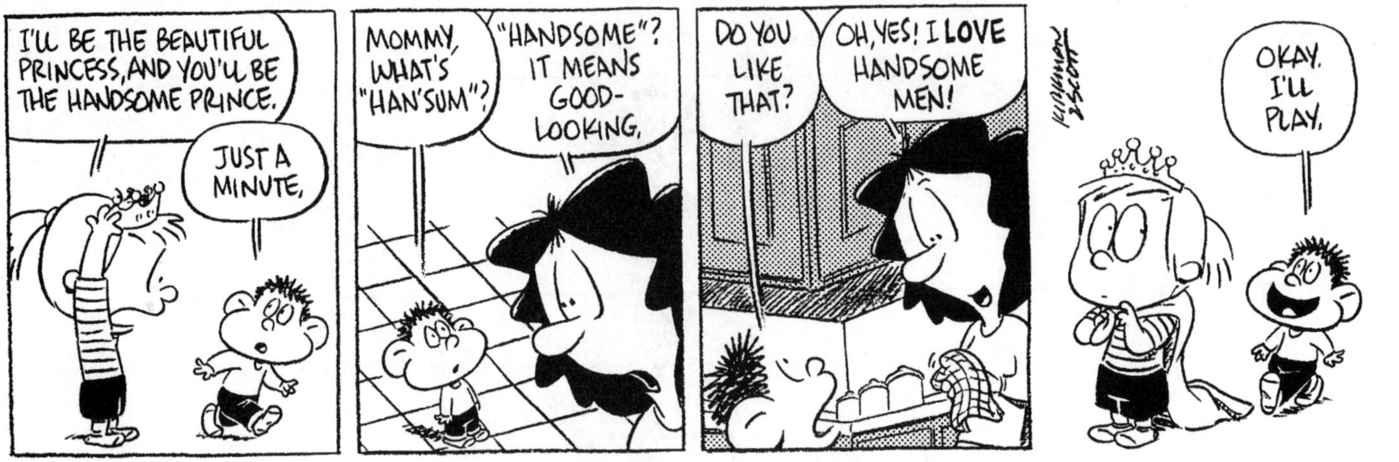
I'LL BE THE BEAUTIFUL PRINCESS, AND YOU'LL BE THE HANDSOME PRINCE.
JUST A MINUTE.
MOMMY, WHAT'S "HAN'SUM"?
"HANDSOME"? IT MEANS GOOD-LOOKING.
DO YOU LIKE THAT?
OH, YES! I LOVE HANDSOME MEN!
KIRKMAN & SCOTT
OKAY. I'LL PLAY.

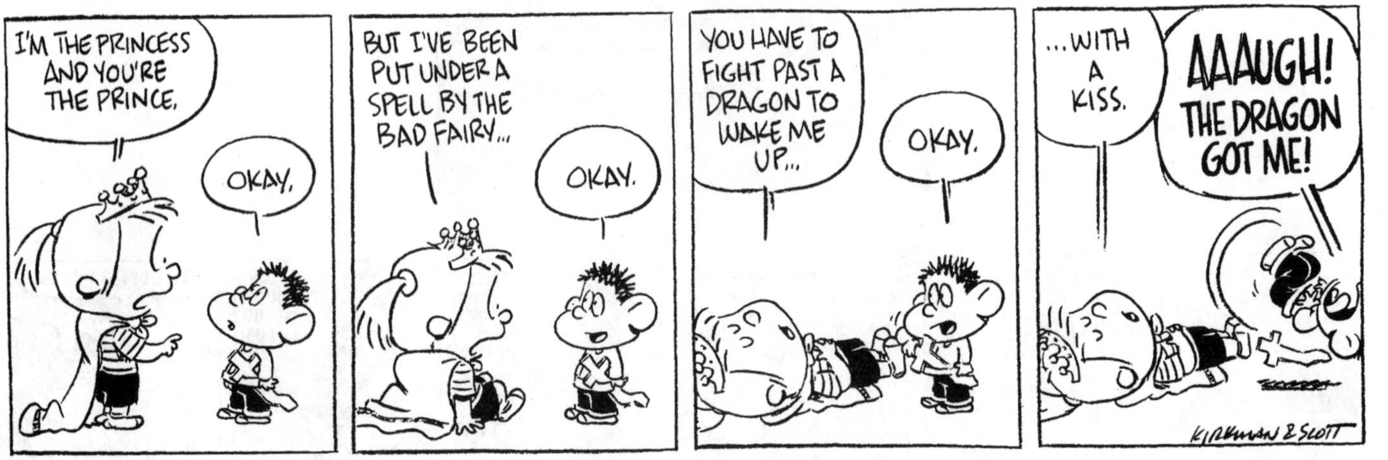
I'M THE PRINCESS AND YOU'RE THE PRINCE.
OKAY.
BUT I'VE BEEN PUT UNDER A SPELL BY THE BAD FAIRY...
OKAY.
YOU HAVE TO FIGHT PAST A DRAGON TO WAKE ME UP...
OKAY.
...WITH A KISS.
AAAUGH! THE DRAGON GOT ME!
KIRKMAN & SCOTT

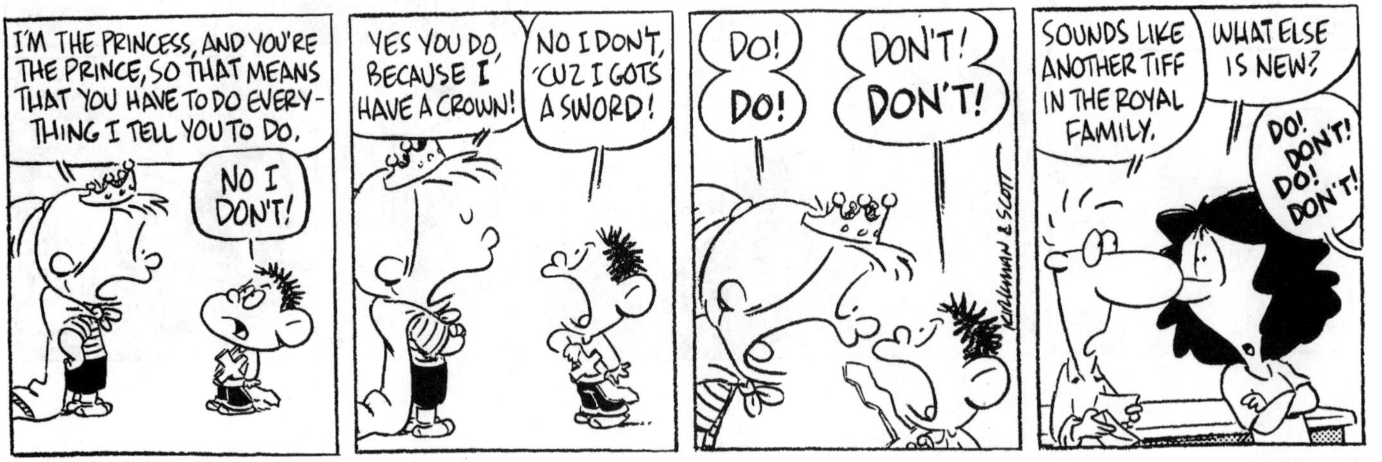
I'M THE PRINCESS, AND YOU'RE THE PRINCE, SO THAT MEANS THAT YOU HAVE TO DO EVERYTHING I TELL YOU TO DO.
NO I DON'T!
YES YOU DO, BECAUSE I HAVE A CROWN!
NO I DON'T, 'CUZ I GOTS A SWORD!
DO! DO!
DON'T! DON'T!
KIRKMAN & SCOTT
SOUNDS LIKE ANOTHER TIFF IN THE ROYAL FAMILY.
WHAT ELSE IS NEW?
DO! DON'T! DO! DON'T!

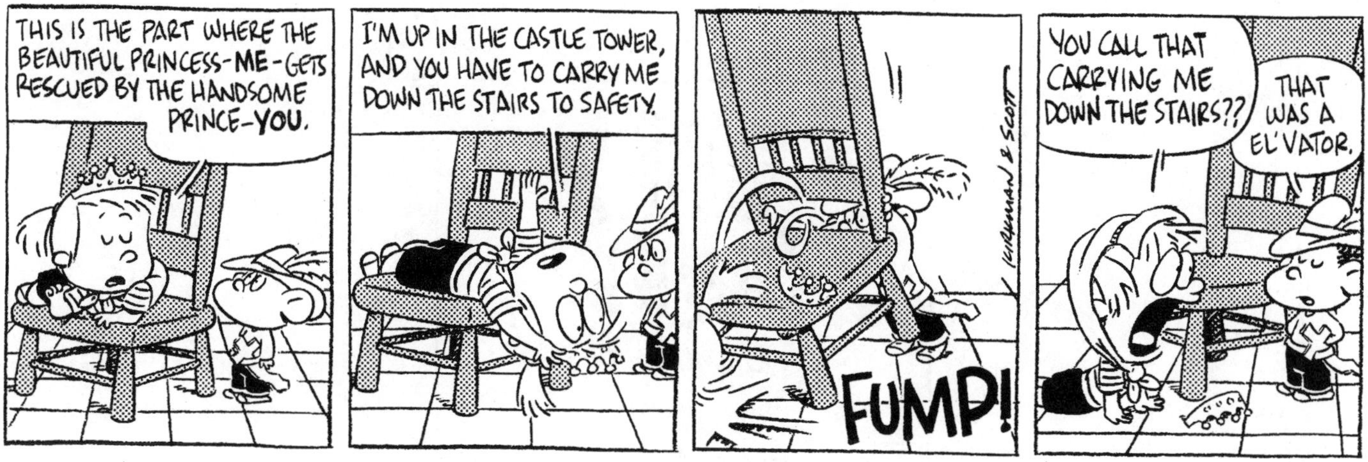
THIS IS THE PART WHERE THE BEAUTIFUL PRINCESS-ME-GETS RESCUED BY THE HANDSOME PRINCE-YOU.
I'M UP IN THE CASTLE TOWER, AND YOU HAVE TO CARRY ME DOWN THE STAIRS TO SAFETY.
FUMP!
KIRKMAN & SCOTT
YOU CALL THAT CARRYING ME DOWN THE STAIRS??
THAT WAS A EL'VATOR.

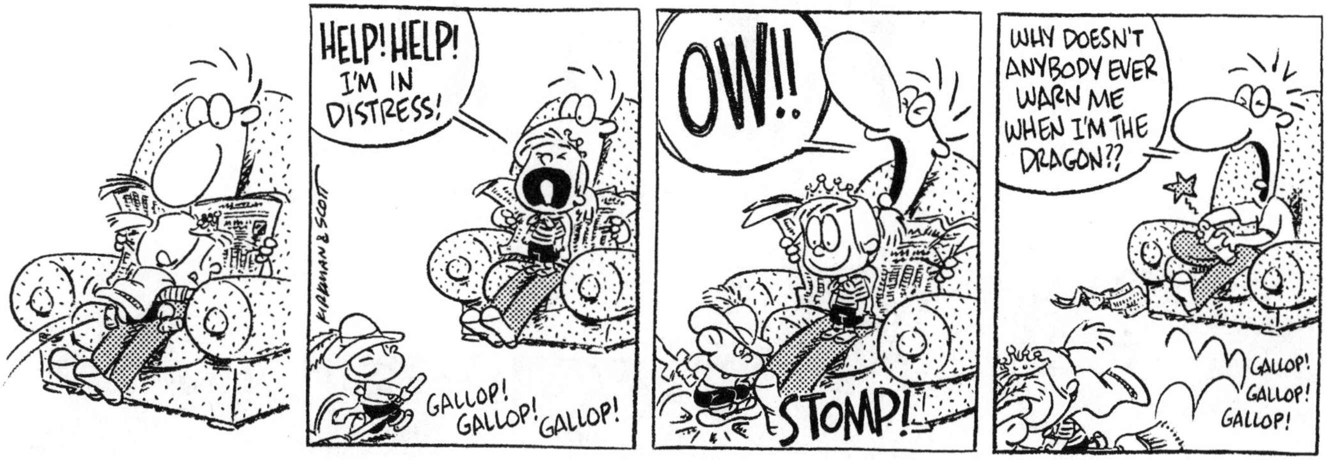
HELP! HELP! I'M IN DISTRESS!
KIRKMAN & SCOTT
GALLOP! GALLOP! GALLOP!
OW!!
STOMP!
WHY DOESN'T ANYBODY EVER WARN ME WHEN I'M THE DRAGON??
GALLOP! GALLOP! GALLOP!

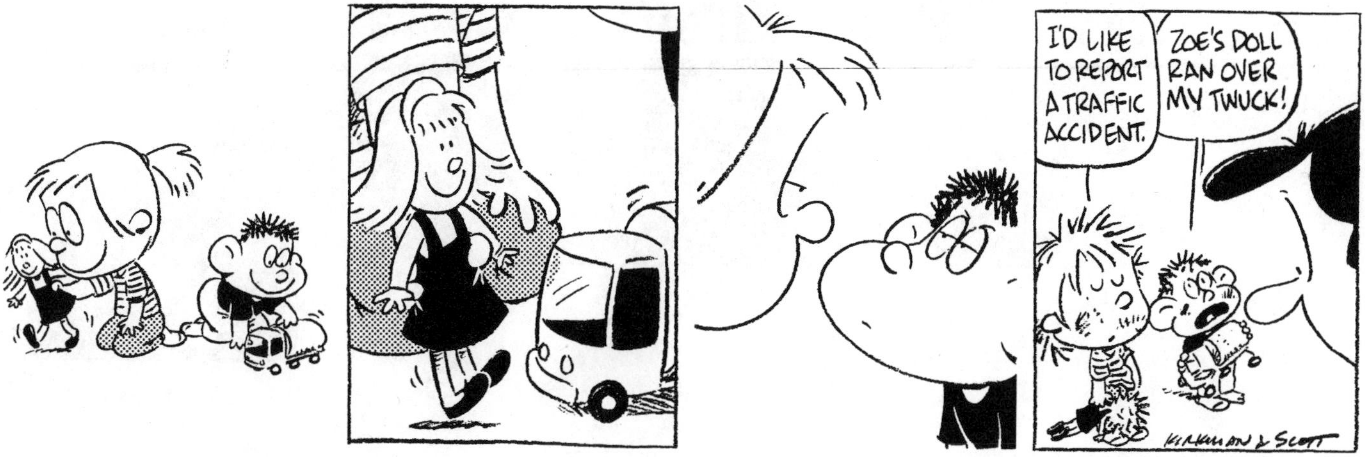
I'D LIKE TO REPORT A TRAFFIC ACCIDENT.
ZOE'S DOLL RAN OVER MY TWUCK!
KIRKMAN & SCOTT

BABY BLUES®
BY RICK KIRKMAN / JERRY SCOTT

DARRYL?
MFGLBM?
WOULD YOU GET ME A DRINK OF WATER?
UH, YEAH. SURE... OKAY.
OW!
OUCH! OOCH!
YEOW!
OW! OW! OW! OW!
OUCH!
OW! OOH!
AAGHK!
NFVH!
MAYBE NEXT TIME I'LL TELL YOU TO GET YOUR OWN WATER.
AND MAYBE NEXT TIME YOU PROMISE TO PICK UP THE KIDS' LEGOS, YOU'LL DO IT.

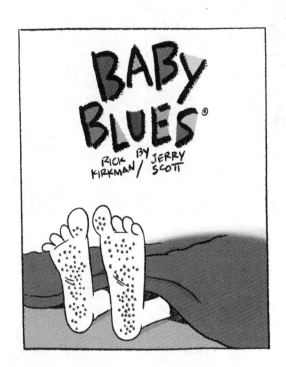

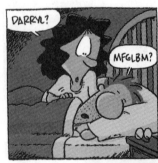

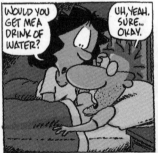

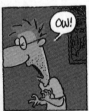

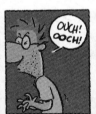

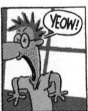

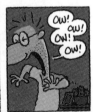

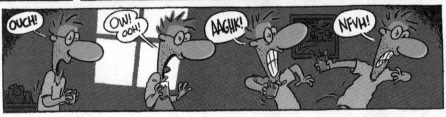

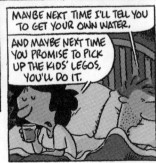

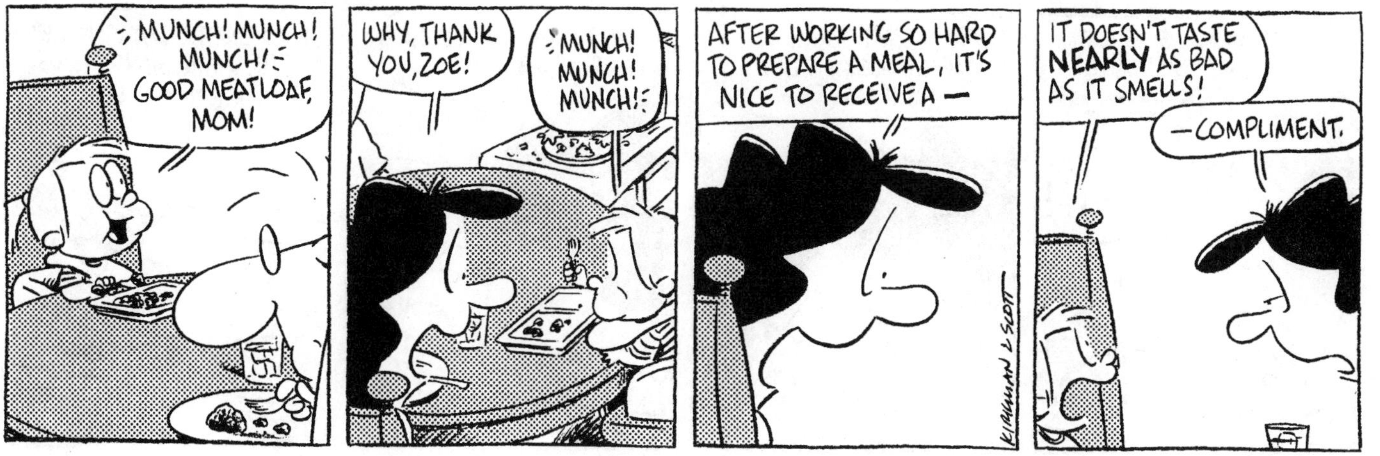
MUNCH! MUNCH! MUNCH! GOOD MEATLOAF, MOM!
WHY, THANK YOU, ZOE!
MUNCH! MUNCH! MUNCH!
AFTER WORKING SO HARD TO PREPARE A MEAL, IT'S NICE TO RECEIVE A —
KIRKMAN & SCOTT
IT DOESN'T TASTE NEARLY AS BAD AS IT SMELLS!
—COMPLIMENT.

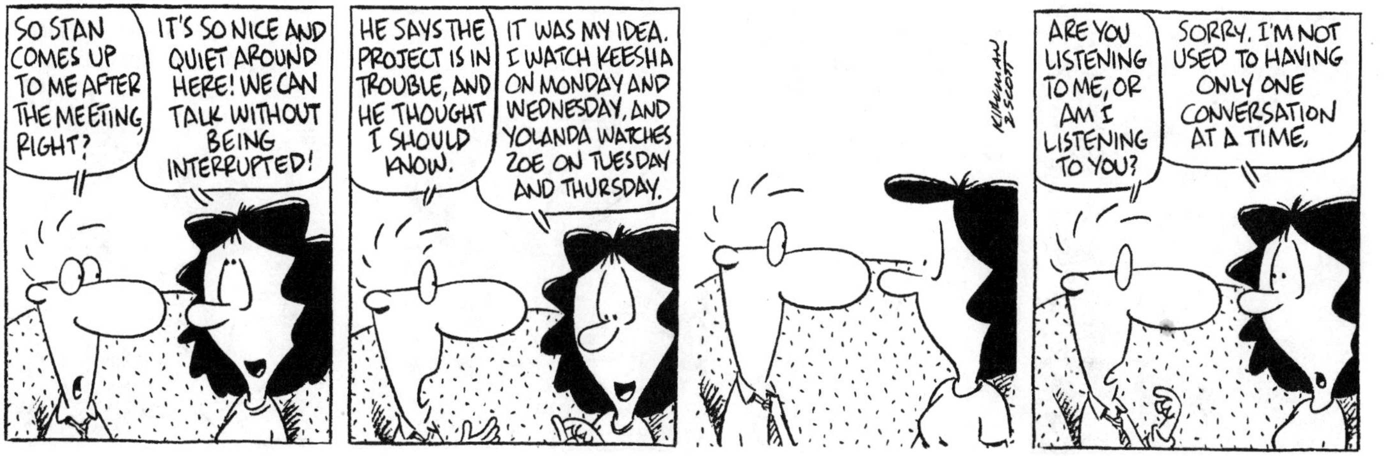
SO STAN COMES UP TO ME AFTER THE MEETING, RIGHT?
IT'S SO NICE AND QUIET AROUND HERE! WE CAN TALK WITHOUT BEING INTERRUPTED!
HE SAYS THE PROJECT IS IN TROUBLE, AND HE THOUGHT I SHOULD KNOW.
IT WAS MY IDEA. I WATCH KEESHA ON MONDAY AND WEDNESDAY, AND YOLANDA WATCHES ZOE ON TUESDAY AND THURSDAY.
KIRKMAN & SCOTT
ARE YOU LISTENING TO ME, OR AM I LISTENING TO YOU?
SORRY. I'M NOT USED TO HAVING ONLY ONE CONVERSATION AT A TIME.

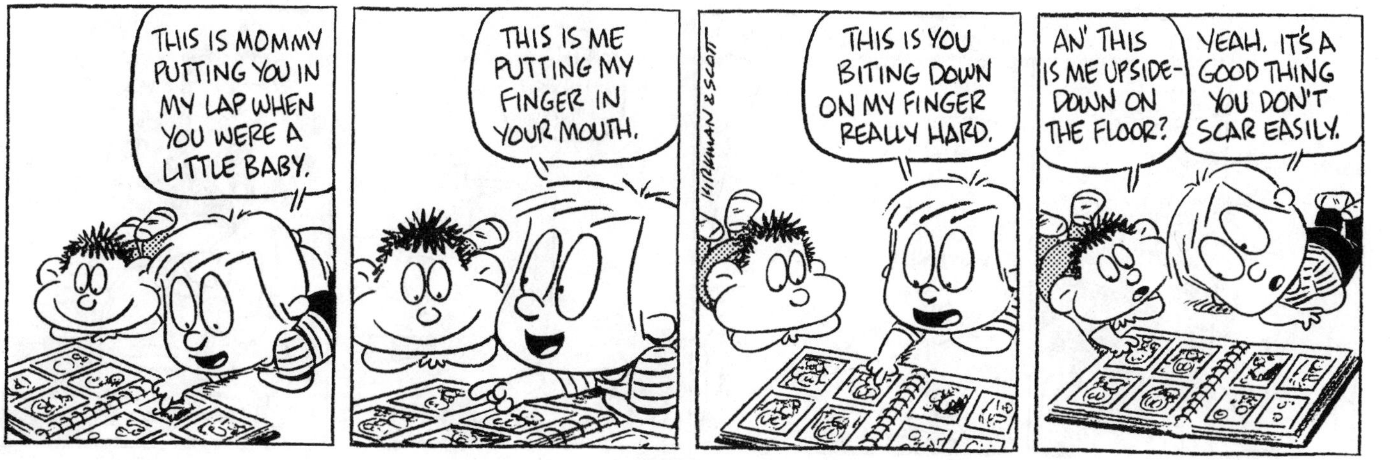
THIS IS MOMMY PUTTING YOU IN MY LAP WHEN YOU WERE A LITTLE BABY.
THIS IS ME PUTTING MY FINGER IN YOUR MOUTH.
KIRKMAN & SCOTT
THIS IS YOU BITING DOWN ON MY FINGER REALLY HARD.
AN' THIS IS ME UPSIDE-DOWN ON THE FLOOR?
YEAH. IT'S A GOOD THING YOU DON'T SCAR EASILY.

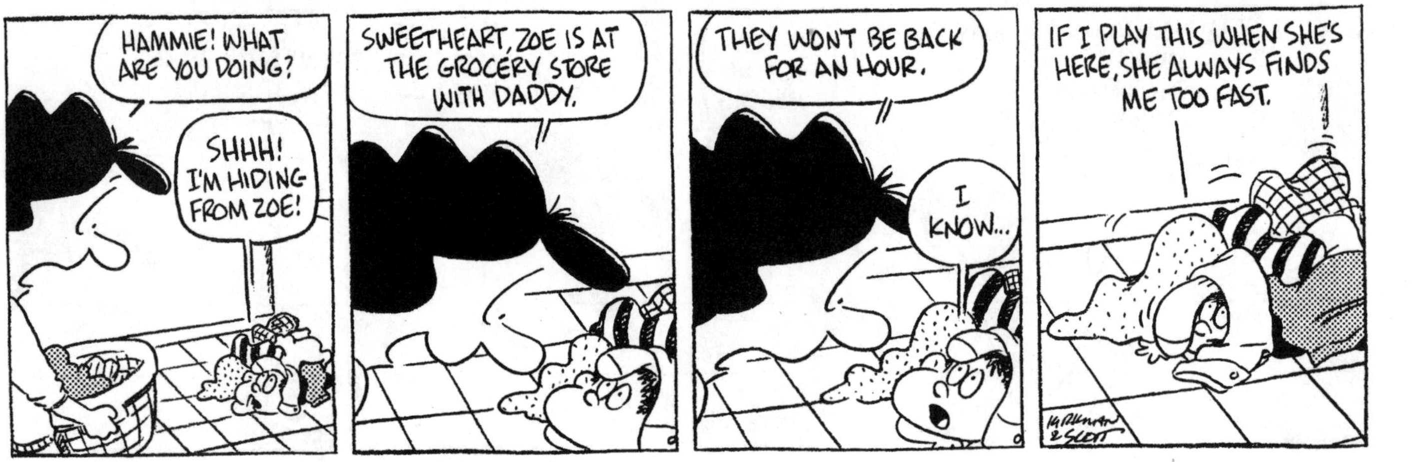
HAMMIE! WHAT ARE YOU DOING?
SHHH! I'M HIDING FROM ZOE!
SWEETHEART, ZOE IS AT THE GROCERY STORE WITH DADDY.
THEY WON'T BE BACK FOR AN HOUR.
I KNOW...
IF I PLAY THIS WHEN SHE'S HERE, SHE ALWAYS FINDS ME TOO FAST.

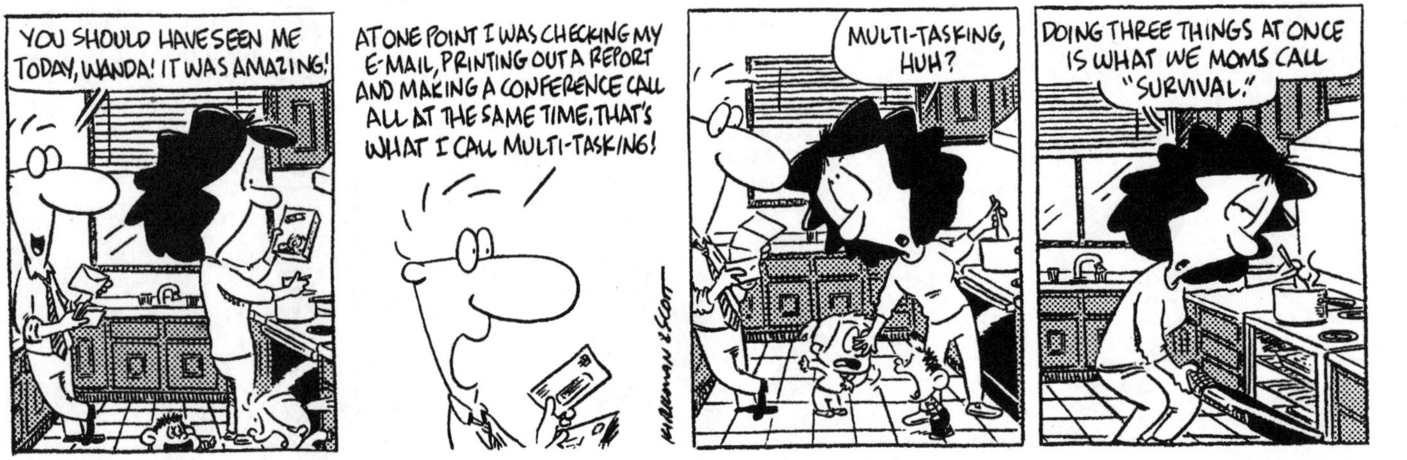
YOU SHOULD HAVE SEEN ME TODAY, WANDA! IT WAS AMAZING!
AT ONE POINT I WAS CHECKING MY E-MAIL, PRINTING OUT A REPORT AND MAKING A CONFERENCE CALL ALL AT THE SAME TIME. THAT'S WHAT I CALL MULTI-TASKING!
MULTI-TASKING, HUH?
DOING THREE THINGS AT ONCE IS WHAT WE MOMS CALL "SURVIVAL."

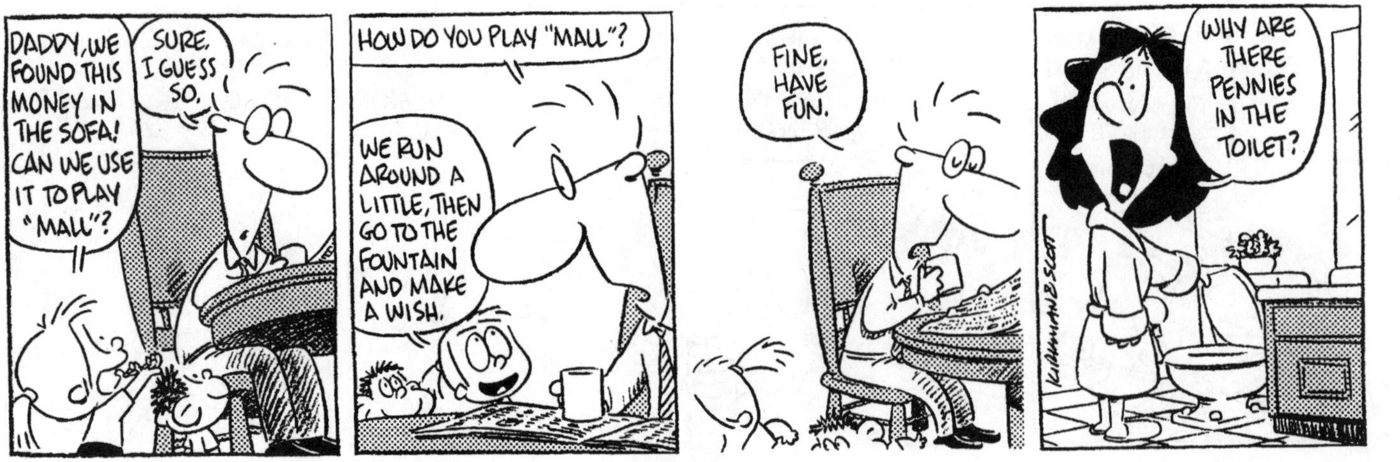
DADDY, WE FOUND THIS MONEY IN THE SOFA! CAN WE USE IT TO PLAY "MALL"?
SURE. I GUESS SO.
HOW DO YOU PLAY "MALL"?
WE RUN AROUND A LITTLE, THEN GO TO THE FOUNTAIN AND MAKE A WISH.
FINE. HAVE FUN.
WHY ARE THERE PENNIES IN THE TOILET?

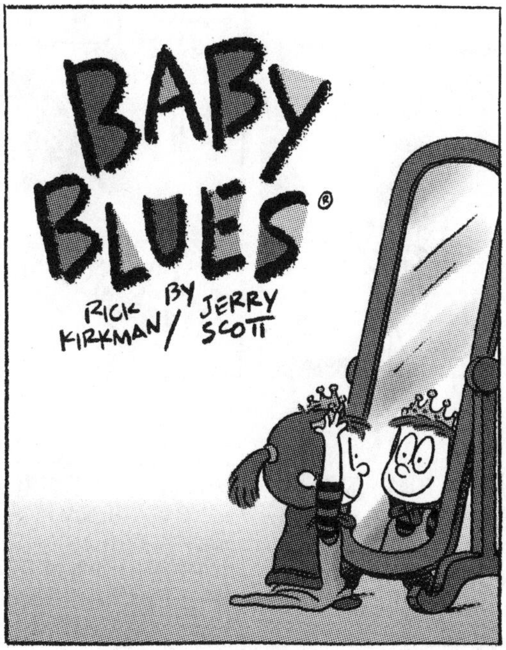
BABY BLUES®
BY RICK KIRKMAN / JERRY SCOTT

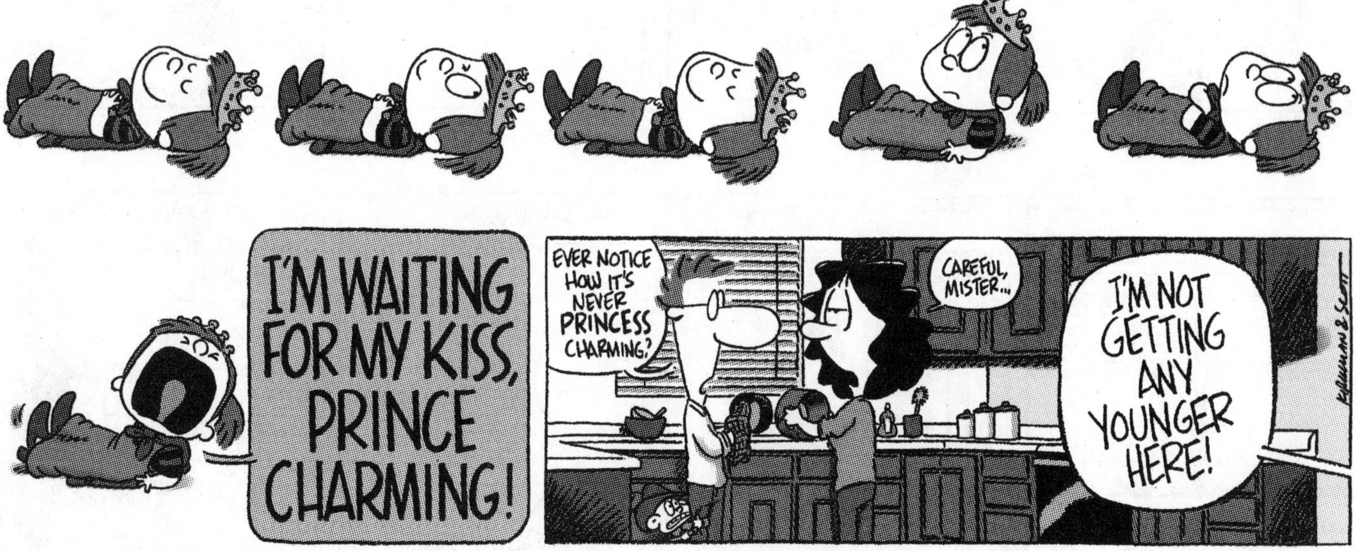
I'M WAITING FOR MY KISS, PRINCE CHARMING!
EVER NOTICE HOW IT'S NEVER PRINCESS CHARMING?
CAREFUL, MISTER...
I'M NOT GETTING ANY YOUNGER HERE!

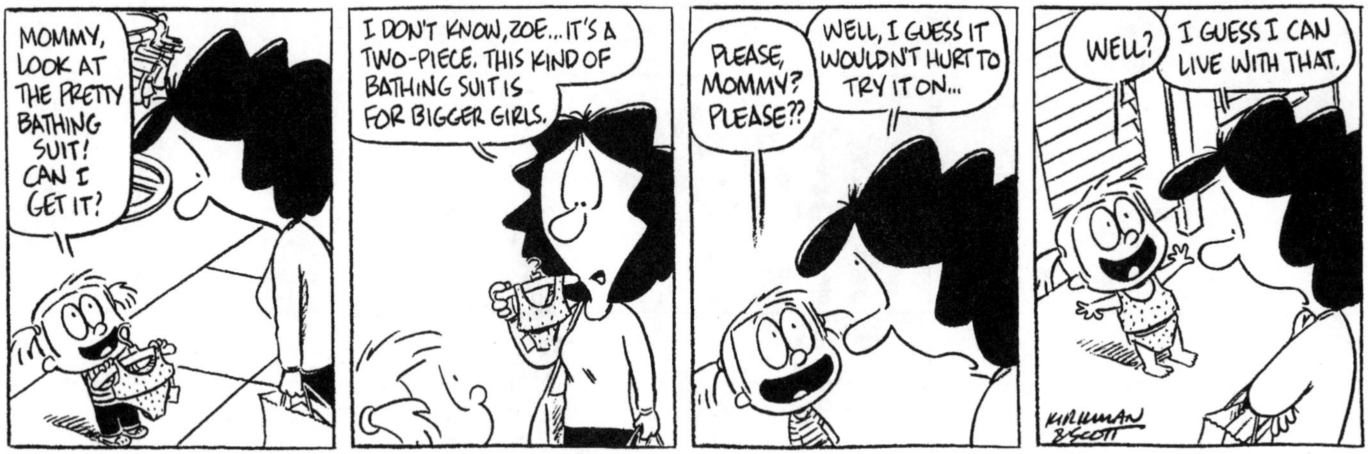
MOMMY, LOOK AT THE PRETTY BATHING SUIT! CAN I GET IT?
I DON'T KNOW, ZOE... IT'S A TWO-PIECE. THIS KIND OF BATHING SUIT IS FOR BIGGER GIRLS.
PLEASE, MOMMY? PLEASE??
WELL, I GUESS IT WOULDN'T HURT TO TRY IT ON...
WELL?
I GUESS I CAN LIVE WITH THAT.
KIRKMAN & SCOTT

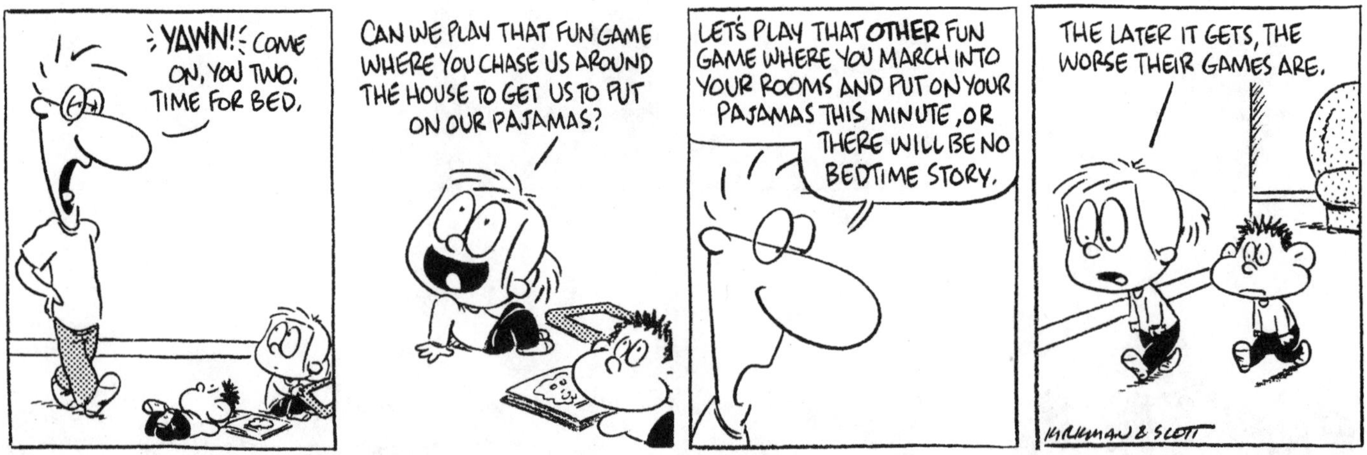
YAWN! COME ON, YOU TWO. TIME FOR BED.
CAN WE PLAY THAT FUN GAME WHERE YOU CHASE US AROUND THE HOUSE TO GET US TO PUT ON OUR PAJAMAS?
LET'S PLAY THAT OTHER FUN GAME WHERE YOU MARCH INTO YOUR ROOMS AND PUT ON YOUR PAJAMAS THIS MINUTE, OR THERE WILL BE NO BEDTIME STORY.
THE LATER IT GETS, THE WORSE THEIR GAMES ARE.
KIRKMAN & SCOTT

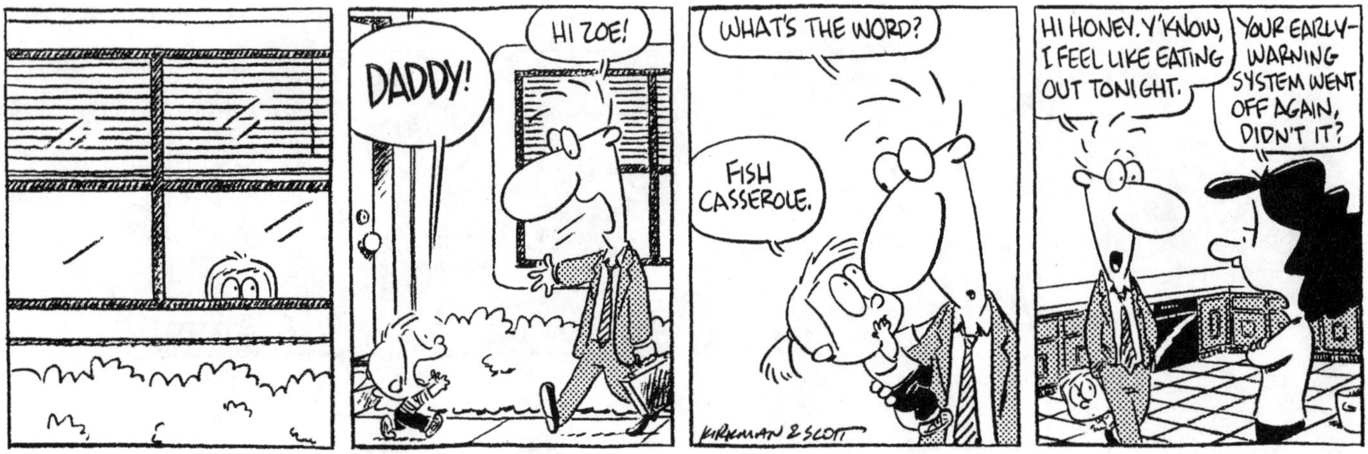
DADDY!
HI ZOE!
WHAT'S THE WORD?
FISH CASSEROLE.
KIRKMAN & SCOTT
HI HONEY. Y'KNOW, I FEEL LIKE EATING OUT TONIGHT.
YOUR EARLY-WARNING SYSTEM WENT OFF AGAIN, DIDN'T IT?

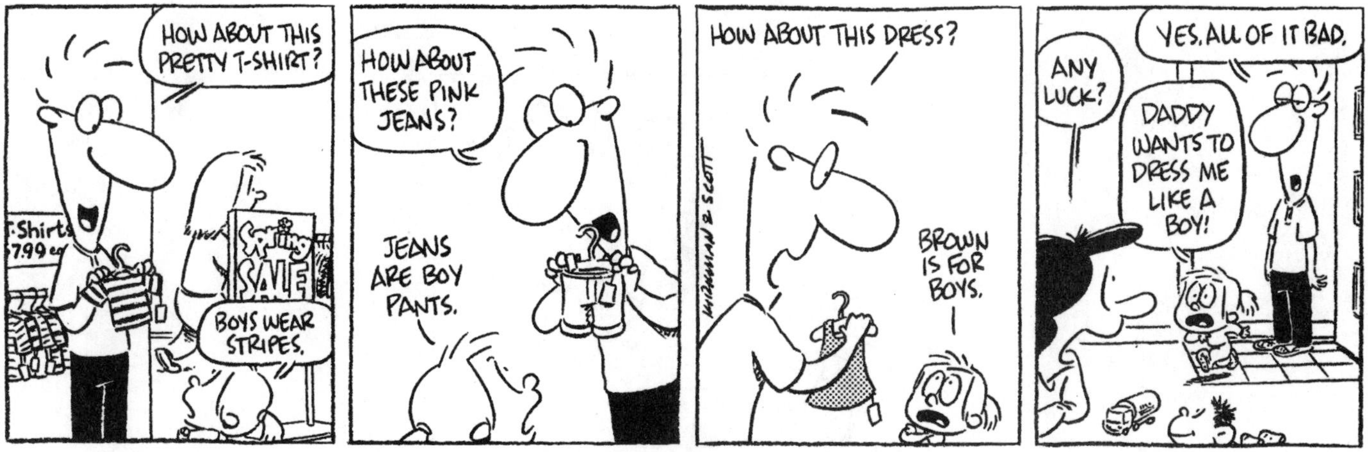
HOW ABOUT THIS PRETTY T-SHIRT?
Spring SALE
BOYS WEAR STRIPES.
HOW ABOUT THESE PINK JEANS?
JEANS ARE BOY PANTS.
HOW ABOUT THIS DRESS?
BROWN IS FOR BOYS.
KIRKMAN & SCOTT
ANY LUCK?
YES. ALL OF IT BAD.
DADDY WANTS TO DRESS ME LIKE A BOY!

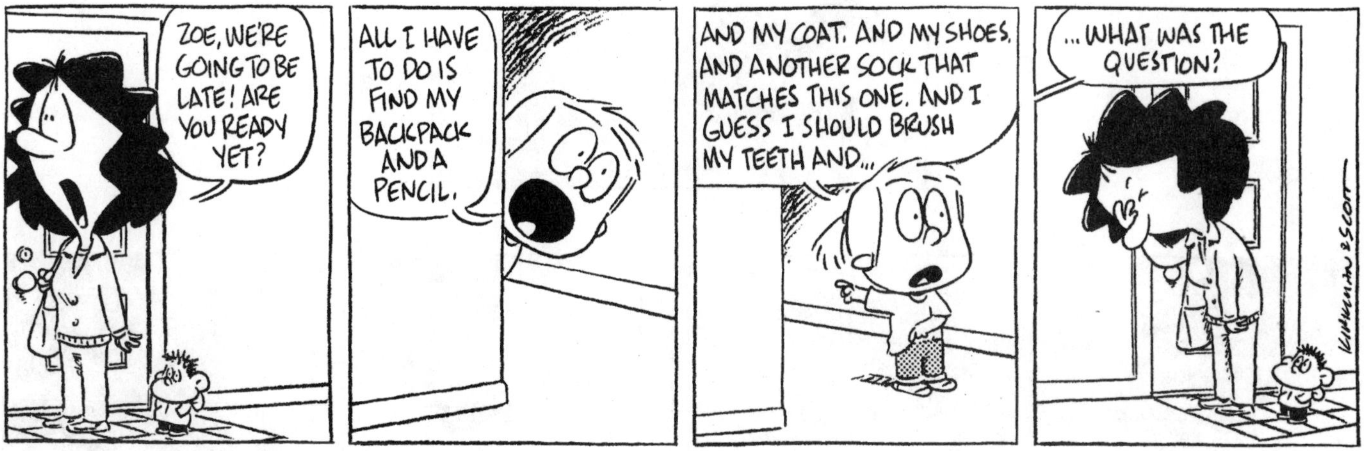
ZOE, WE'RE GOING TO BE LATE! ARE YOU READY YET?
ALL I HAVE TO DO IS FIND MY BACKPACK AND A PENCIL.
AND MY COAT. AND MY SHOES. AND ANOTHER SOCK THAT MATCHES THIS ONE. AND I GUESS I SHOULD BRUSH MY TEETH AND...
...WHAT WAS THE QUESTION?
KIRKMAN & SCOTT

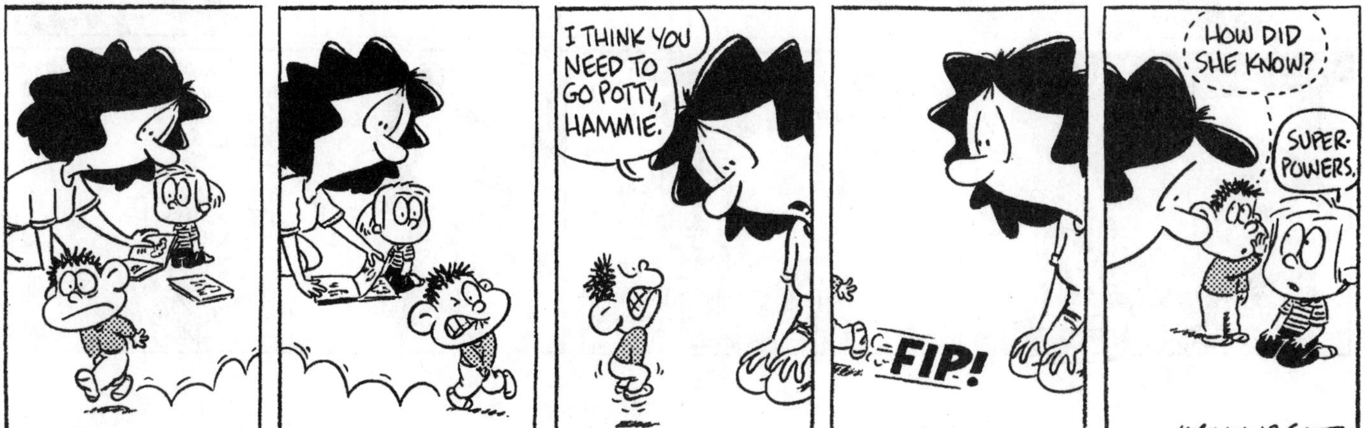
I THINK YOU NEED TO GO POTTY, HAMMIE.
FIP!
HOW DID SHE KNOW?
SUPER-POWERS.
KIRKMAN & SCOTT

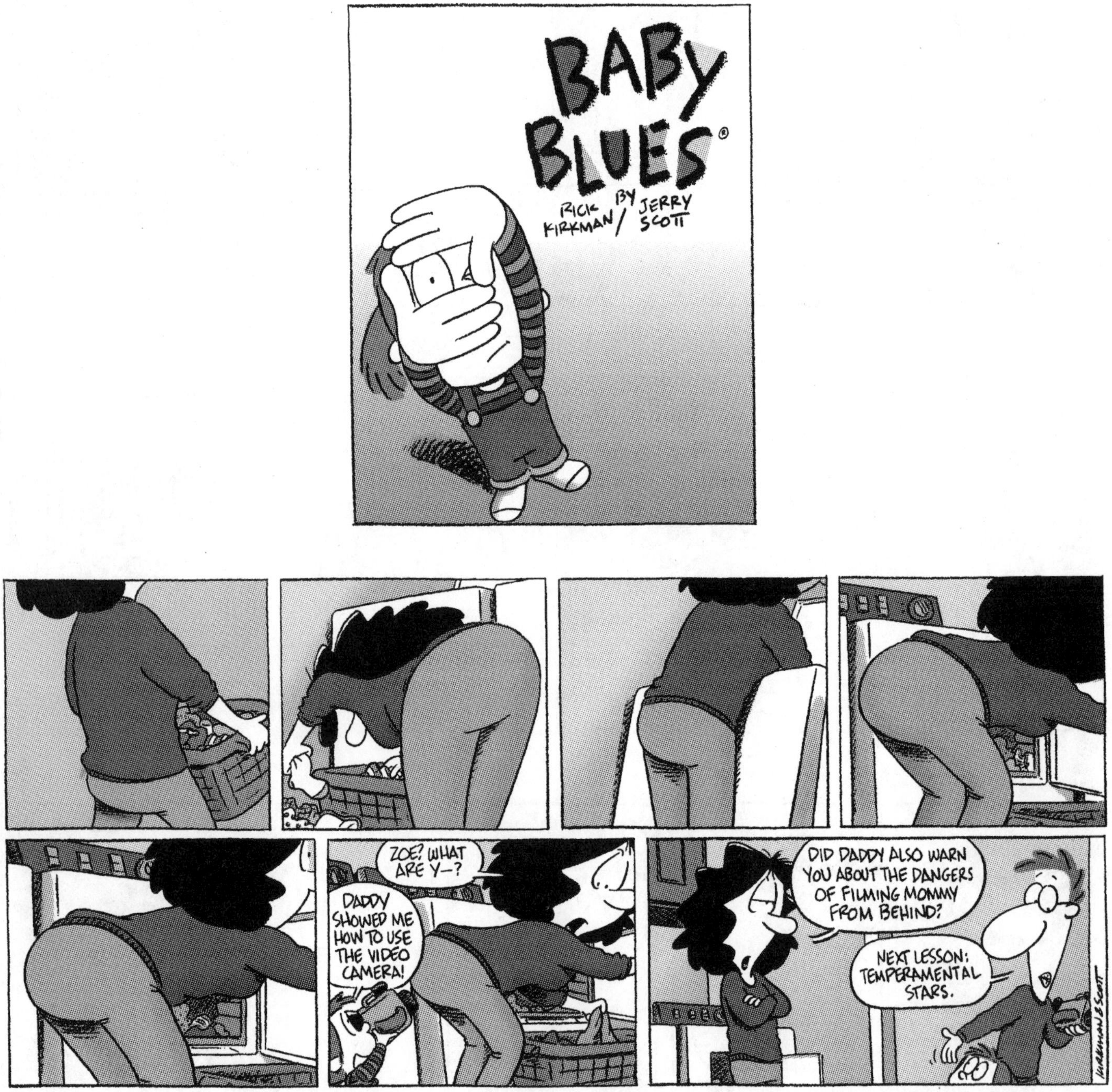
BABY BLUES®
BY RICK KIRKMAN / JERRY SCOTT
ZOE? WHAT ARE Y–?
DADDY SHOWED ME HOW TO USE THE VIDEO CAMERA!
DID DADDY ALSO WARN YOU ABOUT THE DANGERS OF FILMING MOMMY FROM BEHIND?
NEXT LESSON: TEMPERAMENTAL STARS.

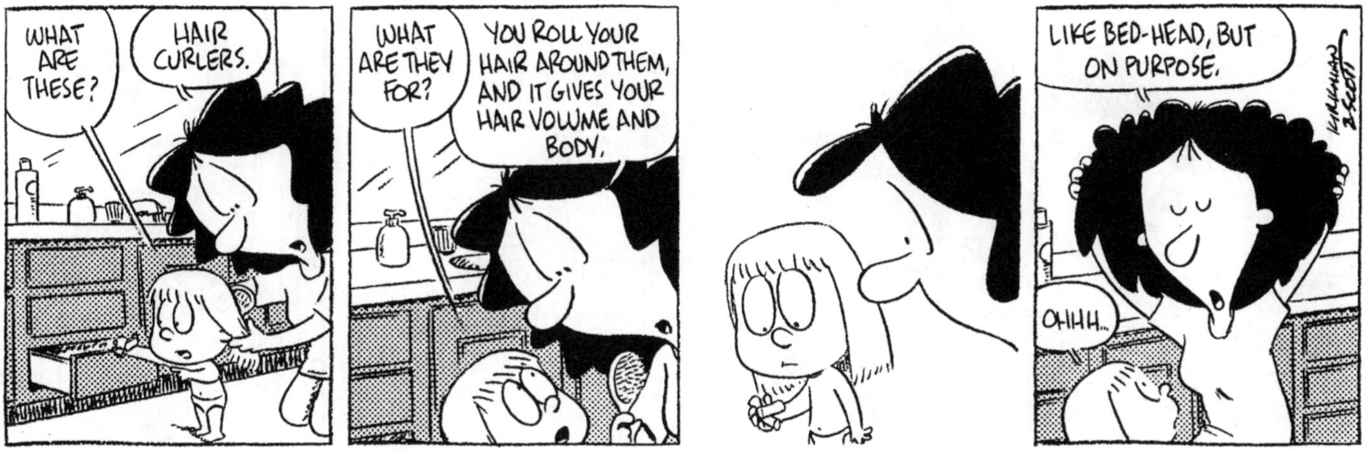
WHAT ARE THESE?
HAIR CURLERS.
WHAT ARE THEY FOR?
YOU ROLL YOUR HAIR AROUND THEM, AND IT GIVES YOUR HAIR VOLUME AND BODY.
LIKE BED-HEAD, BUT ON PURPOSE.
OHHH...

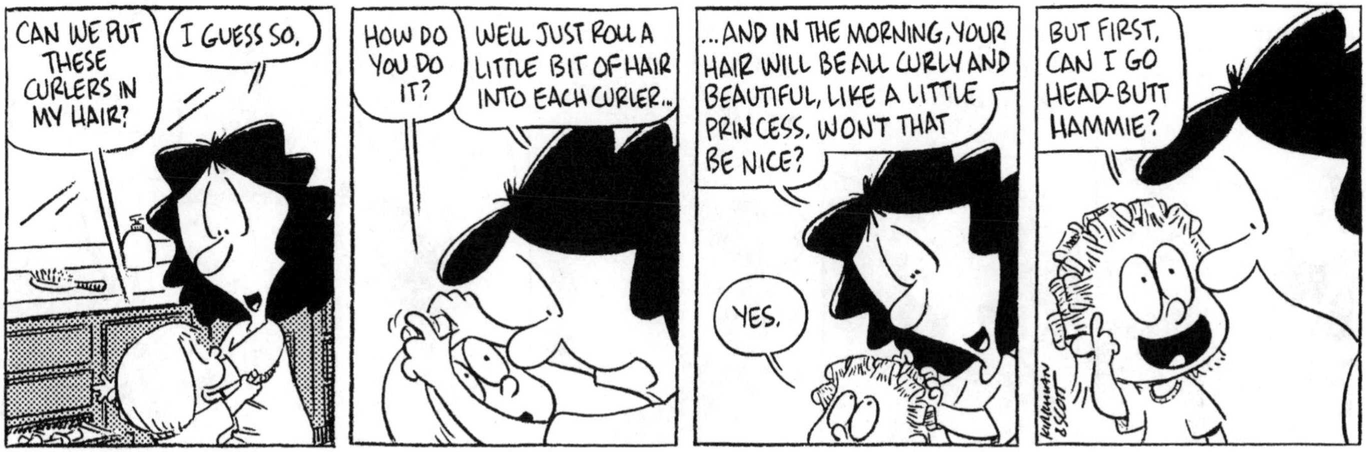
CAN WE PUT THESE CURLERS IN MY HAIR?
I GUESS SO.
HOW DO YOU DO IT?
WE'LL JUST ROLL A LITTLE BIT OF HAIR INTO EACH CURLER...
...AND IN THE MORNING, YOUR HAIR WILL BE ALL CURLY AND BEAUTIFUL, LIKE A LITTLE PRINCESS. WON'T THAT BE NICE?
YES.
BUT FIRST, CAN I GO HEAD-BUTT HAMMIE?

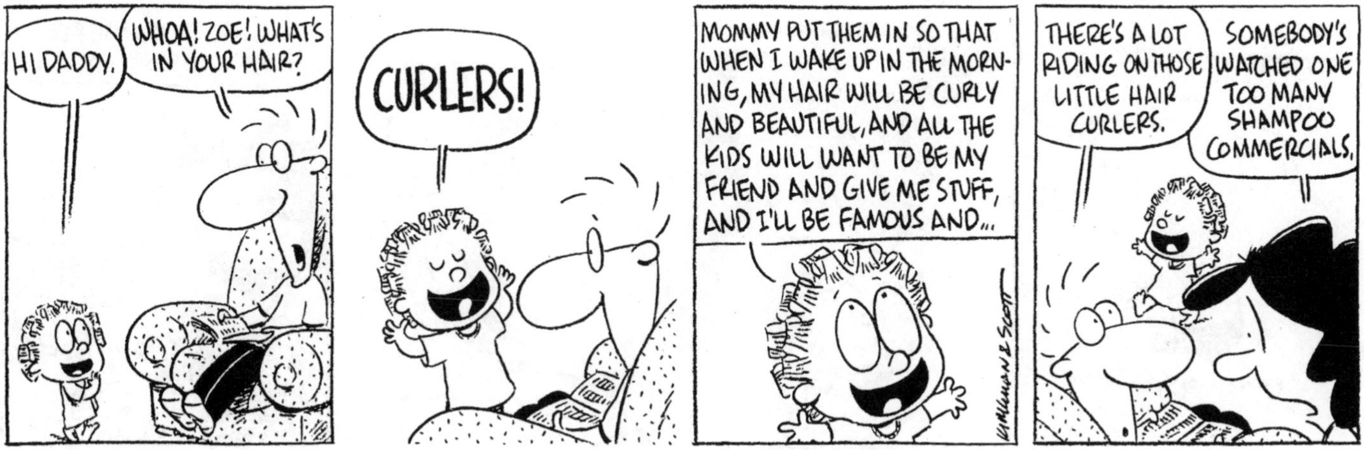
HI DADDY.
WHOA! ZOE! WHAT'S IN YOUR HAIR?
CURLERS!
MOMMY PUT THEM IN SO THAT WHEN I WAKE UP IN THE MORNING, MY HAIR WILL BE CURLY AND BEAUTIFUL, AND ALL THE KIDS WILL WANT TO BE MY FRIEND AND GIVE ME STUFF, AND I'LL BE FAMOUS AND...
THERE'S A LOT RIDING ON THOSE LITTLE HAIR CURLERS.
SOMEBODY'S WATCHED ONE TOO MANY SHAMPOO COMMERCIALS.

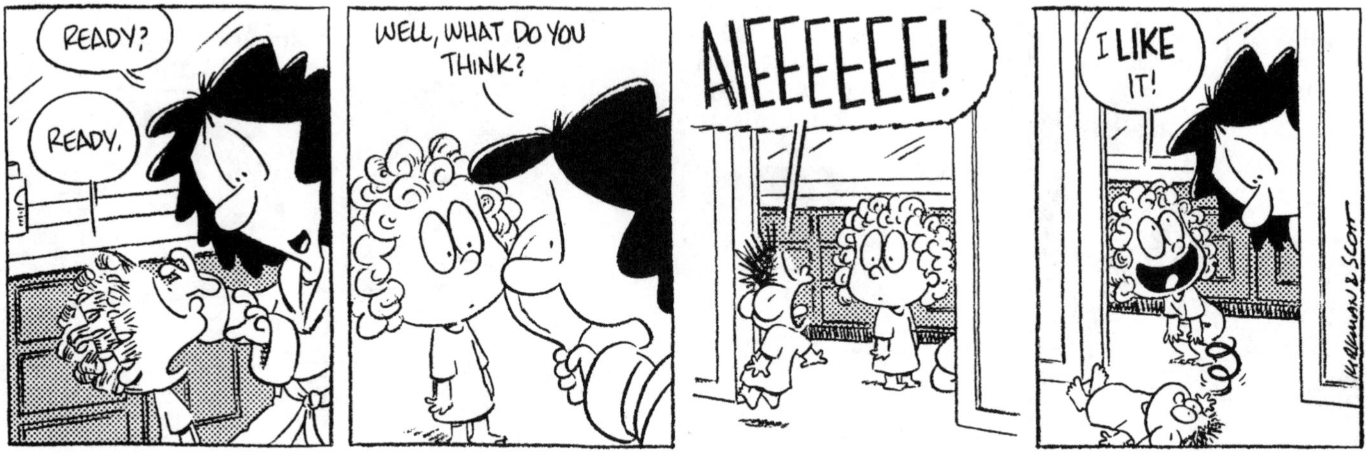
READY?
READY.
WELL, WHAT DO YOU THINK?
AIEEEEEE!
I LIKE IT!
KIRKMAN & SCOTT

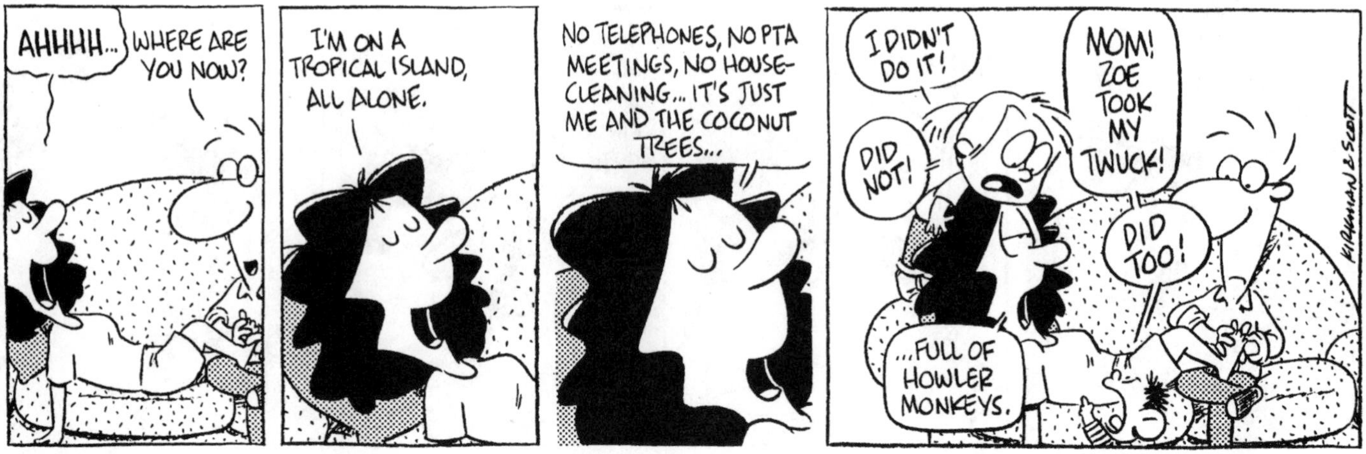
AHHHH...
WHERE ARE YOU NOW?
I'M ON A TROPICAL ISLAND, ALL ALONE.
NO TELEPHONES, NO PTA MEETINGS, NO HOUSE-CLEANING... IT'S JUST ME AND THE COCONUT TREES...
I DIDN'T DO IT!
MOM! ZOE TOOK MY TWUCK!
DID NOT!
DID TOO!
...FULL OF HOWLER MONKEYS.
KIRKMAN & SCOTT

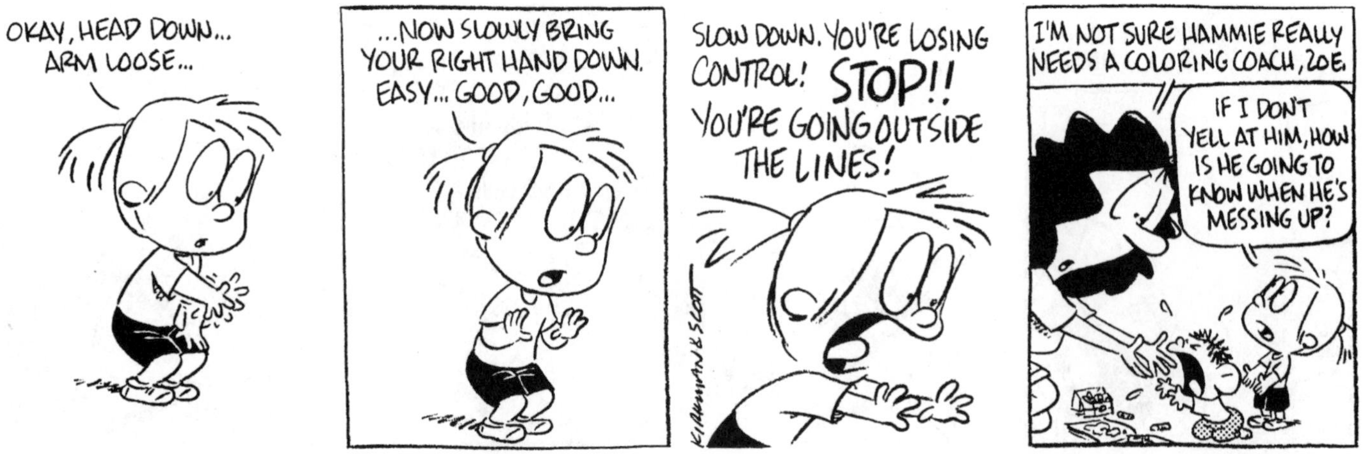
OKAY, HEAD DOWN... ARM LOOSE...
...NOW SLOWLY BRING YOUR RIGHT HAND DOWN. EASY... GOOD, GOOD...
SLOW DOWN. YOU'RE LOSING CONTROL! STOP!! YOU'RE GOING OUTSIDE THE LINES!
KIRKMAN & SCOTT
I'M NOT SURE HAMMIE REALLY NEEDS A COLORING COACH, ZOE.
IF I DON'T YELL AT HIM, HOW IS HE GOING TO KNOW WHEN HE'S MESSING UP?

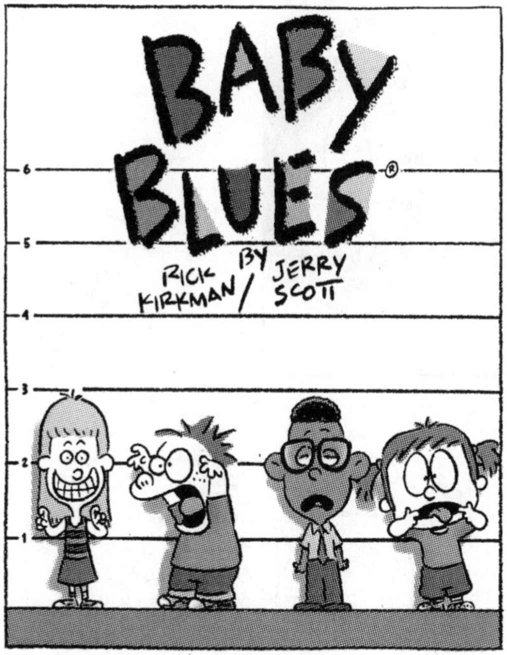
BABY BLUES®
BY
RICK KIRKMAN / JERRY SCOTT

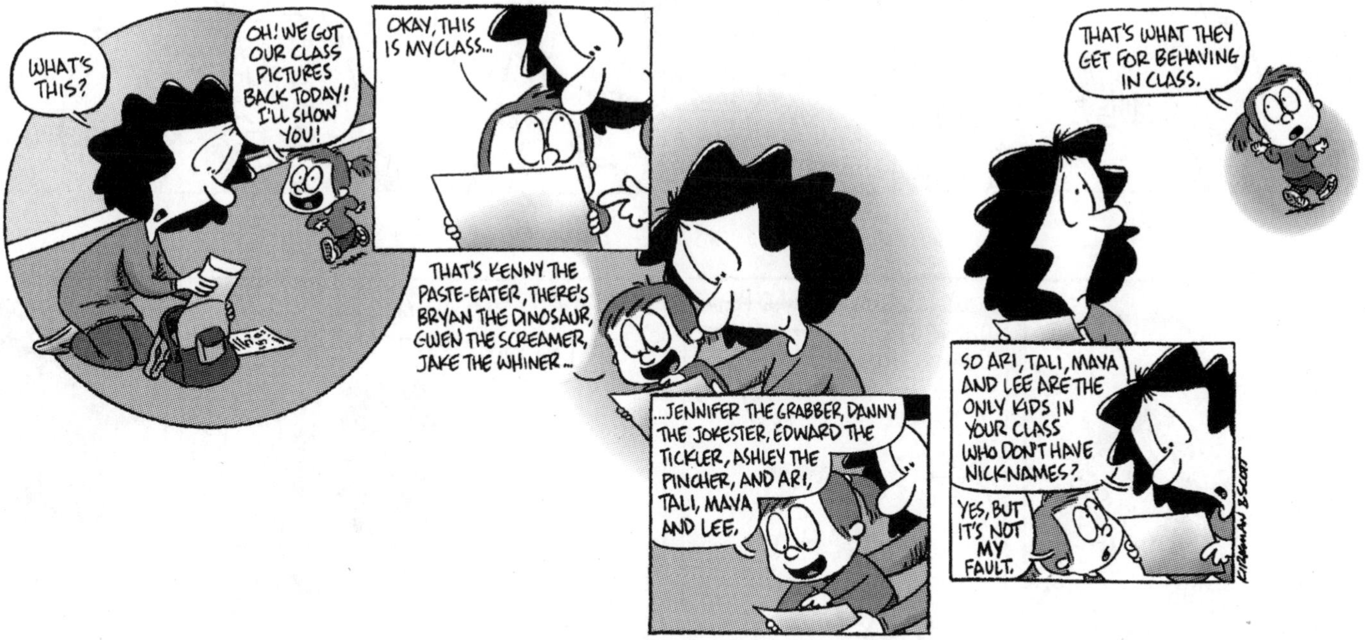
WHAT'S THIS?
OH! WE GOT OUR CLASS PICTURES BACK TODAY! I'LL SHOW YOU!
OKAY, THIS IS MY CLASS...
THAT'S KENNY THE PASTE-EATER, THERE'S BRYAN THE DINOSAUR, GWEN THE SCREAMER, JAKE THE WHINER...
...JENNIFER THE GRABBER, DANNY THE JOKESTER, EDWARD THE TICKLER, ASHLEY THE PINCHER, AND ARI, TALI, MAYA AND LEE.
SO ARI, TALI, MAYA AND LEE ARE THE ONLY KIDS IN YOUR CLASS WHO DON'T HAVE NICKNAMES?
YES, BUT IT'S NOT MY FAULT.
THAT'S WHAT THEY GET FOR BEHAVING IN CLASS.
KIRKMAN & SCOTT

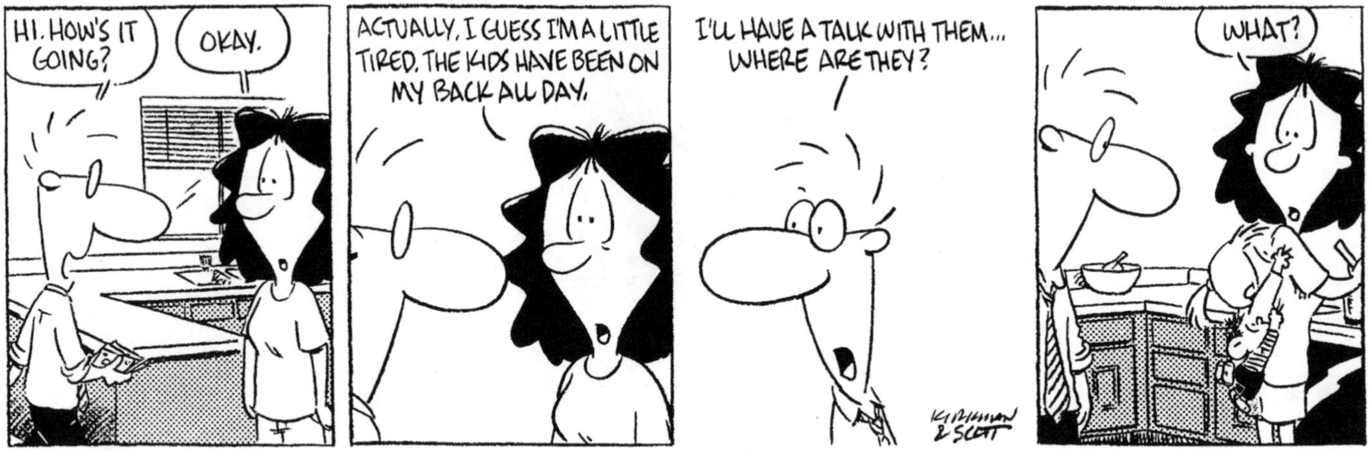
HI. HOW'S IT GOING?
OKAY.
ACTUALLY, I GUESS I'M A LITTLE TIRED. THE KIDS HAVE BEEN ON MY BACK ALL DAY.
I'LL HAVE A TALK WITH THEM... WHERE ARE THEY?
KIRKMAN & SCOTT
WHAT?

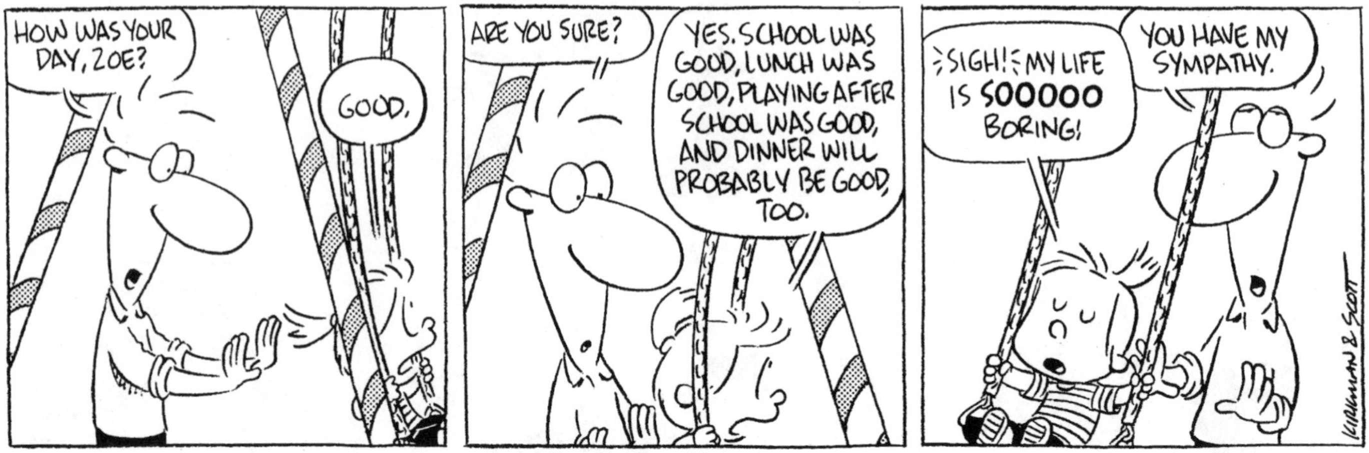
HOW WAS YOUR DAY, ZOE?
GOOD.
ARE YOU SURE?
YES. SCHOOL WAS GOOD, LUNCH WAS GOOD, PLAYING AFTER SCHOOL WAS GOOD, AND DINNER WILL PROBABLY BE GOOD, TOO.
SIGH! MY LIFE IS SOOOOO BORING!
YOU HAVE MY SYMPATHY.
KIRKMAN & SCOTT

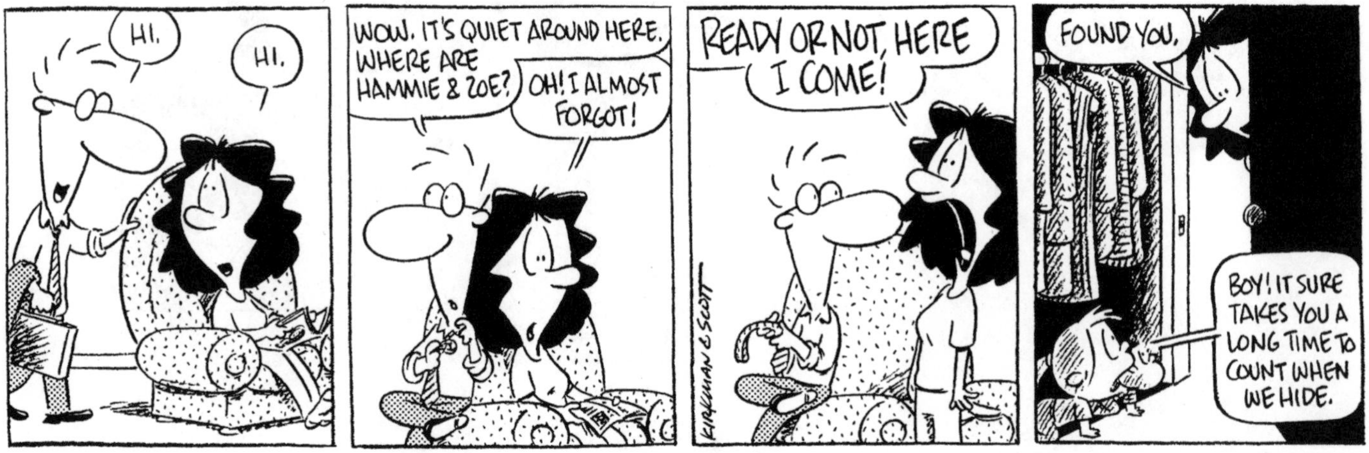
HI.
HI.
WOW. IT'S QUIET AROUND HERE. WHERE ARE HAMMIE & ZOE?
OH! I ALMOST FORGOT!
KIRKMAN & SCOTT
READY OR NOT, HERE I COME!
FOUND YOU.
BOY! IT SURE TAKES YOU A LONG TIME TO COUNT WHEN WE HIDE.

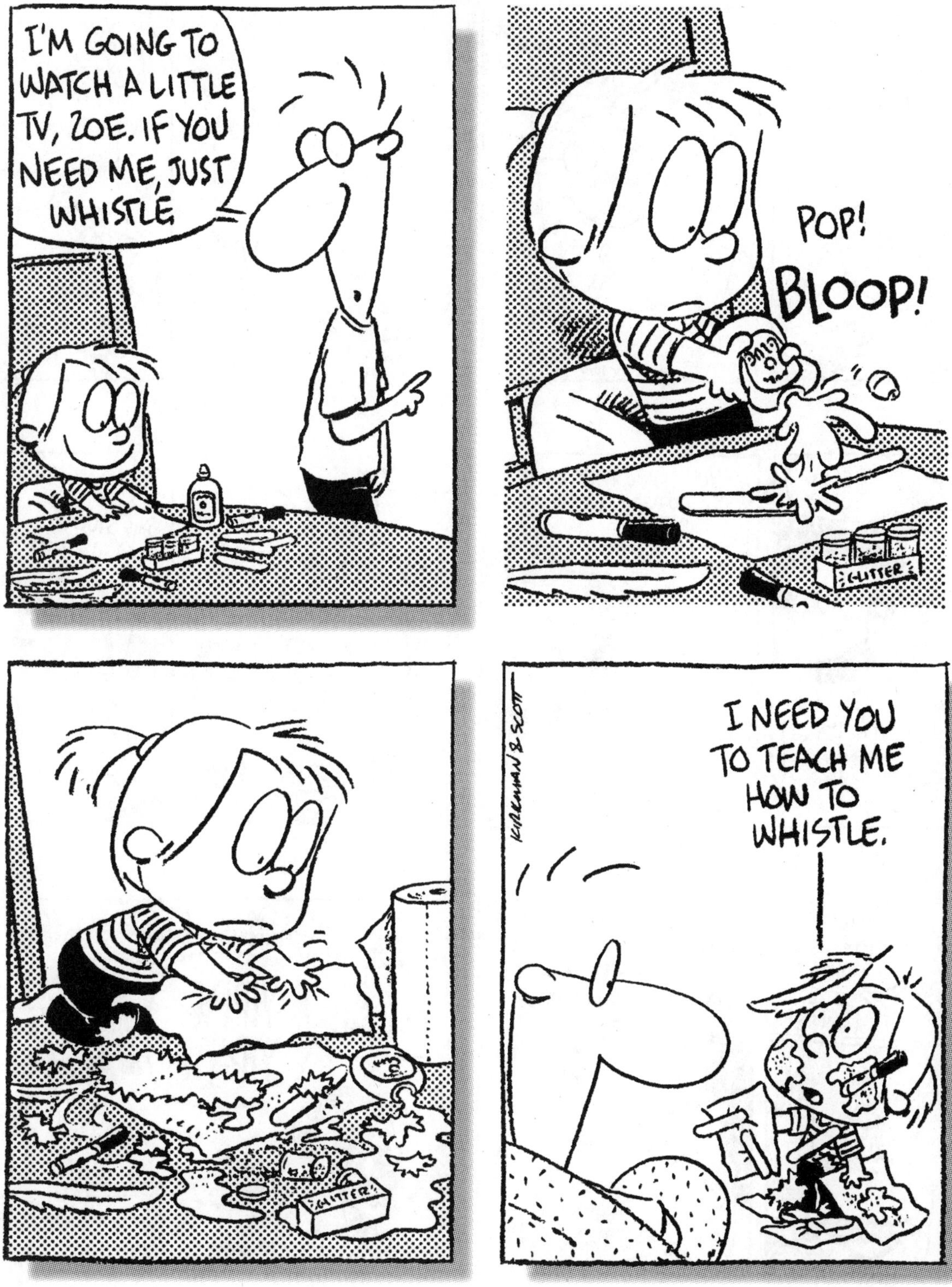
I'M GOING TO WATCH A LITTLE TV, ZOE. IF YOU NEED ME, JUST WHISTLE.
POP!
BLOOP!
GLITTER
GLITTER
KIRKMAN & SCOTT
I NEED YOU TO TEACH ME HOW TO WHISTLE.

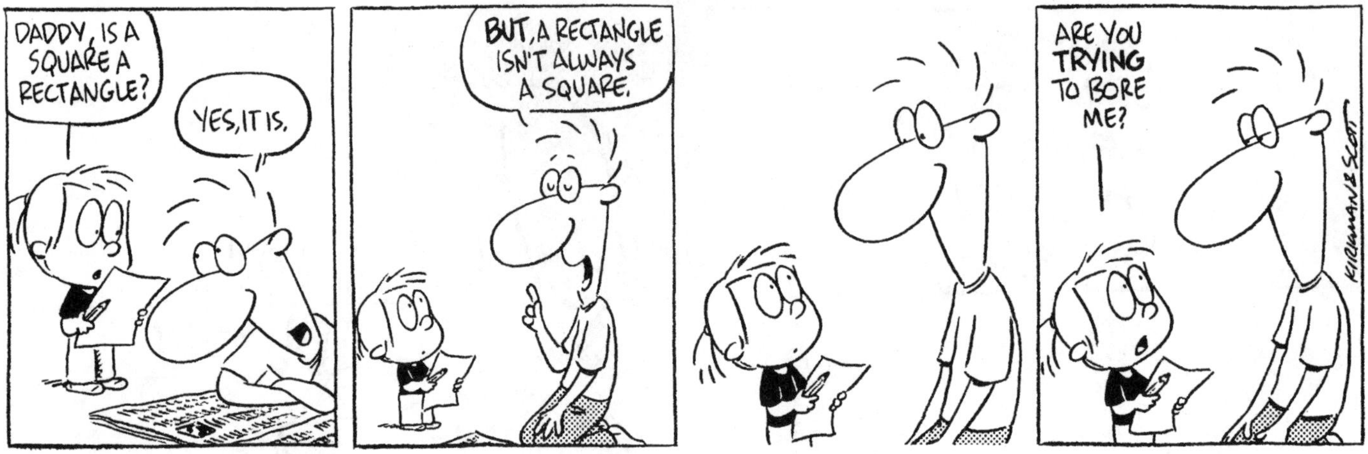
DADDY, IS A SQUARE A RECTANGLE?
YES, IT IS.
BUT, A RECTANGLE ISN'T ALWAYS A SQUARE.
ARE YOU TRYING TO BORE ME?
KIRKMAN & SCOTT

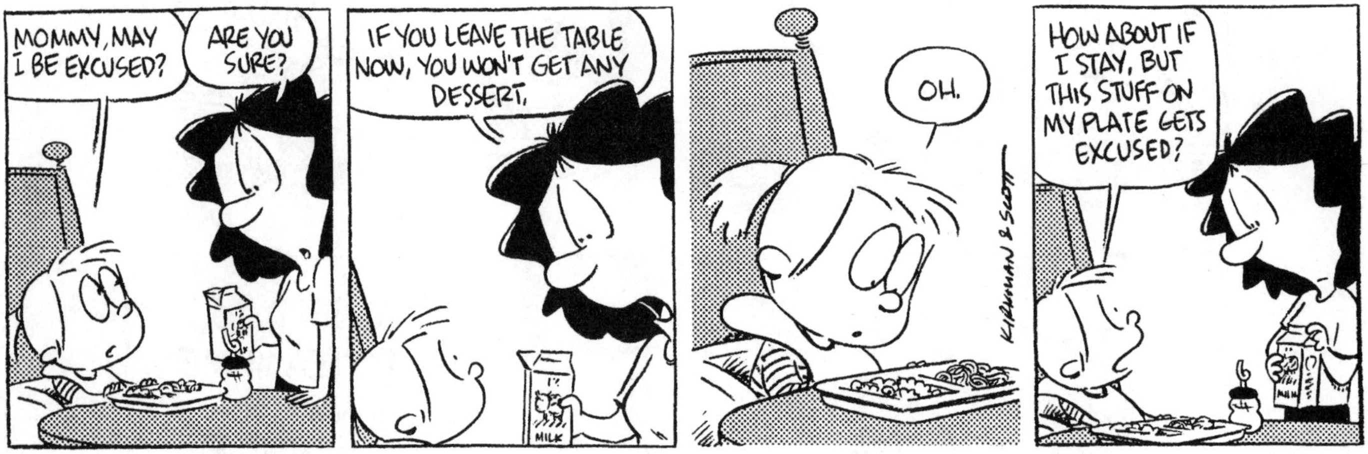
MOMMY, MAY I BE EXCUSED?
ARE YOU SURE?
IF YOU LEAVE THE TABLE NOW, YOU WON'T GET ANY DESSERT.
MILK
OH.
KIRKMAN & SCOTT
HOW ABOUT IF I STAY, BUT THIS STUFF ON MY PLATE GETS EXCUSED?

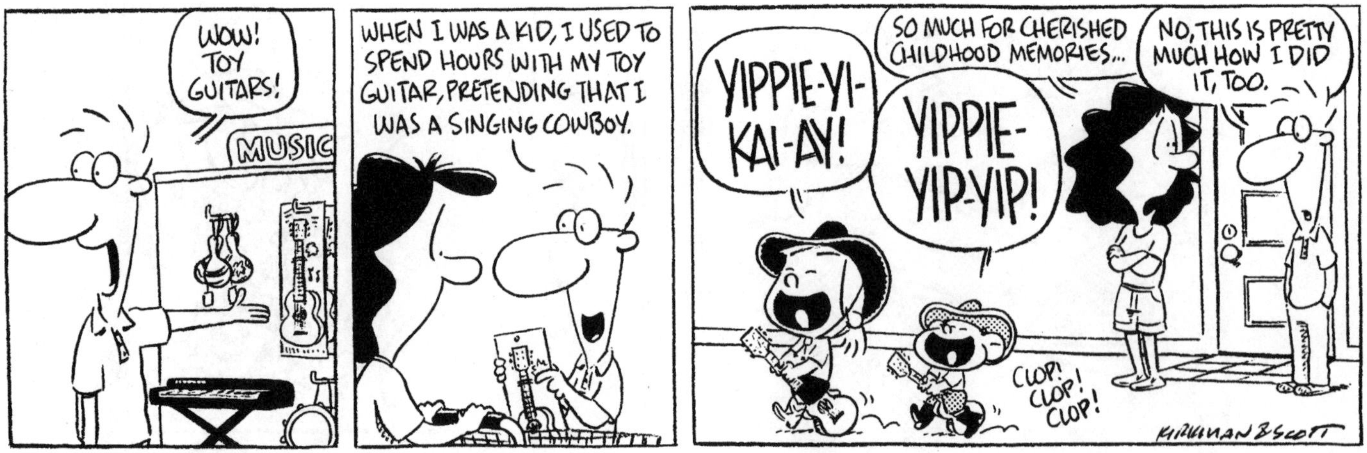
WOW! TOY GUITARS!
MUSIC
WHEN I WAS A KID, I USED TO SPEND HOURS WITH MY TOY GUITAR, PRETENDING THAT I WAS A SINGING COWBOY.
YIPPIE-YI-KAI-AY!
SO MUCH FOR CHERISHED CHILDHOOD MEMORIES...
YIPPIE-YIP-YIP!
NO, THIS IS PRETTY MUCH HOW I DID IT, TOO.
CLOP! CLOP! CLOP!
KIRKMAN & SCOTT

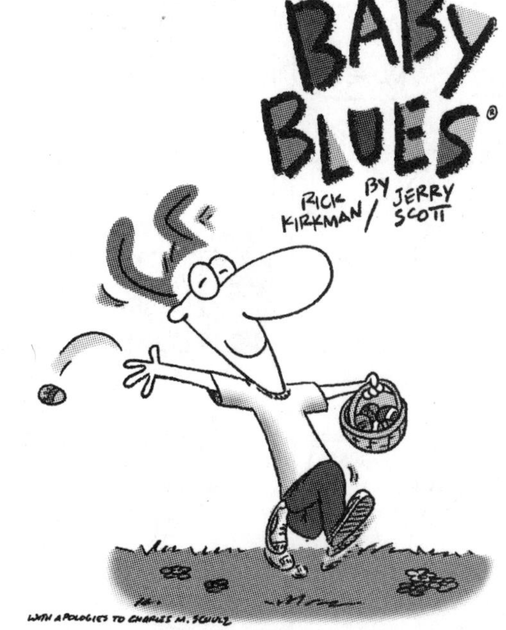
BABY BLUES®
RICK KIRKMAN / BY JERRY SCOTT
WITH APOLOGIES TO CHARLES M. SCHULZ

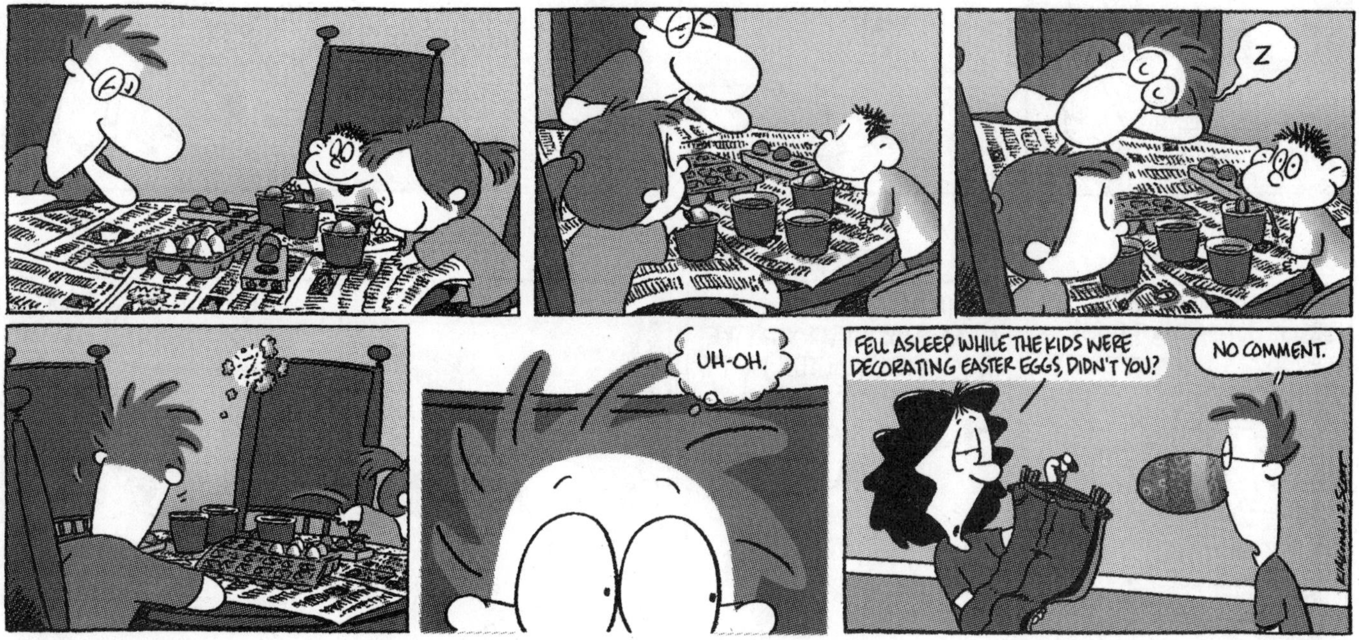
Z
UH-OH.
FELL ASLEEP WHILE THE KIDS WERE DECORATING EASTER EGGS, DIDN'T YOU?
NO COMMENT.

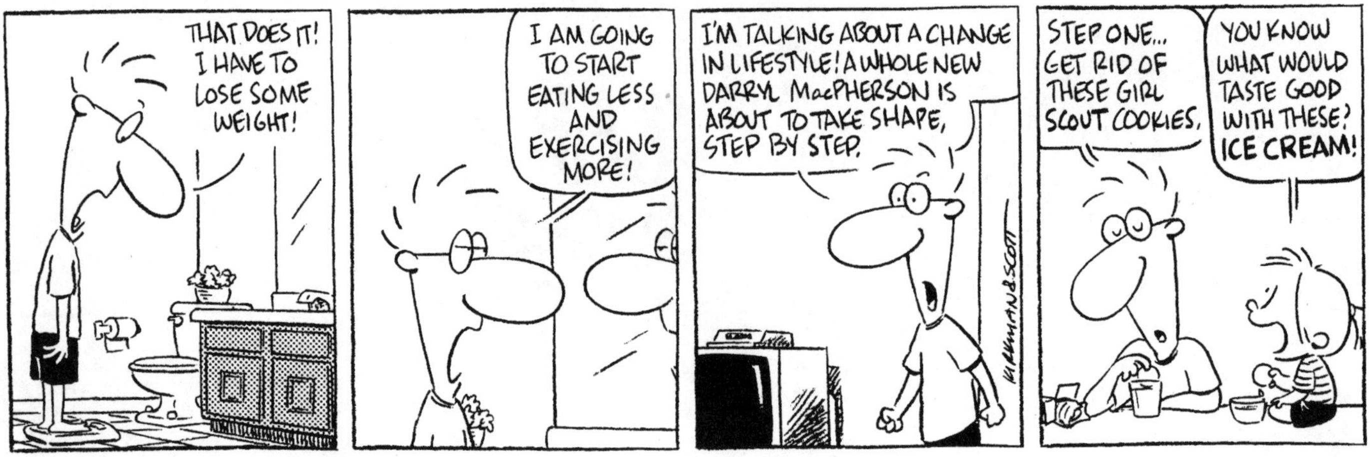
THAT DOES IT! I HAVE TO LOSE SOME WEIGHT!
I AM GOING TO START EATING LESS AND EXERCISING MORE!
I'M TALKING ABOUT A CHANGE IN LIFESTYLE! A WHOLE NEW DARRYL MacPHERSON IS ABOUT TO TAKE SHAPE, STEP BY STEP.
KIRKMAN & SCOTT
STEP ONE... GET RID OF THESE GIRL SCOUT COOKIES.
YOU KNOW WHAT WOULD TASTE GOOD WITH THESE? ICE CREAM!

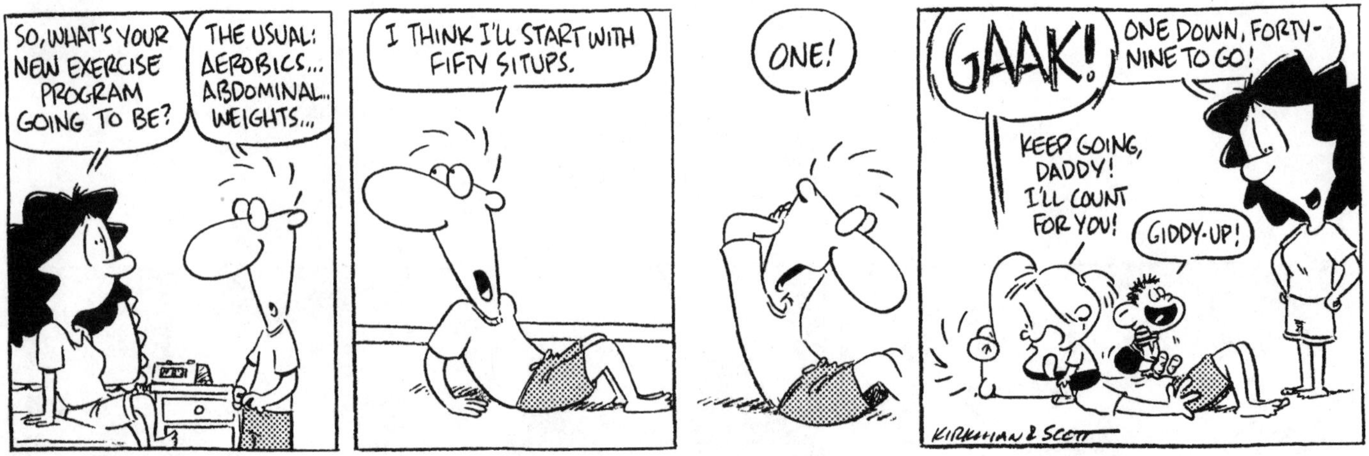
SO, WHAT'S YOUR NEW EXERCISE PROGRAM GOING TO BE?
THE USUAL: AEROBICS... ABDOMINAL... WEIGHTS...
I THINK I'LL START WITH FIFTY SITUPS.
ONE!
GAAK!
ONE DOWN, FORTY-NINE TO GO!
KEEP GOING, DADDY! I'LL COUNT FOR YOU!
GIDDY-UP!
KIRKMAN & SCOTT

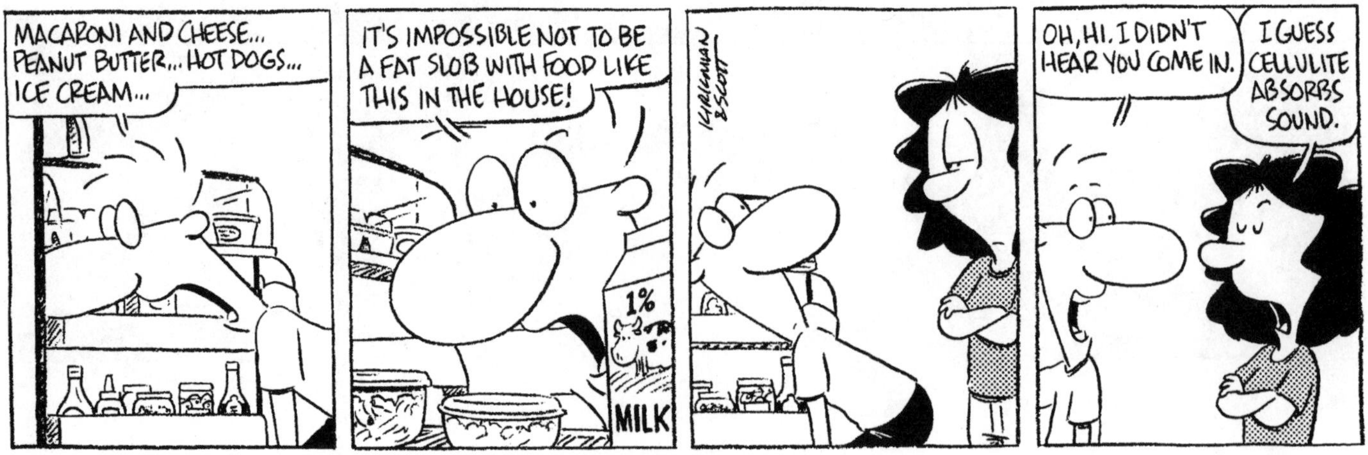
MACARONI AND CHEESE... PEANUT BUTTER... HOT DOGS... ICE CREAM...
IT'S IMPOSSIBLE NOT TO BE A FAT SLOB WITH FOOD LIKE THIS IN THE HOUSE!
1%
MILK
KIRKMAN & SCOTT
OH, HI. I DIDN'T HEAR YOU COME IN.
I GUESS CELLULITE ABSORBS SOUND.

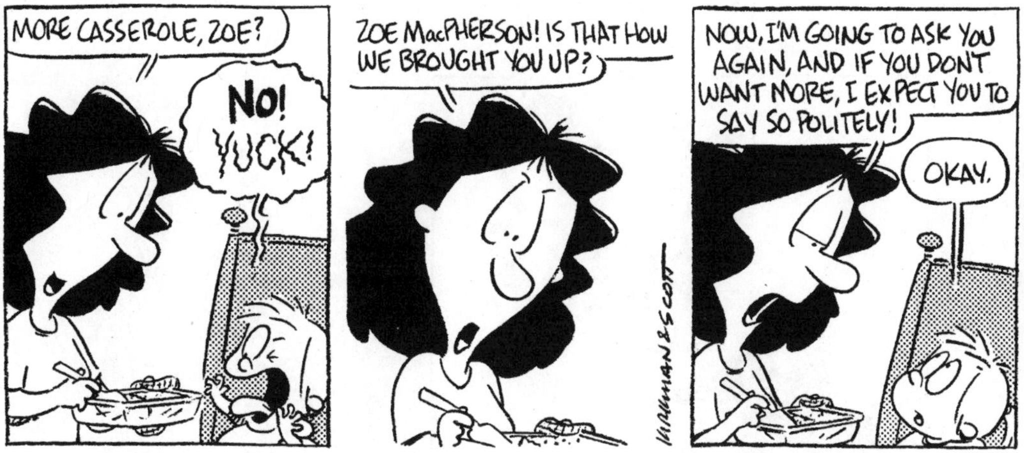
MORE CASSEROLE, ZOE?
NO! YUCK!
ZOE MacPHERSON! IS THAT HOW WE BROUGHT YOU UP?
KIRKMAN & SCOTT
NOW, I'M GOING TO ASK YOU AGAIN, AND IF YOU DON'T WANT MORE, I EXPECT YOU TO SAY SO POLITELY!
OKAY.
MORE CASSEROLE, ZOE?
NO, THANK YOU.

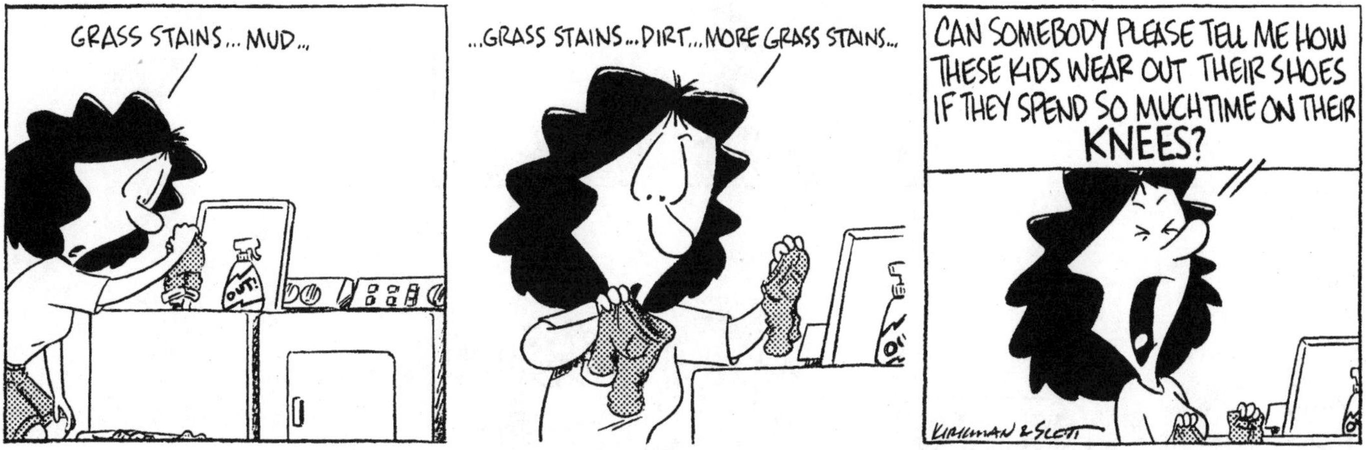
GRASS STAINS... MUD...
OUT!
...GRASS STAINS... DIRT... MORE GRASS STAINS...
CAN SOMEBODY PLEASE TELL ME HOW THESE KIDS WEAR OUT THEIR SHOES IF THEY SPEND SO MUCH TIME ON THEIR KNEES?
KIRKMAN & SCOTT

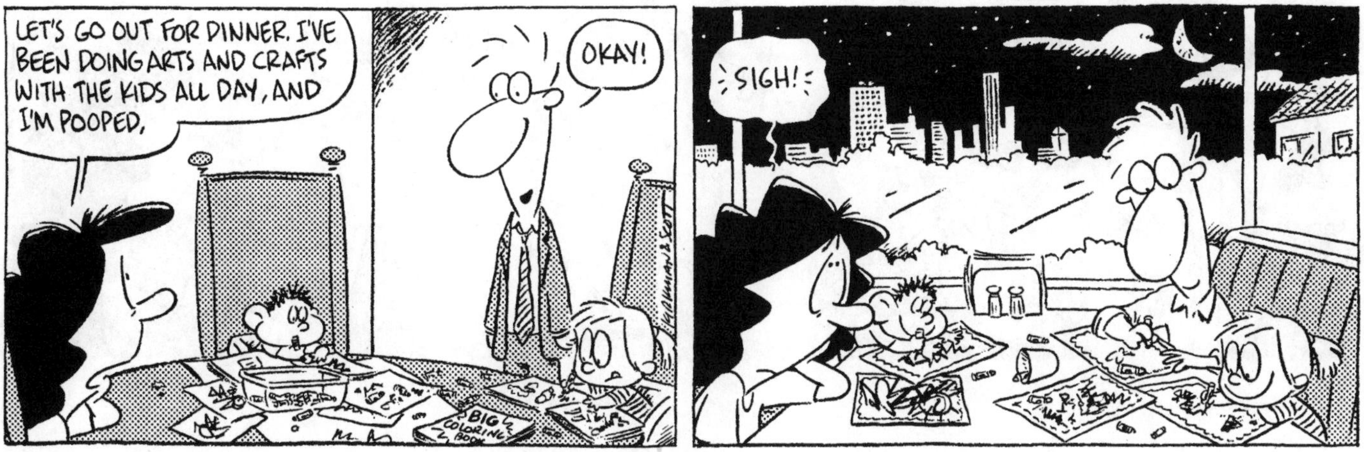
LET'S GO OUT FOR DINNER. I'VE BEEN DOING ARTS AND CRAFTS WITH THE KIDS ALL DAY, AND I'M POOPED.
OKAY!
KIRKMAN & SCOTT
BIG COLORING BOOK
SIGH!

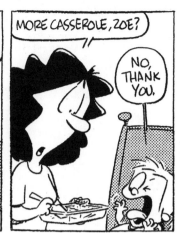

BABY BLUES®
BY RICK KIRKMAN / JERRY SCOTT

WOW! WE'RE ALMOST OUT OF MUSTARD AND KETCHUP AGAIN!
WHENEVER WE BUY STUFF IN SQUEEZE BOTTLES, WE SEEM TO USE MORE OF IT.
REALLY?
PPPPBBTH!
PWUUT!
PBBBBT!
I WONDER WHY?
HA-HA! HA HA! HAHAHA!
HEE HEE! HEEEEE!
DO IT AGAIN!!
KIRKMAN & SCOTT

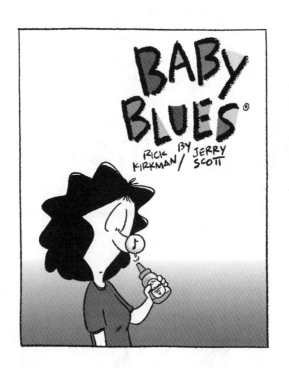

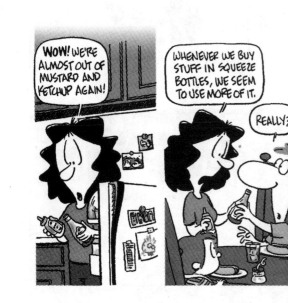

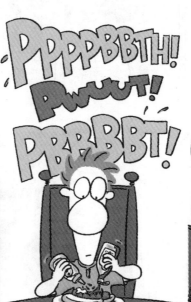

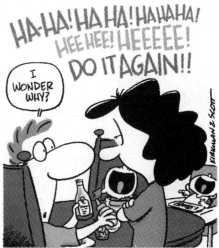

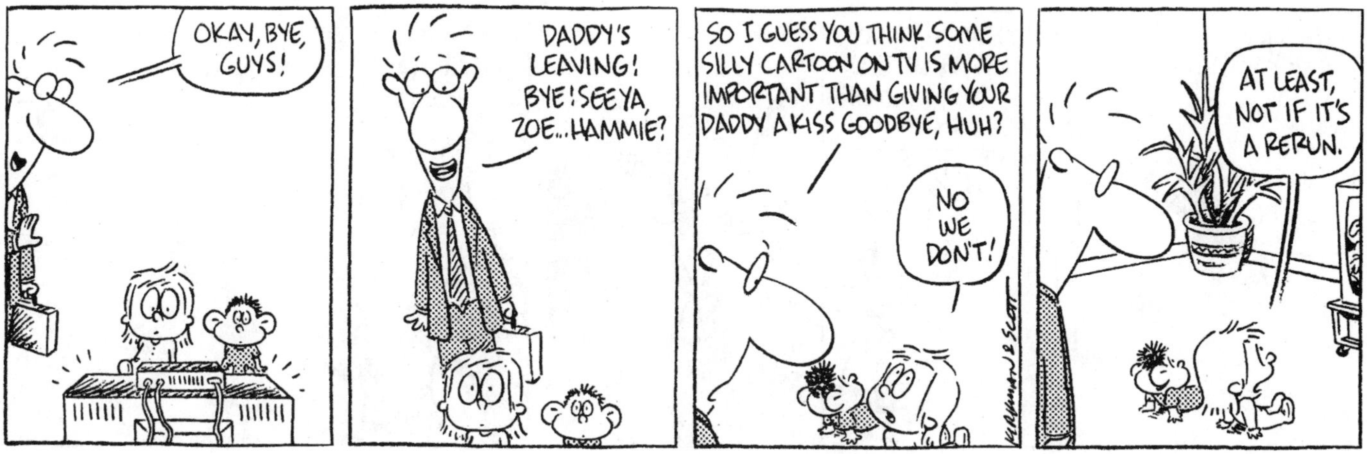
OKAY, BYE, GUYS!
DADDY'S LEAVING! BYE! SEE YA, ZOE... HAMMIE?
SO I GUESS YOU THINK SOME SILLY CARTOON ON TV IS MORE IMPORTANT THAN GIVING YOUR DADDY A KISS GOODBYE, HUH?
NO WE DON'T!
AT LEAST, NOT IF IT'S A RERUN.
KIRKMAN & SCOTT

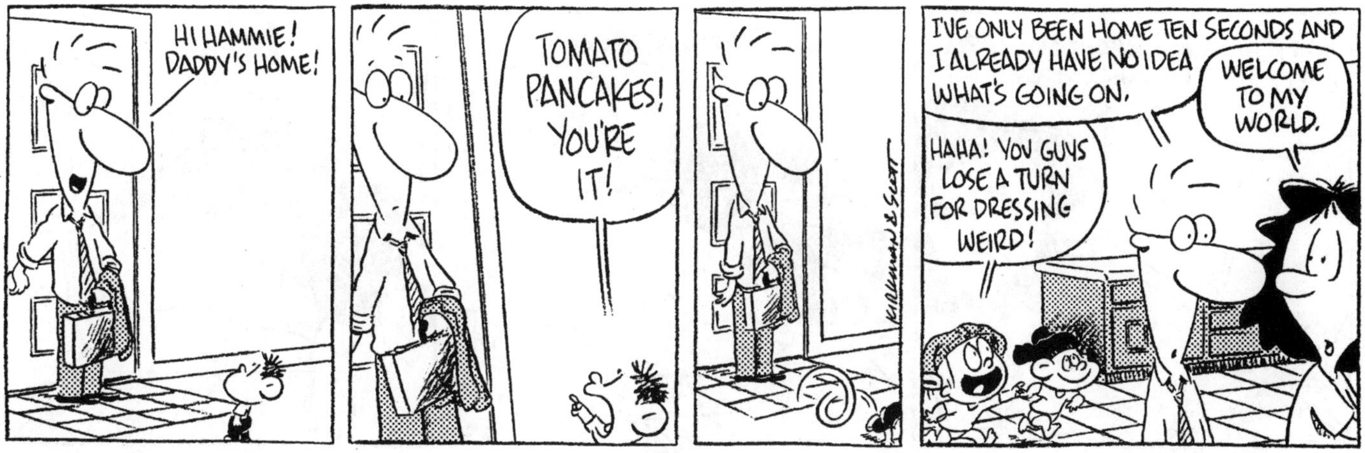
HI HAMMIE! DADDY'S HOME!
TOMATO PANCAKES! YOU'RE IT!
KIRKMAN & SCOTT
I'VE ONLY BEEN HOME TEN SECONDS AND I ALREADY HAVE NO IDEA WHAT'S GOING ON.
WELCOME TO MY WORLD.
HAHA! YOU GUYS LOSE A TURN FOR DRESSING WEIRD!

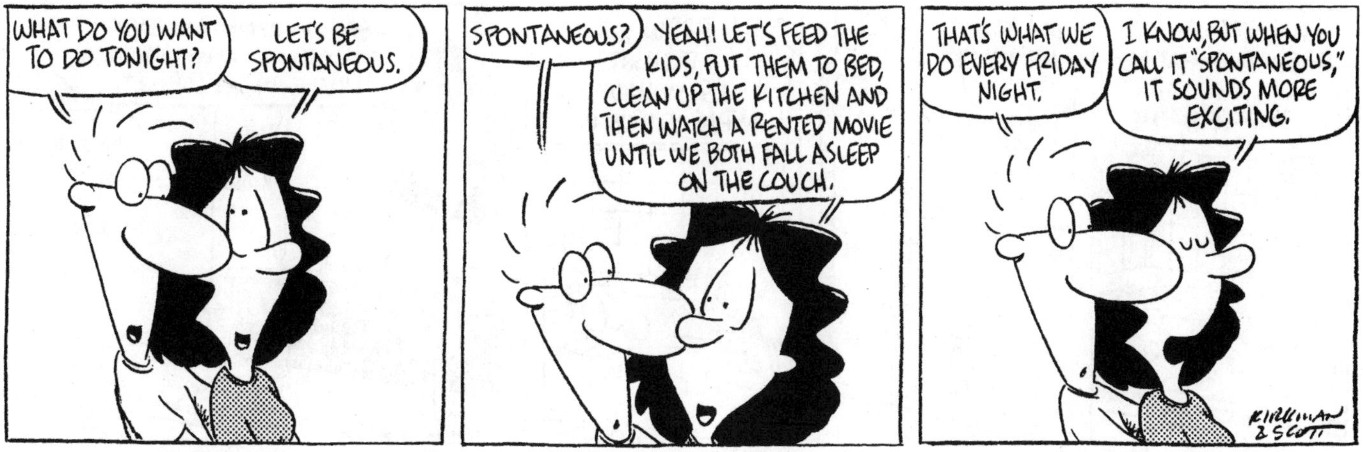
WHAT DO YOU WANT TO DO TONIGHT?
LET'S BE SPONTANEOUS.
SPONTANEOUS?
YEAH! LET'S FEED THE KIDS, PUT THEM TO BED, CLEAN UP THE KITCHEN AND THEN WATCH A RENTED MOVIE UNTIL WE BOTH FALL ASLEEP ON THE COUCH.
THAT'S WHAT WE DO EVERY FRIDAY NIGHT.
I KNOW, BUT WHEN YOU CALL IT "SPONTANEOUS," IT SOUNDS MORE EXCITING.
KIRKMAN & SCOTT

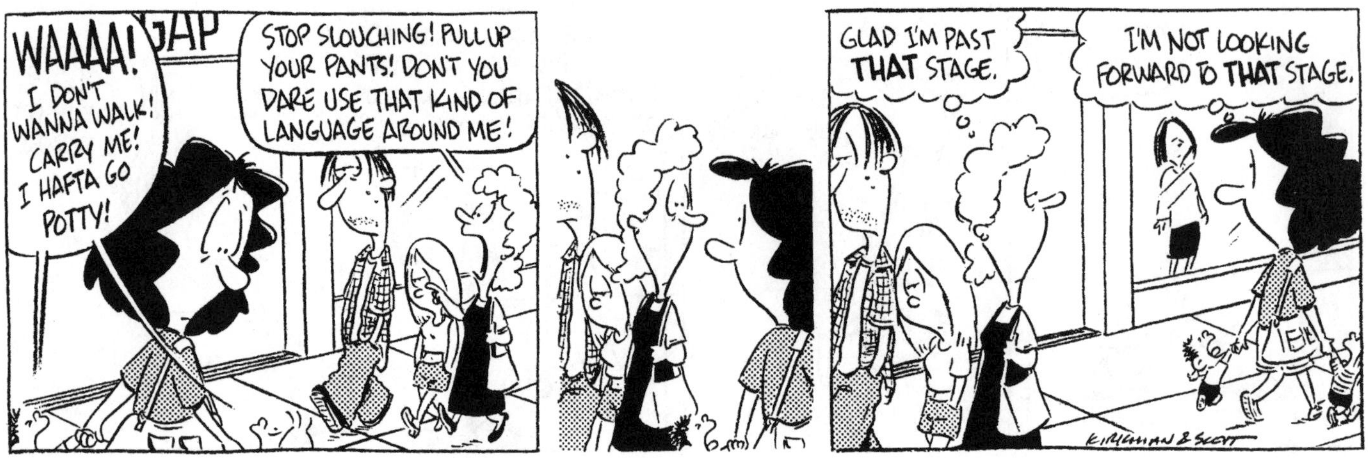
GAP
WAAAA! I DON'T WANNA WALK! CARRY ME! I HAFTA GO POTTY!
STOP SLOUCHING! PULL UP YOUR PANTS! DON'T YOU DARE USE THAT KIND OF LANGUAGE AROUND ME!
GLAD I'M PAST **THAT** STAGE.
I'M NOT LOOKING FORWARD TO **THAT** STAGE.
KIRKMAN & SCOTT

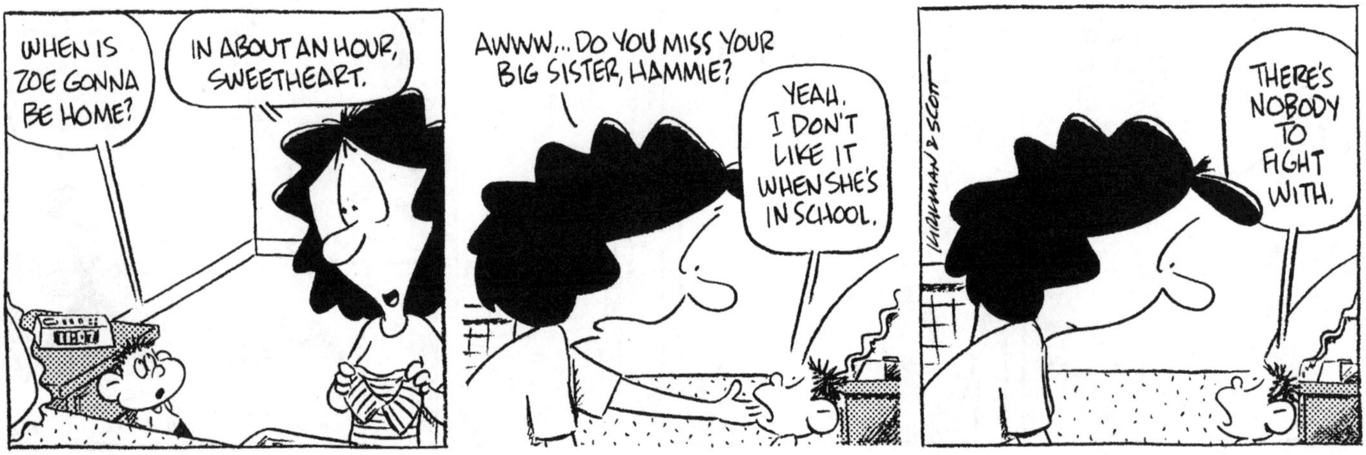
WHEN IS ZOE GONNA BE HOME?
IN ABOUT AN HOUR, SWEETHEART.
AWWW... DO YOU MISS YOUR BIG SISTER, HAMMIE?
YEAH. I DON'T LIKE IT WHEN SHE'S IN SCHOOL.
KIRKMAN & SCOTT
THERE'S NOBODY TO FIGHT WITH.

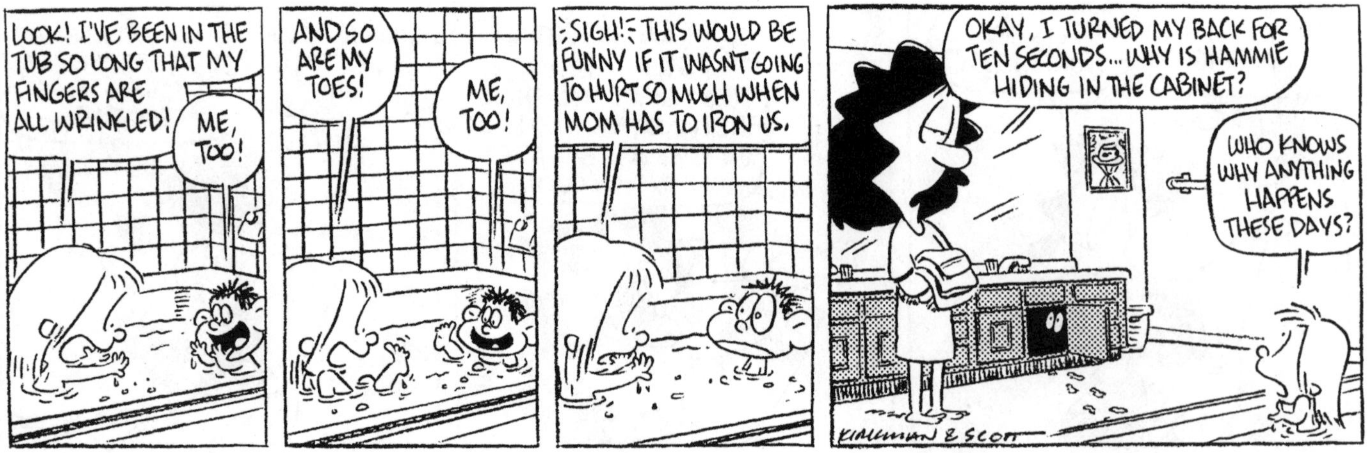
LOOK! I'VE BEEN IN THE TUB SO LONG THAT MY FINGERS ARE ALL WRINKLED!
ME, TOO!
AND SO ARE MY TOES!
ME, TOO!
:SIGH!: THIS WOULD BE FUNNY IF IT WASN'T GOING TO HURT SO MUCH WHEN MOM HAS TO IRON US.
OKAY, I TURNED MY BACK FOR TEN SECONDS... WHY IS HAMMIE HIDING IN THE CABINET?
WHO KNOWS WHY ANYTHING HAPPENS THESE DAYS?
KIRKMAN & SCOTT

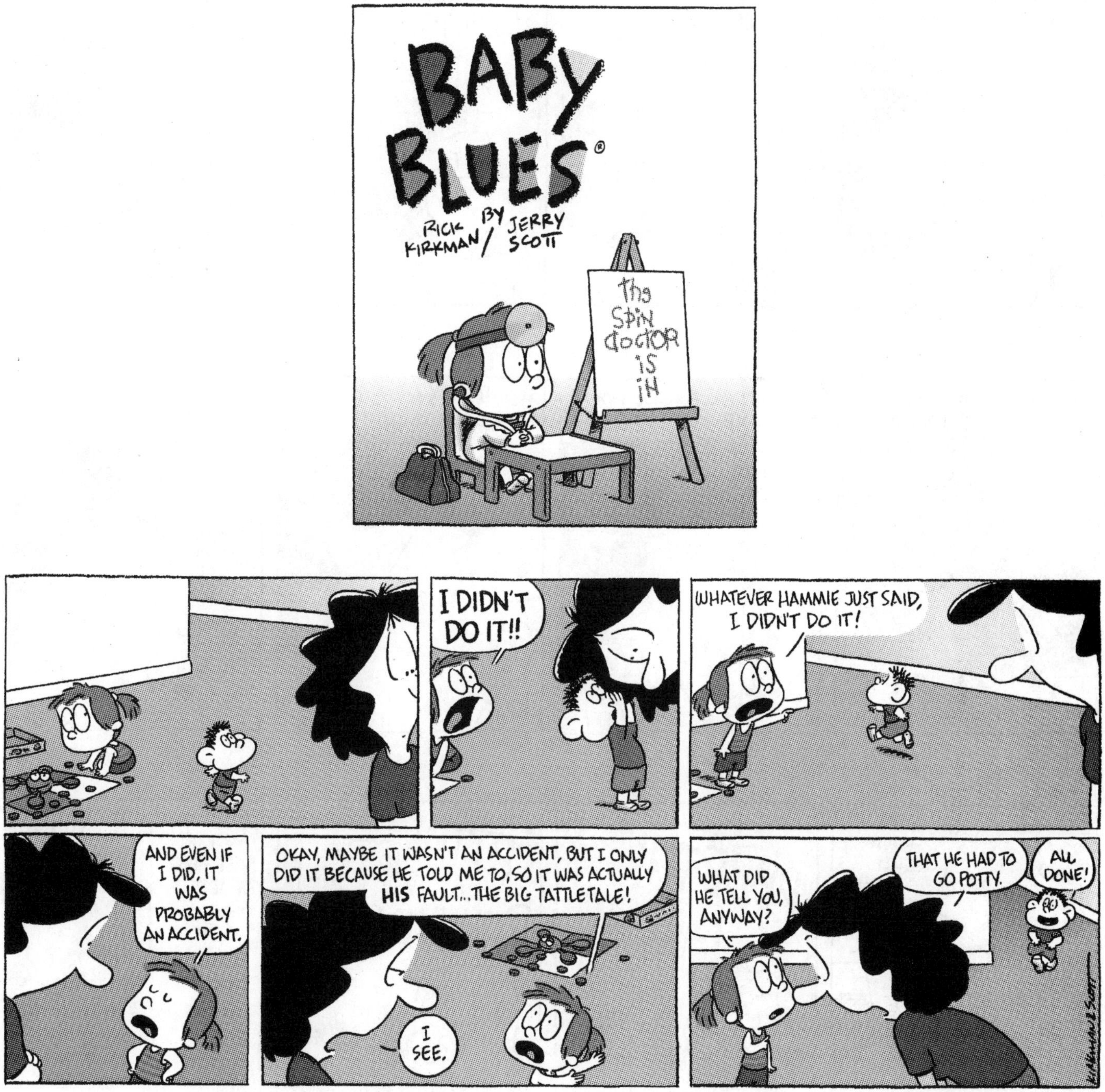
BABY BLUES®
BY RICK KIRKMAN / JERRY SCOTT
The SPIN doctor is iN
I DIDN'T DO IT!!
WHATEVER HAMMIE JUST SAID, I DIDN'T DO IT!
AND EVEN IF I DID, IT WAS PROBABLY AN ACCIDENT.
OKAY, MAYBE IT WASN'T AN ACCIDENT, BUT I ONLY DID IT BECAUSE HE TOLD ME TO, SO IT WAS ACTUALLY HIS FAULT... THE BIG TATTLETALE!
I SEE.
WHAT DID HE TELL YOU, ANYWAY?
THAT HE HAD TO GO POTTY.
ALL DONE!

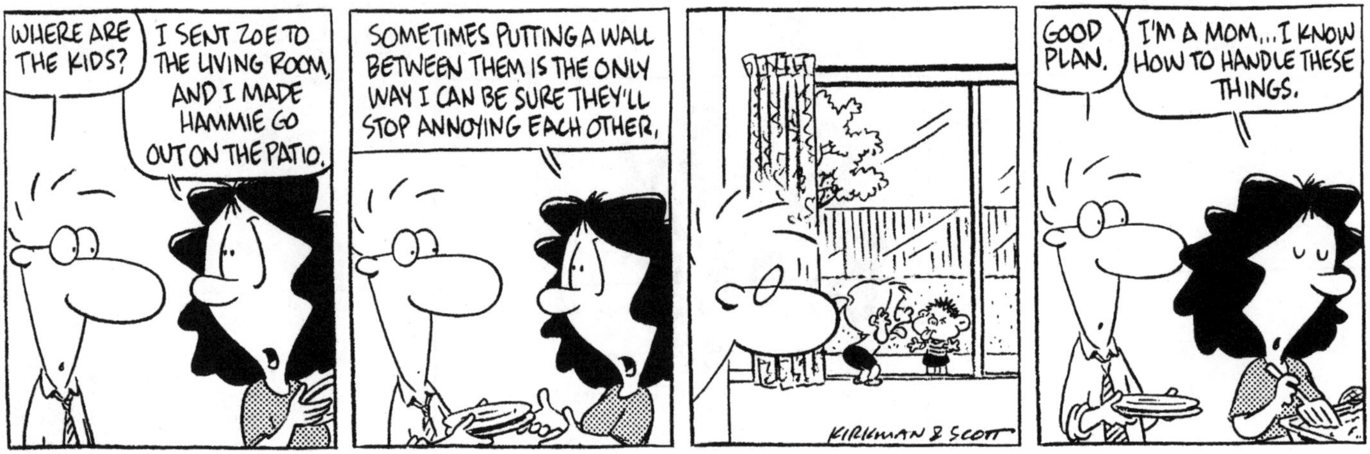
WHERE ARE THE KIDS?
I SENT ZOE TO THE LIVING ROOM, AND I MADE HAMMIE GO OUT ON THE PATIO.
SOMETIMES PUTTING A WALL BETWEEN THEM IS THE ONLY WAY I CAN BE SURE THEY'LL STOP ANNOYING EACH OTHER.
KIRKMAN & SCOTT
GOOD PLAN.
I'M A MOM... I KNOW HOW TO HANDLE THESE THINGS.

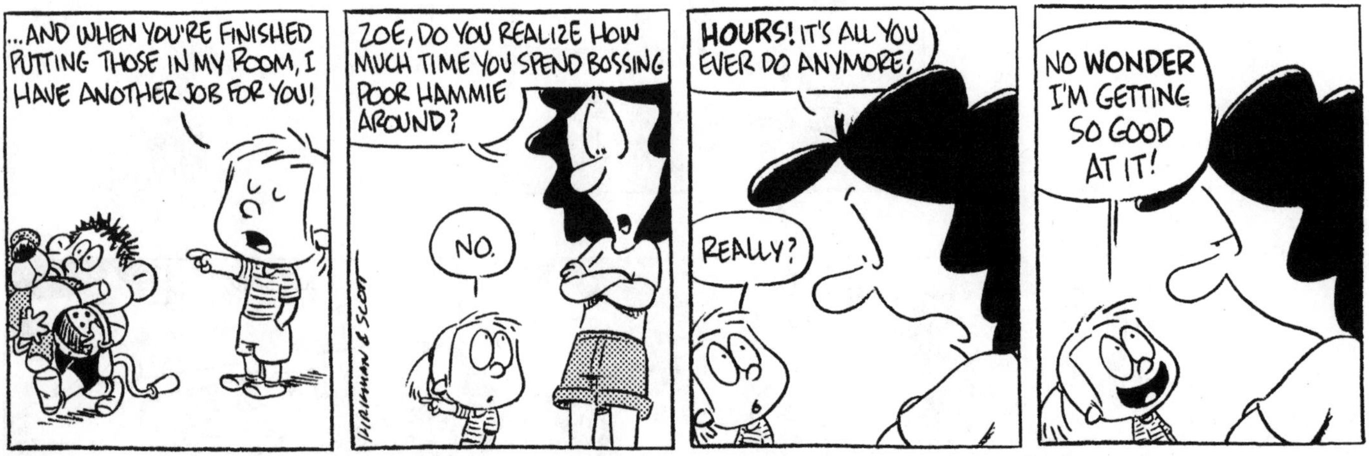
...AND WHEN YOU'RE FINISHED PUTTING THOSE IN MY ROOM, I HAVE ANOTHER JOB FOR YOU!
ZOE, DO YOU REALIZE HOW MUCH TIME YOU SPEND BOSSING POOR HAMMIE AROUND?
NO.
KIRKMAN & SCOTT
HOURS! IT'S ALL YOU EVER DO ANYMORE!
REALLY?
NO WONDER I'M GETTING SO GOOD AT IT!

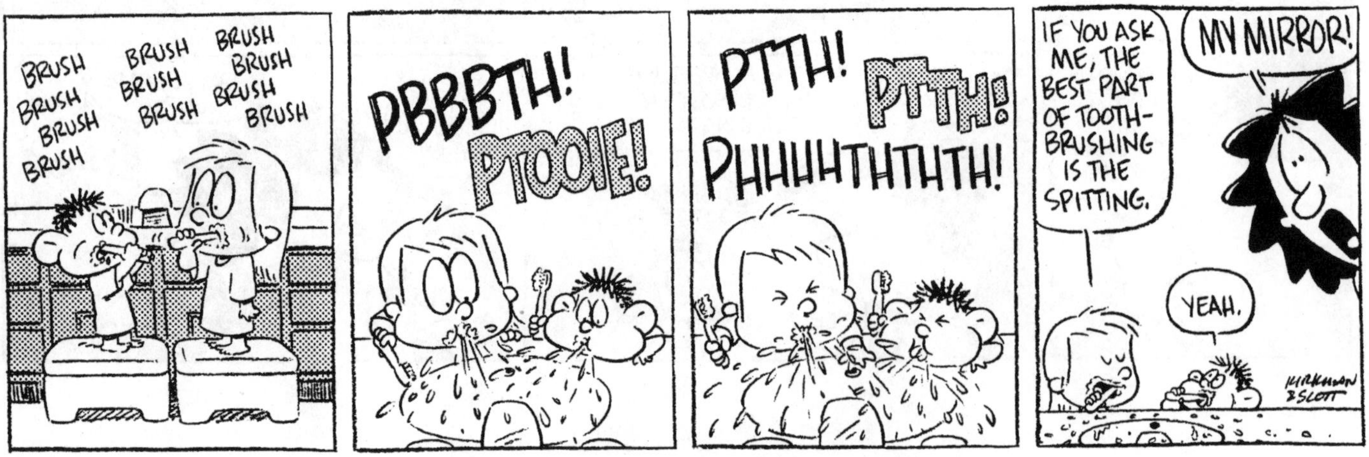
BRUSH BRUSH BRUSH BRUSH BRUSH BRUSH BRUSH BRUSH BRUSH BRUSH BRUSH BRUSH
PBBBTH!
PTOOIE!
PTTH!
PTTH!
PHHHTHTHTH!
IF YOU ASK ME, THE BEST PART OF TOOTH-BRUSHING IS THE SPITTING.
MY MIRROR!
YEAH.
KIRKMAN & SCOTT

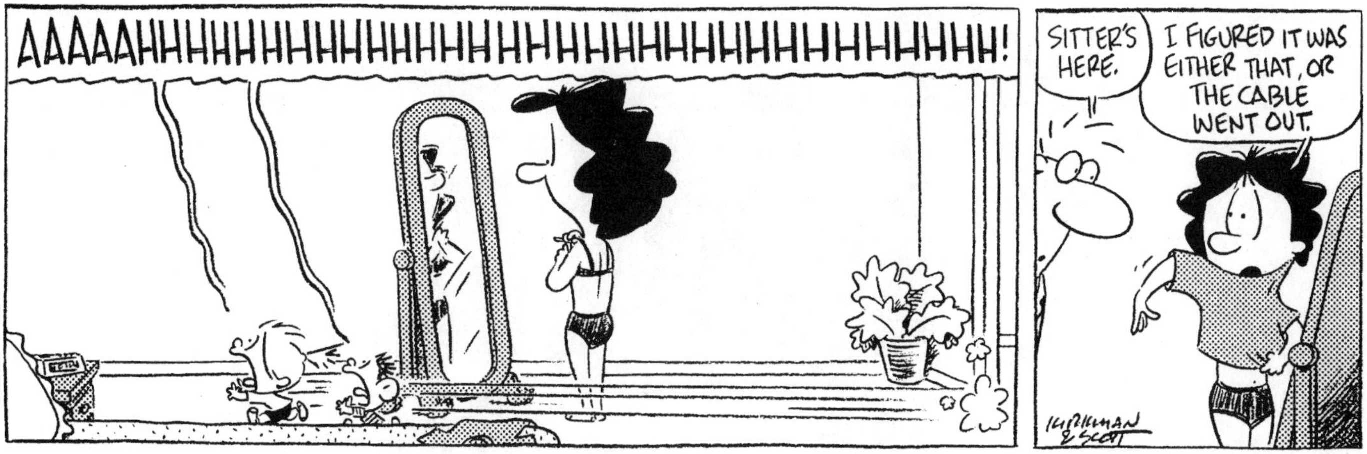
AAAAAHHHHHHHHHHHHHHHHHHHHHHHHHHHHHHHHHHHHHH!
SITTER'S HERE.
I FIGURED IT WAS EITHER THAT, OR THE CABLE WENT OUT.

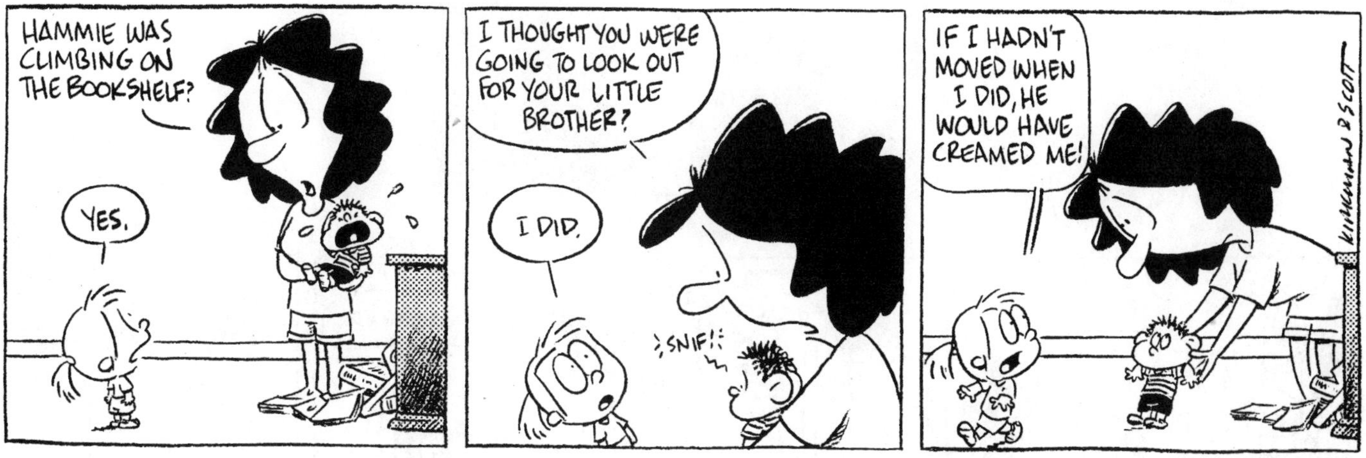
HAMMIE WAS CLIMBING ON THE BOOKSHELF?
YES.
I THOUGHT YOU WERE GOING TO LOOK OUT FOR YOUR LITTLE BROTHER?
I DID.
SNIF!
IF I HADN'T MOVED WHEN I DID, HE WOULD HAVE CREAMED ME!

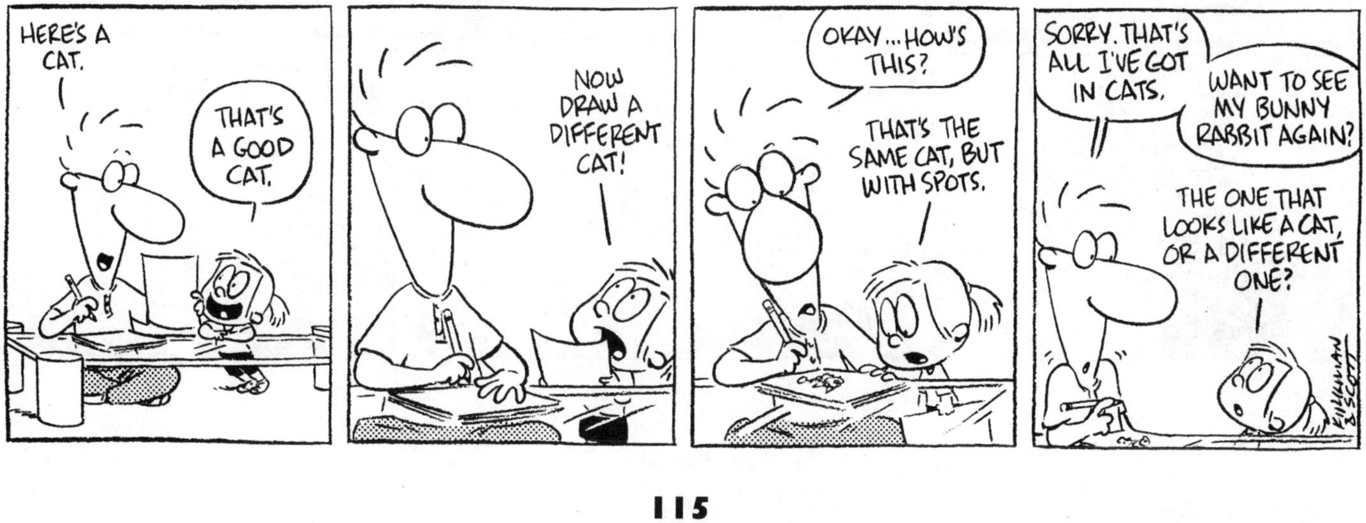
HERE'S A CAT.
THAT'S A GOOD CAT.
NOW DRAW A DIFFERENT CAT!
OKAY... HOW'S THIS?
THAT'S THE SAME CAT, BUT WITH SPOTS.
SORRY. THAT'S ALL I'VE GOT IN CATS.
WANT TO SEE MY BUNNY RABBIT AGAIN?
THE ONE THAT LOOKS LIKE A CAT, OR A DIFFERENT ONE?

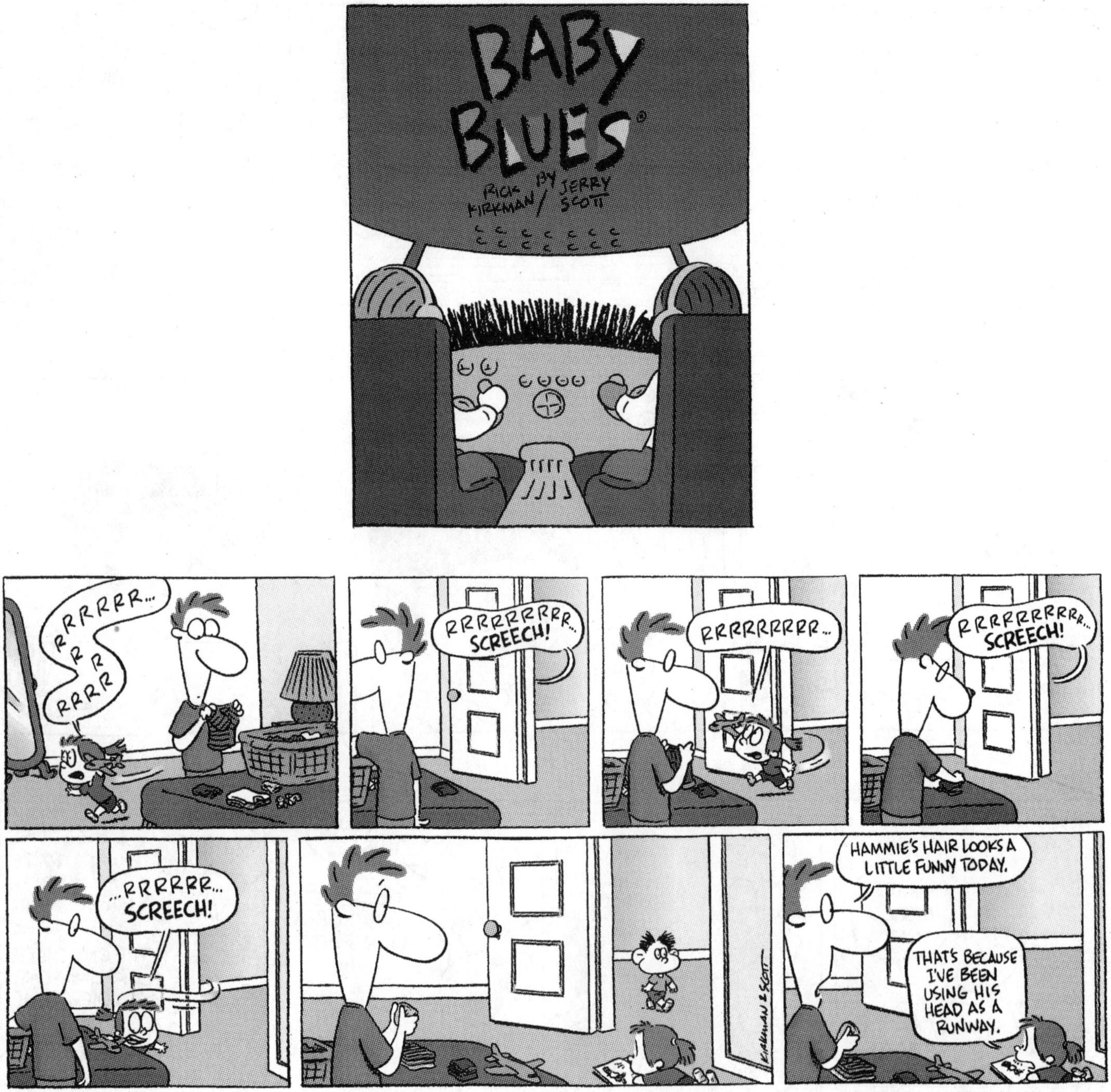
BABY BLUES®
BY RICK KIRKMAN / JERRY SCOTT
RRRRRR... R R R RRRR
RRRRRRRRR... SCREECH!
RRRRRRRRR...
RRRRRRRRR... SCREECH!
...RRRRRR... SCREECH!
KIRKMAN & SCOTT
HAMMIE'S HAIR LOOKS A LITTLE FUNNY TODAY.
THAT'S BECAUSE I'VE BEEN USING HIS HEAD AS A RUNWAY.

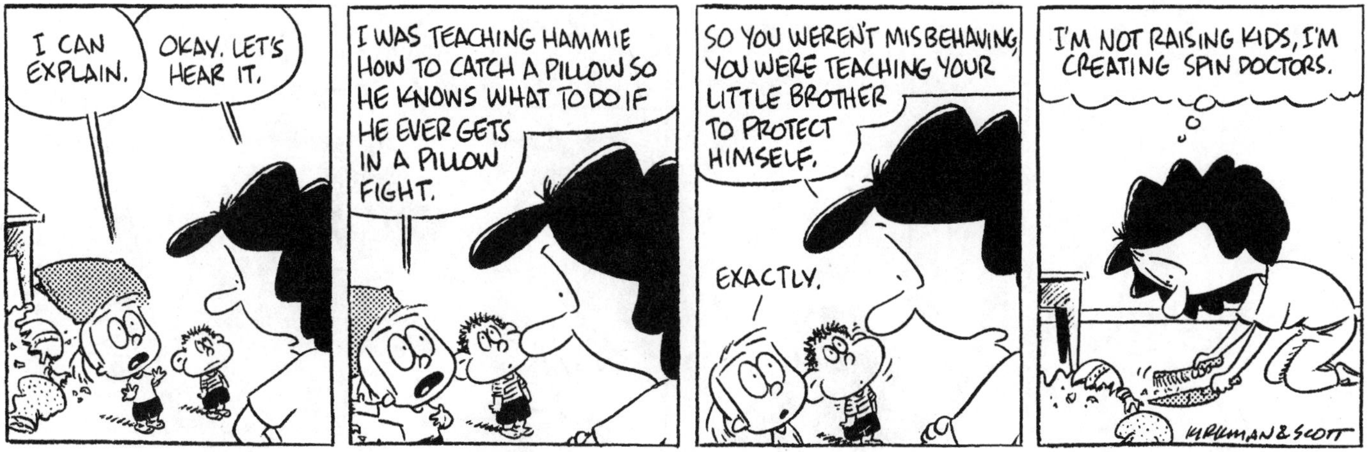
I CAN EXPLAIN.
OKAY. LET'S HEAR IT.
I WAS TEACHING HAMMIE HOW TO CATCH A PILLOW SO HE KNOWS WHAT TO DO IF HE EVER GETS IN A PILLOW FIGHT.
SO YOU WEREN'T MISBEHAVING, YOU WERE TEACHING YOUR LITTLE BROTHER TO PROTECT HIMSELF.
EXACTLY.
I'M NOT RAISING KIDS, I'M CREATING SPIN DOCTORS.
KIRKMAN & SCOTT

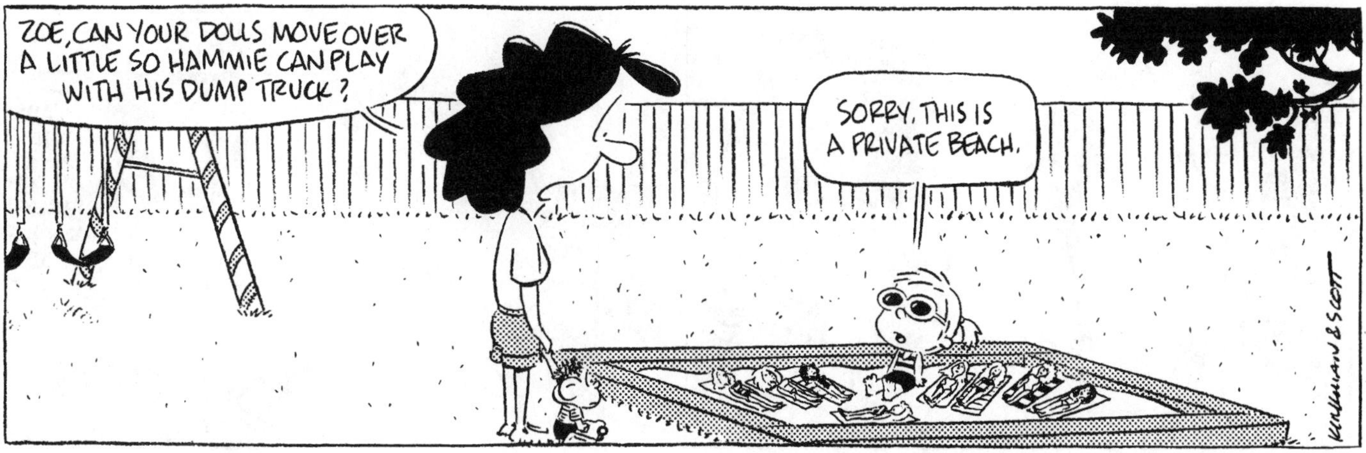
ZOE, CAN YOUR DOLLS MOVE OVER A LITTLE SO HAMMIE CAN PLAY WITH HIS DUMP TRUCK?
SORRY. THIS IS A PRIVATE BEACH.
KIRKMAN & SCOTT

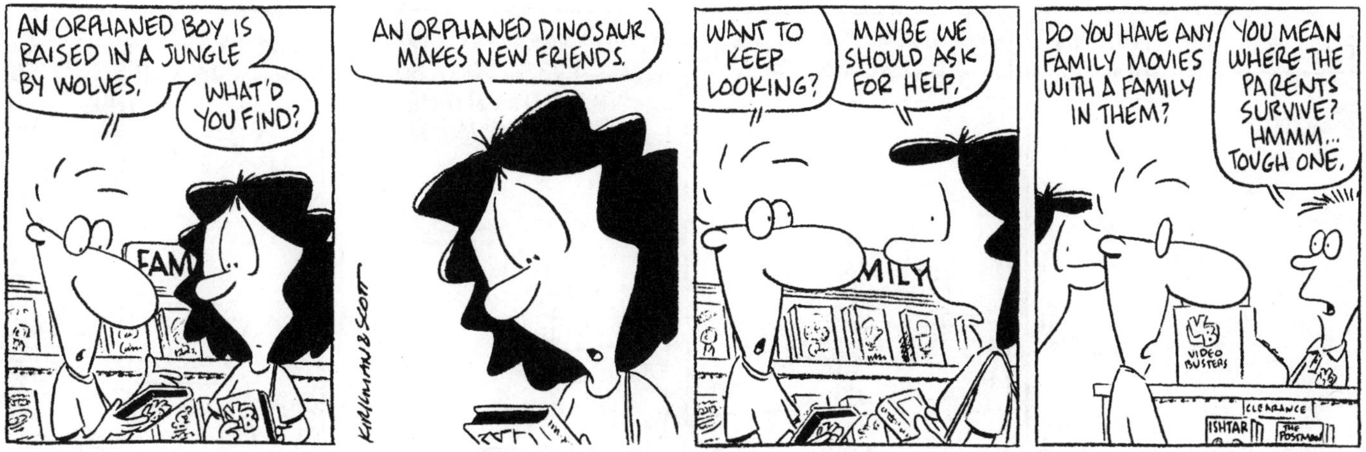
AN ORPHANED BOY IS RAISED IN A JUNGLE BY WOLVES.
WHAT'D YOU FIND?
KIRKMAN & SCOTT
AN ORPHANED DINOSAUR MAKES NEW FRIENDS.
WANT TO KEEP LOOKING?
MAYBE WE SHOULD ASK FOR HELP.
DO YOU HAVE ANY FAMILY MOVIES WITH A FAMILY IN THEM?
YOU MEAN WHERE THE PARENTS SURVIVE? HMMM... TOUGH ONE.
VIDEO BUSTERS
CLEARANCE
ISHTAR
THE POSTMAN

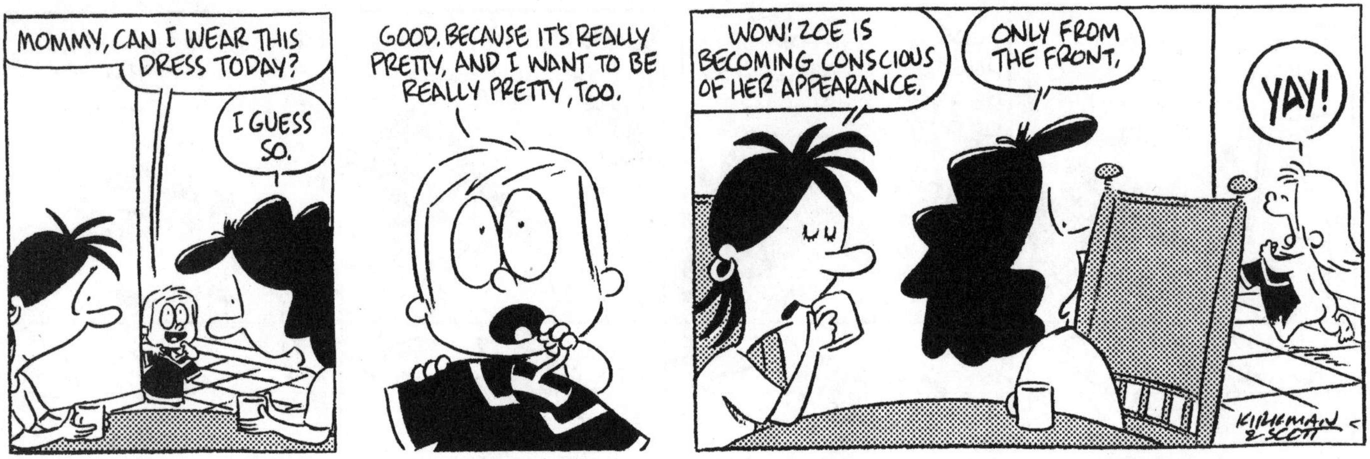
MOMMY, CAN I WEAR THIS DRESS TODAY?
I GUESS SO.
GOOD. BECAUSE IT'S REALLY PRETTY, AND I WANT TO BE REALLY PRETTY, TOO.
WOW! ZOE IS BECOMING CONSCIOUS OF HER APPEARANCE.
ONLY FROM THE FRONT.
YAY!
KIRKMAN & SCOTT

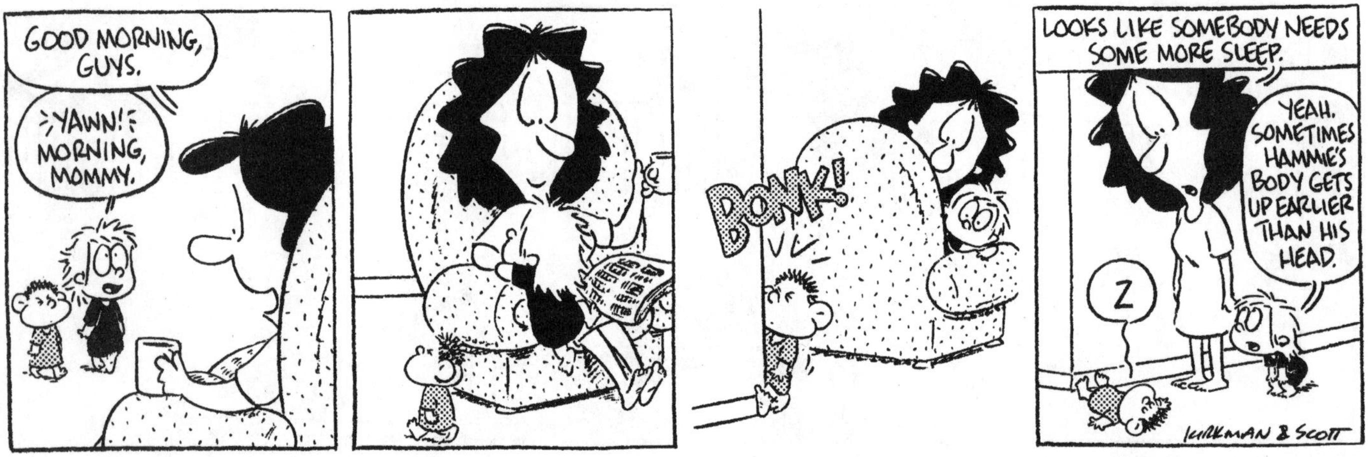
GOOD MORNING, GUYS.
YAWN! MORNING, MOMMY.
BONK!
LOOKS LIKE SOMEBODY NEEDS SOME MORE SLEEP.
YEAH. SOMETIMES HAMMIE'S BODY GETS UP EARLIER THAN HIS HEAD.
Z
KIRKMAN & SCOTT

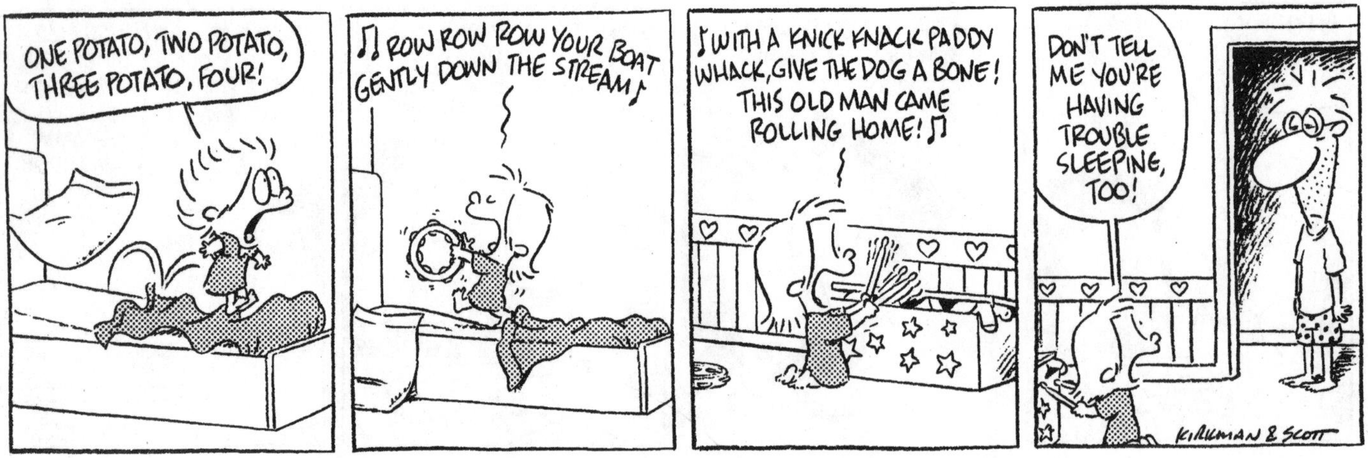
ONE POTATO, TWO POTATO, THREE POTATO, FOUR!
♫ ROW ROW ROW YOUR BOAT GENTLY DOWN THE STREAM ♪
♪ WITH A KNICK KNACK PADDY WHACK, GIVE THE DOG A BONE! THIS OLD MAN CAME ROLLING HOME! ♫
DON'T TELL ME YOU'RE HAVING TROUBLE SLEEPING, TOO!
KIRKMAN & SCOTT

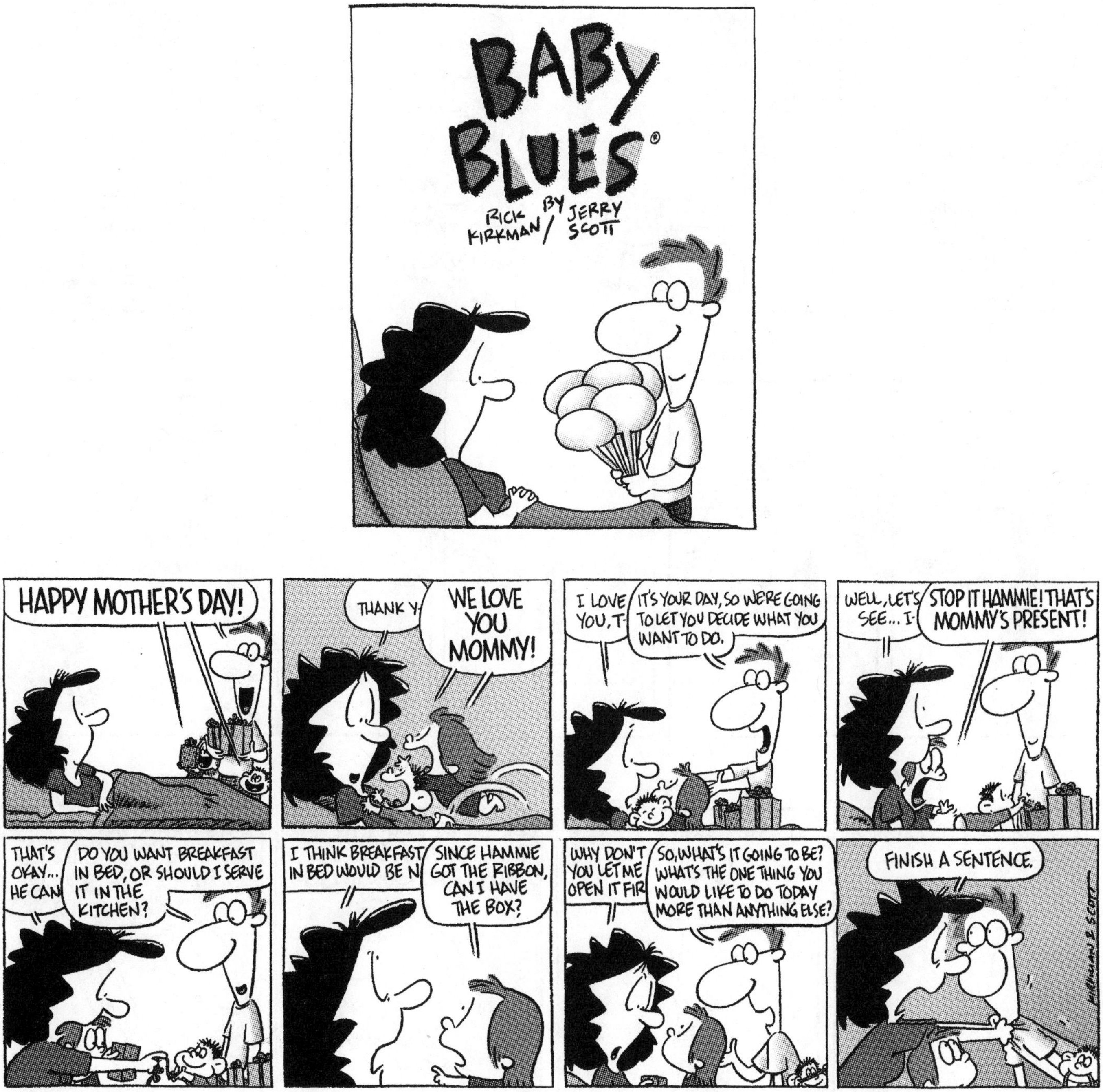
BABY BLUES®
BY RICK KIRKMAN / JERRY SCOTT
HAPPY MOTHER'S DAY!
THANK Y-
WE LOVE YOU MOMMY!
I LOVE YOU, T-
IT'S YOUR DAY, SO WE'RE GOING TO LET YOU DECIDE WHAT YOU WANT TO DO.
WELL, LET'S SEE... I-
STOP IT HAMMIE! THAT'S MOMMY'S PRESENT!
THAT'S OKAY... HE CAN
DO YOU WANT BREAKFAST IN BED, OR SHOULD I SERVE IT IN THE KITCHEN?
I THINK BREAKFAST IN BED WOULD BE N
SINCE HAMMIE GOT THE RIBBON, CAN I HAVE THE BOX?
WHY DON'T YOU LET ME OPEN IT FIR
SO, WHAT'S IT GOING TO BE? WHAT'S THE ONE THING YOU WOULD LIKE TO DO TODAY MORE THAN ANYTHING ELSE?
FINISH A SENTENCE.

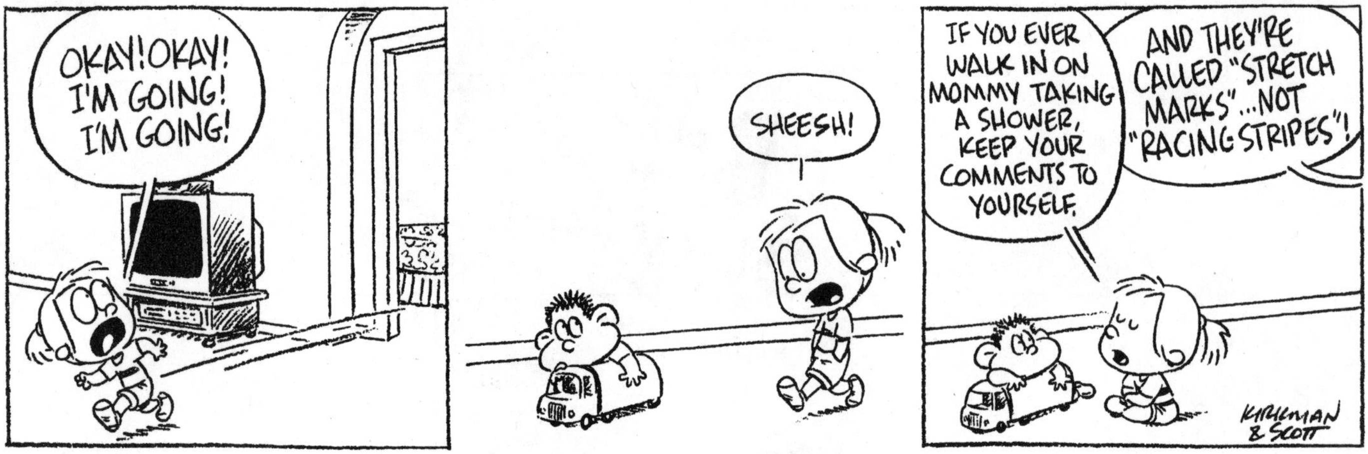
OKAY! OKAY! I'M GOING! I'M GOING!
SHEESH!
IF YOU EVER WALK IN ON MOMMY TAKING A SHOWER, KEEP YOUR COMMENTS TO YOURSELF.
AND THEY'RE CALLED "STRETCH MARKS"...NOT "RACING STRIPES"!
KIRKMAN & SCOTT

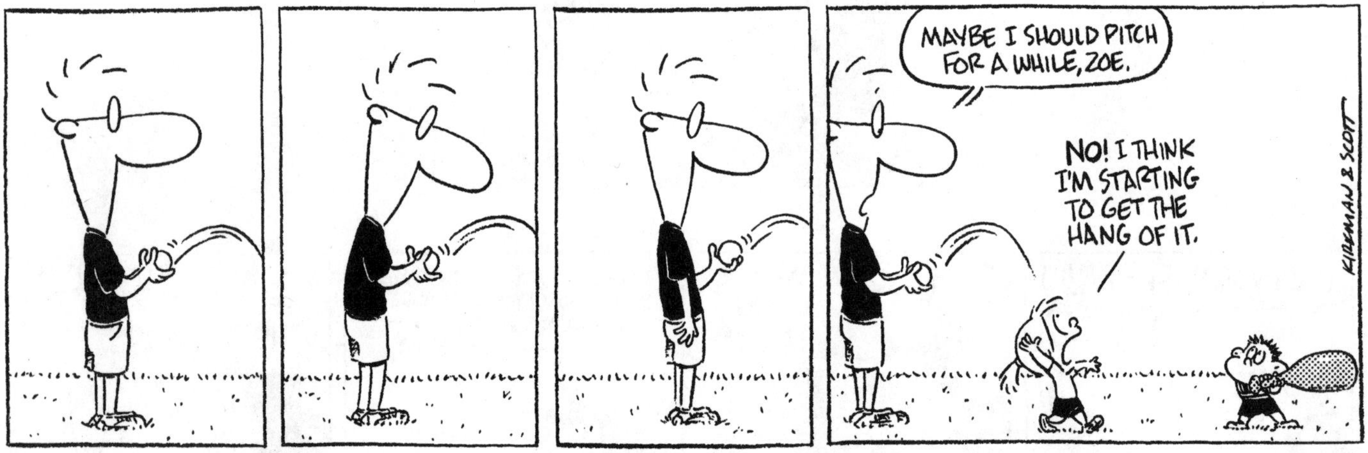
MAYBE I SHOULD PITCH FOR A WHILE, ZOE.
NO! I THINK I'M STARTING TO GET THE HANG OF IT.
KIRKMAN & SCOTT

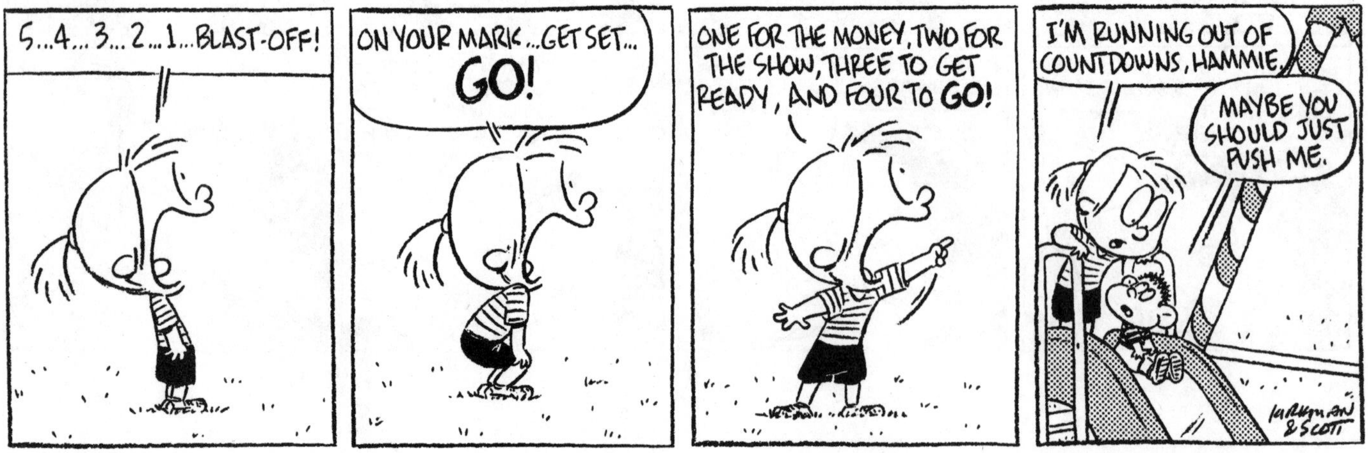
5...4...3...2...1...BLAST-OFF!
ON YOUR MARK...GET SET... GO!
ONE FOR THE MONEY, TWO FOR THE SHOW, THREE TO GET READY, AND FOUR TO GO!
I'M RUNNING OUT OF COUNTDOWNS, HAMMIE.
MAYBE YOU SHOULD JUST PUSH ME.
KIRKMAN & SCOTT

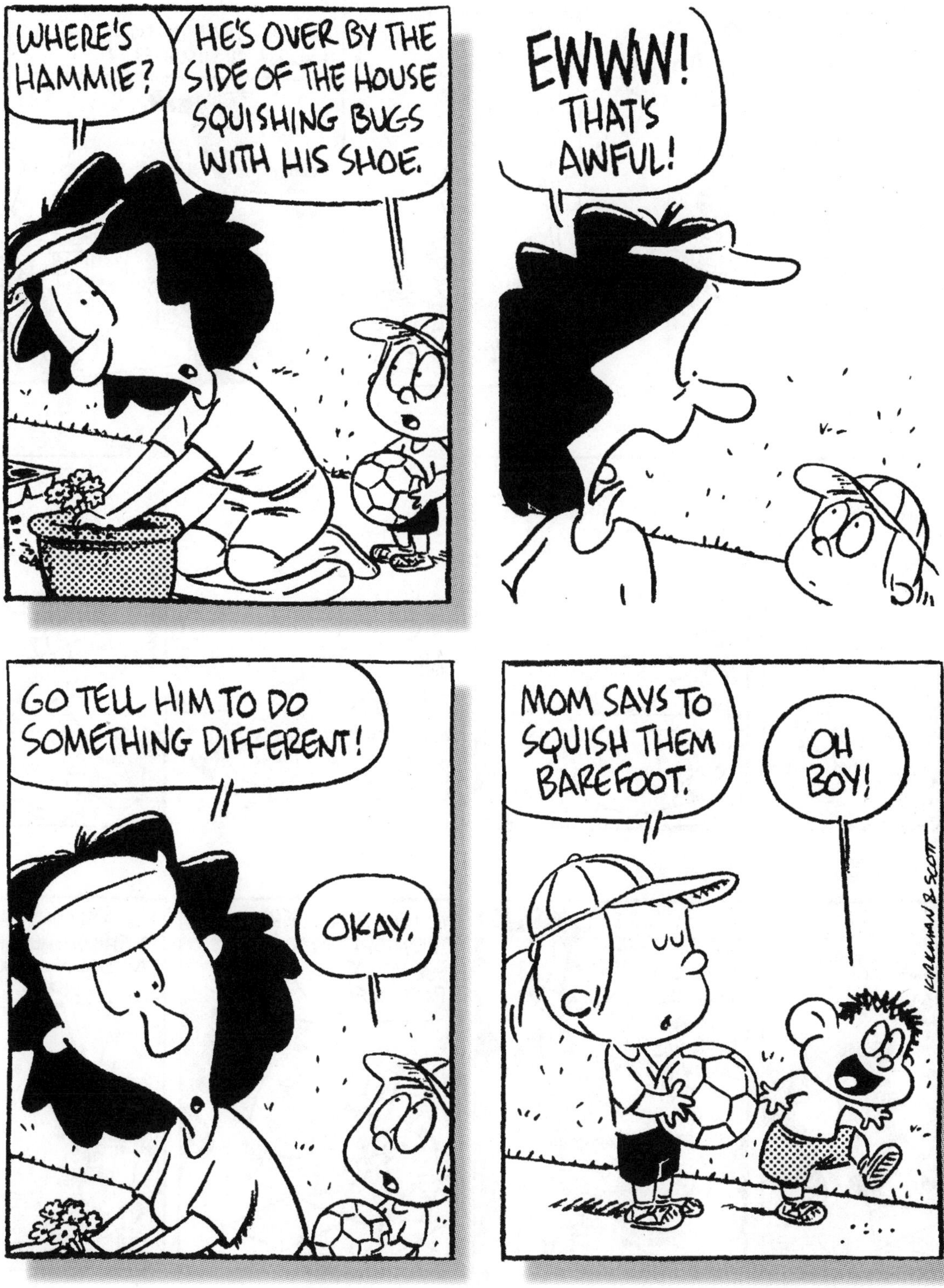
WHERE'S HAMMIE?
HE'S OVER BY THE SIDE OF THE HOUSE SQUISHING BUGS WITH HIS SHOE.
EWWW! THAT'S AWFUL!
GO TELL HIM TO DO SOMETHING DIFFERENT!
OKAY.
MOM SAYS TO SQUISH THEM BAREFOOT.
OH BOY!
KIRKMAN & SCOTT

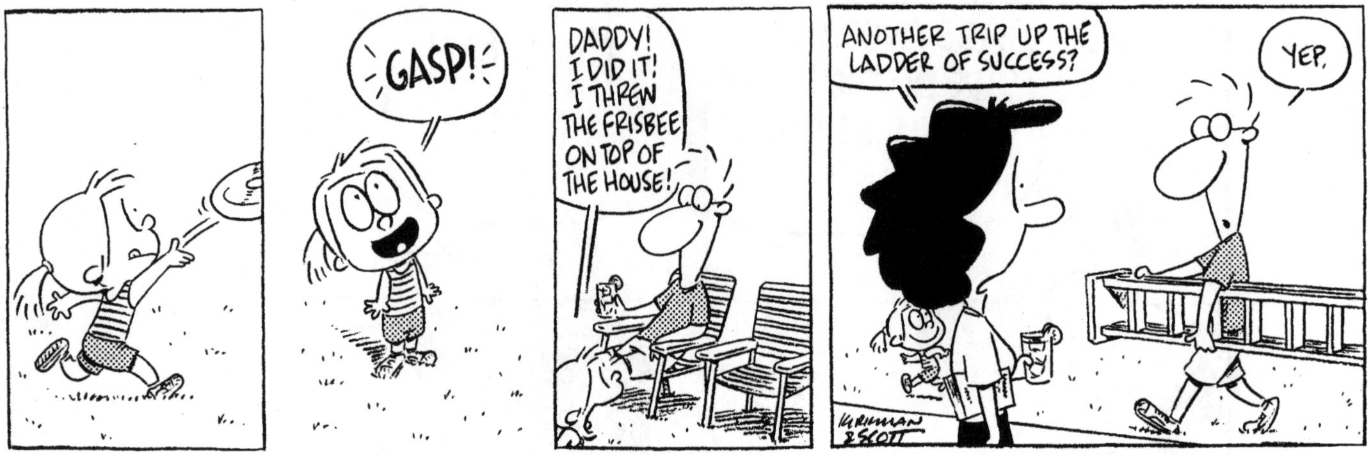
GASP!
DADDY! I DID IT! I THREW THE FRISBEE ON TOP OF THE HOUSE!
ANOTHER TRIP UP THE LADDER OF SUCCESS?
YEP.
KIRKMAN & SCOTT

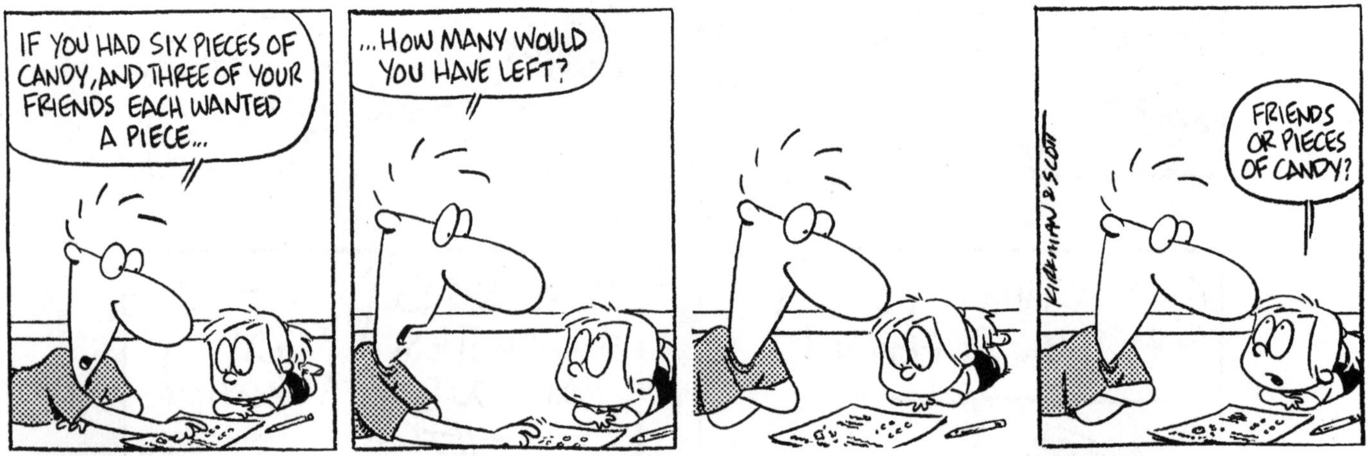
IF YOU HAD SIX PIECES OF CANDY, AND THREE OF YOUR FRIENDS EACH WANTED A PIECE...
...HOW MANY WOULD YOU HAVE LEFT?
KIRKMAN & SCOTT
FRIENDS OR PIECES OF CANDY?

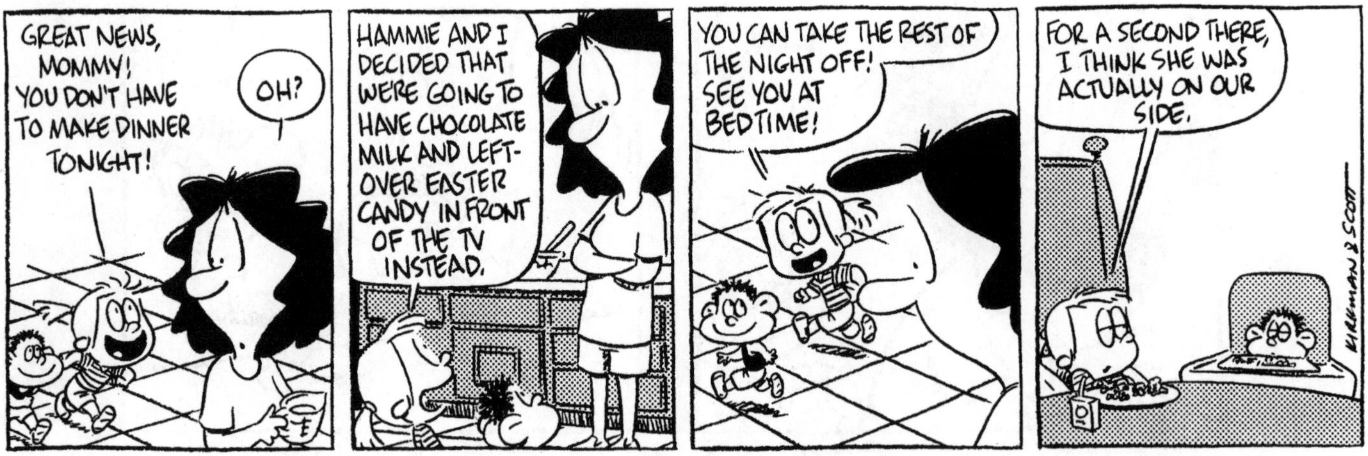
GREAT NEWS, MOMMY! YOU DON'T HAVE TO MAKE DINNER TONIGHT!
OH?
HAMMIE AND I DECIDED THAT WE'RE GOING TO HAVE CHOCOLATE MILK AND LEFT-OVER EASTER CANDY IN FRONT OF THE TV INSTEAD.
YOU CAN TAKE THE REST OF THE NIGHT OFF! SEE YOU AT BEDTIME!
FOR A SECOND THERE, I THINK SHE WAS ACTUALLY ON OUR SIDE.
KIRKMAN & SCOTT

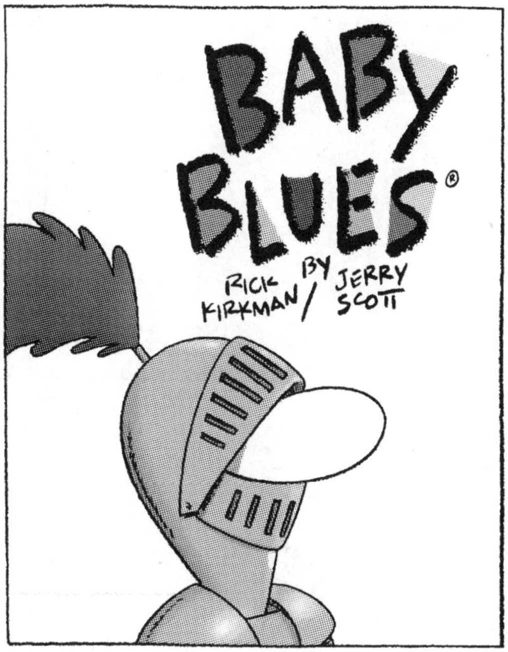
BABY BLUES®
BY
RICK KIRKMAN / JERRY SCOTT

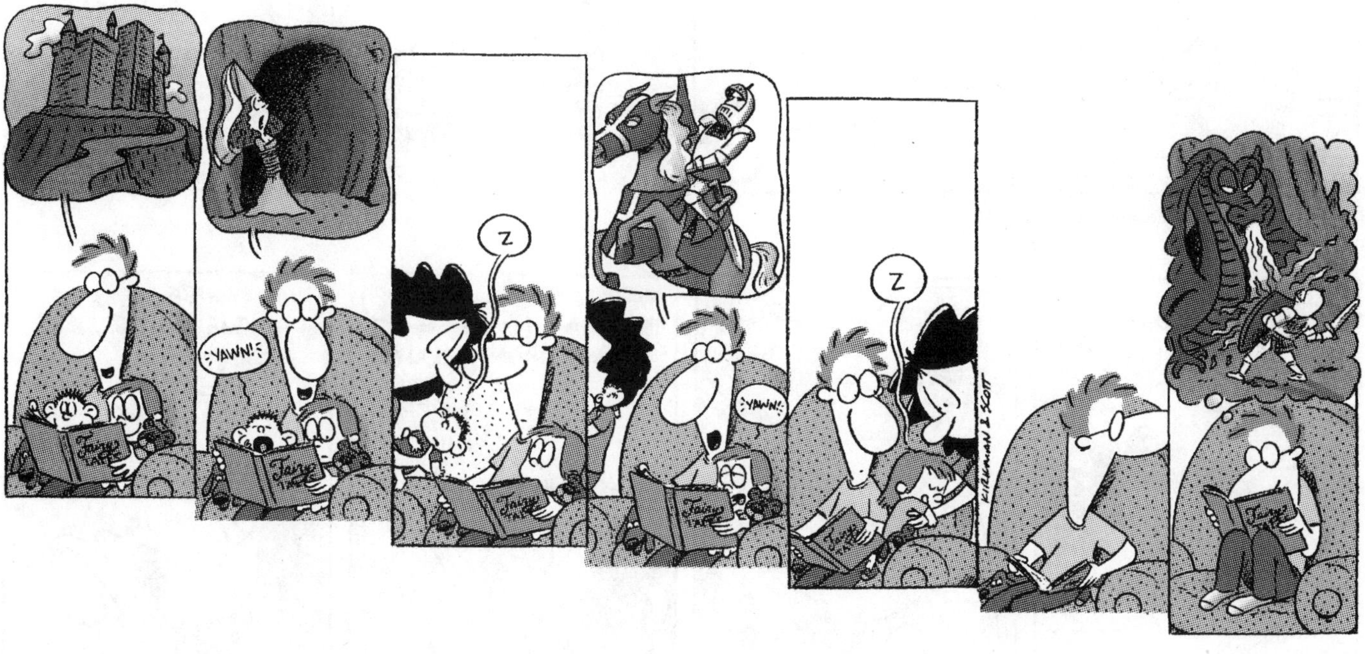
YAWN!
Z
YAWN!
Z

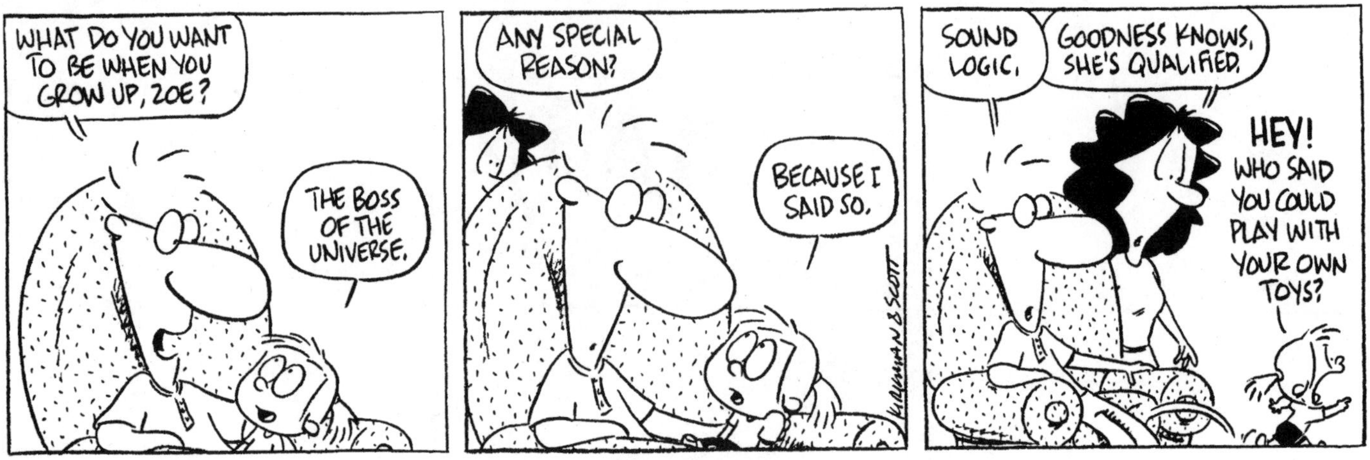
WHAT DO YOU WANT TO BE WHEN YOU GROW UP, ZOE?
THE BOSS OF THE UNIVERSE.
ANY SPECIAL REASON?
BECAUSE I SAID SO.
SOUND LOGIC.
GOODNESS KNOWS, SHE'S QUALIFIED.
HEY! WHO SAID YOU COULD PLAY WITH YOUR OWN TOYS?

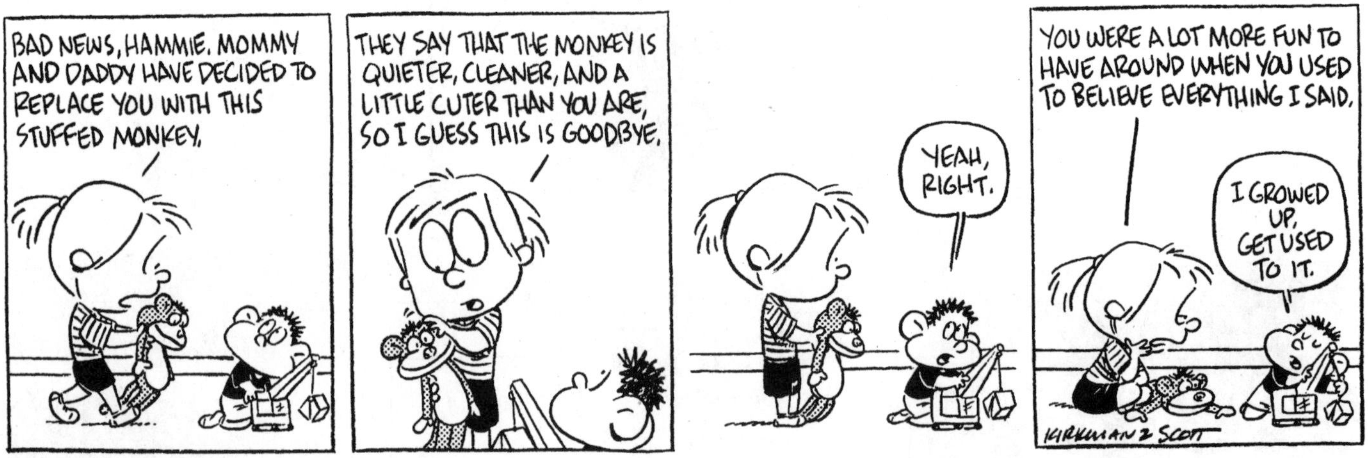
BAD NEWS, HAMMIE. MOMMY AND DADDY HAVE DECIDED TO REPLACE YOU WITH THIS STUFFED MONKEY.
THEY SAY THAT THE MONKEY IS QUIETER, CLEANER, AND A LITTLE CUTER THAN YOU ARE, SO I GUESS THIS IS GOODBYE.
YEAH, RIGHT.
YOU WERE A LOT MORE FUN TO HAVE AROUND WHEN YOU USED TO BELIEVE EVERYTHING I SAID.
I GROWED UP, GET USED TO IT.
KIRKMAN & SCOTT

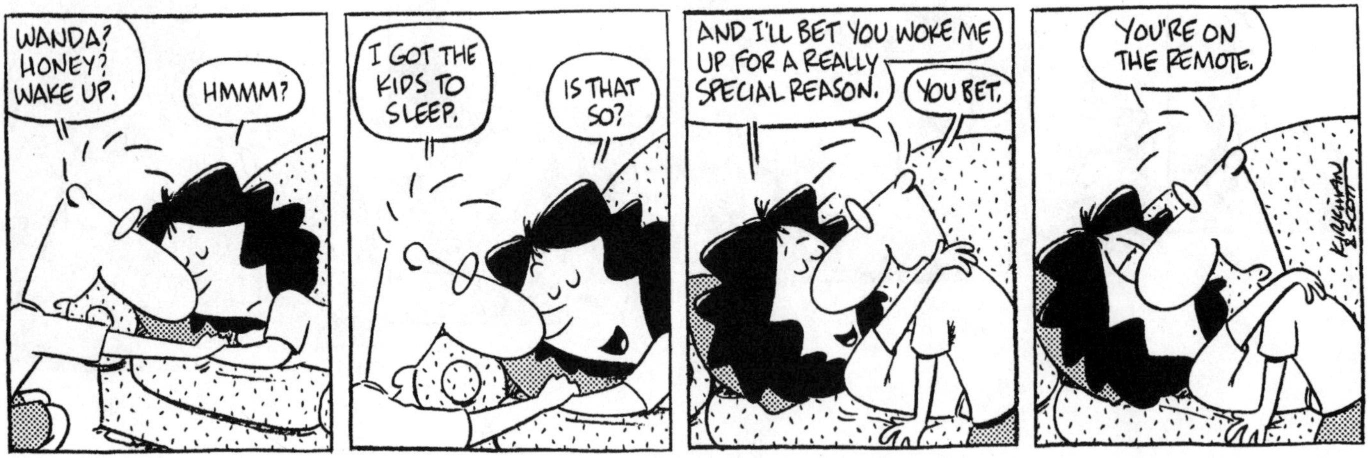
WANDA? HONEY? WAKE UP.
HMMM?
I GOT THE KIDS TO SLEEP.
IS THAT SO?
AND I'LL BET YOU WOKE ME UP FOR A REALLY SPECIAL REASON.
YOU BET.
YOU'RE ON THE REMOTE.

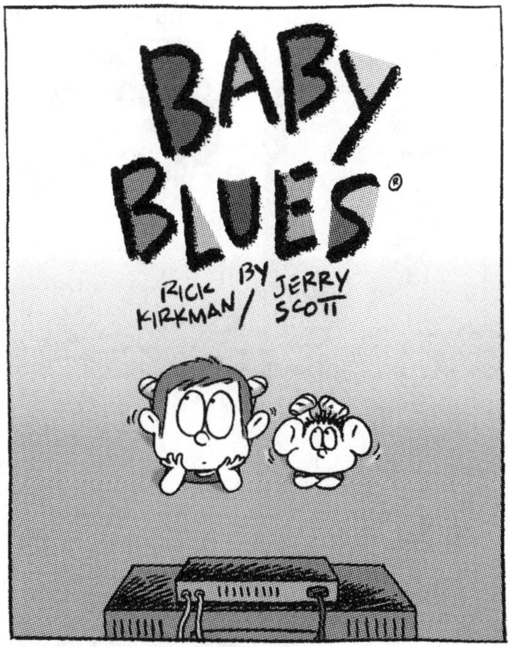
BABY BLUES®
BY RICK KIRKMAN / JERRY SCOTT

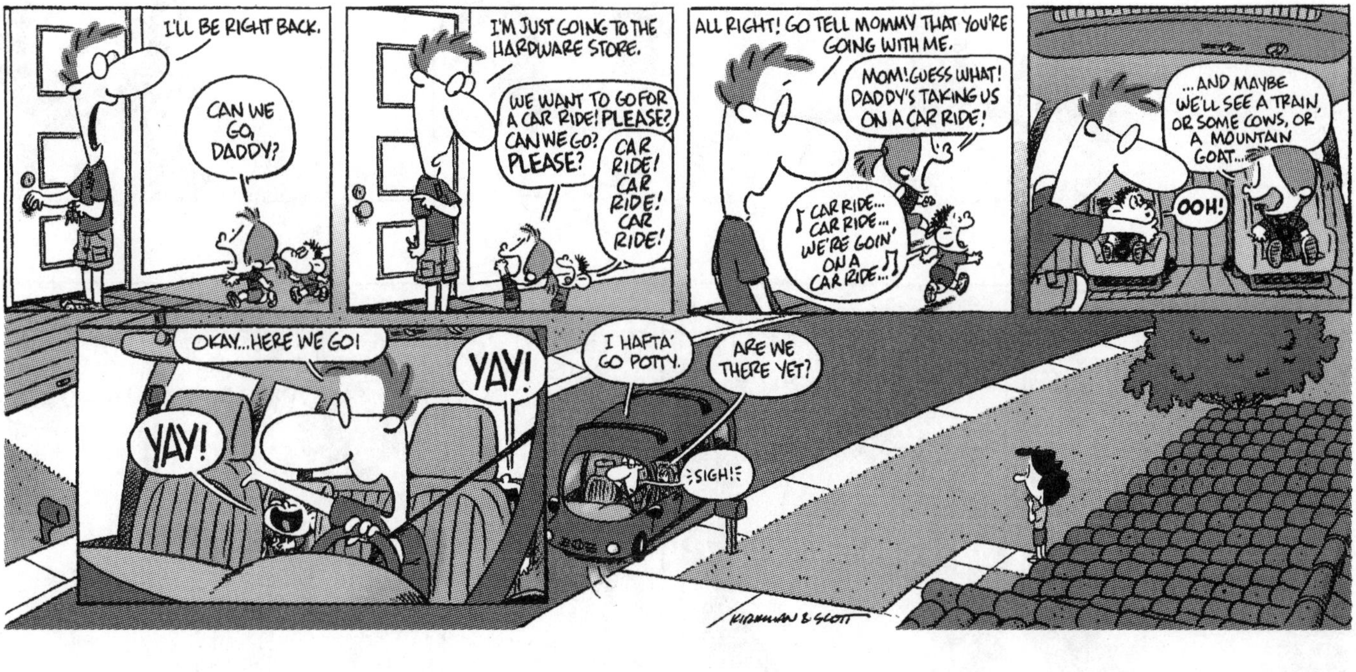
I'LL BE RIGHT BACK.
CAN WE GO, DADDY?
I'M JUST GOING TO THE HARDWARE STORE.
WE WANT TO GO FOR A CAR RIDE! PLEASE? CAN WE GO? PLEASE?
CAR RIDE! CAR RIDE! CAR RIDE!
ALL RIGHT! GO TELL MOMMY THAT YOU'RE GOING WITH ME.
MOM! GUESS WHAT! DADDY'S TAKING US ON A CAR RIDE!
CAR RIDE... CAR RIDE... WE'RE GOIN' ON A CAR RIDE...
...AND MAYBE WE'LL SEE A TRAIN, OR SOME COWS, OR A MOUNTAIN GOAT...
OOH!
OKAY...HERE WE GO!
YAY!
YAY!
I HAFTA' GO POTTY.
ARE WE THERE YET?
SIGH!
KIRKMAN & SCOTT

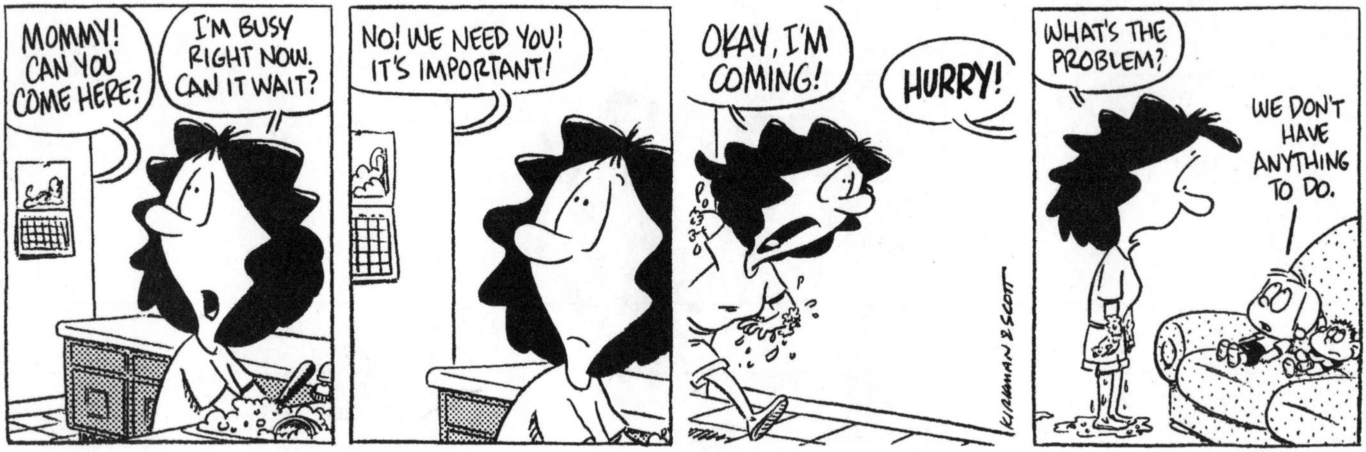
MOMMY! CAN YOU COME HERE?
I'M BUSY RIGHT NOW. CAN IT WAIT?
NO! WE NEED YOU! IT'S IMPORTANT!
OKAY, I'M COMING!
HURRY!
KIRKMAN & SCOTT
WHAT'S THE PROBLEM?
WE DON'T HAVE ANYTHING TO DO.

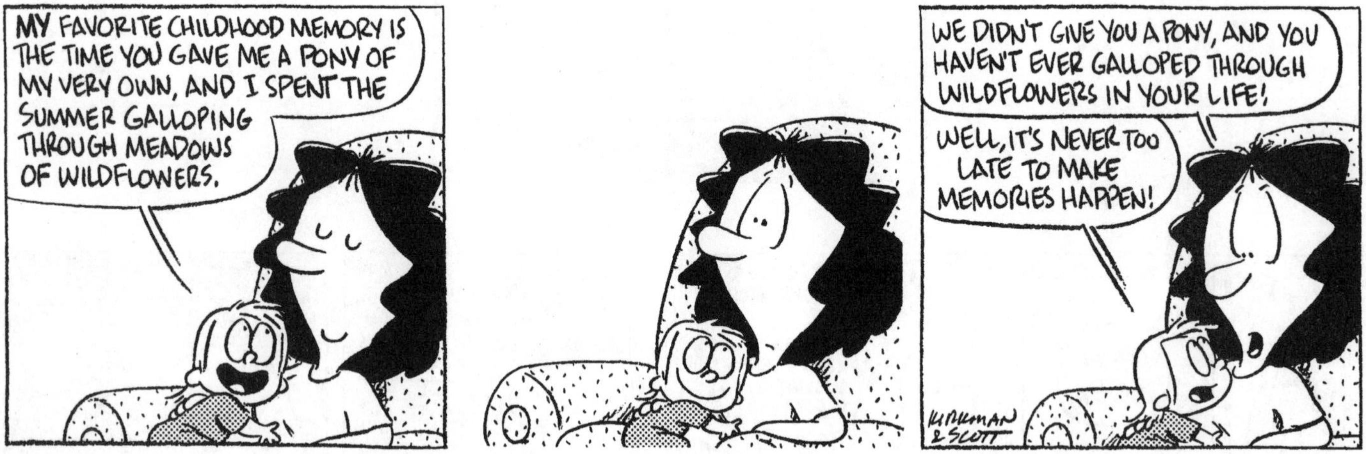
MY FAVORITE CHILDHOOD MEMORY IS THE TIME YOU GAVE ME A PONY OF MY VERY OWN, AND I SPENT THE SUMMER GALLOPING THROUGH MEADOWS OF WILDFLOWERS.
WE DIDN'T GIVE YOU A PONY, AND YOU HAVEN'T EVER GALLOPED THROUGH WILDFLOWERS IN YOUR LIFE!
WELL, IT'S NEVER TOO LATE TO MAKE MEMORIES HAPPEN!
KIRKMAN & SCOTT

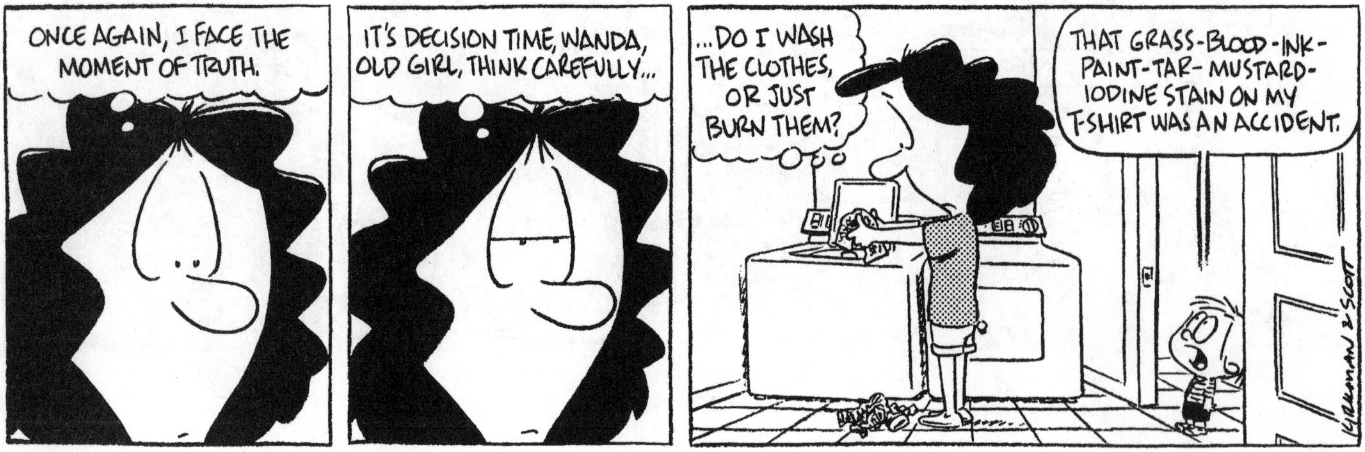
ONCE AGAIN, I FACE THE MOMENT OF TRUTH.
IT'S DECISION TIME, WANDA, OLD GIRL, THINK CAREFULLY...
...DO I WASH THE CLOTHES, OR JUST BURN THEM?
THAT GRASS-BLOOD-INK-PAINT-TAR-MUSTARD-IODINE STAIN ON MY T-SHIRT WAS AN ACCIDENT.
KIRKMAN & SCOTT

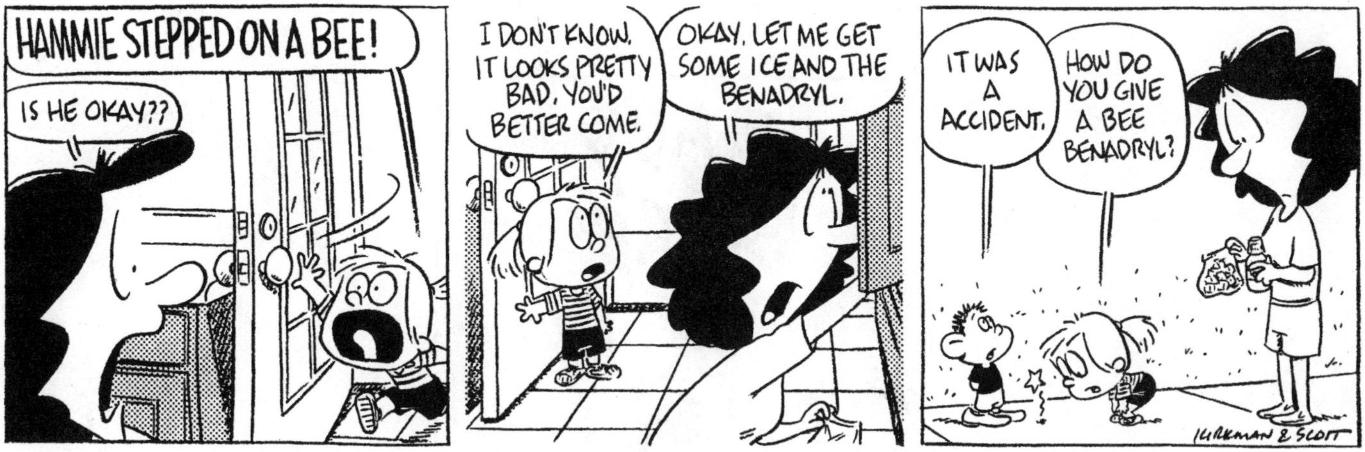
HAMMIE STEPPED ON A BEE!
IS HE OKAY??
I DON'T KNOW. IT LOOKS PRETTY BAD. YOU'D BETTER COME.
OKAY. LET ME GET SOME ICE AND THE BENADRYL.
IT WAS A ACCIDENT.
HOW DO YOU GIVE A BEE BENADRYL?
KIRKMAN & SCOTT

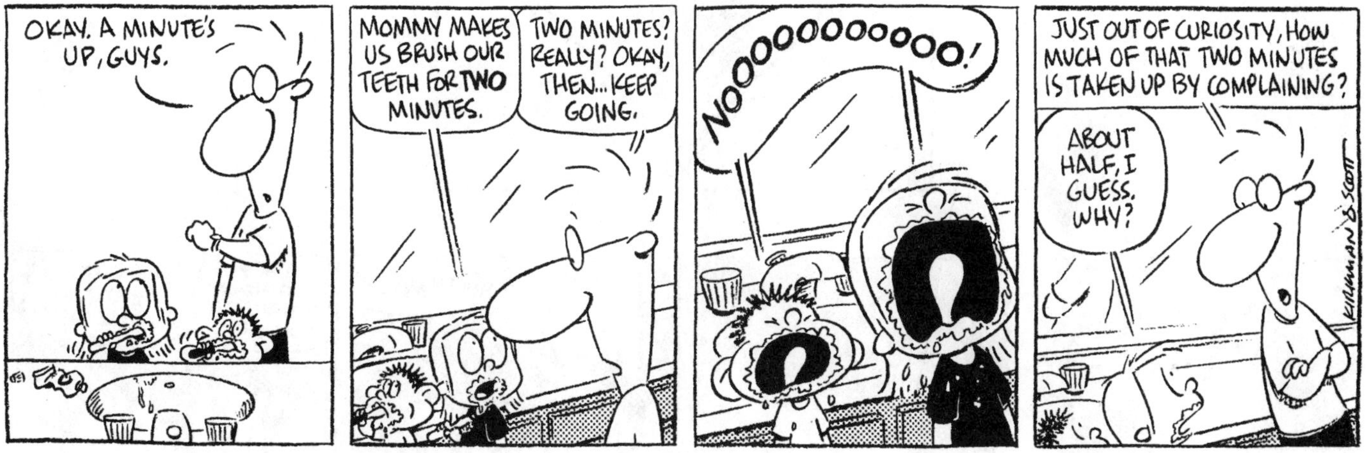
OKAY. A MINUTE'S UP, GUYS.
MOMMY MAKES US BRUSH OUR TEETH FOR **TWO** MINUTES.
TWO MINUTES? REALLY? OKAY, THEN... KEEP GOING.
NOOOOOOOOOOOO!
JUST OUT OF CURIOSITY, HOW MUCH OF THAT TWO MINUTES IS TAKEN UP BY COMPLAINING?
ABOUT HALF, I GUESS. WHY?
KIRKMAN & SCOTT

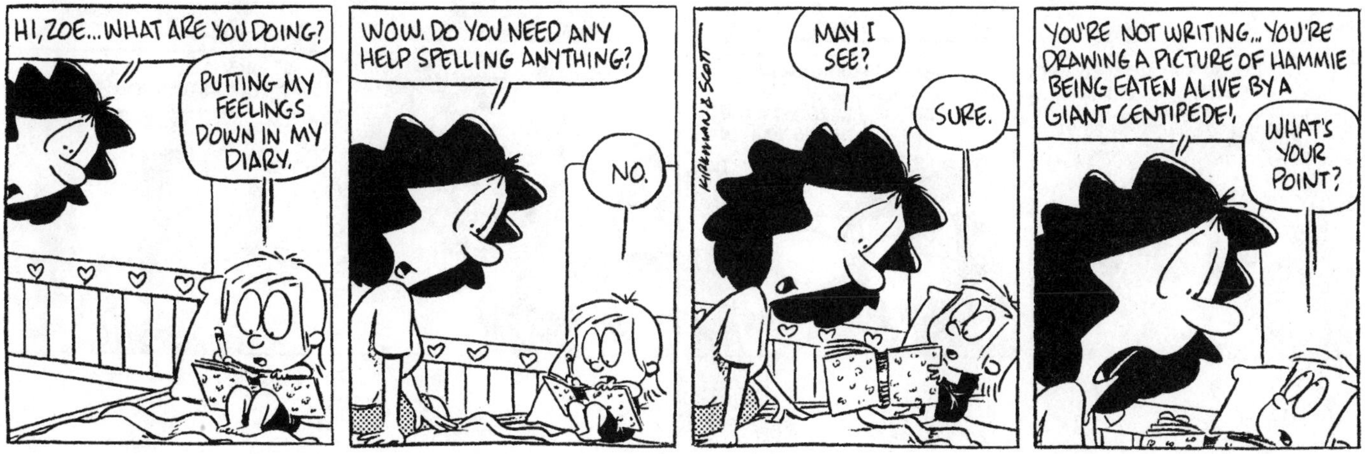
HI, ZOE... WHAT ARE YOU DOING?
PUTTING MY FEELINGS DOWN IN MY DIARY.
WOW. DO YOU NEED ANY HELP SPELLING ANYTHING?
NO.
KIRKMAN & SCOTT
MAY I SEE?
SURE.
YOU'RE NOT WRITING... YOU'RE DRAWING A PICTURE OF HAMMIE BEING EATEN ALIVE BY A GIANT CENTIPEDE!
WHAT'S YOUR POINT?

BABY BLUES®
BY RICK KIRKMAN / JERRY SCOTT

WHOA! BRENDA! IS THAT YOU??
HOLEY-MOLEY!
LOOK AT YOU! WOOO-HOOO! YOU'RE IN FOR IT NOW, GIRL!
AH-OOGA! AH-OOGA! WIDE LOAD AHEAD!
I SEE YOU TWO HAVE BEEN BUSY!
YEAH! NICE GOING, ROB! HA! HA! HA!
UNBELIEVEABLE! WELL, GOOD LUCK... YOU'RE GOING TO NEED IT!
HEY, LOOK AT IT THIS WAY... YOU'RE A THIRD OF THE WAY TO HAVING YOUR OWN BASEBALL TEAM!
MAYBE WE SHOULD HAVE JUST SAID "CONGRATULATIONS"...
NAH... AFTER TWO KIDS IT'S OPEN SEASON.

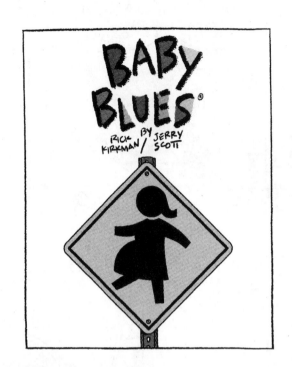

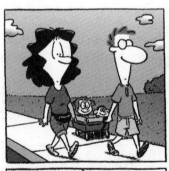

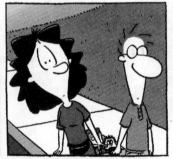

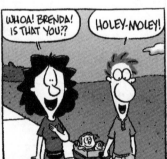

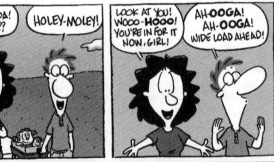

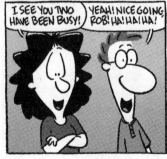

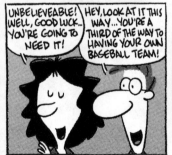

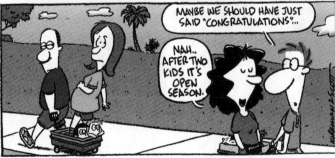